GEM Desktop
Publisher

Bill Lawrence

Scott, Foresman and Company
Glenview, Illinois   London

Cover photo courtesy of International Business Machines Corporation.

AutoCAD is a trademark of Autodesk, Inc.
Click Art is a trademark of T/Maker.
dBase II is a trademark of Ashton-Tate, Inc.
DesqView and DesqView Companions are trademarks of Quarterdeck Office Systems.
Epson is a trademark of Epson America, Inc.
Fontware is a trademark of Bitstream, Inc.
GEM, GEM Paint, GEM 1st Word Plus, GEM Draw Plus, GEM Write, GEM Scan, GEM WordChart,
    GEM Diary, GEM Graph, and GEM Desktop Publisher are trademarks of Digital Research, Inc.
Genius is a trademark of Micro Display Systems.
Hercules Graphics Card is a trademark of Hercules Computer Technology.
IBM PC and Proprinter are trademarks of International Business Machines Corp.
LaserJet is a trademark of Hewlett-Packard Corp.
LaserWriter is a trademark of Apple Computers, Inc.
Linotronic is a trademark of Allied Corp.
Logi-Mouse is a trademark of Logitech Inc.
Lotus 1-2-3 is a trademark of Lotus Development Corporation.
NEC 890 is a trademark of NEC Information Systems.
Office Publisher is a trademark of Laser Friendly.
PC Quick-Art and The Graphics Link are trademarks of PC Quick-Art, Inc.
PostScript is a trademark of Adobe Systems Inc.
Ventura Publisher is a trademark of Ventura Software, Inc.
Windows and Word are trademarks of Microsoft Corp.
WordPerfect is a trademark of WordPerfect Corp.
WordStar is a trademark of Micropro International Corp.
Wyse is a trademark of Wyse Technology, Inc.

Library of Congress Cataloging-in-Publication Data

Lawrence, Bill
    GEM desktop publisher.
    Includes index.
    1. Desktop publishing. 2. GEM (Computer operating system) I. Title.
Z286.D47L38 1989   686.2'2   88-33630
ISBN 0-673-38147-1

1 2 3 4 5 6 KPF 93 92 91 90 89 88

ISBN 0-673-38147-1

Copyright © 1989 Bill Lawrence.
All Rights Reserved.
Printed in the United States of America.

Notice of Liability

The information in this book is distributed on an "As Is" basis, without warranty. Neither the author nor Scott, Foresman and Company shall have any liability to customer or any other person or entity with respect to any liability, loss, or damage caused or alleged to be caused directly or indirectly by the programs contained herein. This includes, but is not limited to, interruption of service, loss of data, loss of business or anticipatory profits, or consequential damages from the use of the programs.

Scott, Foresman professional books are available for bulk sales at quantity discounts. For information, please contact Marketing Manager, Professional Books Group, Scott, Foresman and Company, 1900 East Lake Avenue, Glenview, IL 60025.

CONTENTS

CHAPTER 1
Background and Selecting Hardware   1

WHAT SORT OF BOOK IS THIS? • WHY GEM? • COMPUTERS AND GEM • STANDARD MONITORS AND GRAPHICS CARDS • PRINTERS AND PLOTTERS • POINTING DEVICES • GRAPHICS TABLETS

CHAPTER 2
Putting GEM/3 on Your System   13

INTRODUCTION • STARTING THE INSTALLATION • CHANGING THE CONFIGURATION

CHAPTER 3
Welcome to the Top of Your Desk   20

INTRODUCTION • MOUSE TECHNIQUES • CRANKING UP • WELCOME TO THE GRAPHIC ENVIRONMENT MANAGER • HOW TO OPERATE YOUR DESK • THE MENUS • DESKTOP • KEYBOARD COMMANDS • OUTPUT • PULL-DOWN MENUS • PREFERENCES

CHAPTER 4
Fontware and FontMerge: Things You Need to Know   49

BEYOND SWISS AND DUTCH • INSTALLATION • ADDING FONTS • MAKING FONTS • MODIFYING FONTWARE • FONT CODES • THE CHARACTER SET • FONTMERGE

CHAPTER 5
GEM Paint II 64

A VERSATILE PUBLISHER'S TOOL • OPENERS • TOOLBOX • TEXT • OTHER ARTIST'S TOOLS • PULL-DOWNS • TOOLS • PATTERNS • DESIGNING WITH GEM PAINT II

CHAPTER 6
Welcome to GEM Draw Plus 84

INTRODUCTION • TOOLKIT • PULL-DOWN MENUS • YOUR FIRST ASSIGNMENT • SECOND ASSIGNMENT: THE ORGANIZATIONAL CHART

CHAPTER 7
GEM Draw Plus Techniques 116

LEARNING VS. DABBLING • LAYERING EXAMPLE: THE BOX • DRAWING THE TRAFFIC LIGHT • CLIP-ART • LABELING THE ILLUSTRATION • A WORD ABOUT SIZE

CHAPTER 8
A New Dimension 133

TOOLING UP FOR 3-D • ISOMETRIC PROJECTIONS • SINGLE VANISHING POINT PERSPECTIVE • DUAL VANISHING POINT PERSPECTIVE • FINAL REVIEW

CHAPTER 9
GEM Graph 143

A POWERFUL PRESENTATION TOOL • STARTING UP • DATA ENTRY • GRAPHING: SCREEN TWO • PULL-DOWN MENU REFERENCE • GRAPHING WINDOW • THE MAP EDITOR

CHAPTER 10
Advanced Graphing   169

TURNING YOUR CREATIVITY LOOSE • WHICH GRAPH? • PUTTING THE RULES TO USE

CHAPTER 11
WordChart   176

A REAL PAGING PROGRAM? • THE CHARTING AREA • TOOLKIT • MENUS • WORDCHART • CHARTING YOUR COURSE • OUTLINES • DECIMAL TABS • BORDERING ON INSANITY • ENHANCING YOUR WORDCHARTS WITH GEM DRAW PLUS

CHAPTER 12
GEM Write, the Original GEM Word Processor   203

PLUSES AND MINUSES • GETTING STARTED • MOUSE TECHNIQUES • PULL-DOWN MENUS • USING THE RULER • INSERT • SECRETS WITHIN • DOT-DOT COMMANDS

CHAPTER 13
GEM 1st Word Plus: Professional Editing Power for GEM   225

A TOOL FOR WORDSMITHS? • IN THE FOYER • INTO THE FILE • PULL-DOWN MENUS • SPELLING • GRAPHICS • HELP • KEYBOARD COMMANDS

CHAPTER 14
Publishing With 1st Word Plus   253

SPEAKING GRAPHICALLY • STATIONERY-ON-DEMAND • PUBLICATION DESIGN WITH 1ST WORD PLUS • DOING SOMETHING • SUMMING UP

CHAPTER 15
GEM Desktop Publisher: The Basics   260

SIMPLY SUPERIOR • SYSTEM REQUIREMENTS • WHAT TO FEED DESKTOP PUBLISHER • OPENING UP • THE TOOLKIT • PULL-DOWN MENUS • ATTRIBUTES • PAGE NUMBERS • OPTIONS • KEYBOARD COMMANDS • EMBEDDED COMMANDS

CHAPTER 16
Desktop Publisher: Advanced Techniques   301

A FEATURE-LADEN PACKAGE • TASTE IN TYPOGRAPHY • A FEW RULES FOR SINGLE-COLUMN MATERIAL • MULTI-COLUMN WORK • BROCHURE: HANGING GRAPHICS ON THE GRID • SUMMING UP

CHAPTER 17
Other GEM Applications   320

WIDER HORIZONS • OFFICE PUBLISHER • VENTURA PUBLISHER • SUPERBASE • MASTERPLAN

CHAPTER 18
Non-GEM Programs You Can Use   338

BEYOND GEM • HALO DPE • THE GRAPHICS LINK • PC QUICK-ART • T/MAKER • COREL • DESQVIEW

Appendix: Directory of Manufacturers and Vendors 350

Glossary of GEM Terminology 353

ASCII Chart 356

Index 357

ACKNOWLEDGMENTS

First and foremost, to Kathy—my lovely and loving wife—I want to express my endless gratitude and love for all your help, support, bearing the family burdens while I devoted myself to this project, and for just being you. At least half the credit for this book belongs to you.

Thanks to Digital Research in general and to Gale Steiner of DRI in particular for consistent support throughout the preparation of this book; it's greatly appreciated.

Additional thanks to Pava Cohen at Media Cybernetics. All of the screen images were captured with HALO DPE; without HALO DPE, I wouldn't have any graphics.

Thanks to Jack Sheets for the help, counsel, hardware loans, etc. Every time part of my system went down, Jack was there.

All of the people who provided software—too numerous, unfortunately, to mention individually—deserve thanks also. Likewise, I want to express appreciation to Marlene Konnar of PC Technologies for the RamRacer board.

Hank Walker deserves mention for his wise counsel and help. If you really want to keep up to date on GEM, subscribe to Hank's *GEM Facets Journal.*

My ex-boss Bob Davis also merits mention here. In addition to reviewing the manuscript, he provided much help and wise counsel, gave me constant support, and served as a good sounding board.

Finally, thanks to Amy Davis at Scott, Foresman. Her patience and ready advice have been much appreciated.

—BILL LAWRENCE

CHAPTER 1

Background and Selecting Hardware

WHAT SORT OF BOOK IS THIS?	2
WHY GEM?	2
COMPUTERS AND GEM	3
STANDARD MONITORS AND GRAPHICS CARDS	4
PRINTERS AND PLOTTERS	7
POINTING DEVICES	11
GRAPHICS TABLETS	12

WHAT SORT OF BOOK IS THIS?

This book is designed to do four things for you:

1. Help you select and configure hardware to run GEM. I'll go over the pros and cons concerning computers, pointing devices, graphics cards and monitors, and output devices.
2. Provide a single volume quick-reference for all of the Digital Research GEM applications. All of the commands, functions, and dialogs are covered. Each application also has a page or two that can be photocopied to provide a quick reference.
3. Teach you the techniques and tricks that will make the GEM applications really useful for you. Learning these took me several years; why should you wait that long?
4. Introduce you to some other very useful programs that run under GEM or separately. I've found programs that make my life easier, and you should know about them. I'll also tell you about any "gotchas" in using them.

The book was written around GEM/3. If you are using an earlier release, most of the things you'll find here still apply. I've been careful to mention when something applies only to GEM/3.

WHY GEM?

If you use your computer to create presentations, reports, newsletters, or heftier publications, you know how important it is to be able to mesh text, illustrations, and layout capabilities. You need something that makes all of the pieces work together. That something shouldn't be a burden to use, or even a sluggish inconvenience, on fairly ordinary hardware. That working environment is GEM. GEM/3, the current release, has been refined so that it is an intuitive working partner.

This book was written and illustrated with GEM/3 applications and Media Cybernetics HALO DPE. Most of the text was originally written with WordStar 4, which is by any measure an excellent writer's tool. It was finished with GEM 1st Word Plus. I find Word Plus to be an elegant writing tool, and it's now my standard word processor. Nearly all of the illustrations were created with GEM applications, with a few exceptions from Media Cybernetics' HALO DPE program. While not a GEM application, HALO DPE can write GEM format image files.

COMPUTERS AND GEM

GEM is fast, efficient software. Many other desktop publishing environments require at least a '286-based computer (AT type) to run in something better than geologic time. GEM can run passably on a standard PC. On a '286 machine, it's really amazing. On a '386 machine, it's dazzling.

GEM also can run with a standard color graphics card and without a mouse. Technically, you don't even need a hard disk drive. But then, you can drive a car while sitting on one hand.

I changed my computer three times in the course of writing this book. It started as a modest XT clone, with a meager eight megahertz 8088 (actually a V20). If you don't understand that jargon, it means that my computer was twice as fast as an IBM PC. I then added a RamRacer '286 board that PC Technologies loaned to me. That kicked my system up to processing speeds equivalent to the original IBM AT. If you have an XT-type machine, this is a good and inexpensive way to increase your performance.

My final attempt at hot-rodding was to buy a permanent upgrade that would let me run slow applications (specifically Office Publisher, the only really slothful GEM application I know). I swapped the main board in my computer for a Wave Mate Bullet '286. Now I'm really cruising.

In addition, my machine has a rather slow (65-millisecond) 30-megabyte hard disk drive. Graphics are provided by a Hercules-compatible graphics card driving a soft-white, 14-inch monitor. This provides high resolution graphics at much less expense than a good color system. For pointing and drawing I use a serial mouse of the roller-ball persuasion.

Bottom line: a little under $1500 in hardware provides an excellent desktop publishing computer. If you check current mail order prices, I'm sure you'll be able to equal or better my price for a similar system.

The rest of this chapter is devoted to a discussion of the various hardware devices supported by GEM, including their pros and cons. If you don't already have a computer to run GEM, by all means read this chapter before buying anything. If you have a computer system, look this over anyway. You might find something you want to add to your system to enhance its performance.

OF CPU'S AND SPEED

My home machine now has an 80286 processor rather than the 8088 type I started with. A '286-based machine is faster than an 8088 for two reasons:

1. The '286 is a more efficient processor than the '88 or '86. It can process more information per instruction, and it has more instructions available.

2. Information is shuffled about in 16-bit words instead of 8-bit bytes.

The speed improvement is most noticeable in the time it takes to redraw the screen and the time it takes to process images (GEM Paint and scanned files) in Desktop Publisher. AT-type machines usually have faster hard drives than the XT class, so loading and accessing data is faster. Sometimes such machines run at very fast clock rates, which is the speed that the processor and memory are cycled. This further improves performance.

The '386-based machines run even faster, though GEM can't take advantage of the 32-bit capabilities. Actually, the increased performance you get with GEM from a '386 over a fast '286 is hardly worth mentioning.

Many graphics programs can use the math co-processor chip (if installed) to greatly increase their performance. GEM does not use the co-processor. It's so fast on its own that you don't need one.

PS/2

The Model 30 has a fast 8086 processor, giving it about the same performance as the AT&T 6300 or a turbo-XT. Models 40 and up are '286-based machines or better. Any of the PS/2's will run GEM quite elegantly. As GEM is a product carried by IBM, you'll see even heavier support for these computers in the future. In fact, GEM/3 has hooks built in for the new OS/2 operating system.

STANDARD MONITORS AND GRAPHICS CARDS

Right out of the box, GEM/3 supports standard EGA, CGA, VGA, Hercules-compatible, and Vega Video-compatible graphics cards.

CGA

Color Graphics Adapter. The old standby. Many older computers have this card and either a composite (monochrome or color) or RGB color monitor. You can use this combination, but I wouldn't. It provides the lowest resolution, no color, and it must be run in monochrome mode to achieve its meager 640x200-dot resolution.

While CGA graphics are usable, you won't want to live with the results over any length of time. Type is difficult to read. You'll also find that you need to use the zoom-in features in the graphics applications a good deal of the time.

EGA

This is really quite nice, and not nearly as expensive as it once was. You can get eight or 16 colors (let the capabilities of your monitor be your guide) and very useful resolution. I've used a standard EGA board and monitor and had no complaints. It's even more useful if you have a color printer. If you don't, the colors are pretty but really don't serve any function.

Hercules

The Hercules graphics card is one of the pieces of hardware that made desktop publishing on PC's possible. It has excellent resolution, something you really need with layout programs and detailed graphics. Since most laser printers are black-and-white, its monochrome display is quite appropriate to black-and-white output. This is the best bargain for resolution versus cost.

    I recommend that you buy a 14-inch TTL monitor to go with this card. I look at computer screens all day (and usually all evening), and I love big screens. If you use a computer for extended periods, you'll love a big screen too.

3270 PC

The resolution is high enough to make the 3270 PC useful, but I wouldn't buy one just for publishing. This comes under the class of "I've got one and I want to use it." So use it.

AT&T

Excellent resolution, but not as well supported by software and vendors as many other cards. If that doesn't bother you, these are pretty slick.

Video Seven Vega Deluxe and Quadram Prosync

These are super EGA cards that provide better resolution than standard EGA—but only when used with an expensive multi-sync monitor. Typical vendors are NEC and Sony. If high resolution and full color are very important to you, and your wallet can stand the strain, this is the way to go.

VGA

The new standard in high resolution color. Very nice indeed. If you are using a 256 gray level scanner, this type of monitor/graphics card combination can display the grays.

MONITORS SUPPORTED THROUGH GEM DRIVER PACKS

Currently, Digital Research supports just three monitors through its driver packs.

EGA Monochrome Display

Why would anyone run monochrome from an EGA? Well, suppose you can't afford an EGA monitor yet, but you do want to get one eventually. A low-cost, interim solution is to buy an EGA card and a monochrome TTL monitor. Then you can enjoy pretty decent monochrome resolution before upgrading to full color sometime in the future.

EGA 16 Color

The tradeoff is 16 colors for lower resolution (640x200).

Amstrad PC1512

A 16-color monitor peculiar to the European Amstrad computer, the PC1512 is supported because Amstrad is a major distributor of GEM products.

MONITORS SUPPORTED BY THIRD-PARTY DRIVERS

Before we get into this, let me tell you my philosophy about third-party drivers. They are usually quite well done, and can often provide you with some very useful display options. However, they make you dependent on the third party for updates. Since the drivers are not supported by Digital Research, that leaves me a little jumpy.

If lots of other software companies are supporting a monitor, or if it's selling like mad, then it's very likely a safe bet. But if you end up with a monitor that for some reason doesn't catch on, you could eventually be stuck. The third party may not continue to support it, and neither will Digital Research. Be careful.

The following list of third-party drivers is not complete, but it covers most of the major options. The appendix at the rear of the book tells you how to contact the manufacturers.

AT&T DEB Card

One of the original, really nice color graphics cards. AT&T and Xerox both get their computers from Olivetti (so much for all the hoopla about buying real AT&T technology). Unless you have one of these computers or can get a really good deal, don't buy this graphics combination. It really is quite nonstandard, and therefore not well supported.

AT&T Monochrome Card

Not really as good as a Hercules-compatible card, and also nonstandard. The same warning given above applies here.

Wyse WY-700

Offering extremely high resolution (1280x800), this is a monochrome monitor and graphics card combination that you will also see under the Amdek 1280 label. While it's great for graphics programs, I don't like it for page layout. It uses a 15-inch horizontal format monitor to display a full page, and the result is teeny, tiny letters on the screen. Eye strain city.

The Genius

My personal favorite for page layout. This is a vertical format monitor and card combination that displays a full page (66 lines of text). Resolution is 1008x736.

Verticom 480

Another high resolution EGA board (640x480) that supports multi-sync EGA monitors. Lots of colors at about Hercules resolution.

Viking 1

Wow. A 19-inch, horizontal format monochrome monitor driven at a resolution of 1280x960. No eye strain here.

Xerox Full Page Display

This is a 15-inch vertical format monitor that provides a very readable full-page display. Not quite as sharp as the Genius, but not quite as expensive either. Since Xerox markets Ventura Publisher (a GEM application), you can bet that Xerox will continue to support GEM well into the future.

PRINTERS AND PLOTTERS

This is probably your most important piece of hardware for desktop publishing. After all, output is your product. Your printer provides your masters for offset printing or photocopying. GEM comes with drivers to support five major classes of printers:

1. PostScript-based laser printers
2. HP LaserJet+ compatible laser printers
3. IBM/Epson graphics compatible dot-matrix printers
4. Color printers
5. Diablo 630 compatible daisywheel and laser printers

POSTSCRIPT-BASED LASER PRINTERS

These are the best printers you can use with GEM. Typical models are the venerable Apple LaserWriter and the NEC 890. Using Adobe's page description language PostScript, these printers render pages at a full 300 dots by 300 dots, for what the industry calls near typeset quality. Graphics are very sharp, with almost no apparent jagged edges. Examples of PostScript output abound in this book. Almost every illustration was printed with a NEC 890 in PostScript mode. If you are serious about desktop publishing, this is the way to go.

Without getting too deeply into PostScript, I want to explain why this works so well. PostScript is the de facto industry standard for page description languages. A page description language tells the printer, in very great detail, about everything that falls on the page. It covers the size, weight, style, and position of type. It describes the weight, length, and position of each line. It also controls the bit map for GEM Paint images.

PostScript is actually an interpreter computer language, and it's executed by a computer in the printer (which is one of the reasons why PostScript-equipped laser printers are more expensive than other laser printers). For those who care about such things, PostScript is distantly related to Forth, and has common roots with Xerox Interpress.

You can also use the PostScript driver to create files for high-resolution typesetters. Such devices can provide resolution in excess of 2500 dots per inch.

HEWLETT-PACKARD LASERJET+ COMPATIBLE LASER PRINTERS

Your second best choice, and somewhat less expensive, is a Hewlett-Packard compatible laser printer. It must have enough memory to allow it to print graphics at a resolution of 300x300 dots per inch. Otherwise, you'll have to settle for 150x150 dots to the inch.

LaserJet compatible printers outperform PostScript printers in two areas:

1. They print bitmapped graphics (.IMG files) faster. You might want to consider this if you use a lot of scanned images.
2. They produce finer screens. Actually, though, these screens are too fine for the average photocopier to reproduce without problems.

IBM/EPSON DOT-MATRIX PRINTERS

For most home users, this is the printer type of choice. The only real drawback to dot-matrix printers is that it takes several minutes to print a page. To work with GEM, your printer must emulate (or be) one of the following printers: Epson MX80, IBM Graphics Printer, IBM Proprinter, Epson LQ Series Printers.

My home printer is a Citizen MSP-10, which does a very nice job with GEM output in its IBM Graphics Printer mode. Most dot-matrix printers have IBM Graphics emulation (check the manual), but if yours doesn't, don't despair. There are a few other drivers available from Digital Research.

If you are doing a school, club, or church newsletter, you may find the output from an inexpensive dot-matrix printer quite adequate. I use my MSP-10 as a proof printer, and take my GEM files to a computer with a PostScript laser printer for final output.

COLOR PRINTERS

GEM supports the Xerox 4020. I'm sorry I can't show you the output from this directly; you'll just have to imagine the colors. This printer isn't exactly cheap, and it's also quite specialized. You can't use it to make masters for color printing because color printing requires color separations (separate layers for each printing color). Besides, it's just too slow to mass produce color documents. The 4020 can, however, make color overhead projection masters, as well as color comps to show what a final printed piece will look like.

DIABLO 630 AND ITS EMULATORS

Selecting this printing option means that you can't print graphics, thereby reducing GEM's usefulness by about 90 percent. So why would anyone do this? If you are using GEM 1st Word Plus, a 630 will get you access to a letter-quality printer.

Many daisywheel and laser printers emulate the 630. Even the Apple LaserWriter emulates a 630. As a result, you can use the LaserWriter or other printers from both GEM Write and other non-GEM applications that can't speak in PostScript.

PLOTTERS

Pen plotters use servo-driven mechanical arms to whiz pens across the page, literally drawing the graphics and text. They do a very nice job with graphics, although they set no speed records. They are far too slow to use with anything text intensive. You definitely wouldn't produce a newsletter with a pen plotter.

GEM is shipped with a driver for Hewlett-Packard plotters or any plotter that can use Hewlett-Packard Graphics Language (HPGL). Additional plotter drivers are available from Digital Research.

PRINTER, PLOTTER, AND CAMERA DRIVERS FROM DRI

While the following list was up to date at the time of printing, Digital Research is constantly adding drivers to the list. To find out if there are any additional drivers, call 1-800-433-4200. Have your GEM serial number ready.

Driver Pack #1

IBM EGA monochrome (640x350 dots per inch)
IBM EGA 16 colors (640x200 dots per inch)

Driver Pack #2

Hewlett-Packard and DM/PL plotter drivers

Driver Pack #3

IBM 3812 PagePrinter (240x240 dots per inch)
IBM Quietwriter II and III (240x240 dots per inch)
Diablo C150 Color Inkjet (120x120 dots per inch)

Driver Pack #4

Epson LQ 2500C (180x180 dots per inch)
Toshiba P351C (180x180 dots per inch)
Hewlett-Packard PaintJet (180x180 dots per inch)

Driver Pack #5

Epson JX80 (120x144 dots per inch)

Driver Pack #6

Quadram Quadjet (84 dots per inch)

Driver Pack #7

Hewlett-Packard ThinkJet (96 dots per inch)

Driver Pack #8

AST Laser (300x300 dots per inch)
Tall Tree Laser (300x300 dots per inch)

Driver Pack #9

(Not shown in current Digital Research lists.)

Driver Pack #10

Polaroid Palette and Palette Plus Color Imaging Systems

Driver Pack #11

Ricoh P6000 Laser (300x300 dots per inch)
Xerox 4045 Laser (300x300 dots per inch)

Driver Pack #12

IBM Color Jetprinter (100x96 dots per inch)

Driver Pack #13

IBM Proprinter X24 and XL24 (180 dots per inch)

Driver Pack #14

Amstrad PC1512, 16-color monitor

POINTING DEVICES

Ok, okay you can run GEM without a pointing device. You can also pound nails into wood with your bare hand. Once I had to do a number of book illustrations without a mouse. I won't do it again. This seems to be one of the corners people on a very tight budget always try to cut. Don't. To run GEM efficiently, you need a good pointing device. I use mice. At home I have a Logitech C7 serial mouse, while at work I use a Microsoft Bus Mouse. Both work very well.

Like keyboards, mice are very personal things. You should pick one that has a good feel to it. Play with several types from different manufacturers. Mice come in two basic flavors:

Roller ball

These use a hard rubber ball in their base to track your hand movement across the desk. Very old models had steel balls. Although very sensitive and reliable, they do require a periodic grooming. You must remove the ball occasionally and clean any accumulated crud from the directional rollers inside. A minor inconvenience.

Optical

These run over a special pad with grid. The mouse has an optical sensor and light source, and it tracks your hand movement by watching the grid. These require careful handling because if you scratch the pad you'll have a dead spot—i.e., the mouse won't see the grid through the scratch. Of course, if you get too many potholes in your pad, you can get a new one.

Optical mice also require a power source. This is provided with the mouse, but it means that you'll have two wires hanging out of your mouse instead of one.

GRAPHICS TABLETS

GEM supports the SummaGraphics line of tablets. I tried to get one to let you know what it's like, but the manufacturer just wouldn't lend me one. Oh well . . . .

CHAPTER

2

Putting GEM/3 on Your System

INTRODUCTION	14
STARTING THE INSTALLATION	14
CHANGING THE CONFIGURATION	18

INTRODUCTION

GEM was never difficult to install, but GEM/3 is a snap. Aside from being easier to install, it's also much easier to update. If you are a previous GEM user, you're also going to find that you can eliminate many of the previously created GEM directories. Now all of the GEM files and directories live under GEMAPPS. You can delete GEMBOOT, GEMSYS, GEMDESK, and GEMSCRAP (if you have this one).

Before we get into the nitty-gritty of GEM/3 installation, make sure of two things:

1. You have all of the disks that you need. In addition to the GEM installation disks, you may need a GEM driver pack disk. These disks hold the drivers for *all* plotters, cameras, and scanners, as well as for some exotic graphics card/monitor combinations and printers.
2. You know the types of hardware that make up your system, including: graphics card and monitor; pointing device (mouse or graphics tablet); printer or printers (and the ports that they use); and plotter, camera system, or scanner type (if you are installing any of these).

If you don't know this sort of information, you'll need to call your computer dealer or your friendly neighborhood PC guru for help.

STARTING THE INSTALLATION

To begin the installation, put the *system disk* (disk #1) into drive A:. Log to A: (type A, followed by Return at the DOS command prompt), and then type the following:

GEMPREP (Return)

The installation program will now prompt you to swap disks and supply information. The disk swapping part is fairly simple, but you will need to know the right answers when GEM/3 wants to know about your system. The first screen will ask if you are installing GEM/3 as a brand new program on your computer, or if you are merely changing an existing GEM/3 program. If you have a previous version of GEM on the computer, you are still installing this as a new configuration. See Figure 2.1.

Note that the bottom of the screen displays a bit of help in maneuvering through all of this. Pressing function key F1 will give you a bit more information about the selected device. Sometimes this will have a list of com-

Figure 2.1

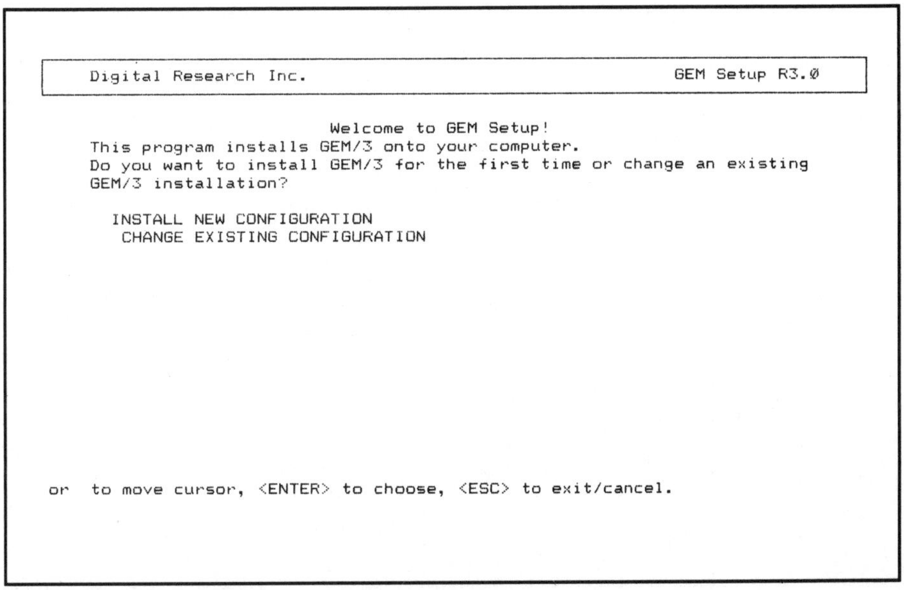

```
┌─────────────────────────────────────────────────────────────────┐
│    Digital Research Inc.                         GEM Setup R3.0 │
│                                                                 │
│                     Welcome to GEM Setup!                       │
│        This program installs GEM/3 onto your computer.          │
│        Do you want to install GEM/3 for the first time or change an existing
│        GEM/3 installation?                                      │
│                                                                 │
│           INSTALL NEW CONFIGURATION                             │
│           CHANGE EXISTING CONFIGURATION                         │
│                                                                 │
│                                                                 │
│                                                                 │
│                                                                 │
│        or   to move cursor, <ENTER> to choose, <ESC> to exit/cancel. │
│                                                                 │
└─────────────────────────────────────────────────────────────────┘
```

patible devices. You can use the up or down arrow keys to move your selector up or down through any menus. When you have the selection you want, just press Return. If you want to back up one screen, press the Escape key. At this point, pressing Escape will give you an opportunity to bail out of the setup program.

Now comes the fun part. GEM/3 will ask you for that hardware information we talked about previously. The first thing you'll need to tell it is about the disk drives you'll be installing GEM/3 on.

GEM/3 and its applications take up a lot of storage real estate, so the best way to do this is with a hard drive. If you have a high-density 5¼-inch floppy, or a 3½-inch microfloppy, GEM/3 won't be terribly inconvenient to run. At least you can get the Desktop on a single disk. If you have the 360-kilobyte, PC-type floppies, you can still install GEM/3. You'll need two blank, formatted floppy disks. Unless you're a true stoic, you'll put up with running GEM/3 that way only as long as it takes for your new hard drive and controller card to arrive in the mail.

After deciding the target media, you'll get to select the choices that match your system. At each selection, simply press Return to go on. See Figures 2.2, 2.3, 2.4, and 2.5.

Figure 2.2

```
┌─────────────────────────────────────────────────────────────────────┐
│  ┌─────────────────────────────────────────────────────────────┐    │
│  │ Digital Research Inc.                        GEM Setup R3.0 │    │
│  └─────────────────────────────────────────────────────────────┘    │
│                                                                     │
│     From the list below, select the graphics card and display       │
│     installed in your system.                                       │
│                                                                     │
│         AT&T DEB Card 16-Color Display (640x400)                    │
│         AT&T Monochrome Card (640x400)                              │
│        Hercules Card / Monochrome PC Display (720x348)              │
│         IBM CGA / Color Display (640x200) - Mono Mode               │
│         IBM EGA / Monochrome Display (640x350)                      │
│         IBM Enhanced Card & 16-Color Display (640x350)              │
│         IBM 16-Color VGA for PS/2 (640x480) or Compatible           │
│         IBM VGA Monochrome for the PS/2 (640x480) or Compatible     │
│         MDS THE GENIUS Monitor / THE GENIUS Monitor Card (728x1008) │
│         Video 7 Vega Deluxe / Quadram Prosync 16-Color Display (640x480) │
│         Video 7 Vega Deluxe / Quadram Prosync 16-Color Display (752x410) │
│         Wyse/Amdek Monochrome Graphics Display (1280x800)           │
│         OTHER (Driver Pack)                                         │
│                                                                     │
│                                                                     │
│    or    to move cursor, <ENTER> to choose.                         │
│                                                                     │
│                                                                     │
│                                                                     │
└─────────────────────────────────────────────────────────────────────┘
```

If you don't see your particular piece of hardware listed, you have two options:

1. If you have a driver pack that has the additional device you need, simply select the *OTHER (Driver Pack)* option and the program will prompt you to put your driver disk in drive A:.
2. The second option is considerably less wonderful. You may have hardware that GEM/3 doesn't directly support, and you may not have a driver pack disk to get you out of this mess. Take heart, you can call Digital Research and for a modest fee they'll send you a driver pack (if they have one). In the meantime, you can press Escape over and over until you get the option of exiting to DOS.

If you discover that Digital Research doesn't have a driver to match your hardware, check with the hardware manufacturer to see if that company might have a driver that it wrote. If not—well, what can I say? Read through the introductory chapter on picking your hardware, and decide what supported hardware best suits your needs. By the way, if you don't see your dot-matrix or laser printer listed, don't despair. Most dot-matrix printers either emulate the Epson/IBM Graphics printers or they can be made to.

Figure 2.3

```
┌─────────────────────────────────────────────────────────────────┐
│  ┌───────────────────────────────────────────────────────────┐  │
│  │   Digital Research Inc.                   GEM Setup R3.0  │  │
│  └───────────────────────────────────────────────────────────┘  │
│                                                                 │
│     Select the mouse or tablet you are using from the list below. │
│                                                                 │
│         No Mouse                                                │
│         Bus Mouse (Requires file MOUSE.COM )                    │
│         IBM Personal System/2 Mouse                             │
│         Microsoft Serial Mouse (RS232 )                         │
│         Mouse Systems PC Mouse / SummaMouse / Compatibles       │
│         SummaSketch 961 Cursor-Type Tablet                      │
│         SummaSketch 961 Stylus-Type Tablet                      │
│         SummaSketch 1201 Cursor-Type Tablet                     │
│         SummaSketch 1201 Stylus-Type Tablet                     │
│         Summagraphics MM1812 Cursor-Type Tablet                 │
│         Summagraphics MM1812 Stylus-Type Tablet                 │
│                                                                 │
│                                                                 │
│                                                                 │
│    or    to move cursor, <ENTER> to choose.                     │
│                                                                 │
│                                                                 │
└─────────────────────────────────────────────────────────────────┘
```

For instance, the Okidata Microline series will work just fine with the plug'n'play read-only memory chips installed.

As for laser printers, most will either emulate one of the Hewlett-Packard LaserJet models or speak PostScript. If not, you're probably stuck. Digital Research might be able to help you out, but you might also have an oddball printer.

The same goes for mice. Most mice will emulate the Microsoft mouse, and will have a MOUSE.COM program just for that purpose. I selected Microsoft BUS mouse for my system, even though I have a Logitech serial mouse. Isn't emulation a wonderful thing?

Remember as you go through the installation that you can have multiple printers and plotters. You can also have a printer or plotter not really attached to your computer, although you'll need to lie to GEM/3 to make this installation. A typical example might be a laser printer tied to a network. Install it as a printer with a port that you don't use and might not even have. LPT3: is usually a good choice. Just remember to redirect the output to a file with the *Printer Preferences* options in Output when you print with this device.

When you're all done, just tell the setup program to save everything, and it will ask you for various disks as it copies everything it needs. Don't

Figure 2.4

```
┌─────────────────────────────────────────────────────────────────┐
│                                                                 │
│    Digital Research Inc.                      GEM Setup R3.0    │
│                                                                 │
│   Select the printer that you intend to use from the list below.│
│                                                                 │
│     Epson GQ-3500 Laser Printer (300 x 300 Dots/Inch)           │
│       Epson LQ Series Printers (180 x 180 Dots/Inch)            │
│       Hewlett Packard Laserjet II Printer (300 x 300 Dots/Inch) │
│       Hewlett Packard LaserJet+ (150 x 150 Dots/Inch)           │
│       IBM/Epson High Resolution Printers (120 x 144 Dots/Inch)  │
│       IBM Proprinter (120 x 144 Dots/Inch)                      │
│       LaserWriter / Postscript Printers                         │
│       LaserWriter Plus / Postscript Printers                    │
│       Toshiba P321, P341, or P351 Printer (180 x 180 Dots/Inch) │
│       Xerox 4020 Color Ink Jet (120 x 240 Dots/Inch)            │
│       OTHER (Driver Pack)                                       │
│                                                                 │
│                                                                 │
│                                                                 │
│   or   to move cursor, <ENTER> to choose.                       │
│                                                                 │
│                                                                 │
└─────────────────────────────────────────────────────────────────┘
```

worry, you'll get one last chance to verify all of your selections before it actually writes the data to the hard drive or floppies.

CHANGING THE CONFIGURATION

That's the great thing about GEM/3. You can easily add, delete, or change the devices installed in GEM without reinstalling the whole GEM system. Marvelous.

To change the configuration, simply put the GEM/3 system disk back in drive A: and log there. Just as you did the first time, type:

GEMPREP (Return)

and away you go. This time, when the first screen comes up, select *Change Existing Configuration.* Now you'll get a chance to change whatever you like, including installing new devices from driver packs. And don't worry if you decide you want to quit in the middle of an update. As long as you haven't actually saved the new configuration, you can always use the Escape key to back up to a point where you can sneak back to DOS.

Figure 2.5

```
┌─────────────────────────────────────────────────────────────────┐
│   ┌─────────────────────────────────────────────────────────┐   │
│   │   Digital Research Inc.                 GEM Setup R3.0  │   │
│   └─────────────────────────────────────────────────────────┘   │
│       Select a communications port for your printer:            │
│                                                                 │
│          Parallel port #1 (LPT1)                                │
│          Parallel port #2 (LPT2)                                │
│          Parallel port #3 (LPT3)                                │
│          Communications port #1 (COM1)                          │
│          Communications port #2 (COM2)                          │
│                                                                 │
│                                                                 │
│                                                                 │
│     or    to move cursor, <ENTER> to choose, <ESC> to exit/cancel. │
│                                                                 │
└─────────────────────────────────────────────────────────────────┘
```

CHAPTER

3

Welcome to the Top of Your Desk

INTRODUCTION	21
MOUSE TECHNIQUES	21
CRANKING UP	23
WELCOME TO THE GRAPHIC ENVIRONMENT MANAGER	23
HOW TO OPERATE YOUR DESK	28
THE MENUS	30
DESKTOP	37
KEYBOARD COMMANDS	41
OUTPUT	42
PULL-DOWN MENUS	44
PREFERENCES	45

INTRODUCTION

When I first saw the GEM Desktop, I was amazed. I couldn't believe graphics that good and that fast were running on an 8088-based computer. I'd used the Macintosh, and here was this program that equaled the fabled Mac desktop running on a PC.

I've been using GEM for several years now, and it still amazes me. It doesn't quite so closely resemble the Mac desktop anymore; it now has a personality very much its own. It's taken me from a die-hard command line user to a person whose computer boots into the Desktop. Not because I like the novelty. Or because I secretly covet a Mac. Just because it is the easiest and most efficient way to run the computer and do the things I do.

In this chapter we'll go over the basics of the GEM/3 Desktop. I'll show you how to operate your computer just as efficiently from GEM as you can from DOS (and with quite a bit less effort). GEM provides a way to control your computer in a more human fashion. Instead of learning lots of commands and arguments, GEM allows you to learn a few common techniques that apply to almost every task. For instance, the mouse techniques you learn in operating the Desktop apply equally well to the applications programs. GEM also has keyboard shortcut commands, and they too are common throughout much of the GEM system.

GEM doesn't have many of the limitations of DOS. When copying or deleting, you aren't limited by DOS's wildcard file selection criteria. When you are at the Desktop, you can see the contents of the disks or directories. You don't have to ask the computer to show them to you.

MOUSE TECHNIQUES

Before we explore the Desktop, you need to know a little about mousing. In GEM, the mouse is just as important as the keyboard. You use it to grab, point, and select. It's really an extension of your hand inside the computer. You use only one mouse button in GEM, the leftmost button. It's used in at least one of five ways in every GEM application.

Click

You just put the pointer over whatever you want to activate and push the mouse button once. This is done to select something.

Figure 3.1

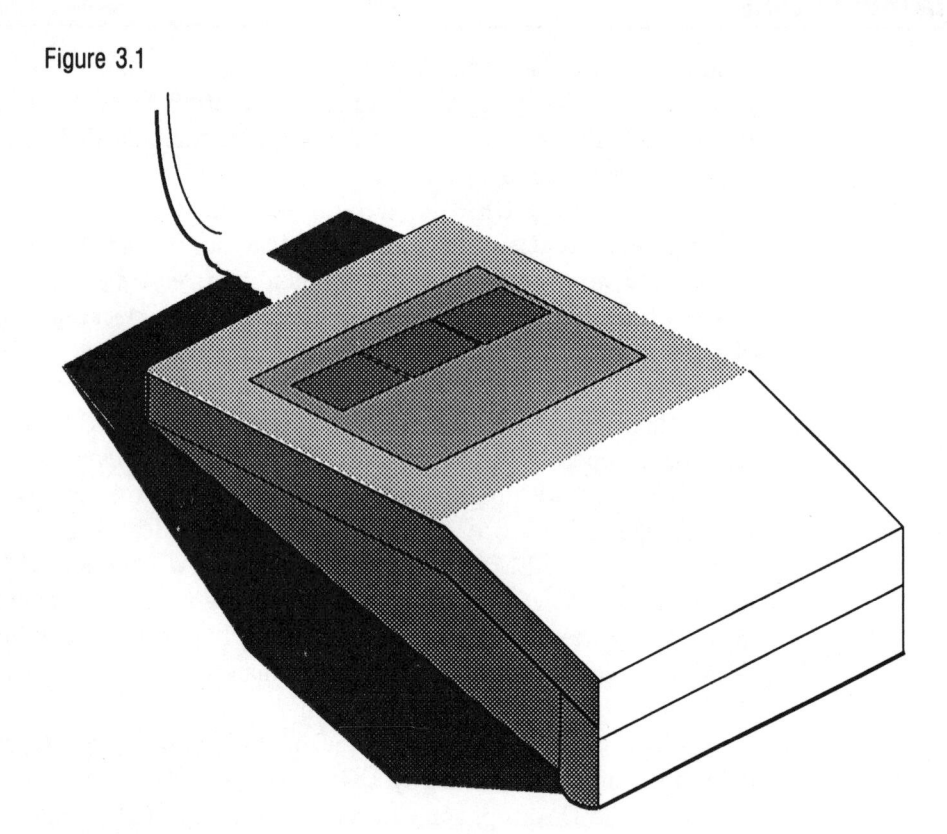

Click and Hold

Like click, except that you hold the button down, click and hold glues the pointer to something. When you move the pointer, the thing you've grabbed will move with it until you release the button.

Double Click

Just push the mouse button twice in rapid succession. You do this to activate something. For instance, if you want to activate an application, you put the pointer over it and double click. You can set the double click speed GEM expects to match your own style (we'll talk about that in configuring the Desktop).

Shift Click

To select more than one thing, you hold the shift key down while you click over several things. You might do this to select several files to print.

Control Click

Suppose you want to select through several things—e.g., when you have layers of things on top of things and you want to select one thing in the stack and leave the others. This really doesn't have much use at the Desktop, but it becomes extremely important with other applications.

That's pretty much all there is to using the mouse. Some GEM applications use variations on the above themes, but they are logical variations. For instance, in Draw Plus, you may click and hold to draw a line. The line will stay glued to the mouse until you release the button.

CRANKING UP

To bring a properly installed version of GEM up on a hard drive, first switch to the root directory. If you have a path command pointing at the root, you don't even have to be there. Now type:

GEM (Return)

A batch file will madly begin switching directories, setting paths, and finally invoke the GEMVDI program. The Desktop will rapidly begin to form on the screen, layer-by-layer. And, as they say in the shopping malls, you are now here.

If you have a floppy-based system, put the Startup disk in drive A: and then type:

GEM (Return)

If you are using 360-kilobyte disks, GEM will tell you when to put the Desktop disk in drive A:. After you load the Desktop disk and press a key, the computer will finish loading GEM.

If you want, you can put the GEM statement as the last line of your AUTOEXEC.BAT file. This will automatically load GEM every time you turn on or reset your computer.

WELCOME TO THE GRAPHIC ENVIRONMENT MANAGER

GEM (the Graphic Environment Manager) relies heavily on graphic images. You don't live in a world of words alone. If people didn't respond to pictures as well as words, all traffic signs would look alike except for their messages. Your computer should be as visual as the rest of your world.

Figure 3.2 shows a typical GEM Desktop (mine). The two "desktops" represent the surfaces of a pair of desks (or desk and table if you prefer). The desks hold various files, file folders, and storage areas. These files are really computer files.

In DOS, a file is identified by its name only. In GEM, files are identified by their names and by symbols called icons. The icons identify:

- Application programs
- Files related to application programs
- Miscellaneous files
- Other things—like directories, floppy drives, and hard disk drives—are also identified with icons.

The icons pictured in Figure 3.3 represent all of the standard GEM applications from Digital Research. You may have all or only some of these applications on your machine, as well as some third-party applications. The total list includes:

GEM Draw Plus

This is the GEM illustration package. It draws crisp straight lines and smooth arcs and circles. Everything drawn becomes an object that you can later

Figure 3.2

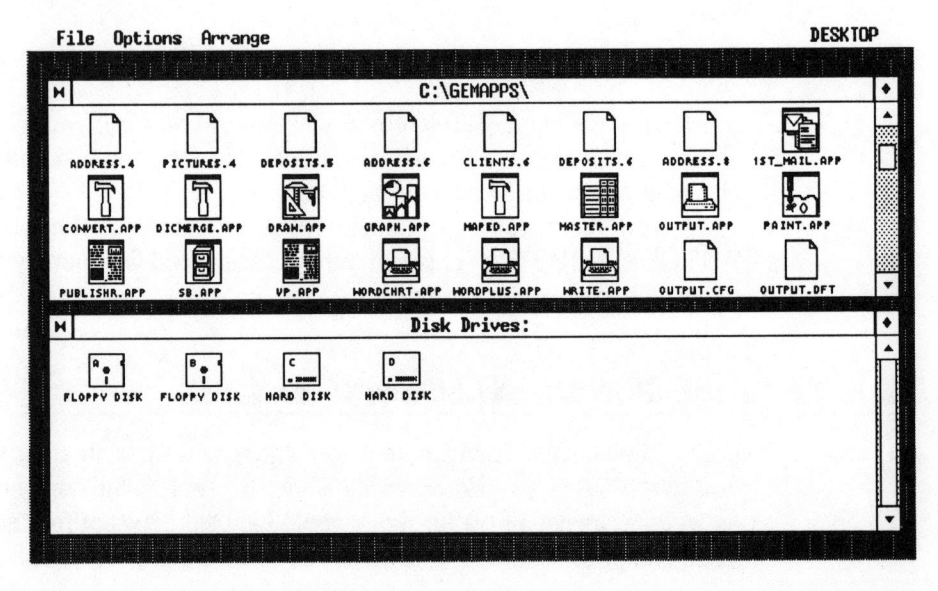

Figure 3.3

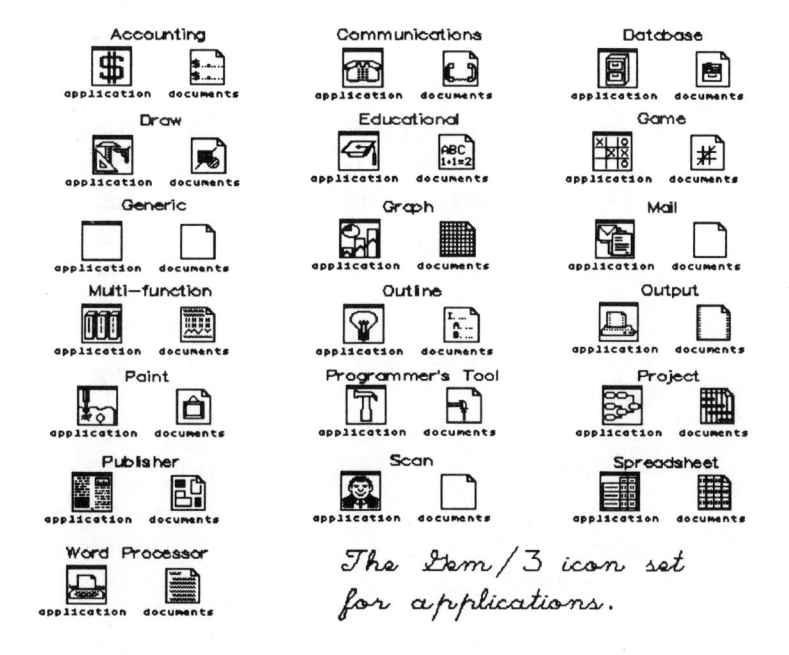

The Gem/3 icon set for applications.

duplicate, modify, or throw away. This icon is applied to any draw (object oriented graphics) application.

GEM Graph

A marvel of a graphing tool, this application allows you to create two- or three-dimensional graphs and charts to illustrate numerical information. It can read data from your favorite spreadsheet, word processor, or even database. You apply this icon to any general-purpose graphing application.

GEM Map Editor

The Map Editor is a tool available to licensed owners of GEM Graph. It lets you break the two maps included with Graph (Europe and the U.S.) into any regions you want. Software tool icon.

GEM Paint II

This is probably the most fun application. It does free-form graphics that have an expressionist quality. Sort of an air brush with fat droplets. An update of the original GEM Paint package, this one has a number of improvements (such as almost infinite control of line weights). It's the bit image graphics application icon.

GEM Desktop Publisher

A powerful page-layout tool, Desktop Publisher can combine text and graphics from all of the various GEM applications into anything from a newsletter to a book. All desktop publishing programs use this icon.

GEM WordChart

You use WordChart to make text-based viewgraphs. These can have multiple columns, borders, numbered points, etc. For lack of a better icon assignment, WordChart uses the word processing icon.

GEM Write

The first GEM word processor, GEM Write is *very* basic. It can, however, combine text and graphics, and it works elegantly with a mouse. Again, the word processing icon.

GEM 1st Word Plus

The current GEM word processor, 1st Word Plus packs fully professional features: a built-in spelling checker, power mailing list utilities, the ability to merge text and graphics, and multiple file editing. It's one of the tools I used to write this book. Another use of the word processing icon.

GEM Convert

This is a 1st Word Plus utility that converts WordStar, GEM Write, or ASCII files into 1st Word Plus files. It works phenomenally well. A software tool.

GEM 1st Mail

The powerful mailing list utility for 1st Word Plus, 1st Mail has the mail list icon.

GEM Dictionary Merge

By using the Dictionary Merge, you can combine your customized 1st Word Plus supplementary dictionaries with the main dictionary. Another software tool.

GEM Scan

I love GEM Scan. It's one of the best and by far the easiest scanner packages I've ever seen. If you use a scanner, you've got to have GEM Scan. The smiling face is the scanner utility icon.

Each application icon has a related file type icon as well. To activate an application, double click on its icon. If you want to activate it and load it with a related file, click on the file. Most applications come with at least one installed related file, and you can install more file types. Just don't install the same file type for more than one application; it will always load into the last application it was installed for. We'll talk about just how to do that in the options menu section.

All other files are shown as either generic programs or batch files (anything that can execute), or generic files. Neatly, GEM allows you to assign icons to programs and batch files, as well as their related files. After you do that, and save the configuration, the programs can be called up from the Desktop as if they were GEM applications.

DISK DRIVES

The three widgets on the bottom desk are storage devices: the A: and B: floppies and the hard drive C:. You'll notice in Figure 3.4 that C: is highlighted, meaning that it is selected. There is a difference between selected and activated. Selected simply means that you can now open it, examine it, delete it, format it, or do any other option available through GEM menus.

By the way, when you install GEM it will find the A: floppy drive and, if present, the C: hard drive on its own. But it's up to you to tell it about any other floppy and hard drives installed. The section on the Options menu explains how to do this.

DIRECTORIES

Directories are shown as neatly arranged file folders, starting from the upper left corner of the desk. (Where else would you keep your files?). To open a folder, place the pointer over it and double click. The contents of the folder will be distributed over the surface of the desk, while all of the previously shown files, etc. are magically put away.

To create a new directory, double click on the folder marked "new folder." See Figure 3.5. GEM will ask you for the name of the folder. New folder is available in any directory.

Figure 3.4

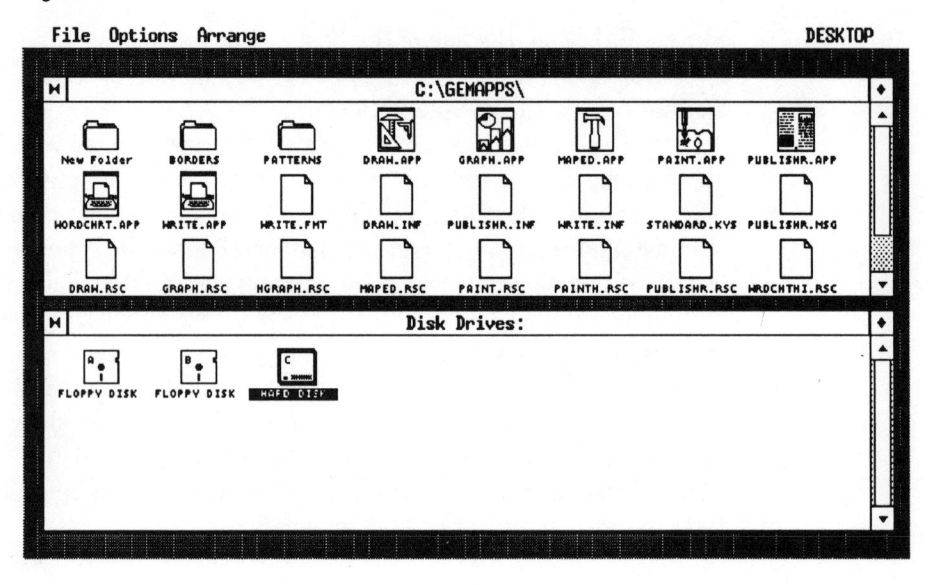

Figure 3.5

HOW TO OPERATE YOUR DESK

This brings us to the Desktop gadgets. Being electronic, these desks have a few features your office desk may lack. See Figure 3.6.

The slider scrolls the window over the surface of the desk up and down. It does this as you run it up and down its track, called a scroll bar. If the slider touches the top and bottom, as in the bottom desk, there's nothing else to see. If it doesn't, you can look at the rest of the contents by simply grabbing it and sliding it down. You do this by:

1. Moving the pointer over the slider.
2. Pressing and holding the left mouse button.
3. Sliding the bar up and down by moving the mouse. As long as you hold the mouse button down, the slider bar will stick to the pointer. Let go

Figure 3.6

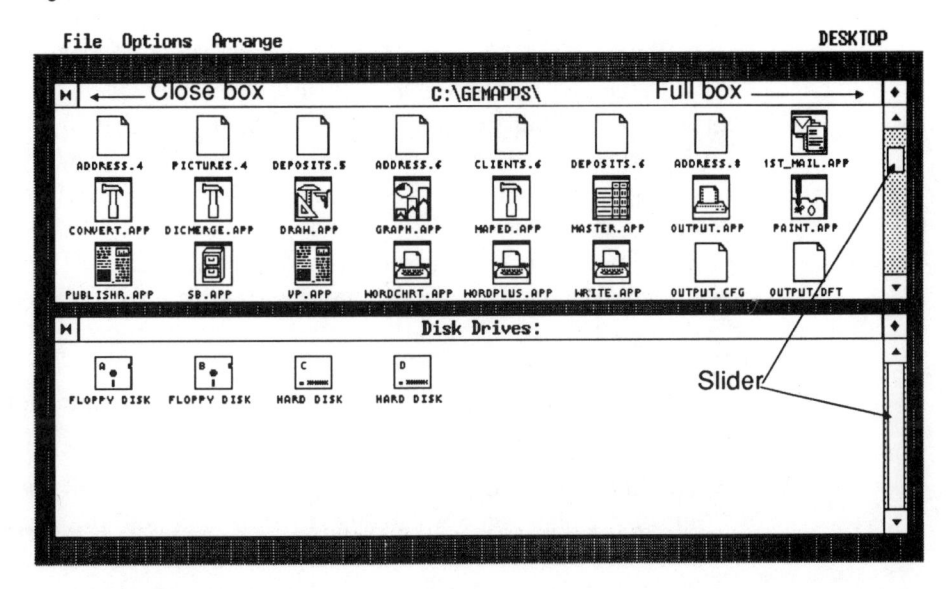

and the pointer will release the slider. The shift arrow at the top and bottom of the scroll bar will shift the slider up or down by one row of icons. Put the pointer over the arrowhead and click to move a row. Hold the mouse button down and the slider will merrily chug along in the proper direction.

The box with the diamond at the upper right of the screen is the full box. If you move the pointer over it and click the left mouse button on it, the Desktop will expand to fill the screen. Click on it again, and it will shrink back to normal size.

The box with the sideways hourglass at the left of each desk is the close box. Click on this and everything on the desk will be put away, revealing the contents of the next directory above. For instance, if you click on the close box in the documents directory, it will close and the contents of the root directory will appear. Close the root directory and you'll see the disk drives.

THE FILING SYSTEM

GEM is quite a bit more capable than DOS at file-handling functions. It's almost intuitive to use. To copy a file, you place the pointer over it, and click and hold. The file will highlight to show that you've selected it. While holding the mouse button, you just drag it to whatever directory or disk you want. When you release the mouse button, the file will be copied.

If there is a name conflict, GEM will tell you. It will also give you the option of canceling the copy or going ahead. Try that in DOS.

Deleting and renaming are just as easy. Click once on the file to highlight it, and then go up to the File menu. Select Info/Rename to rename it or Delete to blow it away.

In DOS, you can select files based only on name. At best, you can put "wildcards" into a name to denote all files with a particular extension or all files with a given combination of letters at a certain position in their names. GEM has no such limitations.

There are two ways to select multiple files, and you can use them both together if you like. See Figure 3.7.

1. The first way is to draw a rectangle around them. Put the pointer to the left of the files you want to select. Press and hold the mouse button, and move the mouse to the right and down until the rectangle trailing from the mouse touches or covers all the files you want to select. Then release the mouse button. All of the files within or touching the rectangle will highlight.
2. The second way is to shift click over the files. Hold the shift key down and click on all the files you want. Each will highlight in turn.

The techniques for manipulating files work just as well with folders and disk drives. Disk-to-disk copying is as simple as grabbing a source disk icon and dragging it to the target disk. One word of caution, though. GEM can actually delete the contents of a hard drive. It will give you adequate warning if you select a hard drive by mistake, but then it will ruthlessly execute the command.

THE MENUS

The bar along the top of the screen is the menu bar. The words in mixed upper and lower case along the top of the screen show the positions of pull-down menus. Actually they're more like fall-down menus since all you need to do is touch the menu title with the pointer and the menu magically drops down. As you move the pointer up and down the menu, the selections alternately turn to white-on-black, marking which one will turn on if you click the mouse button.

Figure 3.7

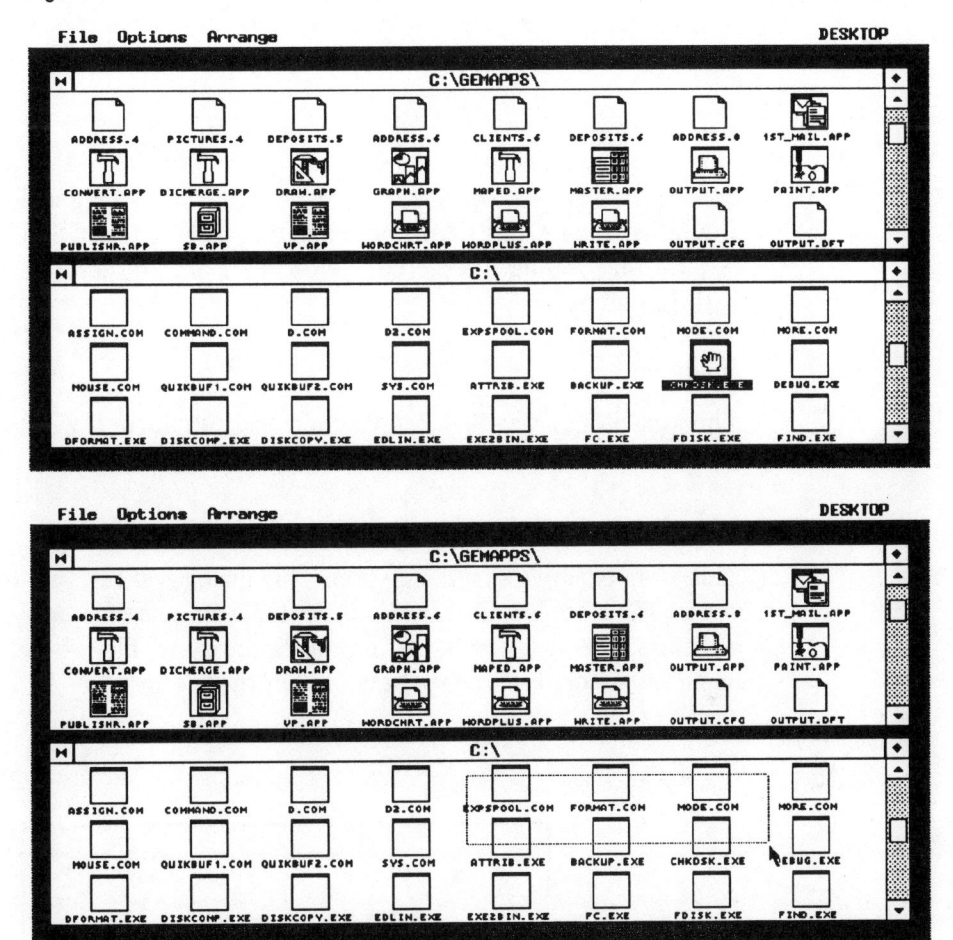

By the way, if you don't like touch-and-drop menus, you can configure GEM to require a click on the menu title to drop the menu. This makes it operate more in tune with the standards set for OS/2.

As you are exploring the menus, you'll notice that some of the selections are followed by an ellipses, such as:

Info/Rename . . .

When you see the ellipses, it means that click on the selection will bring up a *dialog*. A dialog may be a full-blown menu or simply a confirmation that you really want to do this. Whatever it is, it will give you some information and then require you to make some sort of selection (hence the name dialog).

FILE

The file menu lets you handle most of the file management functions in DOS. See Figure 3.8. With the exception of Exit to DOS, all of its options require that you have selected one or more files, directories, or disk drives with the mouse.

Open

This will either activate the application or program, or it will open a directory or disk drive. It is equivalent to double clicking.

Info/Rename . . .

This is an example of a dialog box. This dialog will tell you about the thing you've selected. It will change a little depending on whether you've selected a disk, a directory, or a file. For a directory or file, you can change the name by simply typing in a new one on the file line.

Figure 3.8

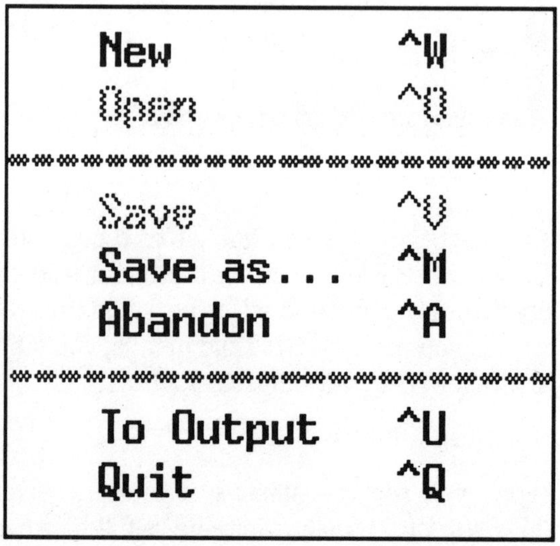

New	^W
Open	^O
Save	^V
Save as...	^M
Abandon	^A
To Output	^U
Quit	^Q

In addition, this box will tell you important information about whatever you've selected. You can find out how big it is, when it was created and so on. See Figures 3.9, 3.10, and 3.11.

You can get to this function by the keyboard command Alt-I (Alt is shown as a diamond in GEM).

Figure 3.9

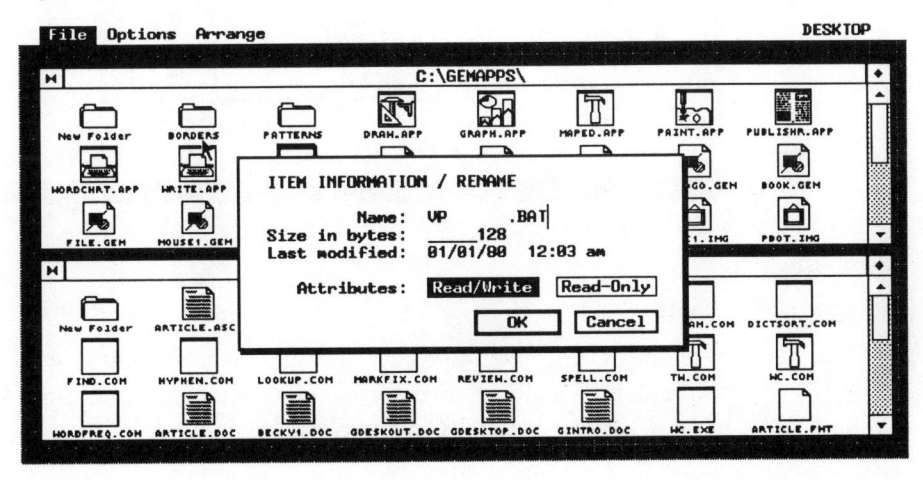

Figure 3.10

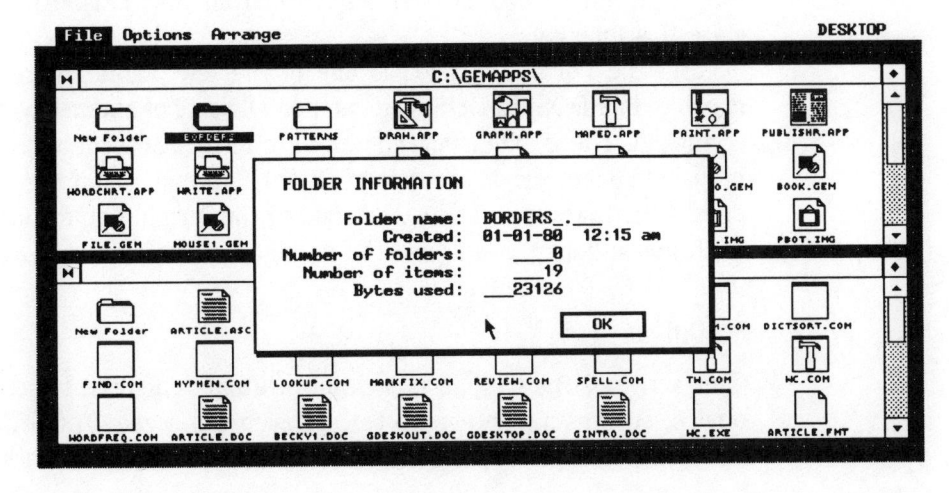

Figure 3.11

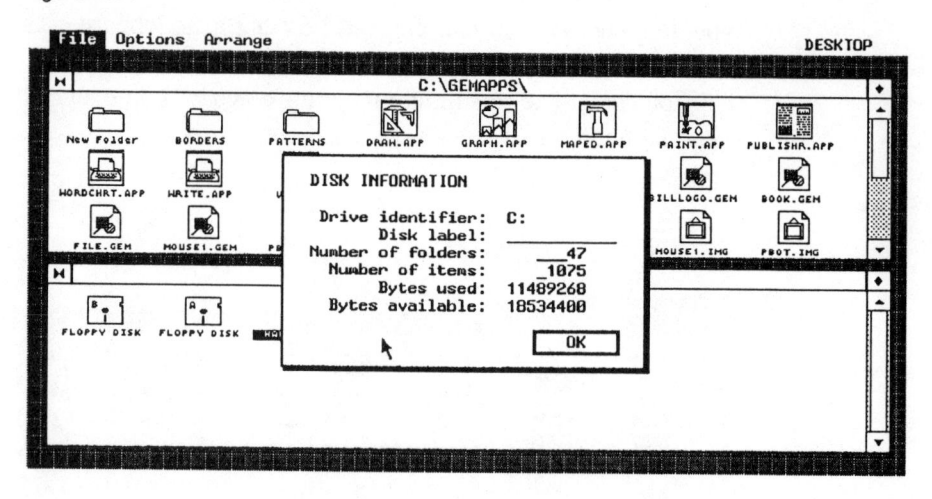

Delete . . .

Selecting Delete will do away with all selected files. It will also delete the contents (including subdirectories) of all selected directories or drives. GEM will ask you to confirm (unless you turn confirm off).

Format . . .

Format the selected drive. GEM will ask you to confirm your decision to format. If you've ever accidentally formatted your hard drive you'll appreciate this function.

But the Format function is one of the few points where GEM is less capable than DOS. In DOS, you can add all sorts of extensions to the format command. These extensions allow you to format 360-kilobyte disks in a 1.2-megabyte floppy drive, use the old DOS 1.0 format, and other niceties. GEM doesn't have a way to add extensions to the format command. If you tell it to format a floppy, it will use the default format for that drive.

To Output

This activates the Output application. Output sends the file to a peripheral device, such as a printer, plotter, or even the screen. In GEM/3, you can also print your file to disk (which is great if you have networked systems).

Exit to DOS

Bye-bye to GEM and back to the DOS command line.

Option

Option let's you tweak GEM until it suits your taste. It also gives you a way to tell GEM about additional drives and assign icons to non-GEM applications. See Figure 3.12.

Install disk drive . . .

If your system has more than one floppy or hard drive, you'll need to use this. Click on the previously installed floppy or hard drive (depending on what you want to install), and then select this option. You'll get a dialog box telling you about the drive you've selected. Use the text cursor (the vertical line) to back over the drive identifier; then type in the drive letter you want to install. Click on Install. Remember to use Save desktop (also in Option) or you'll find that after you exit from GEM the drive is no longer installed. See Figure 3.13.

RAM drives and directories masquerading as drives through the DOS SUBST command should be installed as hard drives.

Configure application . . .

My favorite. Click on an application program (GEM or not) and you can set it up the way you want. Use the arrow keys or the mouse to put the ex-

Figure 3.12

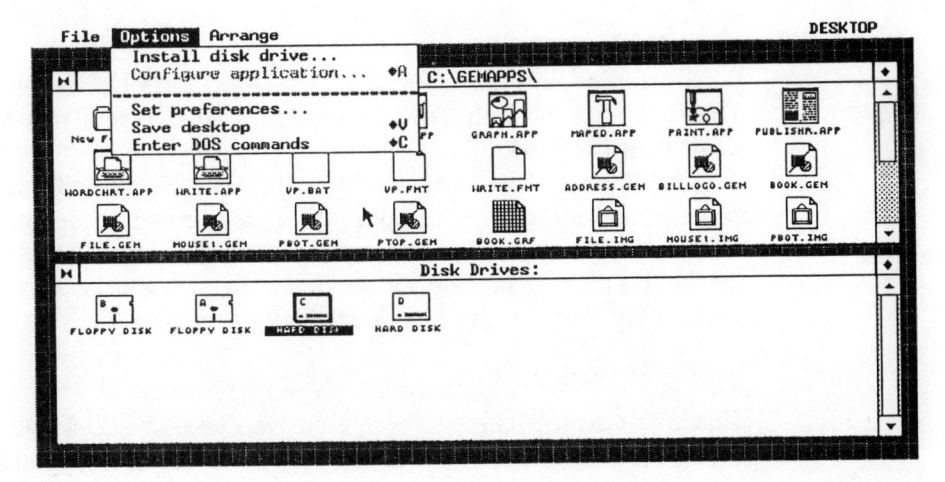

Figure 3.13

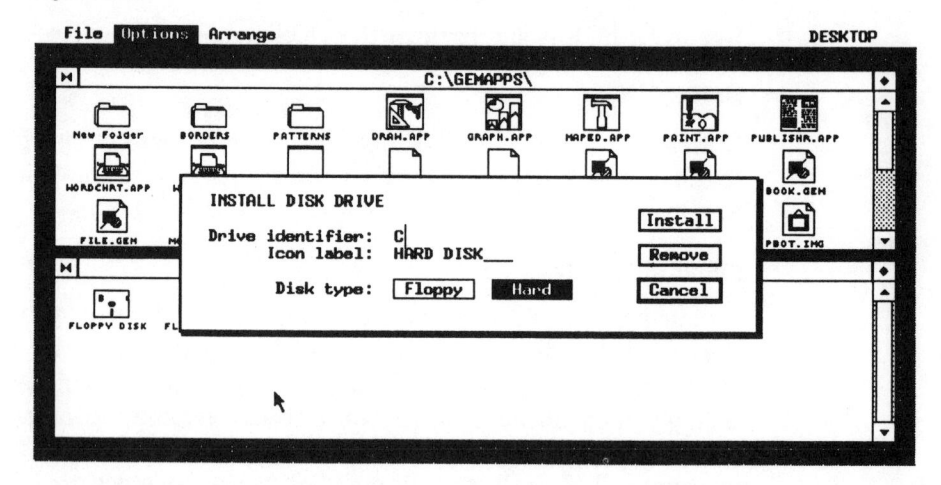

tensions of related files in the Document types spaces. For instance, since I use GEM 1st Word Plus for most word processing, I have 1st Word Plus set for files with the following extensions: DOC, MEM, LET, ME, TXT, and ASC. This assigns all such files the text icon. If I double click on such a file anywhere in the Desktop, it's automatically loaded into 1st Word Plus.

I also use the public domain ARC program to "unpack" compressed files I received over the modem. I have the ARC application program configured to have any files with the ARC extension as Document types. Double clicking on such files sends ARC off to do its thing with a maximum of convenience.

Set DOS-takes parameters if you want GEM to ask you for arguments when you double click on a non-GEM application. If you don't want this, select DOS.

Most non-GEM applications should be set with Needs full memory-Yes. This is just to be safe. (I like safe, especially when unsafe may mean trashing a few hours of work.)

Use the scroll bar and arrows to browse the available icons until you find one that matches your application—or one with a design you like and will remember the new meaning you've mentally assigned to it. For instance, the Font Editor from Specific Solutions installs as the Outline processor because the related files icon looks like a type font file.

Set preferences . . .

This is the main tweaking dialog box. You can be a GEM Rambo and tell it not to confirm deletes or copies (just have a steady eye and hand). If you know someone whose hand and arm movements are impaired, slowing down the click speed can make GEM accessible.

Save desktop

Do this whenever you configure an application or make any changes with Options. If you don't, the changes will last only until you exit from GEM. You can also use this to pick the contents of the twin desks when you crank GEM up. Just select the directories (or whatever you want to display) and save; then these will be the defaults.

Enter DOS commands

Some programs call this a DOS gateway. Select it and you'll apparently drop back to DOS. GEM is still active, however. After you've done whatever you needed to do, enter EXIT at the DOS command line and you'll snap back into GEM.

Watch out when using this. Because GEM is active, it is consuming a little memory. Don't return to GEM with the GEM command. You'll be loading GEM on top of itself with less memory to use. This is a definite crash waiting to happen.

Arrange

I use Arrange all the time, especially in crowded directories. It will sort the directory contents in name (alphabetically), type (file extension), size, or date order. Show as text radically changes the way GEM looks. No zippy icons—just dull, old file names. It's for those who love text and hate pictures. If you use Save desktop under options, the arrange selection you've picked will become the default.

DESKTOP

This is the upper right-hand drawer to the GEM Desktop. See Figure 3.14. It's where all of the accessories live. You can also find the current version of the Desktop or GEM application (and the programmers names) by clicking on the Info selection.

Accessories are pop-up gadgets that serve that occasional invaluable service. You can have any and all of the accessories visible at any given time. You can drag any accessory around the Desktop by clicking and holding on its title bar. If you want the clock visible in your GEM application, just grab

Figure 3.14

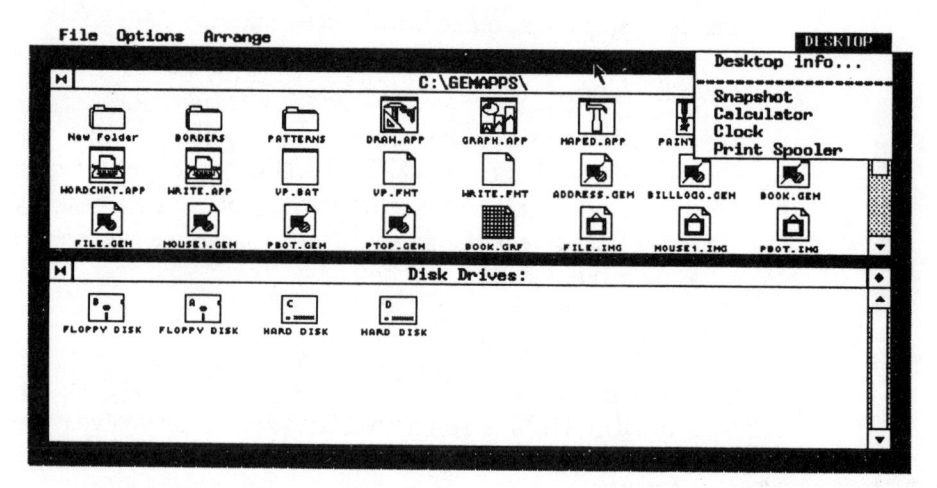

the application by its title bar and shift it down a bit. Then activate the clock and drag it up to the open space.

Click on the close box (upper left) to put the accessory away. If you click on your underlying application, the accessory will remain active but will drop behind the application. Really. Grab the size box at the lower right of the application and push it back if you don't believe me. Anyway, you can pull the accessory out front again by selecting it from the information dialog.

A technical digression: Desktop accessories are loaded into system memory whenever you boot GEM. In previous versions, the accessories inhabited the GEMBOOT directory. With the end of such directories in GEM/3, they were forced to move down the block to /GEMAPPS/GEMSYS. This is good to know because sometimes you may need to clear memory space by removing the accessories.

Accessories always have an .ACC, such as SNAPSHOT.ACC, and they can also have a .RSC file. I remove them by just renaming the files extensions. Select the .ACC and .RSC file icons, and hit the ALT-I. Backspace over the file extension, and put in something else (I usually just reverse the order of the letters to .CCA and .CSR). Exit from GEM and come back in, and the accessories will be gone.

Your ever-handy accessories are:

Calculator

The GEM calculator (see Figure 3.15) is a typical four-function calculator, with memory, that you can pull out of the drawer at any time. You can either

Figure 3.15

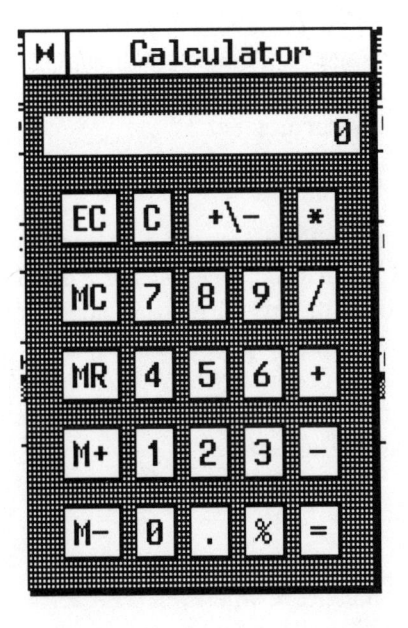

Figure 3.16

press the buttons by clicking on them (which is much like typing with a cane), or you can press the NUMLOCK key and use the numeric keypad on your keyboard. The keys with letters are accessed by pushing the key combination shown. For instance, press M and then R for MR (memory response). Use the \ key for sign change.

Clock

The clock (see Figure 3.16) displays the time and date, read from the system clock. If you don't have a real time clock, you can just set the date and time. Click on the hour, minute, month, etc., and it will highlight. You can now enter the date or time. The clock symbol, am/pm indicator, and the note are *toggles*. Toggles change state when you click on them. The clock symbol will change to the alarm bell, and show you the time and date for the alarm clock. Click on the note and it will change to red or become solid to indicate that the alarm is set.

Print Spooler

Unlike the DOS spooler, this one works in the background while you use a GEM application. See Figure 3.17. It's just a print utility, so don't expect it to execute any formatting codes in a word processor file. Add name and Delete name do just what they say.

If you are using the Apple LaserWriter or any other PostScript printer, forget about the spooler. It can't generate PostScript so your spooled printing will be ignored.

SnapShot

This one comes with GEM Paint, and it's a writer's dream tool. With it, you can capture whatever is on screen (in GEM) and save it as a GEM Paint file (.IMG). Its primary use is to take an object graphic from GEM Draw

Figure 3.17

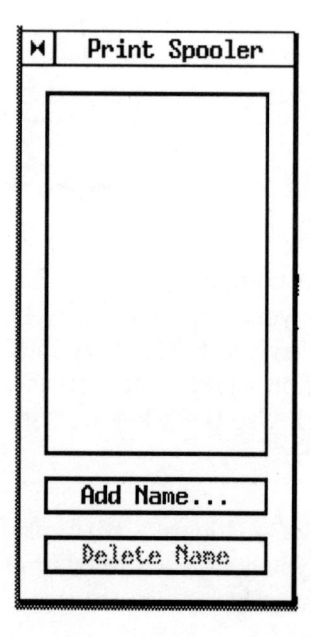

Plus and transfer it to GEM Paint. You may find that it doesn't have enough memory to work in some applications (such as Desktop Publisher). Instructions for its use are available by clicking on the big question mark.

Diary

This is an almost wonderful utility written by Roland Frank of EDTD in Germany. You can get it in this country with AMSTRAD computers. Basically, it's a replacement for the calculator, clock, and printer spooler accessory that comes with GEM. You can keep all of the accessories installed, but they will suck up a fair amount of memory. Since Diary has a calculator and the calendar has a clock, all you'll lose is the print spooler.

What you gain is an appointment calendar, multiple card files, and the ability to set enough alarms and reminders to drive yourself nuts. Unfortunately you can't print any information from it.

Your copy of Diary may not be set to install into GEM/3. To install it, make a GEMBOOT directory, and then use the INSTALL application on the Diary disk. When it's done, copy the DIARY.ACC file to the /GEMAPPS/GEMSYS directory, and then delete GEMBOOT. A little cumbersome, but not terribly difficult.

KEYBOARD COMMANDS

GEM keyboard commands are listed on the pull-down menus, but just for your easy reference the following is a complete list of Desktop keyboard commands.

Configure application	Alt-A
Enter DOS commands	Alt-C
Delete (file, directory, disk contents)	Alt-D
Info/Rename (file)	Alt-I
Sort by name (files)	Alt-N
Sort by type (files)	Alt-P
Show as text (files)	Alt-S
Sort by date (files)	Alt-T
Save desktop (configuration)	Alt-V
Sort by size (file)	Alt-Z

Exit to DOS	Control-Q
To Output	Control-U

OUTPUT

Actually, Output is a separate application called from the Desktop. I've included it with the Desktop because they seem so interrelated. Output does what it says: it outputs something to the selected device. Unlike earlier versions of GEM, GEM/3 allows you to have multiple output devices selected. For instance, let's say that you have a NEC 890 laser and a dot-matrix printer. Because the NEC can be configured either as a PostScript or LaserJet II compatible laser printer, you might want both types of output drivers available. You might also want a dot-matrix printer assigned to parallel port LPT1:. You can have all three printers installed, and pick the one you want when you're ready to print. To pick an output device, merely click on its icon.

Because GEM files are device independent, you can take a disk with files from a machine set up for a Xerox inkjet printer to a machine with an Apple LaserWriter and print them on either device with no problems. Output can also print non-GEM files, as long as they are in an ASCII format.

GEM makes three types of printer files:

1. .GEM files are graphics output files. Even .IMG files will have a matching .GEM file, and that's the one you print.
2. .GMP files are the document output files from Desktop Publisher.
3. .OUT files are the output files from 1st Word Plus and Write.

There are, quite conveniently, four different ways to get to Output:

1. *Go directly to Output from the Desktop with no files selected.* Output is accessed through the File pull-down menu. You might do this to grab your files using Output's own add file feature, or to change the Output's default parameters.
2. *Select files and then go to Output from the Desktop.* You select files by clicking on them, or shift clicking on multiple files. Or you can drag a box around them with click and hold. Up to ten files selected directly from the Desktop.
3. *Double click on a .LIS file.* These are lists of files saved so they can be loaded into Output.

4. *Access Output from within another GEM application, such as Desktop Publisher or Paint.* When you do this, you get the choice of exiting from Output either to the Desktop or back to your application.

Any file that you select for Output—from the Desktop, an application, or from within Output itself—is added to the Output list. Output lists can be modified from within Output, and they can be saved to a file with a .LIS format. This is quite handy, especially if the files are strung across multiple directories.

Once in Output, you'll find an assortment of tools. If you have GEM 2.1 or later, you'll notice output device types along the right. These reflect the devices you've installed. You can have one printer, one plotter, one camera, and one screen device. Version 2.2 has a legend below each device with its name. The highlighted icon is the one that's currently selected, with the printer as the default. GEM/3, of course, allows you to have multiple printers installed.

The left of the screen has two pull-down menus and a set of tools. See Figure 3.18. Click on START to start the output process (it will highlight when selected). Add Name calls up a typical GEM file selector. Click on the close box at the upper right of the selector to jump up a directory level. Click on directory shown if you want to open it, or a file if you find one you

Figure 3.18

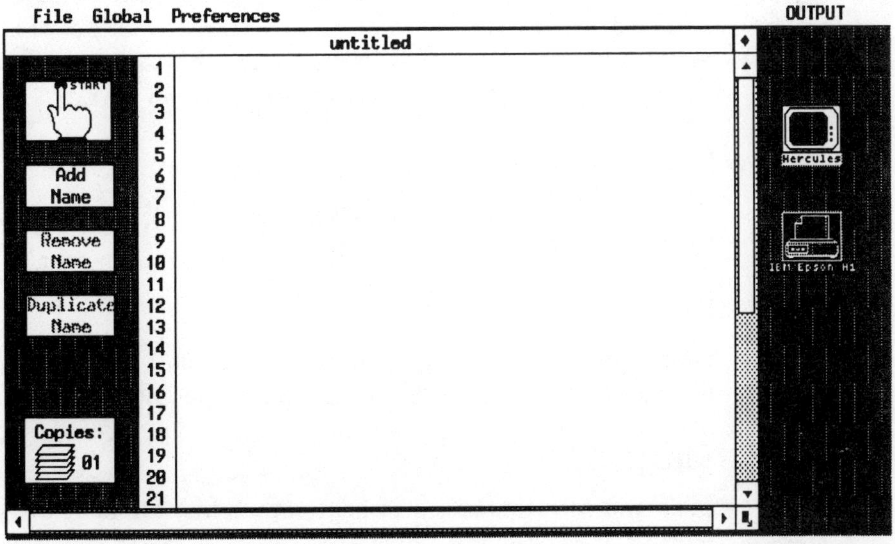

want. You can also click on the directory or file names, backspace over what's currently there, and type in the proper path or file name.

The Delete file tool lets you remove a file from the Output list. First, you must select a file in the list before this tool will become active (otherwise it will stay gray). Click on a file to highlight it; then click on Delete file. If you want to print more than one copy of a file in the list, follow the same rationale.

The Number of copies tool at the bottom lets you print multiple sets of the files in the Output list. Click on the line, backspace over one, and type in the number you want.

PULL-DOWN MENUS

GEM/3 Output has a lot more capability than previous versions, and there are some new menu selections as well.

FILE

An old friend. File shows up in just about every application, although it may have more or less functions depending on the program.

New

Opens a new List file, clearing away anything on the current Output listing. List files are just that, lists of files to load into Output. This makes it easy to output a number of files, even though they are on different directories. Output listings and List files can have up to 36 entries.

Open . . .

Pulls up the file selector so that you hunt about for a previously saved List (.LIS) file.

Save

Saves everything on the current Output listing to a List file. The file selector will appear so that you can assign it a name and a folder to live in.

Save as . . .

Let's you save the listing to some other List file name. If you've modified the List file you might want to do this.

To (whatever)

Pops out of Output and back to the application you were in. This only appears if you've jumped to Output from a GEM application.

Quit

Back to the Desktop.

GLOBAL

Shortcuts . . .

A handy two-screen helper that reminds you of keyboard commands for the Output tools and some handy tips.

Global . . .

One of the really major enhancements in GEM/3. See Figure 3.19. The menu offers three choices, the last of which you'll find is tremendously handy.

1. *Confirm .LIS changes*, if set to Yes, will make you confirm any changes to a .LIS file before they are made.
2. *Auto display:* is something you probably want to stay away from. You definitely don't want to use this if you have Desktop Publisher or 1st Word Plus. When set to Yes, Output will automatically begin printing any selected files. That may seem pretty slick, but it doesn't let you use the next selection.
3. *Print pages numbered 001 through 999.* Use this to set the beginning and ending pages for a Desktop Publisher or 1st Word Plus file. This was a major annoyance with Desktop Publisher, and now there is an elegant and simple solution.

PREFERENCES

This pull-down menu lets you fine tune Output. Unlike other menus, this one changes form depending on what type of output device is currently selected.

SCREEN PREFERENCES

Screen preferences let you use the screen output for a "slide show." These are great for training courses, sales presentations, and the like. If you have

Figure 3.19

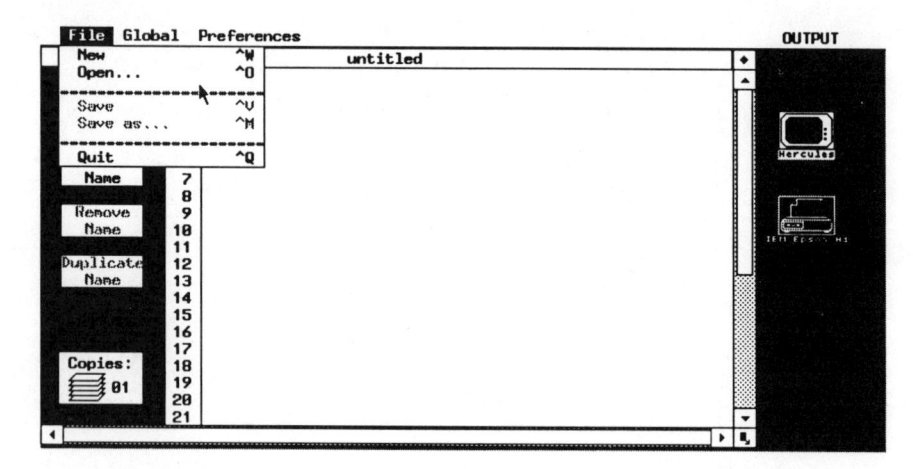

access to a video projector that can take output from a computer, GEM can be the presentation tool of your dreams.

Wait for key means that GEM won't output the next file on the list to the screen until either a key is pressed (other than Shift, Control, or Alt), or the mouse button is clicked.

Selecting either 2, 5, 10, or 20 seconds sets GEM to wait the prescribed time before advancing to the next file in the list. If you set Cycle to Yes, GEM will wrap around to the first file in the list after it outputs the last. It will repeat the list until someone has the decency to press the Escape key.

PRINTER PREFERENCES

The printer preferences pull-down menu gives you a good deal of control over your printer. There are several dialogs.

Page

Scale (see Figure 3.20) has these options:

Full scale literally means that graphics will be printed at the size they were drawn. If your GEM Draw Plus graphic is three inches by seven inches, that's the way it will appear when printed.

Best fit is handy when, after looking at the printed output, you don't like what you see. GEM will stretch the graphic to fill the page.

Figure 3.20

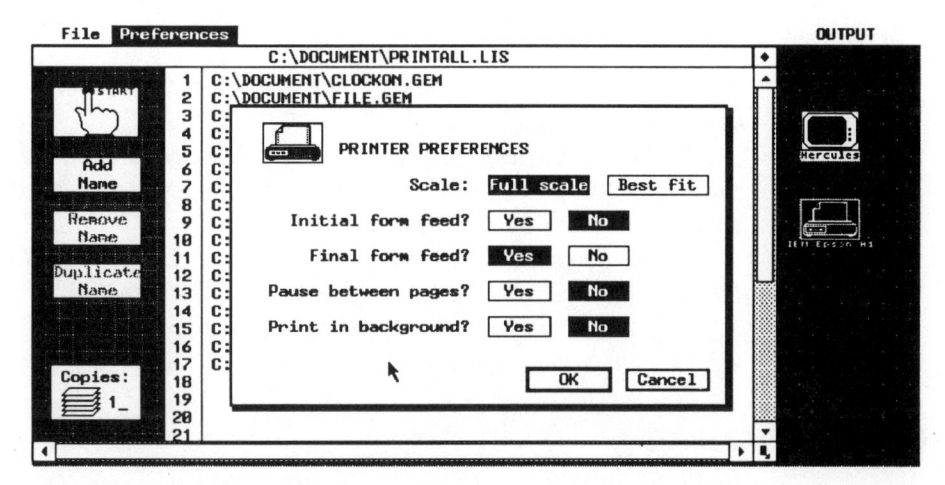

The *Final form feed* option will kick a blank sheet of paper through the printer after printing the output list. If the printer is properly set, then this will make sure that it advances to the top of a page before printing anything else. This is unnecessary with laser printers, unless you want a blank separator sheet between your stuff and the rest of the world's.

Position lets you move the image around a bit on the page. It's a great last minute adjuster if you didn't set your margins correctly.

Paper Size

Units: lets you pick the increments to display for the list of paper sizes. Click on whatever paper size you want, as long as your printer can do it. If you are using a wide carriage printer or a laser printer, this is really handy.

Paper Tray: The title is deceiving because this does more than select paper trays. The Default Paper Tray option works only if you have a laser printer with more than one tray (such as the NEC 890). Continuous form is the normal setting for most printers. Manual feed is useful if you are feeding letterhead stationery one sheet at a time through your printer. GEM/3 will wait until you signal that you're ready. Optional Tray #1 lets you use the second tray if your laser printer has one.

File Redirect

Gosh I'm glad that DRI did this. The old trick was to use the public domain file redirection utility LPTX to snatch the printer information to a file. You'll need this if you are sending files to a printer buffer over a network, or if you want to transmit printer information over the phone line (to someone with a laser printer for instance).

Send output to: lets you pick whether the information should be sent to the printer or a file.

Print file in background? isn't generally a good idea, unless you have a really fast machine. On a PC or XT, your applications will move at glacial speeds while the file is printing.

If you do print in the background mode, *Delete file after printing in background?* will clean up the spooler file GEM created.

The *Directory:* and *File:* options let you pick what the redirected file will be called, and where it will be.

CAMERA PREFERENCES

This sets the relative brightness for the screen and provides a rough initial set up for various common types of slide and print film. The idea is that you can use a 35mm camera and hood to shoot prints or slides directly from the screen. The images are dumped to the screen using the Screen print icon.

The major problem is that GEM doesn't know where you have the monitor brightness and contrast levels set. What you really need to do is to start with the GEM default settings for your film type and work from there.

Setting camera color preferences is something you may want to do even if you don't ever intend to use a camera. If you have a color monitor, this will control the actual displayed colors in your palette. If you have installed an eight color video driver, only the top row of color indexes (0 through 7) can be set. If you've set up a 16-color driver, you can twiddle all of the settings.

Most of the GEM applications let you access the color palette through a pull-down menu marked, cleverly enough, COLOR. The color index numbers are displayed right along with the colors. (If you have a monochrome monitor, go on and read something else.)

The color setting capabilities are quite impressive. You can set a base color, adjust its brightness in one of ten steps, and then even fine tune by adjusting the percentages of red, green, and blue mixed to create the color.

Now you've got GEM in a nutshell (albeit a rather large nut). Practice the techniques and you'll have a large part of learning the GEM applications behind you.

CHAPTER

4

Fontware and FontMerge: Things You Need to Know

BEYOND SWISS AND DUTCH	50
INSTALLATION	50
ADDING FONTS	52
MAKING FONTS	53
MODIFYING FONTWARE	55
FONT CODES	56
THE CHARACTER SET	59
FONTMERGE	59

BEYOND SWISS AND DUTCH

Before the advent of GEM/3, you were absolutely stuck with Swiss and Dutch. Sort of like Henry Ford's Model T: You could get it in any color you wanted as long as it was black. GEM/3 changed all of that, but you still have some restrictions.

This chapter is the Bitstream Tattler, telling all the tales that Bitstream and Digital Research left out. The first part deals with Fontware itself, while the second half covers the FontMerge utility that comes with Desktop Publisher. If you are going to use additional fonts with GEM/3, read this chapter first. If you don't, I won't be responsible for the outcome.

A serious word of warning: If you don't have a computer equipped with an 80286 microprocessor and a full 640 kilobytes of RAM, generating fonts will be a terrible experience. Webster used this software to define both slow and tedious. If you attempt to generate a full range of three or four fonts on an XT, it can literally take days.

INSTALLATION

Although Fontware does not run under GEM/3, installation and operation are very simple. Just put disk #1 of the installation set into the computer and run the Fontware batch file. The installation program will put the Bitstream logo onto the screen (see Figure 4.1) and ask you if it's in color. Answer yes or no and you're on your way.

You are now given the main menu with the option to Set Up Fontware, which is exactly what you want to do. The next questions concern the directories that the Fontware package will make up. See Figure 4.2. They consist of two separate directory structures, one for the Fontware packages and one for fonts. For most purposes, it doesn't matter where Fontware puts its own files. It does matter where it puts fonts, however. Most GEM fonts, including all screen fonts, are resident in the /GEMAPPS/FONTS directory. PostScript fonts end up in /GEMAPPS/PSFONTS. Most GEM applications can only handle four fonts in the FONTS directory. Graph and WordChart get positively weird if you have more than two.

I suggest that you tell the Fontware package to throw all new fonts into a different directory, such as C:/GEMAPPS/ADDFONT. That gives you the opportunity to copy files in and out of the /GEMAPPS/FONTS directory as needed while keeping a number of fonts in a convenient place. You can build batch files to select different font sets. These will do nothing more than

Figure 4.1

```
            Do you see more than two colors?
            Press Y - Yes  or  press N - No

        Installation Kit for GEM - Release 1.1
```

(Bitstream FONTWARE)

Figure 4.2

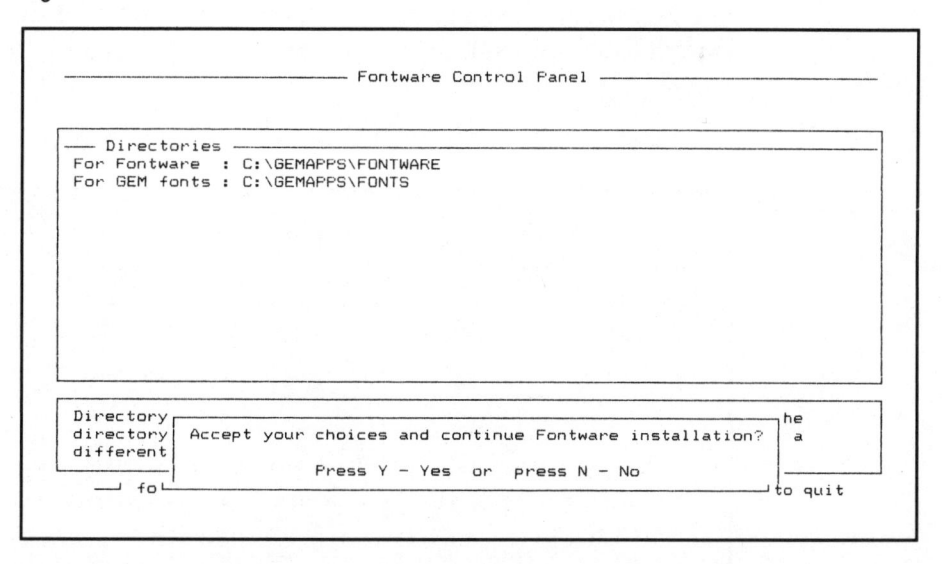

```
┌──────────────── Fontware Control Panel ────────────────┐
│                                                        │
│ ┌── Directories ──────────────────────────────────────┐│
│ │ For Fontware  : C:\GEMAPPS\FONTWARE                 ││
│ │ For GEM fonts : C:\GEMAPPS\FONTS                    ││
│ │                                                     ││
│ │                                                     ││
│ │                                                     ││
│ │                                                     ││
│ └─────────────────────────────────────────────────────┘│
│ ┌Directory┌─────────────────────────────────────────┐he│
│ │directory│ Accept your choices and continue Fontware installation? │a │
│ │different│        Press Y - Yes  or  press N - No  │  │
│ └─ fo ────└─────────────────────────────────────────┘to quit
└────────────────────────────────────────────────────────┘
```

copy fonts between /GEMAPPS/FONTS and /GEMAPPS/ADDFONT. Whatever directories you choose, make certain that they are subdirectories of /GEMAPPS.

If you want to make screen fonts, you'll need to tell Fontware what kind of display you have. See Figure 4.3. Screen fonts are really wonderful things. They are crisp and sharp, whereas GEM's automatically generated fonts look like they were done in GEM Paint II. You also need to tell Fontware what kind of printer you will be using. See Figure 4.4. If you'll be making fonts for several types of printers, don't worry. You can change printers at any time.

For some printers, you'll get a choice concerning what font set to install. Stick with the GEM international character set. It matches everything within the GEM system. See Figure 4.5.

Once you've made your selections, Fontware will copy all of its files from both disks. The program will prompt you when it's time to change disks. After a suitable amount of disk whirring and chugging, you'll find yourself back at the main menu.

ADDING FONTS

The Add/Delete Fontware Typefaces selection lets you pull additional fonts into Fontware. GEM/3 comes with the font primitives for Swiss (Helvetica), Dutch (Times Roman), and the roman or regular face for Bitstream Charter.

Figure 4.3

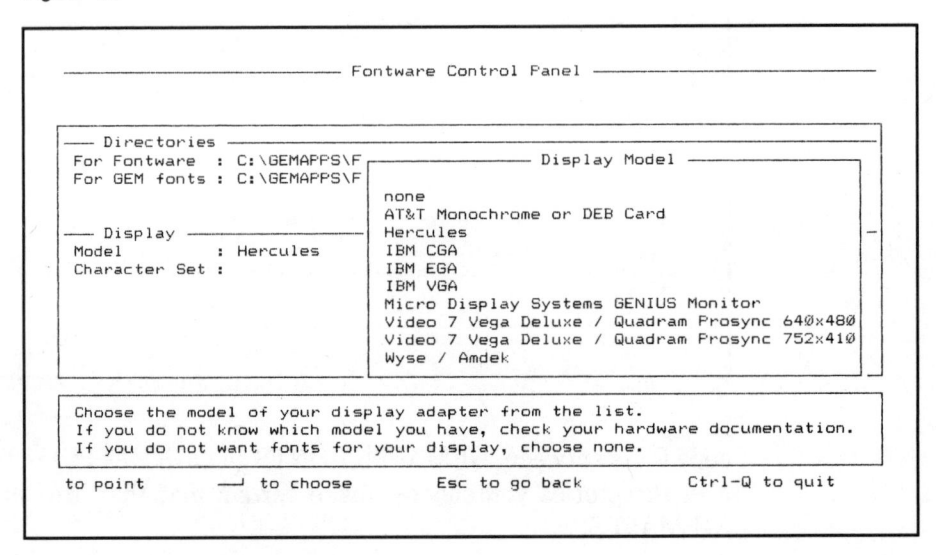

```
┌─────────────────────── Fontware Control Panel ───────────────────────┐
│                                                                       │
│  ┌── Directories ──────────────────┐                                  │
│  │ For Fontware : C:\GEMAPPS\F    │┌── Display Model ──────────────┐  │
│  │ For GEM fonts : C:\GEMAPPS\F   ││                                │  │
│  │                                 ││ none                           │  │
│  │                                 ││ AT&T Monochrome or DEB Card    │  │
│  │ ── Display ──────────────────   ││ Hercules                       │  │
│  │ Model        : Hercules         ││ IBM CGA                        │  │
│  │ Character Set :                 ││ IBM EGA                        │  │
│  │                                 ││ IBM VGA                        │  │
│  │                                 ││ Micro Display Systems GENIUS Monitor │
│  │                                 ││ Video 7 Vega Deluxe / Quadram Prosync 640x480 │
│  │                                 ││ Video 7 Vega Deluxe / Quadram Prosync 752x410 │
│  │                                 ││ Wyse / Amdek                   │  │
│  └─────────────────────────────────┘└────────────────────────────────┘  │
│                                                                       │
│  ┌──────────────────────────────────────────────────────────────────┐ │
│  │ Choose the model of your display adapter from the list.           │ │
│  │ If you do not know which model you have, check your hardware documentation. │ │
│  │ If you do not want fonts for your display, choose none.           │ │
│  └──────────────────────────────────────────────────────────────────┘ │
│                                                                       │
│  to point        ┘ to choose       Esc to go back       Ctrl-Q to quit │
└───────────────────────────────────────────────────────────────────────┘
```

Figure 4.4

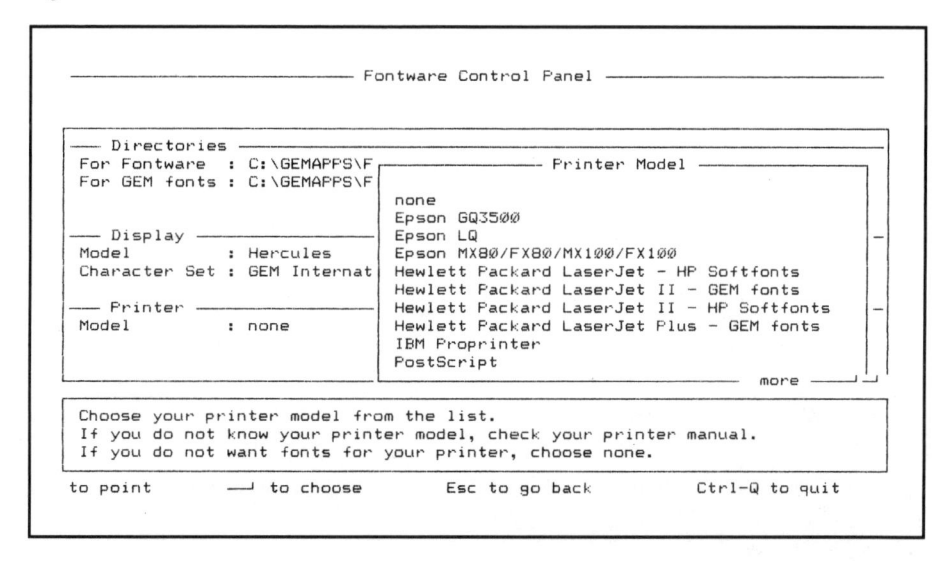

```
┌──────────────────────── Fontware Control Panel ─────────────────────────┐
│ ┌── Directories ───────────────┐                                         │
│ │ For Fontware : C:\GEMAPPS\F  │┌──── Printer Model ─────────────────┐  │
│ │ For GEM fonts : C:\GEMAPPS\F ││                                    │  │
│ │                              ││ none                               │  │
│ │── Display ───────────────────┤│ Epson GQ3500                       │  │
│ │ Model        : Hercules      ││ Epson LQ                           │  │
│ │ Character Set: GEM Internat  ││ Epson MX80/FX80/MX100/FX100        │  │
│ │                              ││ Hewlett Packard LaserJet - HP Softfonts │
│ │── Printer ───────────────────┤│ Hewlett Packard LaserJet II - GEM fonts │
│ │ Model        : none          ││ Hewlett Packard LaserJet II - HP Softfonts │
│ │                              ││ Hewlett Packard LaserJet Plus - GEM fonts │
│ │                              ││ IBM Proprinter                     │  │
│ │                              ││ PostScript                         │  │
│ └──────────────────────────────┘└────────────────────────── more ────┘  │
│ ┌─────────────────────────────────────────────────────────────────────┐ │
│ │ Choose your printer model from the list.                            │ │
│ │ If you do not know your printer model, check your printer manual.   │ │
│ │ If you do not want fonts for your printer, choose none.             │ │
│ │ to point      ─┘ to choose      Esc to go back      Ctrl-Q to quit  │ │
│ └─────────────────────────────────────────────────────────────────────┘ │
└─────────────────────────────────────────────────────────────────────────┘
```

You can buy additional fonts from Bitstream. Check the publishing design chapter for information on selecting fonts.

The Charter roman face is a teaser; it's there in hopes that you'll buy the font. Aside from this font, and the headline fonts, you get roman, bold, italic, and bold italic versions of the fonts—or some variation on this theme. When you select Add/Delete fonts, Fontware will ask you to insert disk #1 of the set in drive A:. It will then ask you which of the faces for the fonts you want to add to Fontware. Normally, you'll want them all.

Usually, you'll be prompted to insert disk #2 of the set. That's really all there is to adding fonts. You can keep stuffing them into Fontware until it can't hold any more.

MAKING FONTS

Here's where the fun starts. To get the maximum from Fontware, you'll want to create fonts to cover a wide range. Fonts are sized in points, with 72 points to the inch. For display fonts, the recommended set of point sizes includes 6, 8, 10, 12, 14, 16, 18, 20, 24, 28, and 36. See Figure 4.6. This covers all of the normally used fonts, and it covers the enlarged and reduced view fonts as well. As a result, no matter what view setting you use in your GEM application, you'll get clear looking fonts.

Figure 4.5

```
┌─────────────────────── Fontware Control Panel ───────────────────────┐
│                                                                      │
│  ┌─ Directories ──────────────────────────────────────────────────┐  │
│  │ For Fontware : C:\GEMAPPS\F ┌── Display Character Set ──────┐  │  │
│  │ For GEM fonts : C:\GEMAPPS\F │                              │  │  │
│  │                              │ GEM International            │  │  │
│  │  ─ Display ─                 │ GEM Character Set for HP Softfonts│
│  │ Model         : Hercules                                        │  │
│  │ Character Set : GEM International                               │  │
│  │                                                                 │  │
│  │                                                                 │  │
│  └─────────────────────────────────────────────────────────────────┘  │
│                                                                      │
│  ┌─────────────────────────────────────────────────────────────────┐  │
│  │ The GEM International character set has 186 characters.         │  │
│  │ Use this set for GEM applications.                              │  │
│  └─────────────────────────────────────────────────────────────────┘  │
│                                                                      │
│   to point        ⏎ to choose      Esc to go back    Ctrl-Q to quit  │
└──────────────────────────────────────────────────────────────────────┘
```

Figure 4.6

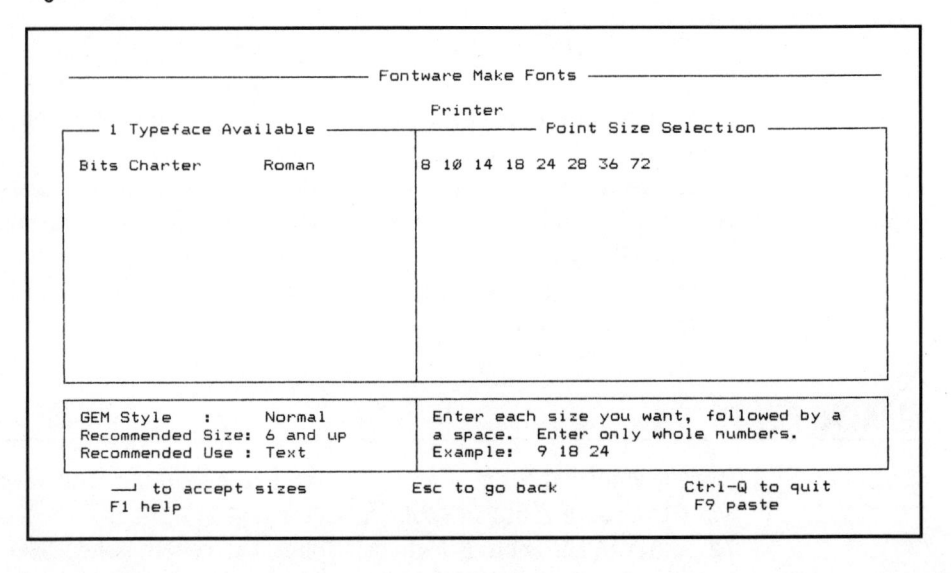

```
┌───────────────────────── Fontware Make Fonts ────────────────────────┐
│                              Printer                                 │
│  ┌─ 1 Typeface Available ──┐ ┌── Point Size Selection ────────────┐ │
│  │                         │ │                                    │ │
│  │ Bits Charter   Roman    │ │ 8 10 14 18 24 28 36 72             │ │
│  │                         │ │                                    │ │
│  │                         │ │                                    │ │
│  │                         │ │                                    │ │
│  │                         │ │                                    │ │
│  │                         │ │                                    │ │
│  └─────────────────────────┘ └────────────────────────────────────┘ │
│  ┌─────────────────────────────┬────────────────────────────────────┐│
│  │ GEM Style      : Normal     │ Enter each size you want, followed by a│
│  │ Recommended Size: 6 and up  │ a space. Enter only whole numbers. ││
│  │ Recommended Use : Text      │ Example:  9 18 24                  ││
│  └─────────────────────────────┴────────────────────────────────────┘│
│   ⏎ to accept sizes       Esc to go back        Ctrl-Q to quit       │
│   F1 help                                       F9 paste             │
└──────────────────────────────────────────────────────────────────────┘
```

To give yourself a bit more latitude for publishing work, you might want to add 9 and 11 point as well because they provide a nice range of body text choices. Remember, if you run Ventura from GEM/3, you'll need to create a full range of fonts for Ventura because it will find only the fonts that are in GEM/3. None of the downloadable fonts that you created specifically for Ventura will be available to it under GEM/3.

The exception to all of this is PostScript. Because PostScript can infinitely scale fonts, it doesn't need fonts for each target size. When Fontware makes up PostScript printer fonts, you get the complete range of fonts automatically.

Font size limitations depend on the printer. The largest font you can make for a LaserJet II printer is 72 points. A LaserJet+ printer can handle anything up to 36 points. Dot-matrix printers can have fonts up to 99 points. The largest display font is 72 points. You can make no font smaller than six points. Of course, PostScript has no limitations except those imposed by the GEM applications themselves.

Now for the catches. Catch number one is disk space. Fonts for all but PostScript printers are disk hogs. For example, a set of four fonts in all of the above sizes for a LaserJet II will take up space in the megabytes. Fontware will check if you have enough room, but don't be surprised when your hard disk real estate vanishes after making fonts.

Catch number two we've already discussed. Most GEM applications can handle four fonts. WordChart and Graph can stand only two. If you make up lots of type fonts, you'll need to limit the number to four at a time in the /GEMAPPS/FONTS directory. This shouldn't pose a serious problem; after all, good taste demands that you don't use a zillion fonts in a single document. But it can be a bit of a pain when you want to change font sets.

Catch number three is time. Fontware estimates how long a set of fonts will take to compile. Fontware is a notorious liar. The actual time, at least in my experience, will be more than double the estimate. I went on a font-making spree to create fonts for four different typefaces in all of the recommended sizes. At the time, I had a lowly eight-megahertz XT. It took almost three days to complete the task. Shortly after that, my hard drive failed. You've been warned. Prudence suggests that you make fonts in small batches.

MODIFYING FONTWARE

The last main entry is View Control Panel. Use this to reconfigure Fontware for different printers and monitors or to change character sets. The program will walk you through your available choices. Just select what you want, and then plunk the disks in the drive when asked. Using this option, you can compile fonts for a variety of printers.

You'll find this feature especially useful if you have a laser printer that can speak both Hewlett-Packard and PostScript. By changing the control panel, you can create fonts for both modes.

FONT CODES

GEM/3 loads the first four fonts, in alphabetical order by font code. The font code is the first two letters of the font file name. If present in /GEM-APPS/FONTS, Swiss will always load because its font codes span AA through AD. Dutch will always load because its codes are AI through AL, although if you have Century Schoolbook it will load before Dutch.

The following is a list of the most commonly found fonts and their codes:

Font Family	*Font Code Prefix*
Swiss Roman	AA
Swiss Italic	AB
Swiss Bold	AC
Swiss Bold Italic	AD
Century Schoolbook Roman	AE
Century Schoolbook Italic	AF
Century Schoolbook Bold	AG
Century Schoolbook Bold Italic	AH
Dutch Roman	AI
Dutch Italic	AJ
Dutch Bold	AK
Dutch Bold Italic	AL
Zaph Calligraphic Roman	AM
Zaph Calligraphic Italic	AN
Zaph Calligraphic Bold	AO
Zaph Calligraphic Bold Italic	AP
Futura Light	AQ
Futura Light Italic	AR
Futura Condensed Medium	AS
Futura Extra Black	AT
Swiss Light	AU
Swiss Light Italic	AV
Swiss Black	AW
Swiss Black Italic	AX
Swiss Condensed Roman	AY

Font Family	Font Code Prefix
Swiss Condensed Italic	AZ
Swiss Condensed Bold	BA
Swiss Condensed Black	BB
Futura Book	BC
Futura Book Italic	BD
Futura Heavy	BE
Futura Heavy Italic	BF
Futura Medium	BG
Futura Medium Italic	BH
Futura Bold	BI
Futura Bold Italic	BJ
Courier 10 Roman	BK
Courier 10 Italic	BL
Courier 10 Bold	BM
Courier 10 Bold Italic	BN
Letter Gothic 12 Roman	BO
Letter Gothic 12 Italic	BP
Letter Gothic 12 Bold	BQ
Letter Gothic 12 Bold Italic	BR
Prestige 12 Roman	BS
Prestige 12 Italic	BT
Prestige 12 Bold	BU
Prestige 12 Bold Italic	BV
ITC Avant Garde Gothic Book	BW
ITC Avant Garde Gothic Medium	BX
ITC Avant Garde Gothic Demi	BY
ITC Avant Garde Gothic Bold	BZ
Zaph Humanist Roman	CA
Zaph Humanist Italic	CB
Zaph Humanist Bold	CC
Zaph Humanist Bold Italic	CD
Bitstream Cooper Black	CE
University Roman	CF
Cloister Black	CG
Broadway Roman	CH
ITC Souvenir Light	CI
ITC Souvenir Light Italic	CJ
ITC Souvenir Demi	CK

Font Family	Font Code Prefix
ITC Souvenir Demi Italic	CL
ITC Korinna Regular	CM
ITC Korinna Kursiv Regular	CN
ITC Korinna Extra Bold	CO
ITC Korinna Kursiv Extra Bold	CP
Bitstream Charter Roman	CQ
Bitstream Charter Italic	CR
Bitstream Charter Bold	CS
Bitstream Charter Bold Italic	CT
ITC Galliard Roman	CU
ITC Galliard Italic	CV
ITC Galliard Bold	CW
ITC Galliard Bold Italic	CX
ITC Garamond Book	CY
ITC Garamond Book Italic	CZ
ITC Garamond Bold	DA
ITC Garamond Bold Italic	DB
Brush Script Italic	DC
Blippo Black	DD
Hobo Roman	DE
Windsor Roman	DF
Swiss Compressed Roman	DG
Swiss Extra Compressed Roman	DH
Exotic Demi	DI
Exotic Bold	DJ
Baskerville Roman	DK
Baskerville Italic	DL
Baskerville Bold	DM
Baskerville Bold Italic	DN
Bitstream Cooper Light	DO
Bitstream Cooper Light Italic	DP
Bitstream Cooper Bold	DQ
Bitstream Cooper Bold Italic	DR
Serifa Roman	DS
Serifa Italic	DT
Serifa Bold	DU
Serifa Black	DV
ITC Garamond Cond Book	DW

Font Family	Font Code Prefix
ITC Garamond Cond Book Italic	DX
ITC Garamond Cond Bold	DY
ITC Garamond Cond Bold Italic	DZ
News Gothic	EA
News Gothic Italic	EB
News Gothic Bold	EC
News Gothic Bold Italic	ED
Goudy Old Style Roman	EE
Goudy Old Style Italic	EF
Goudy Old Style Bold	EG
Goudy Old Style Extra Bold	EH
Coronet Bold	EI
ITC Zaph Chancery Medium Italic	EJ
Clarendon Roman	EK
Clarendon Bold	EL
ITC Bookman Light	EP
ITC Bookman Light Italic	EQ
ITC Bookman Demi	ER
ITC Bookman Demi Italic	ES

THE CHARACTER SET

Figure 4.7 shows the GEM International Character set for both standard type fonts and the PostScript symbol font. Use this listing to look up graphics characters.

FONTMERGE

FontMerge has two rather straightforward functions:

1. To move newly created GEM fonts into a Desktop Publisher width table.
2. To delete fonts from a width table.

Installation is automatic. You'll discover FontMerge in your /GEMAPPS directory. I usually assign the hammer icon for programmer's tool to utilities such as this. Assigning an icon isn't automatic, but it's explained in the chapter about the GEM/3 desktop.

Figure 4.7

Decimal	Char Set 1	Char Set 2
1-31	not used	
32	space	space
33	!	!
34	"	∀
35	#	#
36	$	∃
37	%	%
38	&	&
39	'	∋
40	(	(
41	)	)
42	*	*
43	+	+
44	,	,
45	-	-
46	.	.
47	/	/
48	0	0
49	1	1
50	2	2
51	3	3
52	4	4
53	5	5
54	6	6
55	7	7
56	8	8
57	9	9
58	:	:
59	;	;
60	<	<
61	=	=
62	>	>

Decimal	Char Set 1	Char Set 2
63	?	?
64	@	≅
65	A	A
66	B	B
67	C	X
68	D	Δ
69	E	E
70	F	Φ
71	G	Γ
72	H	H
73	I	I
74	J	ϑ
75	K	K
76	L	Λ
77	M	M
78	N	N
79	O	O
80	P	Π
81	Q	Θ
82	R	P
83	S	Σ
84	T	T
85	U	Y
86	V	ς
87	W	Ω
88	X	Ξ
89	Y	Ψ
90	Z	Z
91	[	[
92	\	∴
93	]	]
94	^	⊥

Decimal	Char Set 1	Char Set 2
95	_	_
96	`	_
97	a	α
98	b	β
99	c	χ
100	d	δ
101	e	ε
102	f	φ
103	g	γ
104	h	η
105	i	ι
106	j	φ
107	k	κ
108	l	λ
109	m	μ
110	n	ν
111	o	o
112	p	π
113	q	θ
114	r	ρ
115	s	σ
116	t	τ
117	u	υ
118	v	ϖ
119	w	ω
120	x	ξ
121	y	ψ
122	z	ζ
123	{	{
124				
125	}	}
126	~	~

Decimal	Char Set 1	Char Set 2
127		
128	Ç	
129	ü	
130	é	
131	â	
132	ä	
133	à	
134	å	
135	ç	
136	ê	
137	ë	
138	è	
139	ï	
140	î	
141	ì	
142	Ä	
143	Å	
144	É	
145	æ	
146	Æ	
147	ô	
148	ö	
149	ò	
150	û	
151	ù	
152	ÿ	
153	Ö	
154	Ü	
155	ø	
156	£	
157	Ø	
158	¤	

Decimal	Char Set 1	Char Set 2
159	ƒ	
160	á	
161	í	ϒ
162	ó	′
163	ú	≤
164	ñ	/
165	Ñ	∞
166	ª	ƒ
167	º	♣
168	¿	♦
169	"	♥
170	"	♠
171	‹	↔
172	›	←
173	¡	↑
174	«	→
175	»	↓
176	ã	°
177	õ	±
178	¥	″
179	¢	≥
180	œ	×
181	Œ	∝
182	À	∂
183	Ã	•
184	Õ	÷
185	§	≠
186	‡	≡
187	†	≈
188	¶	...
189	©		
190	®	—

Decimal	Char Set 1	Char Set 2
191	™	↵
192	„	ℵ
193	...	ℑ
194	‰	ℜ
195	•	℘
196	–	⊗
197	—	⊕
198	°	∅
199	Á	∩
200	Â	∪
201	È	⊃
202	Ê	⊇
203	Ë	⊄
204	Ì	⊂
205	Í	⊆
206	Î	∈
207	Ï	∉
208	Ò	∠
209	Ó	∇
210	Ô	®
211	Š	©
212	š	™
213	Ù	∏
214	Ú	√
215	Û	·
216	Ÿ	¬
217	ß	∧
218		
219		
220		
221		
222		

CARE AND FEEDING

FontMerge deals with specific types of font files. If you're using a PostScript Printer, you'll discover files with .PFA or .PFI extensions. These must be copied into the /GEMAPPS/FONTS subdirectory. In addition to the font files, you'll also need a related .AFM file in /GEMAPPS/FONTS.

For Hewlett-Packard type laser printers, font files end in either .SFL or .SFP. If you're using a 150 dot per inch driver, you'll also need a .HPH file. For the 300 dot per inch driver, you'll need a file with a B30 extension. Again, all files must be in /GEMAPPS/FONTS.

OPERATION

FontMerge has only one dialog, which is always open. See Figure 4.8. It has the following functions:

Add One Font . . .

This brings up the item selector so that you can add a single font to the currently open width table. Remember, only eight fonts to a width table.

Delete Font

Removes the currently highlighted font from the width table.

Figure 4.8

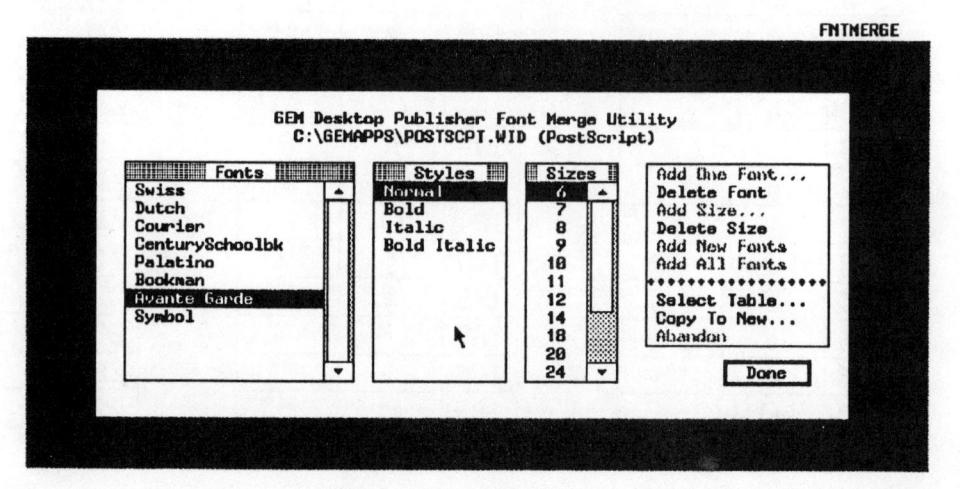

Add Size . . .

Allows you to add a font size. Of course, you must pick a legal size for the printer in question.

Delete Size

Deletes the currently highlighted font size.

Add New Fonts

Adds any and all fonts created through the last run of Fontware. How does it know what these fonts are? They are listed in a file called FWARE.JOB.

Add All Fonts

Adds all font files held in the /GEMAPPS/FONTS subdirectory to the current width table. Be careful with this.

Select Table . . .

Brings up the Item Selector so that you can open a different width table.

Copy To New . . .

Lets you copy the contents of the currently open width table to a new table. You can specify the location and name of the new table.

Abandon

Bail out with no saved changes.

CHAPTER 5

GEM Paint II

A VERSATILE PUBLISHER'S TOOL	65
OPENERS	66
TOOLBOX	66
TEXT	68
OTHER ARTIST'S TOOLS	69
PULL-DOWNS	72
TOOLS	74
PATTERNS	75
DESIGNING WITH GEM PAINT II	76

A VERSATILE PUBLISHER'S TOOL

Paint II is a very recent update of the original GEM Paint program, with some very nice additions. Technically speaking, Paint II is a pixel-based graphics editor. (Oh yeah?) What that line of jargon really means is that Paint II lets you create illustrations by manipulating tiny square dots. Called anything from "fat bits" to "pels" in various other programs, these dots are the basic picture elements (hence *pix*ture *el*ements or pixels). This sort of graphics program has tremendous free-form capability, but it can't create as crisp a graphic as GEM Draw Plus or GEM Graph can.

GEM Paint II is a versatile publisher's tool. Once you master its techniques, you'll discover a zillion uses for it. I've primarily found it useful for:

- Flyers
- Highly stylized illustrations
- Rough page-layout designs
- Manipulating clip art

It is *not* useful as an editor for material scanned at 300 or 200 dots per inch (i.e., the files produced by GEM Scan). GEM Scan itself has some editing capabilities for this sort of thing. Paint II can't handle such big files because of memory limitations. If you really want to edit scanned files, check the section on other useful programs at the rear of this book. It discusses Media Cybernetics HALO DPE program, which I highly recommend as a scanned file editor.

To really understand GEM Paint II, you need to think a bit about Impressionist art. Paint II is good for creating an impression, not a high-resolution technical illustration. Curves and arcs will be jaggedy. Type is only vaguely reminiscent of the type styles that print so clearly from other applications. Distance greatly improves the clarity of the image.

Paint II images are closely related to the Impressionist technique called pointillism. The idea is that you can build a picture from points or dots instead of from lines. That's exactly what Paint II does. The picture is made up of square dots, at a resolution of 75 to the inch. (You can't improve this, no matter what the resolution of your printer.) Not only is the picture made up of dots, but you can zoom in on them and individually turn them on and off. If you don't quite like what you've drawn, therefore, you can zoom in and clean it up. This gives you the ability to sketch with geometric forms (created with the Paint II tools), and then soften the harsh corners and edges. Pretty much like any artist would using oil or acrylic paints.

OPENERS

Paint II opens onto a screen crammed with tools. See Figure 5.1. The icons and lines along the left are your artist's tools. The patterns on the left are your textures. Things that you draw with the tools can later be filled with any of the patterns along the right. You can also load new patterns (there is quite a selection), and you can even design your own.

The pull-down menus on the top give you image manipulation and text tools. These tools let you size your painting area, move things around, and even flip them vertically and horizontally. Block-built versions of the Swiss and Dutch type styles are automatically available, as well as a System font. System is the same font GEM uses in its screens, pull-downs, etc. If you install fonts from Bitstream into GEM/3, you can have a total of four fonts in addition to System.

TOOLBOX

GEM paint has tools no artist ever dreamed of. See Figure 5.2.

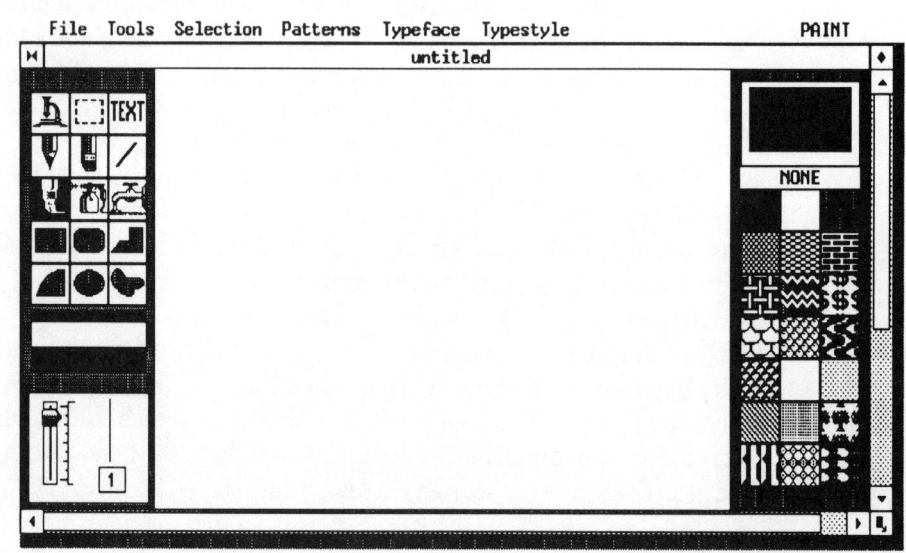

Figure 5.1

Figure 5.2

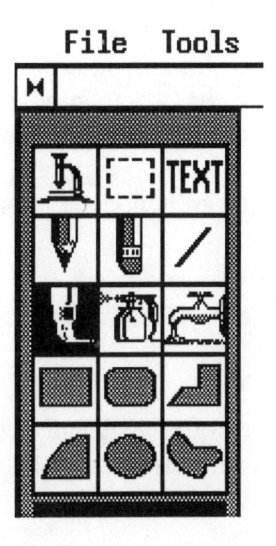

The Microscope

Click on this and the pencil icon will appear in the painting area. Point at the area you want to edit with the pencil, and then click the mouse button. GEM Paint II will zoom in to display the pixels themselves. Off to the left of the screen are your editing tools. At the bottom is your inkwell. Put the pencil over white or black and click. Now when you click on a pixel in the painting area it will either become white or black.

In the center you'll find a "panner." The panner lets you move freely about the entire painting area while zoomed in. Of course, you can also move with the slider bars. Just click and hold over the panner box, and move it around. Your current field of view will show in the box above. When you want to return to normal view, click on the upper box (showing the field of view).

Selector

This is a box you can throw around any part of the picture you want to copy, move, or manipulate. To draw the box, place the pointer at the spot you want to be the upper left corner. Click and hold the mouse, and pull it down and to the right until it covers the area you want. Release the mouse button. And there it is, sort of like a movie marquee.

To copy something, put the pointer within the box and click and hold. You can now drag the copy around. If you want to make multiple copies, this will test your dexterity. Hold the space bar down until you release the mouse button. When you click and hold again, you'll get an additional copy. You can keep that up as long as you like.

Double click on the Selector icon and it will automatically select the entire canvas.

The Selection pull-down menu works with the Selector.

Clear

Whites out everything in the box.

Complement

Provides a reverse image of everything in the box. In black-and-white, a reverse is easy: black becomes white and white goes to black. In color, though, it takes on a different meaning. The complement of the color, not black, is chosen. You can get some really interesting effects with this.

Flip Horizontal

This mirrors the selected image left to right.

Flip Vertical

This turns the image upside down.

TEXT

This is your text selector. As mentioned earlier, Paint supports up to five fonts: System and four others. If you haven't added fonts to GEM, you'll have just Swiss, Dutch, and System. Examples of how they appear in Paint II are shown in Figure 5.3.

Point sizes range from 7 to 72 points by default, but not all selections are available for each font. If you use the Bitstream font loader, you can add fonts in whatever sizes you like between 6 and 72. Sizes and fonts are available from the Font pull-down menu.

The Style menu lets you select bold, italic, underline, or revert to normal. You can also pick how you want text to align: right, left, or centered.

Because text is really just another collection of pixels on the Paint canvas, you can use the microscope tool to zoom in and edit the letters. This is a

Figure 5.3

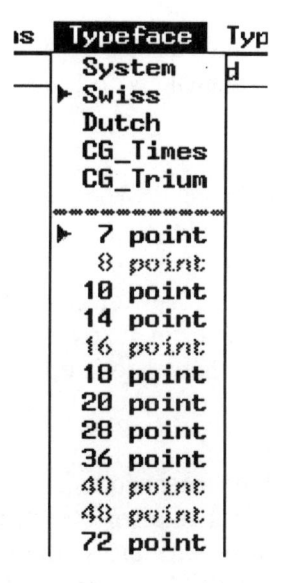

```
ıs │ Typeface │ Typ
    │  System  │ d
  ▶ │  Swiss   │
    │  Dutch   │
    │  CG_Times│
    │  CG_Trium│
    │----------│
  ▶ │  7 point │
    │  8 point │
    │ 10 point │
    │ 14 point │
    │ 16 point │
    │ 18 point │
    │ 20 point │
    │ 28 point │
    │ 36 point │
    │ 40 point │
    │ 48 point │
    │ 72 point │
```

good way to make up your own fonts, letting GEM do most of the work for you.

OTHER ARTIST'S TOOLS

Pencil

This is your freehand line drawing tool. Click on this and the pointer will turn into a pencil when it's over the canvas. Click and hold the mouse button to draw a line from the pencil tip. Sort of a tough tool to use if you haven't had much practice with the mouse, the pencil exactly follows the mouse movement. As a result, it's somewhat like trying to draw a straight line with a pen stuck to the end of a two-by-four.

You can select either a black or white line by clicking on the inkwells over at the left. The line density selections apply to this tool.

Eraser

Use this tool both for cleaning up mistakes and selectively removing patterns, etc. The eraser turns everything in its path white. You can select its shape with Brush Shape under the Tools pull-down menu. If you select one of the airbrush spray patterns, you'll get an eraser that only partially erases. Sort or a reverse airbrush.

If you double click on the eraser, everything on the canvas will disappear. The electronic analogy to crumpling it up and tossing it in the can.

Line

Draws straight lines. When line is selected, the pointer becomes a crosshair. Click and hold to mark the starting point for the line, and release when you've stretched it where you want it. The line weight selector to the left will work for this one. You can select any line weight from 1 at the top (thin) to 45 at the bottom (extremely fat). Just click and hold on the selector indicator, and then slide it up and down.

Paint Brush

This is another freehand tool, but this time you get to pick the brush shape. The paint you use is selected from the palette to the right. You've always wanted to paint with brick wall paint, right? Well, now's your chance.

Select Brush Shape from the Tools pull-down or by double clicking on the brush icon. See Figure 5.4. The airbrush patterns will give you about

Figure 5.4

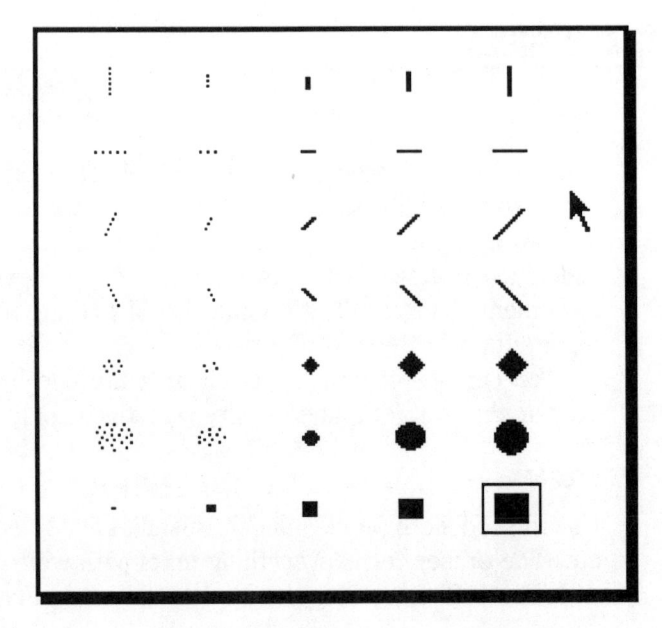

a 90 percent fill-in with the pattern, as opposed to the solid brushes which completely fill wherever you wave them. The lines are like calligraphy nibs, letting you vary the stroke weight depending on the direction you move the brush.

Paint Sprayer

This is subtly different from the brush. If you select the brush and wave it rapidly over the canvas, it will completely cover whatever it touches. But the paint sprayer (even with a solid brush shape) will miss some spots when wiggled rapidly over the canvas. Select an airbrush spray pattern from brush shapes and you'll get a spotty coverage. It works very much like a real air brush.

By the way, you can select brush shapes either from the Tools pull-down or by double clicking on the paint sprayer.

Faucet

The faucet fills the area under the pointer with whatever pattern you select. The pattern will fill until it reaches boundaries. If there's a single pixel gap in any of the boundaries, it will leak through. You can even fill a pattern over a pattern, often with interesting effect.

Rectangle

Draws a rectangle with:

- Line weight picked with the line selector.
- Pattern selected. Whatever pattern is up will completely fill the rectangle.

Click and hold the mouse button to start the upper left corner of the rectangle. Pull the mouse down and to the right until it's the size you want.

Rounded Box

Pretty much the same as the rectangle, except that it has rounded corners. If you make the box narrow enough, you'll get round ends.

Polygon

Use this to draw any multisided figure—as long as it has all straight sides. Click to start the line; click again to mark its end. Double click when you want to mark the end of the last line. Like the rectangle, you can specify the line weight.

Arc

The arc draws arc segments in whatever line weight you want. Click and hold to start the arc; release to stop. If a pattern is selected, the arc will fill with it. Sometimes it's a bit difficult to get the arc to go in the direction you want. Try going in one direction, then the second. For instance, if you want to draw an arc up and to the right of the current position, first go up, then to the right.

Circle

Draws circles and ellipses. Click and hold to start the circle; release when it's the way you want it. If you have a pattern selected, it will fill with the pattern. Any line weight will do.

Free Form

Tracks the mouse movement to draw freehand lines. This is different from the pencil, though. It will use whatever line you have selected on the line selector. It will also fill with the pattern selected.

PULL-DOWNS

We covered the Font, Style, and Selection pull-downs under Tools, but there are still a few others to mention.

FILE

This menu controls file handling. You use this to save, print, and merge paintings. See Figure 5.5.

New

Clears the canvas and starts afresh.

Open . . .

Brings up the file selector so you can bring in a file. You can have two files open at the same time and use the selector to drag parts of the paintings between files.

Close

Closes the file. Close saves the picture if you made any changes.

Figure 5.5

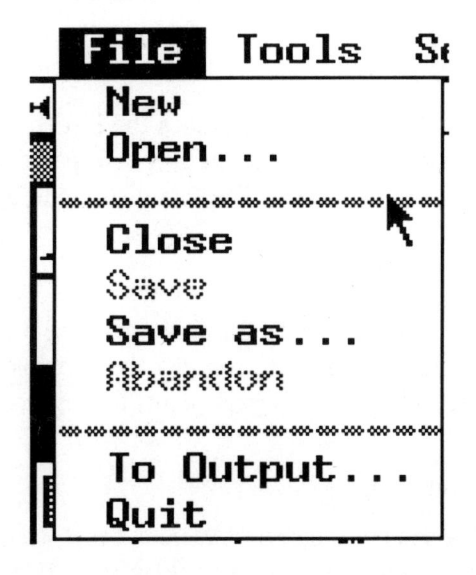

Save

Saves the file to the name you've selected. Paint II won't let you Save until you've first done a Save as . . . and picked a file name.

Save as . . .

Either pick a name for the file or save your changes under a new name.

Abandon

Trash all changes and call up the last saved version of the file.

To Output . . .

Switch to the Output application so that you can print the file. If you haven't saved the file, GEM will ask if you want to (thank goodness). Your current file will load into the output list automatically, and you can bring in additional files or list to print.

Quit

Back to the Desktop. Again, you'll get a chance to save your file if you haven't done so.

TOOLS

Undo

You'll love this one. It erases the last thing you've drawn. If you really mess something up (as I often do), or a pattern leaks out into the main drawing area, this will fix it. You can also Undo by hitting the Escape key.

Grid On/Grid Off

This is a "toggle." Toggles work like a light switch. They turn something on and off. This one toggles the invisible background grid. When on, your lines will snap to a grid point, letting you draw with precision.

Brush Shape

This selects a menu of various brush shapes that apply to the eraser, paint brush, and paint sprayer. Play with this menu until you are familiar with what the different brush types do.

Figure 5.6

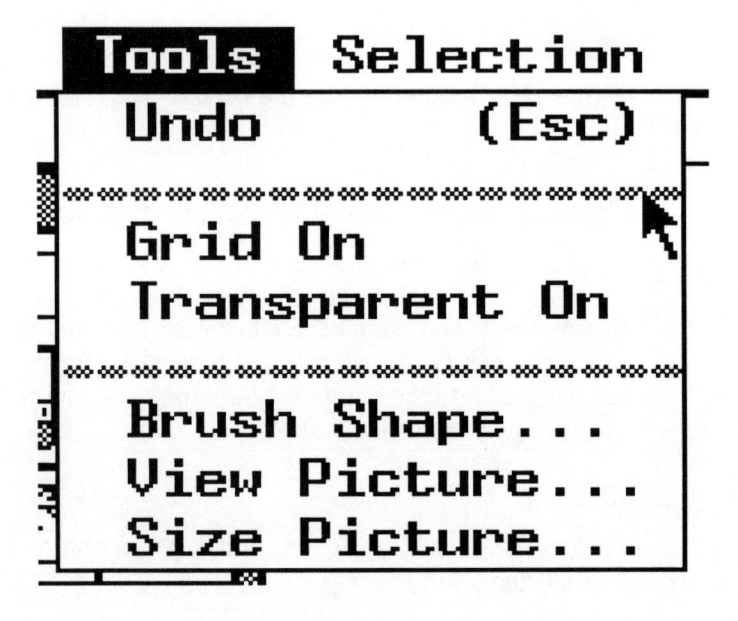

Show Picture

Shows a miniature version of the complete painting on the screen. The box that appears is a panner. Click and hold to grab the box and move it. When you release it, the viewing area on the canvas will shift to match what you've selected.

Size Picture

This selects the canvas size. You can use a one-quarter page, half page, or full page canvas, or you can have a canvas the size of the painting area displayed on the screen. This is really useful with GEM 1st Word Plus, which can import your graphics but cannot size or scale them.

PATTERNS

Without a doubt, GEM Paint II has the best pattern capabilities of any of the popular paint programs. GEM Paint II comes with 13 pattern files, eight for color and five for monochrome, plus the ability to roll your own. Patterns are controlled by the pattern selector at the right. Use the pull-down menu to call up the pattern files, or modify the patterns themselves. See Figure 5.7.

Figure 5.7

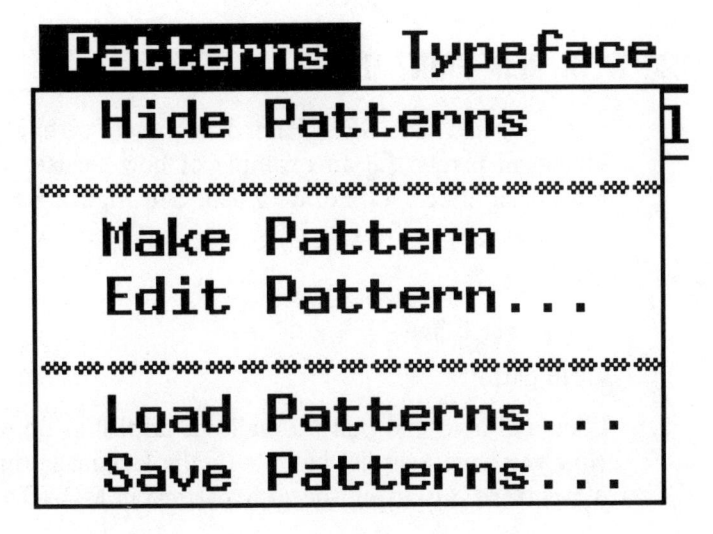

```
┌─────────────────────────────────┐
│  Patterns     Typeface          │
│    Hide Patterns              1 │
│ ─────────────────────────────── │
│    Make Pattern                 │
│    Edit Pattern...              │
│ ─────────────────────────────── │
│    Load Patterns...             │
│    Save Patterns...             │
└─────────────────────────────────┘
```

Hide/Show Patterns

Toggles the display of the pattern selector.

If you want to make your own pattern, you can do it in two ways:

Make Pattern

Use this with the selector icon. Move the selector cross-hair to the upper left corner of the part of the image you want to use. Double click and you'll get a little rectangle just the size of a pattern. Now select Make Pattern from the patterns pull-down, and your pattern will take the place of the one currently selected.

Edit a Pattern

Just select a pattern and edit its pixels. You can turn the individual bits on and off with the pencil tool, and white, black (or colored) pixels.

Save Pattern

Saves the current set of patterns, shown in the selector, to a file so you can call it up again. Use a new name for your home-grown patterns and you won't lose any of the standard patterns. Pattern files always end in .PAT.

Load Pattern

Loads a pattern file into the pattern selector.

DESIGNING WITH GEM PAINT II

Keep in mind that GEM Paint II's biggest strength is its ability to control individual pixels. As an example of how to use this to create a three-dimensional effect, let's draw a ball. See Figure 5.8.

Select:

- Circle icon
- Thin black line
- No pattern

Click and hold and pull the ball out until it's the size and shape you want. Now you have a circle, but it's totally lacking in dimension. First, let's give it a pattern. I'm using the gray pattern in MONO.PAT, but you can use any

Figure 5.8

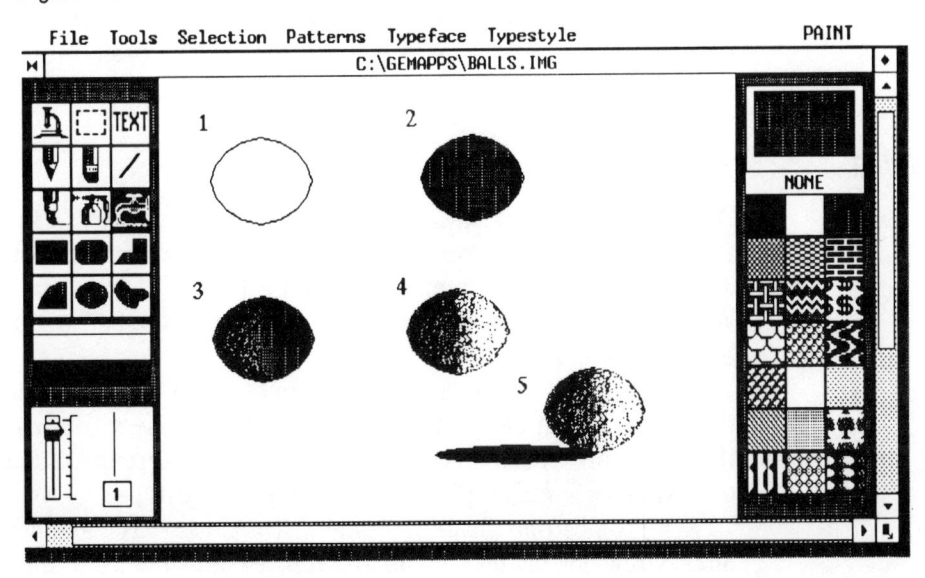

color instead of gray. Select your pattern, and then the paint faucet. Put the cross-hair in the circle and click. Yes, you could have saved this step by selecting the pattern before drawing the circle, but this way you got to play with the faucet as well.

Your ball has a single light source on its right side. Since this means the left is in shadow, select black as the pattern. Double click on the paint sprayer so that the brush shape selection comes up. I used the smallest of the spray patterns on the extreme right, but if you have something in the beach ball range you might want a bigger pattern.

Put the spray pattern over the left half of the circle and click and hold. Wave the sprayer over the left of the ball in smooth arcs, laying down more black as you go left. When the left side suits you, select white and repeat the process in reverse on the right side. Keep laying down more white as you go to the right. If you make any goofs on either side, use the microscope to zoom in and fix them.

Our ball should have a shadow (especially at the price of shadows!). Select black and draw a thin, long ellipse somewhere away from the ball. Turn transparent on (Tools pull-down) and use the selector to box your ball. Drag the ball over to the ellipse, and when it's in place, release it. And there you have it, ready for the Louvre.

Now that you've gotten your feet wet, play around for a while. If you are reading this away from your computer, put it down and go discover what GEM Paint II can do. You'll need to master the basic techniques for using Paint II before you tackle anything involved.

FLYERS

Because GEM Paint II can intermix text and graphics, especially big text that you can see at some distance, it's a great program for making handbills and flyers. For our example, we'll do a handbill for a local theatre group. While this looks quite a bit more complex than the ball we just did, it really isn't; it's only more work.

When doing handbills, etc., remember that the type must be readable from several feet away. A good technique is to use something in the design that you can display type on. As our theatre group is doing *Dracula*, a tombstone will make a lovely backdrop for the type.

The tombstone shape is really just a pair of arcs and a pair of straight lines. Draw one of the arcs for the top, leaving about one-third of the screen above it (we'll need to run type there later). See Figure 5.9. Box it with the selector, and then drag the copy beside the original arc. Use Flip Horizontal under Selection, and then drag the copy into place until it lines up and touches the first arc. Release it and click on the microscope icon. Since the selector always leaves a one-pixel blank border around the image, you'll need to fill in the pixel that will join the arcs together.

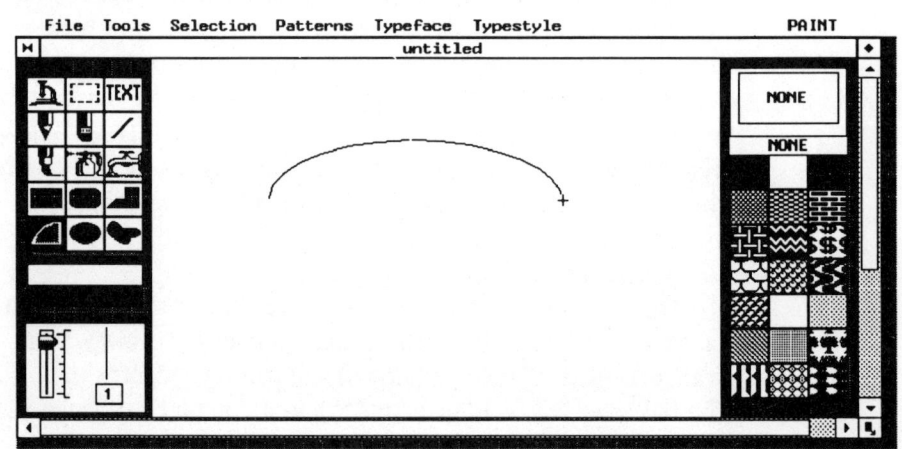

Figure 5.9

Draw two straight lines down, each starting at an end of the arc, about three-quarters of the length of the canvas. Don't worry if they aren't even—neither is the ground around the tombstone. Now you have a proper grave marker.

Use the pencil to draw the ground. Run your line completely from the left to the right of the frame, touching the bottoms of the tombstone lines. Make sure that they touch and that there are no gaps in your line (any open space will allow the patterns to leak through). If you have any gaps, use the microscope to fill them in.

I used the MONO.PAT pattern file for this, and I suggest you stick to the monochrome pattern files (unless you're using a color printer). Even if you have the spiffiest color video around, your output normally will be black-and-white.

Select the black pattern, and click on the faucet icon. Fill the above-ground area around the tombstone with black. Instant night. You'll need to use the slider bar to get to the top of the canvas and fill that with black. Select the 50 percent gray pattern (top right in the pattern selector), and pour this into the ground with the faucet.

Go up to the top. Select 28 point type, Dutch font, and align center. Select white at the selector to the left of the screen. Click on the ABC icon, and then click the cursor over the center of the tombstone, leaving a little room over the text cursor (flashing vertical white line). Type "Spend a quiet evening," hit a return, and type "with . . . ." You'll get two lines of centered, white, and terribly blocky-looking type. See Figure 5.10.

You can smooth the type's blockiness by zooming in with the microscope and turning on a few pixels around the edges. Fill in a little anywhere you see a big step between blocks of pixels.

Now for the text on the white display area. Select: 72 point, Dutch, Bold italic, Align left. Start the text cursor at the left and completely within the white area. Type "Count." If you backspace (your only editing capability in Paint II), you may get some parts of the letters left. Erase these before typing again. If "Count" isn't centered in the area, use the selector to box it and move it to center. You may need to erase some leftovers from the original position. Center "Dracula" under "Count" with the same technique. See Figure 5.11.

To suggest letters cut into stone, fill each letter with the 50 percent gray pattern (using the faucet). This will both lighten the letters and enhance the jaggedy edges, making them look roughly hewn. Depth is provided by using the microscope and turning on the center pixels in the type strokes.

Figure 5.10

Figure 5.11

Age is added to the tombstone with freehand vertical lines, drawn with the pencil icon.

The bulk of the text is done with 14 point type, centered within the white field. You can move the text about to suit yourself.

The fingers along the top of the tombstone are really simple. Double click on the paint brush and select the smallest round brush (bottom of the second row from the left). Select the 50 percent gray pattern, and daub the fingers over the top and lip of the stone. Add nails and finger joint suggestions with the microscope.

The plants along the bottom are drawn with the free-form tool and no line selected. Just suggest the shapes of leaves, filled with the same pattern as the ground. You can add white highlights with the pencil and the microscope.

And there you have it ladies and gentlemen, a handbill produced by GEM Paint II. Really, it didn't take very long. Certainly a fraction of the time that it would take to produce such a handbill by hand. See Figure 5.12.

STYLIZED ART

Because GEM Paint II is so flexible, you can really let your imagination run riot. The following is a large capital to be used as the first letter in an

Figure 5.12

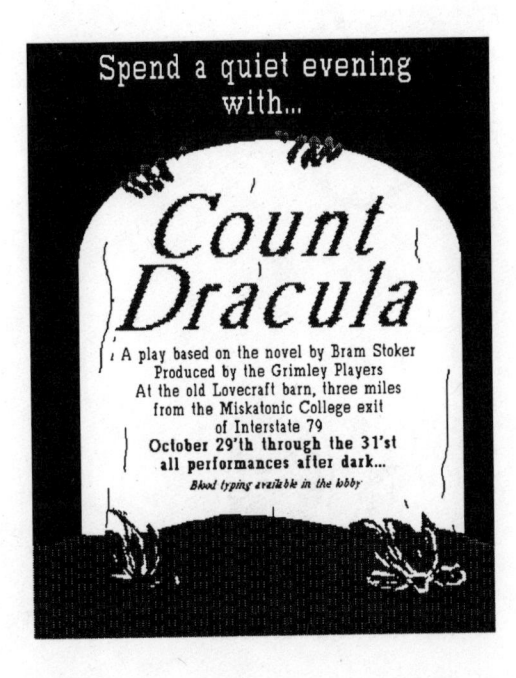

extremely garish layout. The letter is reminiscent of the French manuscript letters of a few centuries ago. It could be used by any of the GEM publishing programs, especially GEM Desktop Publisher.

I created it by simply drawing a bold capital "O" with the Dutch font. Using the microscope, I removed all of the black pixels within the "O," leaving a slightly heavier outline inside. When playing these games, however, you must make sure that you have solid pixel coverage in the outer lines. Otherwise fill patterns will leak in.

The next step is drawing the petals within the "O." I used the ellipse tool and the microscope to clean up where I didn't color inside the lines. I filled the petals with gray and added the white highlights with the microscope. See Figure 5.13.

Done with the petals, I drew the stem and leaves with arcs and the freeform tool. The stem is really just a pair of arcs. Leaf details and shading are easily added with the paint sprayer (fine pattern) and the microscope.

I used the rectangle tool and selected a medium weight line to draw the box. It's a good idea, by the way, to draw the box away from the art so that you don't accidentally paint over your hard work. I used the faucet to fill the box line with 50 percent gray. I then turned transparent on and used

Figure 5.13

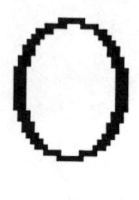

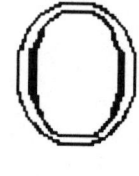

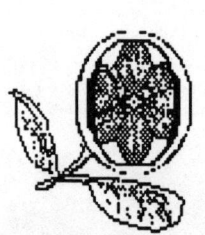

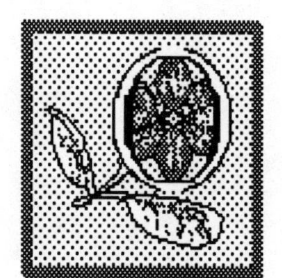

the selector to move it over the flower/letter. I also used the faucet to add the background screen. The final touch was using the microscope to open the top of the "O," something that can't be done until the background pattern has been poured in.

LAYOUT DESIGNS

I really appreciate GEM Paint II's ability to bang out quick thumbnail sketches of page designs. If you are designing a publication, do it here first. You can fiddle and tweak to your heart's content.

Figure 5.14 presents the layout for a newsletter. To show how you can play with the masthead design, I've done three mastheads in the example. Using GEM Paint II lets you play what-if with the number of columns, unifying design features, etc.

One of the big problems designers often face is trying to get people to "visualize" what a publication will look like before it's actually produced. Using GEM Paint II to do the rough layouts solves the problem. People don't have to visualize; they can see the actual design.

Figure 5.14

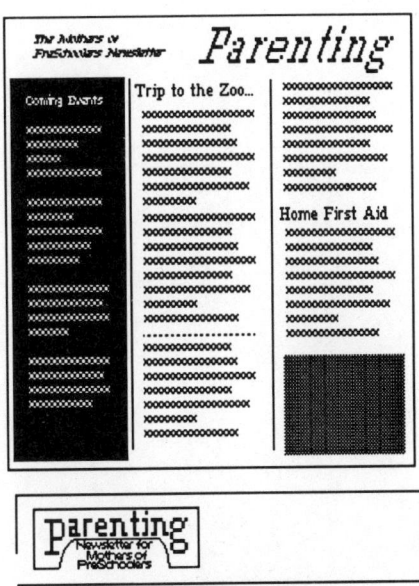

CHAPTER 6

Welcome to GEM Draw Plus

INTRODUCTION	85
TOOLKIT	85
PULL-DOWN MENUS	91
YOUR FIRST ASSIGNMENT	102
SECOND ASSIGNMENT: THE ORGANIZATIONAL CHART	110

INTRODUCTION

GEM Draw Plus is one of the leading PC drawing packages. Its virtues are precision and the ability to move, layer, and size objects you've drawn. Unlike GEM Paint, GEM Draw Plus deals almost entirely with geometric forms. Its fundamental element isn't the pixel; it's the line.

Like GEM Paint II, GEM Draw Plus lets you have two drawings open simultaneously. You can easily take previously drawn elements and incorporate them into your new drawing. This brings to drawing the great advantage word processing introduced to typing: If it's been done once, you can use it over and over again.

GEM Draw Plus requires GEM version 2.1 or later to work. It also requires more memory than most other applications. If you have 640 kilobytes of memory, however, you'll have no problems loading GEM Draw Plus and the desktop accessories. If you have GEM/3 and Specific Solutions or Bitstream fonts, GEM Draw Plus will load up to four fonts.

This chapter is devoted entirely just to learning how to use the package. The following chapters cover advanced techniques. The first few sections of this chapter cover what the various tools and pull-down menus do. Consider it reference material. Later on in the chapter we'll show how the tools and menus are actually used. Of course, there's just no substitute for playing around with the program yourself. Set aside some time to try everything. It's really the best way to learn.

An important point to remember: GEM Draw Plus is the cornerstone to the GEM system and GEM Desktop publishing programs. GEM Desktop Publisher uses Draw Plus not only for art, but also to control headers and footers. Ventura Publisher uses Draw Plus as the medium of exchange for line drawings: Everything from DXF (Drawing eXchange Format) files from CAD systems to MacDraw PICT files are converted to GEM Draw Plus files.

TOOLKIT

Draw Plus has a large toolkit indeed. The left of the screen is filled with geometric-form drawing tools and the top has eight pull-down menus. And, of course, there is the usual full box, size box, and sliders. See Figure 6.1.

Note that the drawing surface has a grid pattern with dots. The dots show you the current grid divisions, which you can adjust or turn off. If on, everything you draw will "snap" to these grid points. This means that every

Figure 6.1

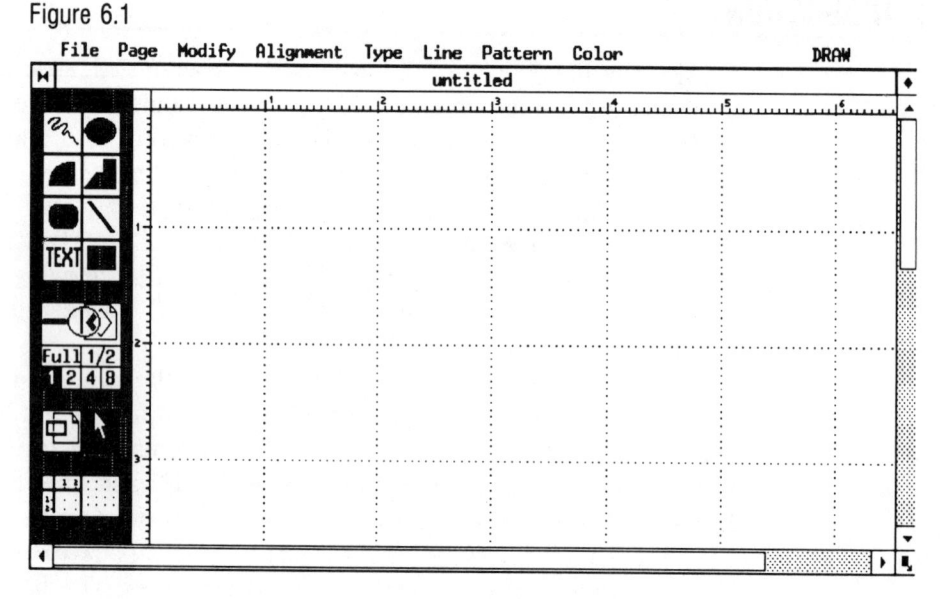

line or side of an object will jump to one or another grid point as you draw. It may take a little getting used to, but this feature can help make your drawings extremely precise.

Remember that with GEM Paint you can select various line weights, fill patterns, colors, and type sizes. The same is true in Draw Plus, and they work pretty much the same way as Paint. Keep this in mind as we describe the drawing tools. See Figure 6.2.

Sketch

Draws a freehand line following the mouse movement. The line is not of infinite length, and sketch will just stop drawing after a certain distance. Click and hold to draw; let go to stop.

Like all of the drawing tools (except text), sketch is affected by the current line weight, color, and fill pattern. Fill patterns get a bit weird with a freehand line.

Circle

Actually, it draws ellipses as well as circles. Click and hold to draw. Release to stop drawing.

Figure 6.2

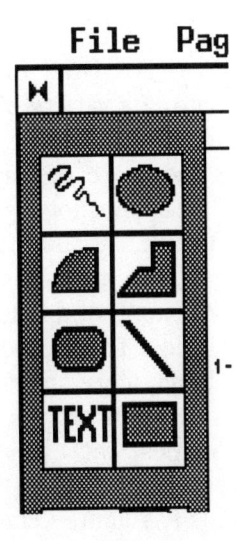

Arc

This is, unfortunately, not as flexible as I would like. Arc draws any arc you want—as long as it's a 90-degree arc. Pretty limiting, but later I'll show you some ways around it. Click and hold to draw; release to stop. If you don't want a fill pattern messing up your curved lines, use a "none" pattern.

Polygon

My favorite, although drawing with it can be a little like stepping in chewing gum (it's sometimes hard to get it to stop drawing). Click to start drawing; click again to mark the end of one line in the polygon. Double click to stop drawing. Caution: If you click one too many times, it will start a new polygon (the stepping-in-gum effect).

Rounded Rectangle

This draws a rectangle with rounded corners. If the rectangle has small enough sides, you'll get a pair of rounded sides instead of rounded corners. Click and hold to draw; release to complete the rounded rectangle.

Line

Draws a line. Click and hold to start the line; release to end it.

Text

Real type. Not just bit mapped approximations like GEM Paint provides. Right out of the box Draw Plus provides both Swiss (Helvetica) and Dutch (Times Roman) in a variety of sizes. Of course, you can add fonts from the Bitstream library.

Because these are the sizes available throughout most of the Digital Research GEM applications, you should get to know them: 7 point, 10 point, 14 point, 20 point, 28 point, 36 point, and 72 point. Since a point is equal to about 1/72 of an inch, 72 point type is an inch high and 7 point type is just shy of one-tenth of an inch.

You can select type to be the usual italic, bold, underline, and combinations. We'll talk more about this when we cover the type pull-down menu.

The text function lets you insert type starting at the current text cursor location (a vertical bar). Position the mouse point and click to make the vertical bar appear.

Draw Plus has limited editing ability, and unlike Paint you can go back and edit your text after you've finished a line. Backspace and delete both erase one character to the left of the cursor. Hit the Escape key and everything to the left of the cursor will disappear. The right and left arrow keys move the cursor along the line.

When you hit Enter, the cursor will drop down one line (spacing varies with type size) and align with the leftmost character of the first line. If you want to edit a line, put the mouse pointer over it and click. The text cursor will snap to that line.

Rectangle

Draws a box. Click and hold to start; release to stop.

VIEWING AND OTHER TOOLS

Below the drawing tools are a set of tools that adjust your viewing area, rulers and grid, plus the all-important pointer. The pointer is your way to select drawing elements for copying, editing, etc.

Zoomer

The zoomer is your way of changing the magnification in your drawing canvas. A setting of 1 provides about a 1:1 view of your picture. Full shows the entire canvas, while 1/2 shows half. The rest are magnifications: 2:1, 4:1, and 8:1. Something to watch out for—the magnified views don't always show true positions. This is especially true for critical alignments when the grid snap is off. Always go back to a 1:1 view to check that you really did line things up the way you wanted.

Click once on the magnification level you want. Double click and Draw Plus will display the panner rectangle (see below) at the selected magnification.

Panner

The panner is an alternate way of zipping around the drawing canvas. Click on the panner and Draw Plus shifts to full drawing area view. A rectangle appears showing the previous viewing area on the canvas.

Put the mouse pointer in the rectangle and click and hold. The pointer will change into an open hand. Move the rectangle around until it's over the viewing area you want. Release the mouse button and the new field of view will snap into place.

Pointer

This selects drawing elements. Click on a drawing element and the extents will suddenly appear around the object. Extents are tiny black boxes placed every 45 degrees around a box. The box completely encloses the drawing element. The wonderful thing about extents is that you can tug at them to stretch or compress the drawing element. The top, bottom, and side extents can be pulled or pushed in one direction. For instance, the top extent can be pulled up or pushed down to stretch or squish the drawing element.

Corner extents move in two directions, letting you adjust the size of the element up-and-down and left-and-right. Isn't technology a marvelous thing!

There are lots of techniques involved in using the pointer, and they're easier to illustrate when we've got something on the canvas. One basic thing you should know, however: If you click on the pointer and then don't select anything, any changes you make to pull-down menu parameters become defaults. The defaults will apply until you leave the drawing or make them permanent.

Rulers

The rulers tool toggles the side and top rulers on and off. Click on it to toggle.

Double click on rulers and you'll get the page size selection menu. The choice between portrait and landscape is simple. Portrait means a canvas higher than it is wide. Landscape is just the opposite: wider than high.

Sizes available vary with letter-, legal-, and ledger-sized paper (or in metric A5, A4, and A3 papers). With most printers, anything over letter (or A5) will print in "titles." For instance, the Apple LaserWriter prints ledger and A3 in two neat halves, which you can trim and paste together.

Borders are, unfortunately, something you can't dispense with. The minimum borders are one-half inch or one centimeter. One-half inch is the minimum an Apple LaserWriter can provide anyway.

Grid

The grid adds precision to your drawing by forcing your drawing element parts to snap to points. While it's helpful to see the grid points when the grid is on, when it's off they can be distracting. If you are going to use SnapShot to transfer part of your drawing to GEM Paint, you probably don't want the grid points showing.

Clicking on the grid icon toggles the grid display on and off. It doesn't turn the grid itself on or off, however, just the visible reference points.

Double clicking invokes the ruler and grid increment menu. Depending on whether your page size is in English or metric, you can select grid increments in 1/32 inch (1/10 cm), 1/16 inch (1/5 cm), 1/8 inch (1/2 cm), 1/4 inch (1 cm), 1/2 inch (2 cm), or 1 inch (3 cm). See Figure 6.3.

Figure 6.3

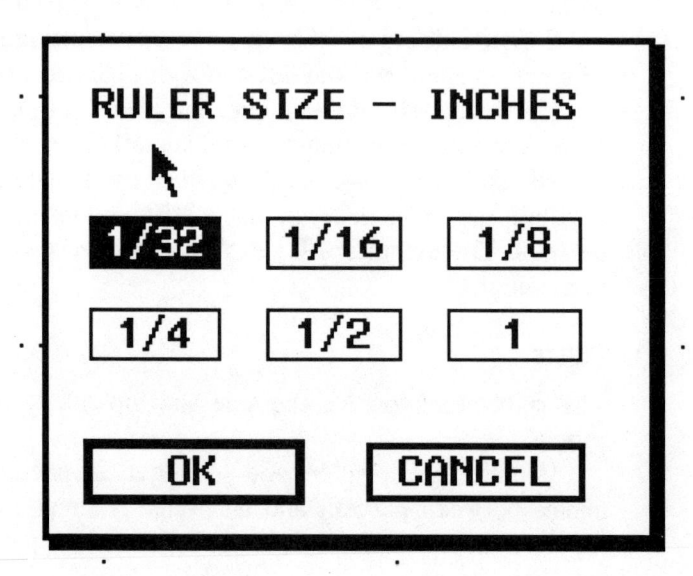

PULL-DOWN MENUS

GEM Draw Plus has a rich collection of pull-down menu functions. These provide a wide variety of patterns, line weights, and image editing functions. As we did with the toolkit, we'll quickly go over the menus and the functions. A bit later on, we'll see how they are actually used.

Most of the pull-down functions can be accessed by control characters, and when you become practiced with the program you'll find this a real time saver. Control codes are listed along the right side of each pull-down menu.

FILE

The File menu is pretty much the same here as in other GEM applications. It controls file naming, opening, closing, and the ever-popular abandoning. See Figure 6.4.

New

Click on this and it clears the canvas. The file title will revert to "untitled." If you have made changes to the drawing since the last time it was saved

Figure 6.4

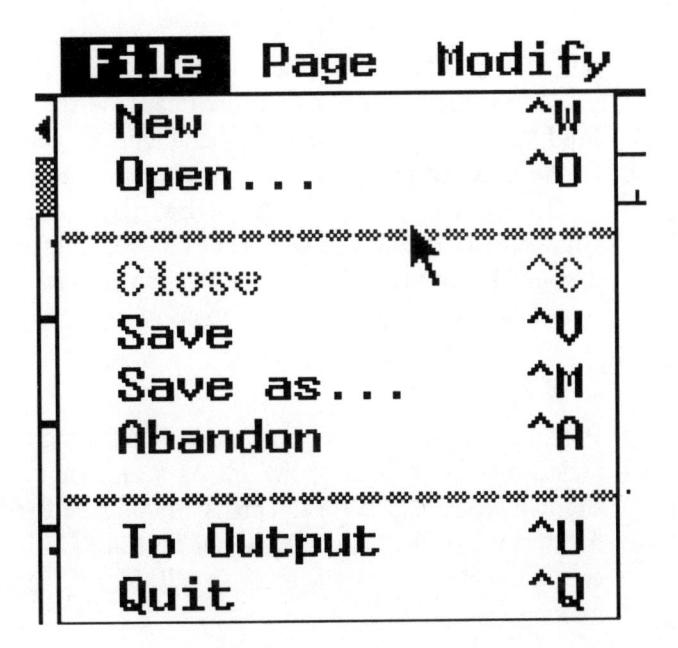

(if ever), Draw Plus will ask you if you want to abandon the file, save it, or cancel the operation before clearing the canvas.

Open

Calls up the file selector so that you can open an existing .GEM file. GEM Draw Plus can only open .GEM files (and .GMP files from Desktop Publisher, although they are layered and opening one can be an extremely messy thing to do). If you open a .GEM file created by Paint, you'll discover it's empty; such a file is created as a pointer file specifically for GEM Write.

If you have "untitled" in the title bar, Draw Plus will simply plop the selected drawing on the canvas. If you already have a drawing with a file name on the canvas, Draw Plus will open a second window for the new drawing. Having two drawings open is a very handy thing. You can move parts of the drawings back and forth at will. But it is a bit tricky. Read through the discussion on pages 113-114 before giving it a try.

Close

Closes the second window if two were open. You can't close the last remaining window.

Save

GEM Draw Plus keeps track of when you last saved the file. If you have made any changes since then, you can use this command to write them to the file. If you haven't made any changes, or you never assigned a file name to the drawing with Save as . . . , you can't access this function.

Every time you save a file, GEM Draw Plus will rename the previous version to a file with a .BAK extension. This is insurance for you. If something dreadful happens to the working file, you can always rename the .BAK version to .GEM and retrieve at least some of your work.

Save as . . .

Pops up the file selector so that you can assign a file name to the file and pick a directory for it to live in. As a general rule, don't save your files to the /GEMAPPS directory. This is a good rule to follow because strange and mysterious things happen to .GEM files in /GEMAPPS, especially with Ventura Publisher. Save the files to PICTURES or a directory of your own making.

Abandon

Throws away all changes since the last save. If you never assigned a file name and save the file, it throws the whole drawing away. Of course, Draw Plus will ask you if you really want to abandon the file, save it, or just forget about the abandon operation.

To Output

Hops off to Output and loads the current drawing into the drawing list. Once again, you can save any recent changes, abandon them, or cancel the output operation.

Quit

Closes up shop and takes you back to the GEM Desktop. Ever vigilant, Draw Plus will ask if you want to save, abandon, or cancel the operation.

PAGE MENU

This controls miscellaneous functions that affect the drawing canvas. It also lets you access a little help pop-up that tells you about double clicking on the panner, zoomer, and ruler icons.

Auto grid Off/On

Toggles the grid on and off. When on, lines and sides or corners of drawing elements will snap to the grid coordinates (which can be displayed as dots). When off, you can put anything anywhere on the canvas.

Page size

The same pop-up menu that you get by double clicking on the ruler icon. It lets you pick portrait or landscape orientation, the size of the page, and the size of the borders. It also lets you select English or metric units for all Draw Plus functions. See Figure 6.5.

Ruler spacing

And more importantly, grid spacing as well. Just click on the spacing you want. Remember, the wider the spacing, the more dramatic the snap to grid coordinates.

Figure 6.5

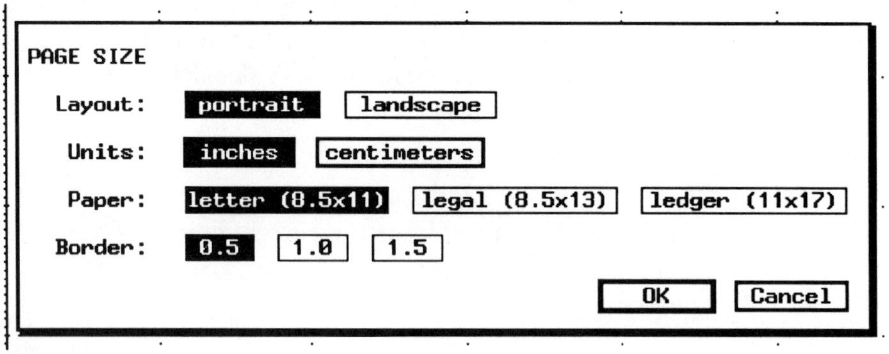

```
PAGE SIZE
  Layout:  portrait   landscape
  Units:   inches     centimeters
  Paper:   letter (8.5x11)   legal (8.5x13)   ledger (11x17)
  Border:  0.5   1.0   1.5
                                    OK    Cancel
```

Shortcuts

A help pop-up that explains what happens when you double click on the panner, zoomer, or ruler.

Save preferences

Saves the current settings for pull-down menus to a file called DRAW.INF in the /GEMAPPS directory. Every time you invoke GEM Draw Plus from then on, it will read those settings from the file and use them as defaults. If you want to revert to the standard settings, just delete the DRAW.INF file.

MODIFY MENU

This menu does what it says: It lets you modify selected drawing elements in very powerful ways. The rotation and mirroring functions are features that were added in GEM Draw Plus. If you like to write letters to software vendors, tell Digital Research how much you appreciate these features and how much more you would appreciate rotation in degree increments. As nice as the 90-degree rotation features are, it won't be too long before you'll say to yourself, "If I could only tilt that element a little bit . . . ."

Delete

Vaporizes the currently selected drawing elements.

Undelete

Restores the last set of deleted drawing elements (or element).

Make copy

Makes a copy of the selected element(s). The copies are then automatically selected for your drawing convenience. The copy is also kicked to the top layer if you have overlapping elements.

Select all

It does. Selects every element on the canvas and displays its extents. If you have plenty of tiny elements concentrated in a single area, they will appear to have grown fuzz.

Rotate

Rotates a single element in 90-degree increments. It will also rotate type.

Flip horizontal

Mirrors drawing elements from right to left. What it does to type is truly interesting, and rather difficult to explain. Look at Figure 6.6. It shows the two columns, figures on the left and ragged right text at the right side. After being horizontally flipped, the text, now at the left, is suddenly right justified.

Figure 6.6

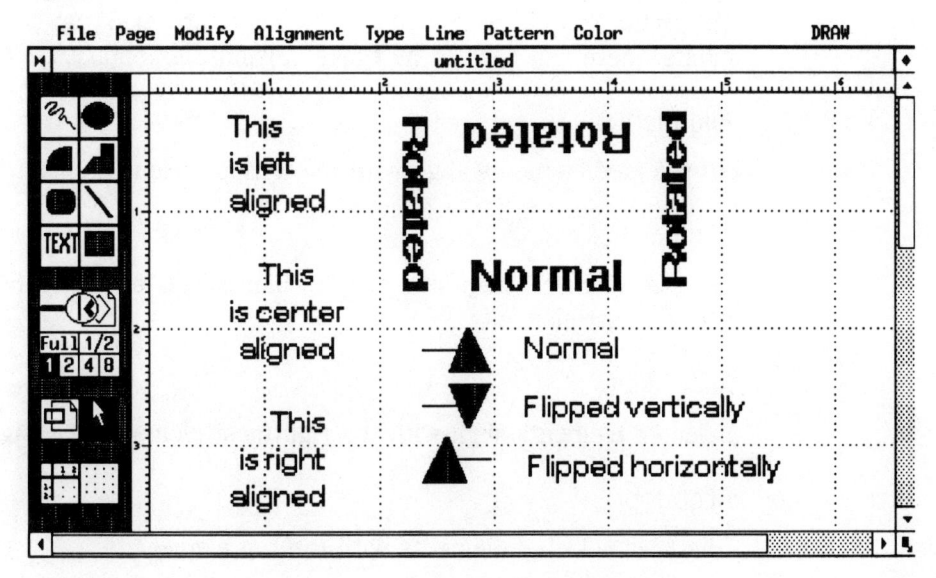

Flip vertical

If we now click on flip vertical, the order of the lines in both columns of type, from top to bottom, is reversed. If you use this on a graphic element, it will be flipped top to bottom.

ALIGNMENT

This one deals strictly with the shuffling about of elements. You can move them in relation to each other, to the page, or move them up and down the stack if they are in layers.

Put in front

Takes the selected element(s) to the front of a layered stack of elements.

Put in back

Moves the selected element(s) to the back of a layered stack of elements.

Make group

Lumps all selected elements into a single element.

Break group

Reduces an element made of other elements to its separate component elements. Now if the component elements are made up of still more elements, these will need to be broken again. Elementary, isn't it?

Align left

All selected elements align with the leftmost element.

Align center

Selected elements align at a center point calculated between the rightmost and leftmost elements.

Align right

Selected elements align with the rightmost element. See Figure 6.7

Align top

Aligns all selected elements with the top element.

Figure 6.7

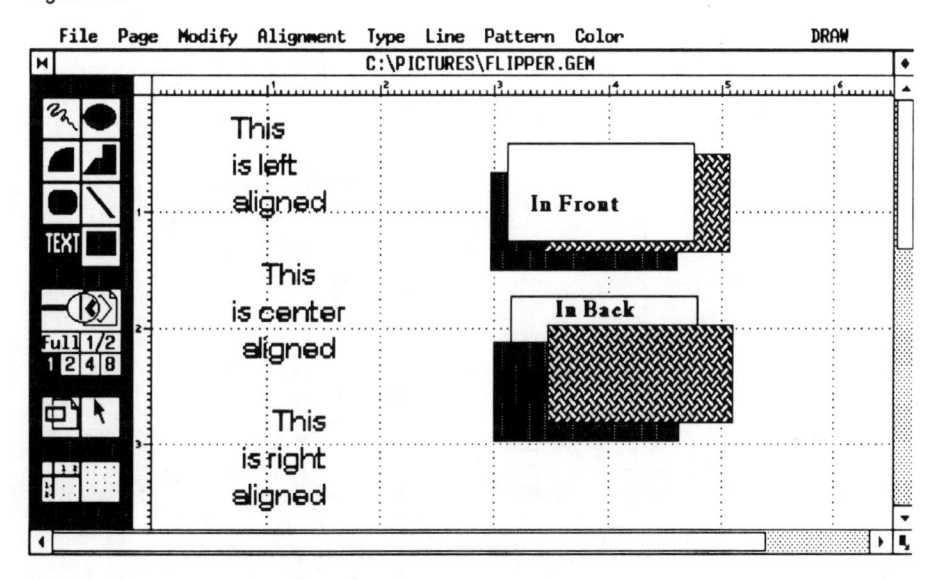

Align middle

Aligns selected elements at a point calculated between the top and bottom elements.

Align bottom

You guessed it; all selected elements line up with the bottom element.

Page center

All selected elements align at the center of the page (calculated from left to right, not top to bottom).

Even spacing

This evenly spaces all selected elements between the top and bottom elements. It only works if elements don't overlap.

TYPE

The type menu selects type size, face, and style. See Figure 6.8. It works for either the line you're currently typing (or about to type), or for any selected lines of type.

Figure 6.8

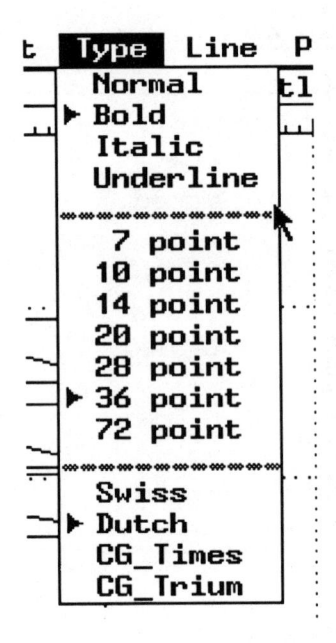

```
t   Type  Line   P
    Normal      t1
  ▶ Bold
    Italic
    Underline
    ⋯⋯⋯⋯⋯⋯⋯⋯
     7 point
    10 point
    14 point
    20 point
    28 point
  ▶ 36 point
    72 point
    ⋯⋯⋯⋯⋯⋯⋯⋯
    Swiss
  ▶ Dutch
    CG_Times
    CG_Trium
```

Normal

Plain, everyday type face. This is sometimes called a "roman" face.

Bold

Heavier, darker version of the type face.

Italic

The roman, or normal, face but pitched at a slant.

Underline

Selects an underscore that runs the length of the line of type. It even underlines spaces between words.

Of course, you can pick any combination of the above, including a combination of bold, italic, and underline.

7-72 point

In printers' lingo, a point is about 1/72 of an inch (a logical unit of measure if ever there was one). Thus 36 point type is about half an inch high, if measured against a capital X.

Swiss

The Bitstream trade name for Helvetica. Helvetica is an extremely popular sans-serif (i.e., no squiggles at the ends of the letters) type face.

Dutch

Another Bitstream trade name, this one for a Times Roman face. This is a serif font, replete with squiggles, designed for newspaper print. It is specifically designed for easy readability even with lousy printing.

Whatever

Any two additional typefaces that you've loaded into GEM/3.

We'll talk a lot more about Swiss and Dutch in the Desktop Publisher chapters. It's sufficient for now to say that both print quite well for all types of printers.

LINES

One of my pet peeves. GEM Draw Plus has rather large jumps in line weights. They go up from a hairline to a 1/4-inch line by 1/32 of an inch (or 0.8 mm). Now I don't often need a 1/4-inch, but I sure could use a couple more line weights between a hairline and 1/16 inch. Anyway, they are what they are, and to Digital Research's credit GEM Draw Plus did pick up a few more line thicknesses over the original GEM Draw. See Figure 6.9.

None

No visible line, but a boundary that the computer remembers. You can see the boundary if you fill the object with a visible pattern.

Dots and Dashes

Useful for phantom lines in mechanical drawings, streets in maps, or different strata in a diagram of rock layers. These are all variations of the hairline.

Hairline

A very thin line (something on the order of 1/100 of an inch, or three dots when printed on a laser printer). This is the standard drawing weight you'll use, and it reproduces quite sharply on both copy machines and offset printing presses.

Figure 6.9

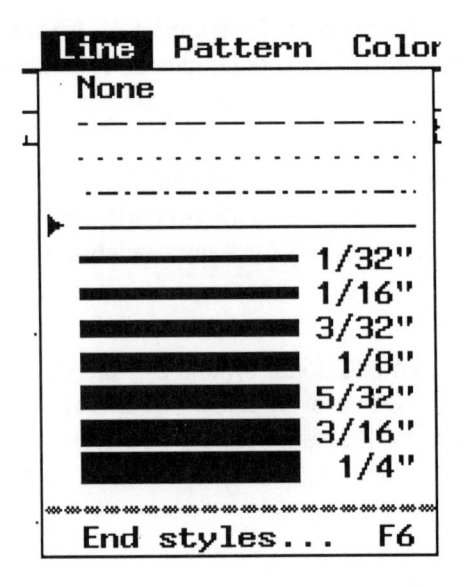

1/32"-1/4"

Varying line thicknesses from heavy to monstrous.

End styles

This selects whether either end of the line should be square, rounded, or have an arrowhead. See Figure 6.10. Click on the selections you want for each end. By the way, the left and right sides of the menu do not correspond to the left and right sides of your line. The left side corresponds to the starting point for the line; the right side corresponds to the ending point.

PATTERNS

These will fill all selected elements with the pattern you click on. See Figure 6.11. A couple need explanation:

None

Transparent. If an object filled with none is placed over another element filled with a visible pattern, the visible pattern will show through.

Figure 6.10

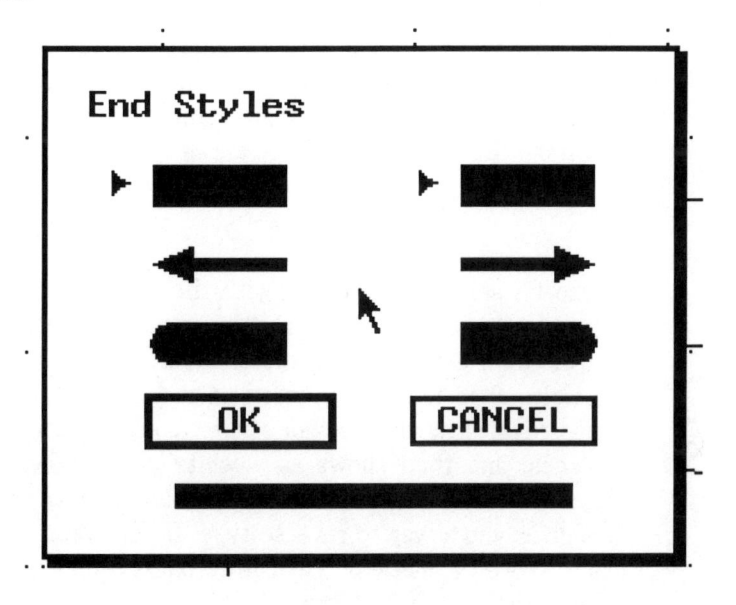

Figure 6.11

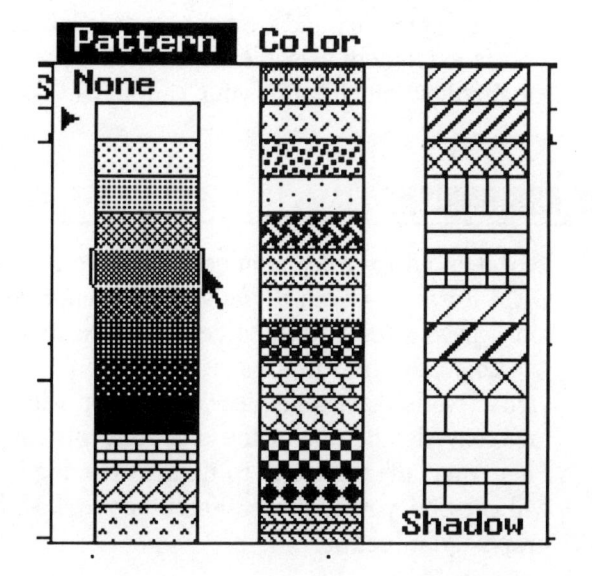

Shadow

Drop shadow. The shadow is a duplicate image of the element, offset a bit to the left and down. The shadow is below the element and filled with black. If you use a drop shadow with an element filled with none, the entire shadow will show through.

COLORS

These fill selected elements with the color you click on. They also color patterns. If you have a monochrome graphics board, or you are using a CGA board, you'll get only two colors: Color 0 and Black.

Color 0 is kind of interesting—a form of GEM Draw Plus sleight of hand—regardless of the video card you're using. An element in color 0 vanishes, and then shows as a white object when placed over any other element. This is very handy if you want to obscure part of a drawing. It also gives you a way to reverse type. If you select color 0 for your type and place it over a black or dark gray background, you'll get white lettering against the darker background.

DRAW

In addition to the usual collection of GEM accessories, you'll find a selection marked GEM Draw info. Click on this and you'll find counters telling you how much memory and element space is left in your current drawing window. This is extremely valuable when working with big drawings. It lets you see roughly how much more your canvas can hold.

YOUR FIRST ASSIGNMENT

Yes, it is an exciting moment. Here you stand ready to create your first GEM drawing. (Even if you've done hundreds of drawings, play along with me. I have a few things to demonstrate that you may have missed.)

Logically, your first piece of art should be your company or organization logo. This is the single piece of art you will use most. Unfortunately, your logo may also be one of the most difficult subjects to render in GEM Draw Plus. Your alternative is to digitize the logo with a scanner (a device that will provide you with a 300x300-dot GEM Paint .IMG file for whatever graphic you feed it).

If you don't have a scanner, you can bite the bullet and draw the logo in GEM Draw Plus. Once done, you have an absolutely painless way to add a logo of any size to your publications.

If you have a difficult logo, however, you may wish to put this off until you've sharpened your GEM Draw Plus techniques. In the case of our mythical company, Frammis International Limited, the logo is relatively simple.

The basic part of the logo is an ellipse, 1 inch high by 3¾ inches wide. See Figure 6.12. This is much easier to draw if you select a 1/4-inch grid (Ruler spacing . . . menu).

You'll want to set a default for the lines for the gridwork on the ellipse. Make sure the ellipse isn't selected (no extents around it) before you do that. With the pointer as your current tool, set up the defaults as follows:

Line weight: 1/32"

Color: 0

Pattern: None

Ruler Setting: 1/16"

Color 0 is white, which will give us our reversed lines against the black ellipse. See Figure 6.13. If you have a color monitor and printer, you can be more creative than black-and-white.

Figure 6.12

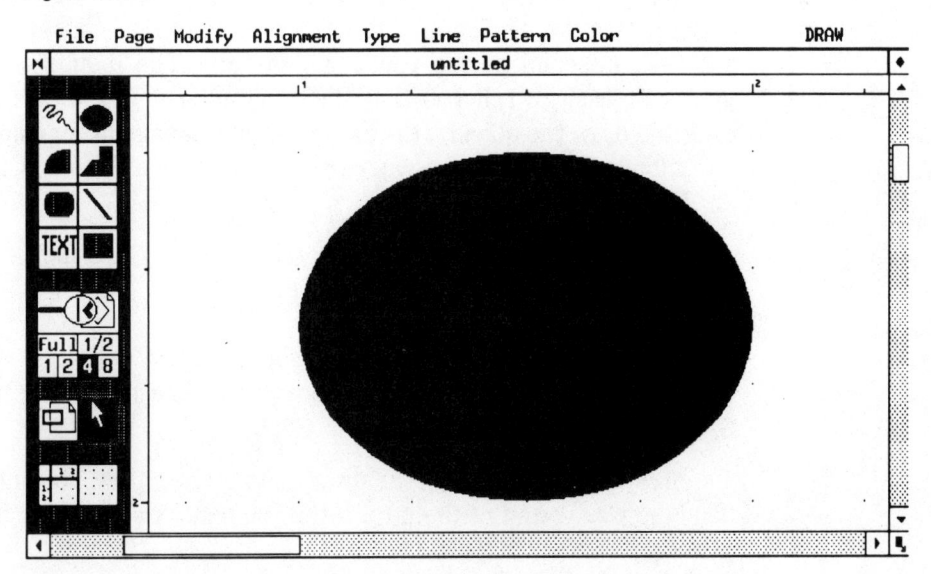

Figure 6.13

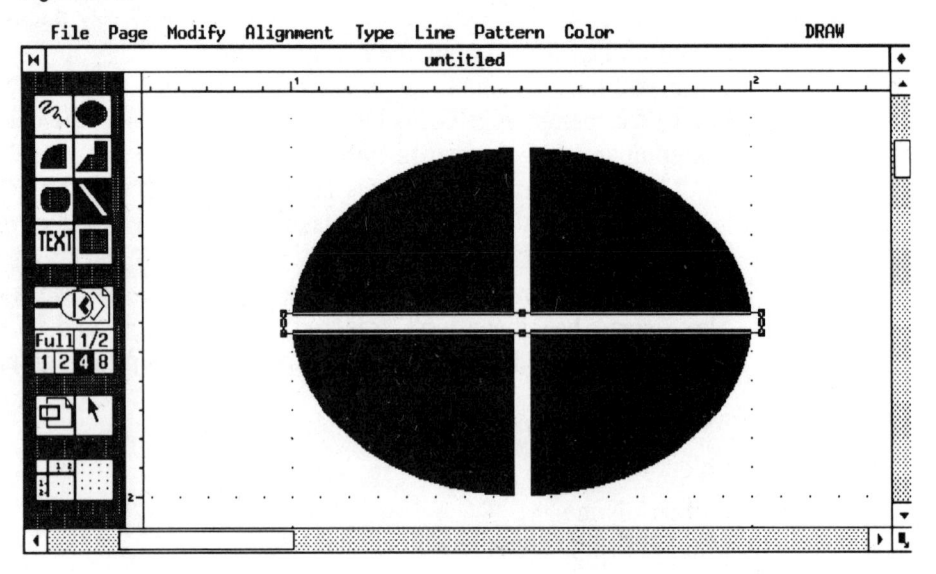

Grab the straight line tool and put the mouse pointer at the top or bottom center point of the ellipse. Click and draw a horizontal line through the ellipse. Now go to the right or left midpoint and draw the horizontal line through the ellipse. Not very hard, is it?

Get the arc tool, and put the mouse pointer at the top center point (right where the vertical line touches the top of the ellipse). Click and hold, but wait a second before you begin the arc. The mouse pointer will momentarily flash to tell you that the arc tool is engaged. Sometimes if you click and draw too quickly, the arc tool won't engage in time and the starting point for the arc won't be where you want it. See Figure 6.14.

Draw the first arc by:

1. Pulling the arc directly left two grid points, or 1/8 inch.
2. Pulling down to the horizontal line.
3. Releasing.
4. Starting a new arc at the end of the first, and pulling it straight down.
5. Joining the new arc to the bottom center line by pulling to the right.
6. Releasing.

Arcs are tricky things to draw. Sometimes they absolutely refuse to bend the way you want them to. If this happens, start the arc from the other side.

Figure 6.14

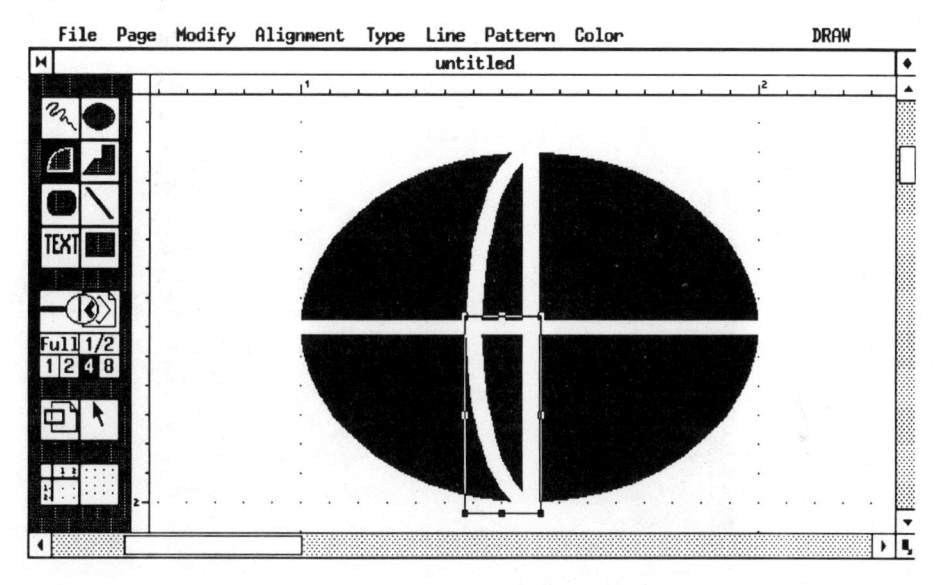

Now draw all of the other vertical arcs, each 1/8 inch further out than the last. Do this only for the left side of the ellipse (we'll let GEM Draw Plus do the right side for us). See Figure 6.15.

To draw the horizontal arcs, put the mouse cursor on the left side of the ellipse, 2/16 of an inch down from the top. Click and draw the arc first down 1/16, and then to the right to touch the center line. Start the bottom arc 2/16 of an inch from the bottom, and you'll have a matched set. See Figure 6.16.

Now we'll use a little of the power of GEM Draw Plus. Get the mouse pointer tool, and start a selection box above and to the left of the ellipse (click and hold). Pull the box down and to the right until it covers the arcs you've drawn and is just to the right of the vertical line. Release. All of the arcs and the vertical line should select and display their extents. Group them with Make group under Alignment. Now use Make copy (under Modify), and copy the group. Use Flip horizontal, under Modify, and you'll get the arcs for the right side of the ellipse. Just drag them over until they snap into position. See Figure 6.17.

TYPE

GEM Draw Plus doesn't treat type like other drawing elements. Type has fixed size (selected with the Type menu) and fixed horizontal spacing. If you

Figure 6.15

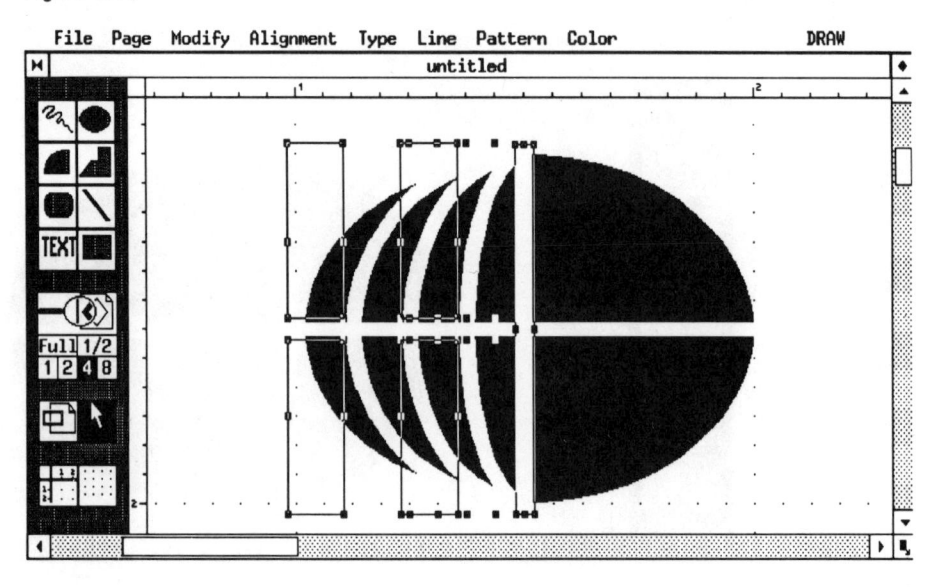

Figure 6.16

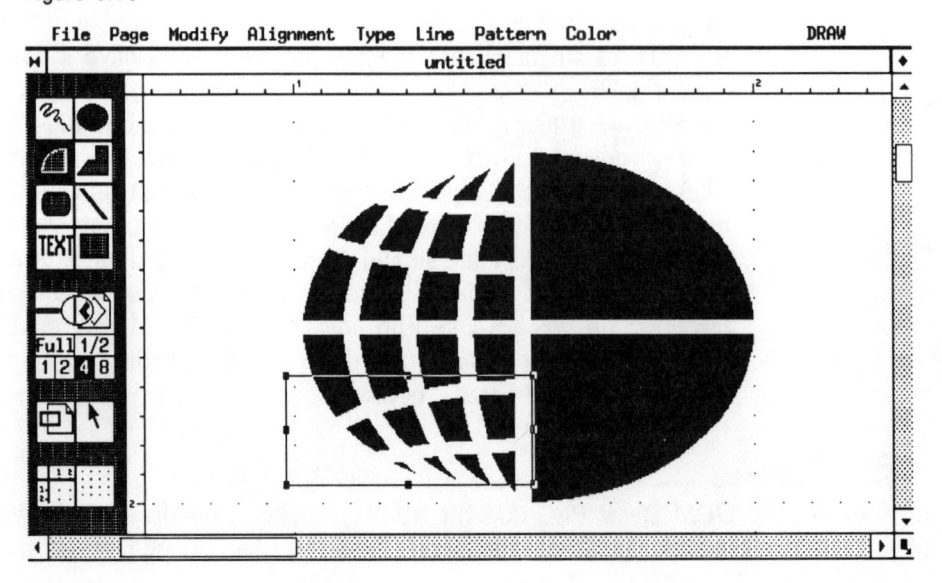

Figure 6.17

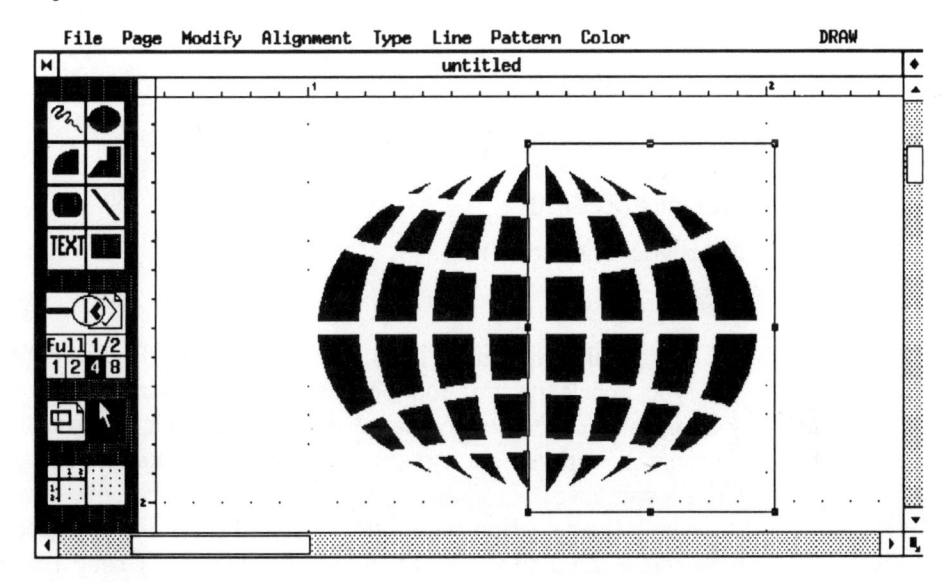

select type and try to stretch it, you can't. You can vary the spacing between lines of type, however, and the Flip horizontal and Flip vertical commands do weird and terribly useful things to type. Flip horizontal changes the order of words from right to left—e.g., "Now is the time . . ." becomes "time the is Now . . . ." Flip vertical changes the order of sentences from top to bottom. For instance:

Frammis

International

Limited

becomes

Limited

International

Frammis

For the Frammis logo, we just need the company name. Select the following as your type:

Color: 1 or whatever you have as black (remember we had set it to 0)

Type size: 14 point

Type face: Dutch

Type font: Bold

Now, in some wide open area of the canvas, type:

Frammis (Return)

International (Return)

Limited (Return)

You should have three lines, left aligned. See Figure 6.18. If you made any typos, click the type tool point over the line you want to fix. The cursor will appear on the line. You can use the left and right arrow keys to position the cursor, and use backspace to delete the mistake. Just type in any additions you have.

Using the selection rectangle, select all three lines of type. Group them. Now move them to the right of the logo ellipse. Group the ellipse and all of its arcs and lines together. Then use the selection rectangle to select the ellipse group and the type group. Click on Align bottom (Alignment), and the word "Limited" will align with the bottom of the ellipse.

Figure 6.18

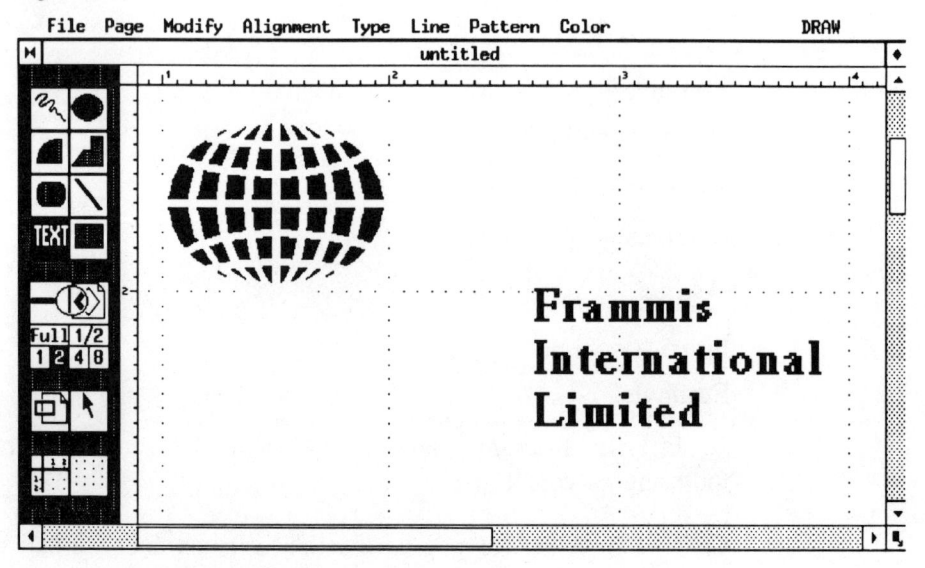

Great, except that the word "Frammis" doesn't align with the top of the ellipse. We need to increase the space between the lines of type. With the pointer tool, click on an open area of the canvas to "de-select" the type and the ellipse. Click on the type group to select it alone. Put the point tip exactly on the top, middle extent box. Click and hold, and wait for the pointer to change into a pointing finger. Now stretch the extents up until the tops of "Frammis" and the ellipse are aligned. See Figure 6.19.

Save the file as FRAMLOGO.GEM. You've created your first piece of infinitely reusable art. By the way, save it in the PICTURES subdirectory or anywhere other than the /GEMAPPS directory. Aside from cluttering up /GEMAPPS (which should be reserved for your GEM applications), you risk strange things happening by using files from /GEMAPPS with some programs. Ventura Publisher will always look for a file in /GEMAPPS first.

I once spent 15 minutes nearly convinced that I had indeed gone completely 'round the bend with this one. I modified the GEM Draw Plus file, loaded it into Ventura, and found the modification wasn't there. I exited Ventura, re-opened the file with GEM Draw Plus, and there was the modification again. I even checked where Ventura said the file was: Sure enough, it said it was getting the file from the PICTURES subdirectory. Finally, I discovered an old version of the file in /GEMAPPS, and that was the file Ventura stubbornly insisted on using.

Figure 6.19

SECOND ASSIGNMENT: THE ORGANIZATIONAL CHART

Have you ever noticed how organizations love charts? Charts provide the warm feeling that perhaps there is some order to all of the apparent chaos. They portray the system as it is supposed to work. Lovely.

If you want to impress people with what your GEM-equipped computer can do, crank out an organizational chart and give it to your personnel or human resource department. They will more than likely publish it across the organization—and certainly all of the managers will get one.

Organizational charts are really pretty simple in GEM Draw Plus. And if you've ever tried to do one using technical pens, a straight edge, and press-on type, you know what a disaster even an ordinary organzational chart can turn out to be.

Since the pages of this book don't lend themselves to extremely large illustrations, the example here is a fairly small organizational chart. We'll only show the top management at the world headquarters of Frammis International Limited.

Start with a clean canvas by using the New command under File, and set the page size to letter (8.5x11), landscape. This will size a canvas that is wider than it is tall. The trick to creating an organizational chart is to make everything look uniform while giving visual cues to each person's position in the corporate hierarchy.

There are two ways to do this:

1. The higher the plane on the chart, the loftier the person.
2. The type of box. You can use bolder lines, drop shadows, etc., to denote status.

Since the president and CEO is definitely the biggie, he or she gets the spiffiest box. The size of the box itself is determined by the size of the name and title. Because it is a grander box, it need not be larger than those below.

To make the type as clear and official-looking as possible, set as follows:

Type face: Swiss

Type font: Normal

Type size: 10 point

This will also fit a goodly amount of information on my rather small example page. When you do your own organizational chart, feel free to make it as large as your organization and patience will allow.

Defaults for the box are:

Line: Thin

Pattern: White

Color: 1 or whatever your black is

Ruler spacing: 1/32

After typing the president's name and title, select, center align, and group them. Now draw the box around the name, leaving a sufficient border along all sides. When you finish the box, note that it obscures the type. No problem, just use Put in back (Alignment) and the box will jump behind the type. Select the box and the type group, and align middle and center.

Now for the Hollywood part. With the box selected (type can be selected too; it won't matter), select a 1/32-inch line and the Shadow pattern. See Figure 6.20. It's a good idea not to select the Shadow pattern until you've aligned the text in the box. The alignment tools will use the right and bottom edges of the shadow in their alignment calculations, and the type won't be quite where you want it.

Try to select a standard box size for each management level. In the example, we had to use the larger box in one instance simply because there was too much type. The visual cue for the next level is a box with a drop shadow, but using the thinner line weight. Again, type is centered, grouped, and then middle and center aligned in each box. See Figure 6.21.

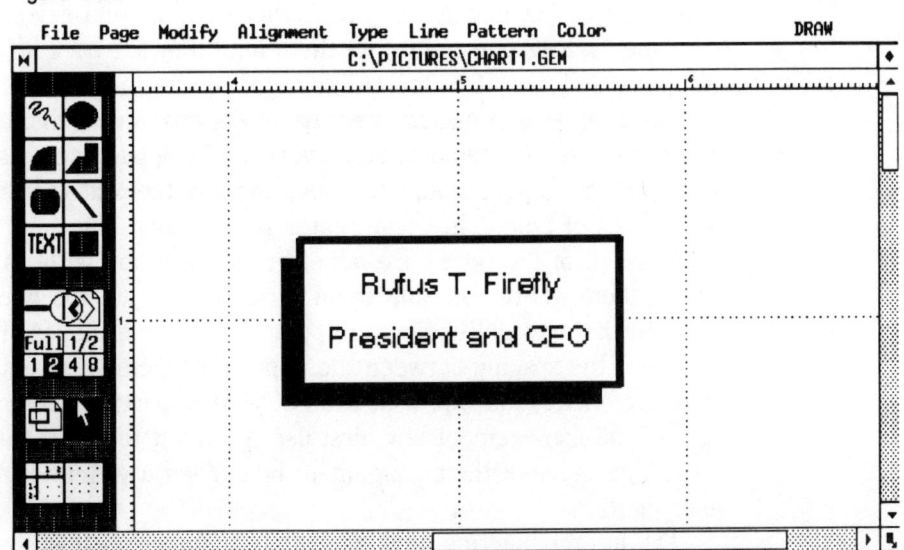

Figure 6.20

Figure 6.21

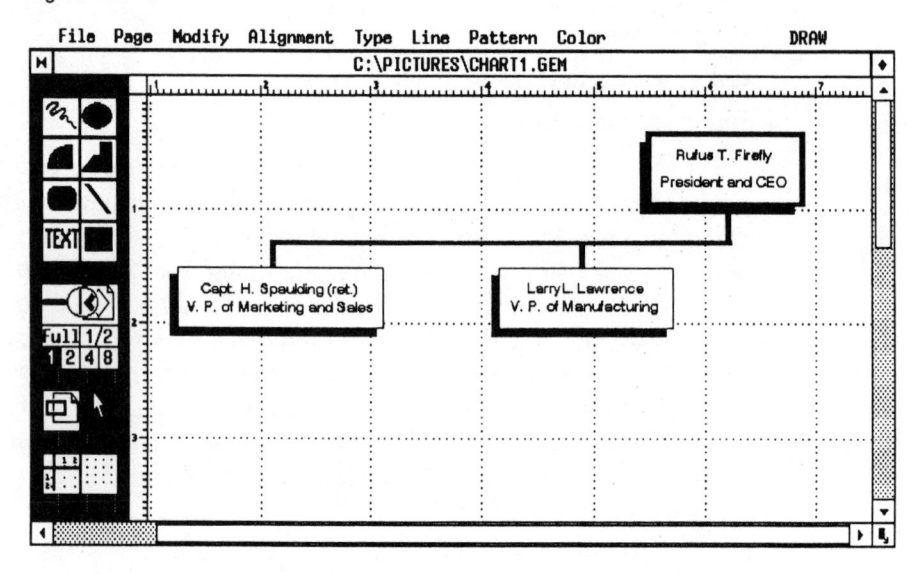

Even horizontal spacing is a little tricky. You can try doing it by eye, but I prefer to let the computer do the hard work. When you complete the second management level boxes, group them. Now use the Rotate tool (Modify) to flip them over. Suddenly you have four vertical boxes, which GEM Draw Plus can evenly space. Break the grouping and select Even spacing (Alignment). Regroup and rotate them until they are back in position. Break the group and use Align top (Alignment) to line them all up.

The final level of management has mere boxes with thin lines. All of the techniques used for the first two levels can be applied here as well. To save time, you can copy a completed box, and use the text tool to change each of the lines of type. Then just center realign them.

After all of the boxes are done, group each box with its type, roughly placing them where you want them. Now you can use the Even spacing tool to space them evenly under the upper management boxes. You don't want to disturb the spacing between the upper management boxes, so be careful what alignment tools you use. If all of your departmental boxes are to the right of the management box, first use Align left to pull them all to the left of the right edge of the management box. Then use Align right to set them flush right.

The interconnecting lines are set as follows:

Line weight: 1/32"

Pattern: None

Color: 1 or whatever your black is

Use the polygon tool wherever possible. You can use it to draw "L" shapes, creating the long interconnecting line and the line running over to the furthest box. Use the line tool to draw short lines, and then snap to the long interconnecting lines. When you draw each line, use Put in back (Alignment) to put any extra part of the line under the boxes.

Now for the logo. Since that's already done and stored in a file, we can just pull it in. Use Open (File) and the GEM file selector will appear. Find the FRAMLOGO.GEM file, and double click on it. You'll suddenly find that there are now two canvases on the screen, one overlaying the other. See Figure 6.22. You can drag the top canvas around the screen by putting the mouse pointer over the title bar, and then clicking and holding. This attaches the pointer to the top canvas, which now slides easily.

Working with two drawing screens takes a little thinking. If you click the mouse pointer anywhere over the bottom screen, it will snap to the top. It will also completely obscure the bottom canvas. However, the bottom canvas is still open. If you find yourself in this mess, grab the current top

Figure 6.22

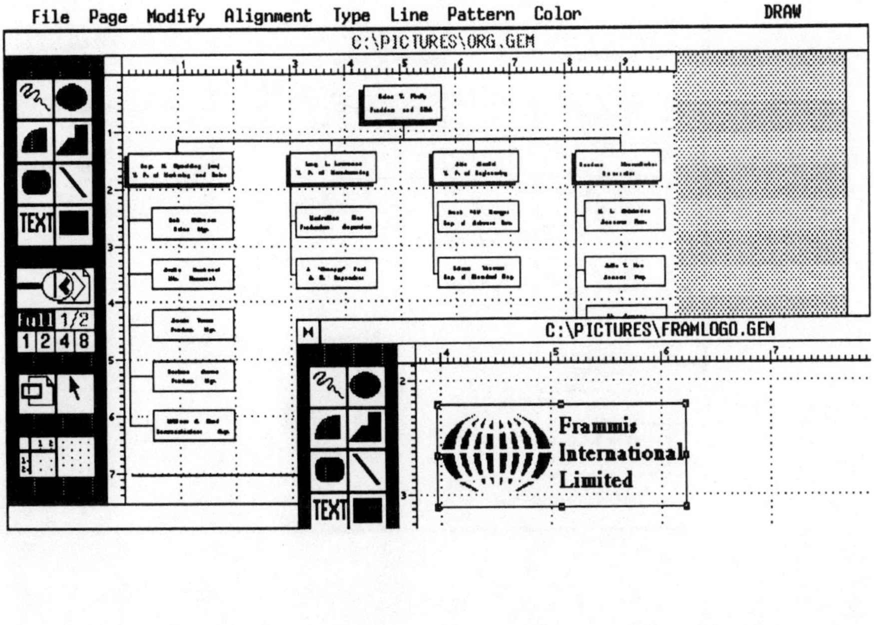

canvas by the title bar and slide it down a bit. When you can see part of the bottom screen, click on it. It will come back to the top.

Pulling things off the top screen sometimes requires a little maneuvering. If the element or elements you want are visible, just throw a selection box around them. If they aren't, you'll need to use the zoomer and the panner. Try clicking on Full first. If that doesn't work, select 1 or 2 on the zoomer and use the panner to put the objects into the left side of the panner rectangle.

Once you have your elements selected, simply click and drag them across to the other screen. When you release the mouse button, they'll drop into place. You can then click on the close box for the top canvas. If you have made any changes to the top drawing during the selection process, such as grouping elements, GEM Draw Plus will ask you if you want to save the changes. Usually you don't—especially if you are pulling in "clip-art" like a logo.

Just drag the logo into position. I also added a 1/32-inch line under the logo, and a 14 point title in the big open space toward the center of the drawing. And there you have it, a fine (almost classic) organizational chart. See Figure 6.23.

Figure 6.23

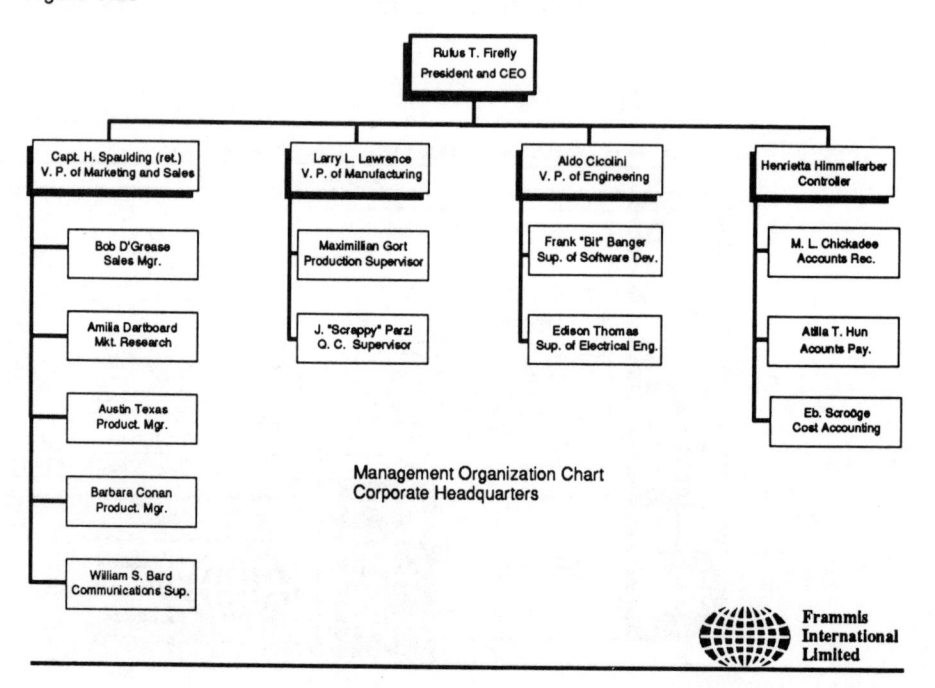

Let's quickly go over what we've covered:

- Color 0 shows as white through any background color.
- Lines and objects can be stretched, copied, rotated, and flipped.
- Type can be moved, rotated, flipped (sort of), and copied, but it can't be stretched.
- You can pull objects from other files.
- Don't save your graphics files to the /GEMAPPS directory.

CHAPTER 7

GEM Draw Plus Techniques

LEARNING VS. DABBLING	117
LAYERING EXAMPLE: THE BOX	117
DRAWING THE TRAFFIC LIGHT	122
CLIP-ART	126
LABELING THE ILLUSTRATION	130
A WORD ABOUT SIZE	132

LEARNING VS. DABBLING

This chapter covers the techniques that will really add speed to your drawing. A lot of people dabble at GEM Draw Plus just long enough to learn how to draw lines, circles, and boxes. Then they stop learning and go off to attack really complex drawing projects. This leads to two things:

1. Intense frustration, both for the artist and his or her boss. It becomes pretty obvious that the drawing could have been done in about half the time with pen and pencil.
2. Less than professional-looking output (and I'm being polite with this statement).

If you work for one of those organizations that can't possibly spare the time to train their people to use something, you've already committed a subversive act by buying this book. Why don't you go all the way and spend a few hours learning techniques? You might even need to do your learning on your own time (horrid thought, but sometimes it's your only option). Believe me, you'll save lots of crisis overtime hours later.

LAYERING EXAMPLE: THE BOX

GEM Draw Plus has extensive features for grouping and layering, and we went over the basics in the last chapter. This example shows exactly how to use these features with many layered elements. It entails drawing a pseudo three-dimensional box (an "orthographic projection" for you graphics types). After we complete the box, we'll hide the secret message, "Hi There!" inside it.

First, set the ruler increments to 1/4 inch, and make sure grid snap is on. This will really show off grid snap, and we don't need any more resolution than this. Pick a solid, visible pattern from the Pattern menu. Select a 1:1 magnification and get the box tool out of the tool box.

Place the mouse pointer at the intersection of two grid lines, click and hold, and draw a rectangle one inch by two inches. See Figure 7.1. Simple, right?

Now copy the rectangle (Alt-C), and drag the copy over 3/4 of an inch to the right and above the original. Go up to the Alignment menu and select Put in back. The copied rectangle will jump behind the original. See Figure 7.2. This is how layering works. Overlapping elements, such as these rectangles, can be bounced back and forth to the front and rear of the overlapping set.

Figure 7.1

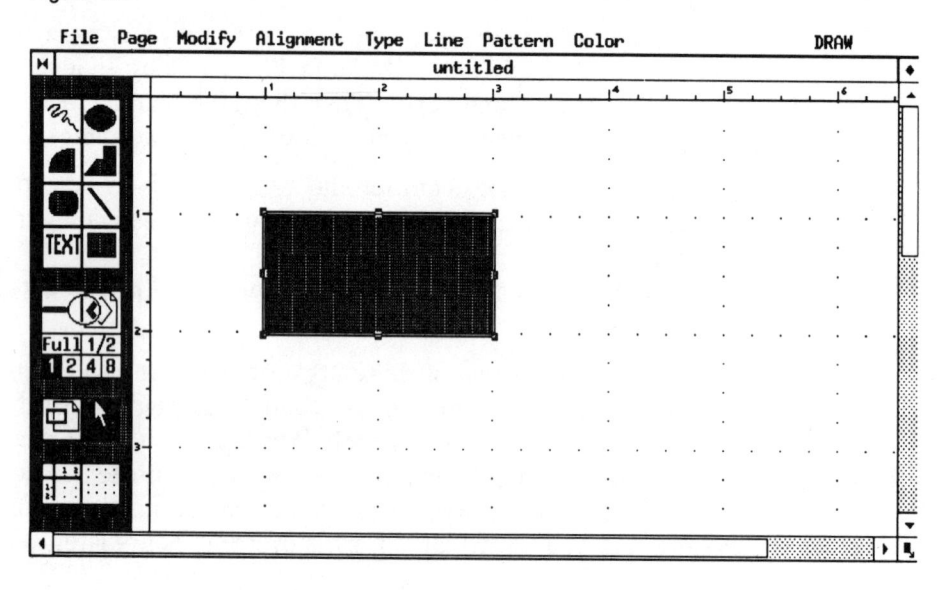

Figure 7.2

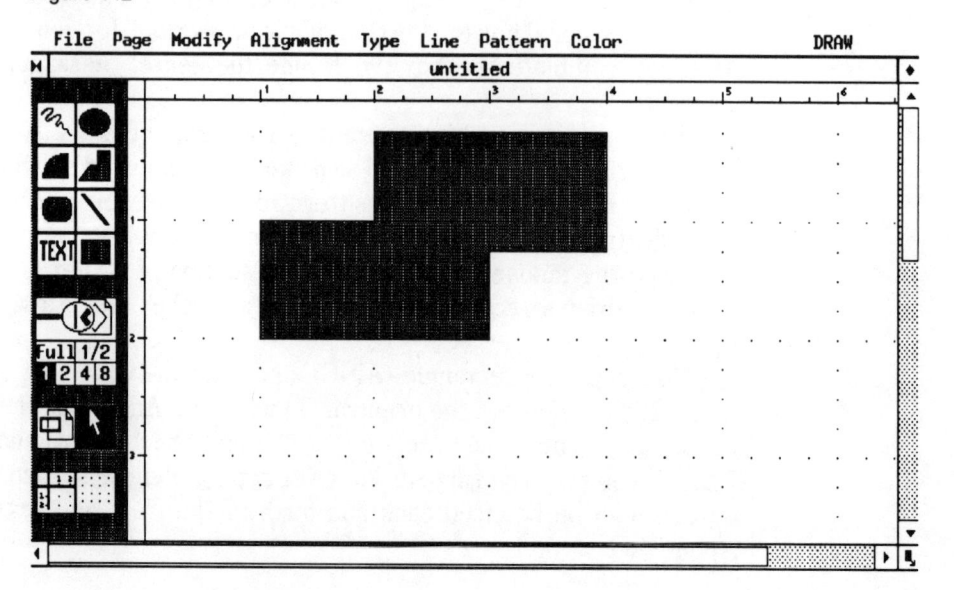

Our box needs sides, a top, and a bottom. If you were drawing this with a pencil and paper, you would probably connect the corners with straight lines. But this is a computer, and it has a lot more capabilities than a pencil (aside from the fact that it rarely rolls off your desk). We'll add real sides, top, and bottom instead of the mere suggestion.

Get the polygon tool and click over the top left corner of the rear rectangle. Put the pointer over the top left corner of the front rectangle, and continue this around the corners until you are at your starting point. Double click. You now have a genuine side. See Figure 7.3.

Copy the side and drag it over until it's in position at the right side of the rectangles. You'll need to use Alignment Put in back to pop it into its proper place. Draw the top the same way, copy it, and move the copy to the bottom. You'll end up with a box like the one shown in Figure 7.4.

So why use the polygon tool instead of lines? Polys are easier to manipulate. You saw how easy it was to duplicate and position them. They're easier to stretch and compress than a collection of lines. They also take up less element space in your drawing.

Now for the fun part. Select 14 point type (big enough to readily see), and type the message "Hi There!" somewhere on the canvas. Use the pointer to select and drag the message over in front of the box. To get it into the

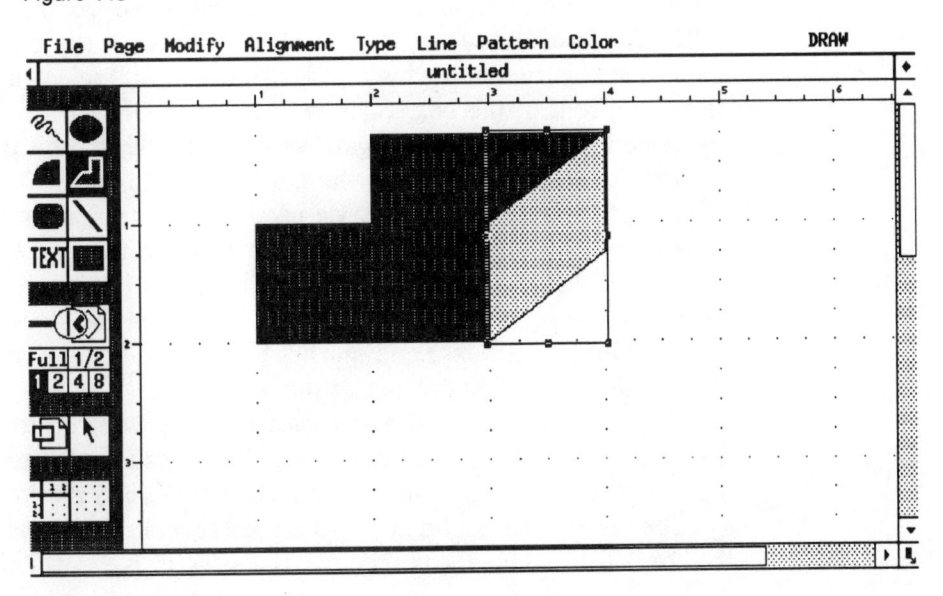

Figure 7.3

Figure 7.4

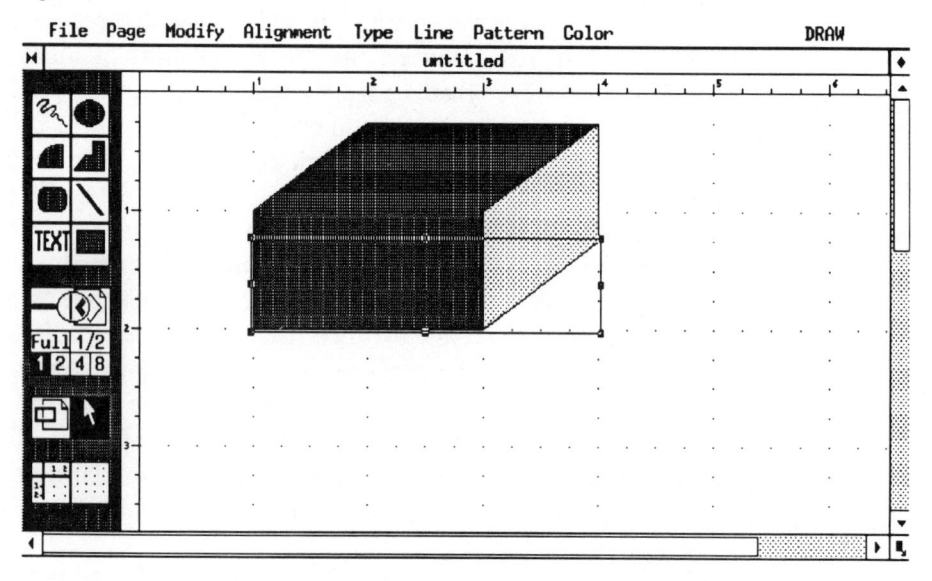

box, we'll use one of the special pointer techniques in GEM Draw Plus: selecting through elements.

We want to select the front of the box, which is behind the type. To reach it, place the pointer over the text. Hold the Control key down and click. Instead of the type, the next element beneath the type is selected—in this case the front of the box. Click again and you'll select another element below the front of the box. Click yet again and GEM Draw Plus will start the selection sequence over again with the top layer: the type. Click one last time to select the front of the box.

To put the type in the box, we need to shift its relative position in the stack of overlapping objects. We want it to be in front of the back of the box, but behind the front of the box. This turns out to be easy. Just use Put in front to pop the front of the box to the top of the stack. The message is now safely in the box. See Figure 7.5. If you want to prove it, select the front of the box and pull it out of the way.

Now put the front of the box back because we need to make the box medium gray. The easiest way to do this—because all the elements are lumped in one area—is to drag a selector box around the lot of them.

Get the pointer tool and put the pointer well above and to the left of the box. Click and hold, and then pull the selector box down and to the right

Figure 7.5

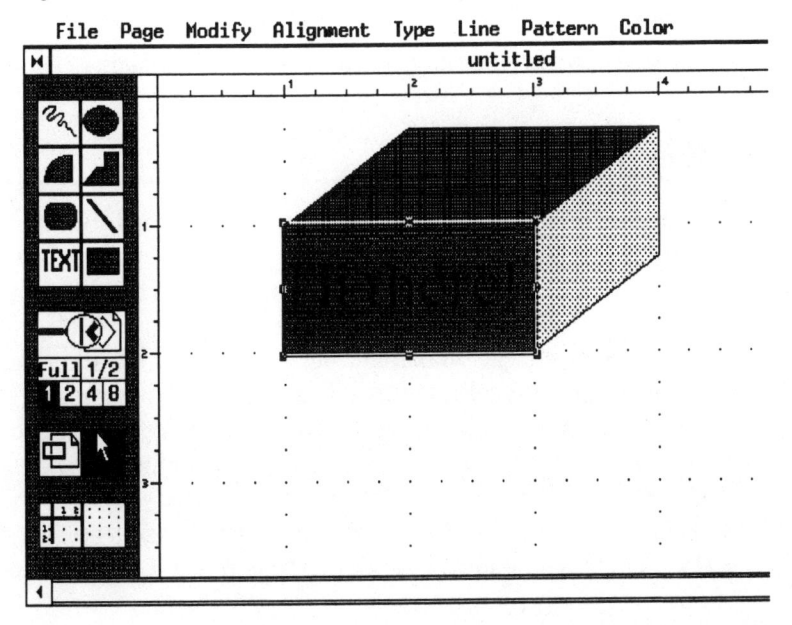

until it's over the rectangle. Release. All of the elements in the box should select, and their extents should appear. Select medium gray from the pattern menu, and they will all fill with this pattern.

That was easy too, right? But what if we want to make the top and the front dark gray? You can't use the selector box because you'll have trouble just getting the elements you want. You could select and change them individually, but that's tedious. Fortunately, Draw Plus lets you select multiple elements with a shift click.

Hold down the shift key and click over the front of the back. Now click over the top. As long as you hold the shift key, each newly selected element will be added to the set. Click on the dark gray pattern and both will change.

SO WHAT HAVE WE COVERED?

- Use polygons instead of collections of straight lines.
- Use snap to place parts with precision.
- To select a single element, get the pointer and click over the element.
- To select several elements in a confined area, enclose them with a selector box.

- To select a single element within a layered set of elements, use control click.
- To select several elements within a set of elements, use shift click.

DRAWING THE TRAFFIC LIGHT

The traffic light figure doesn't appear to be too hard. But look at the version in Figure 7.6 with all of the element extents showing. It's a lot busier than it first appears. To draw this fairly simply object you really need to think about what you're doing. Which leads me to more words of wisdom.

To really get the maximum out of GEM Draw Plus (and most of the other packages as well), you need to plan just how you are going to draw a piece. GEM Draw Plus is a very capable drawing package, but it does have its limitations. You can drive yourself nuts running up against them, or you can overcome them with a little creativity. Once you learn the trick of using a technique and a little thought, you'll be amazed at the power of GEM Draw Plus. For instance, look at the base of the traffic light. At first glance,

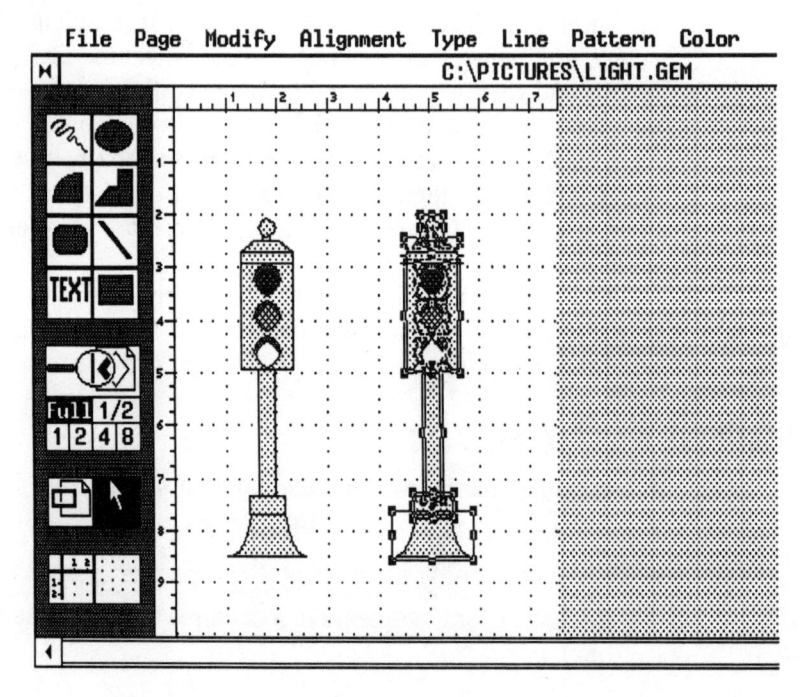

Figure 7.6

it seems impossible to draw that shape and fill it with a pattern. The sides of the base are arcs, and arcs fill in the opposite direction from the way the base is filled.

Another reason to think about what you are doing is to reduce the number of steps. The three signal lights are actually clones of one signal light. Some of the components of the lights are copies of other components. If you plan your drawing, you can save a lot of effort by capitalizing on pieces you've already drawn.

DRAWING THE TOP

The top is the easiest part to draw, but we'll make it even easier. Select the lightest gray as the default pattern (click on the lightest gray with the pointer as your current tool). Now, set the grid to something coarse, like 1/4 inch. Draw a circle by click and holding on a grid point and pulling the circle into shape. Release when you have a 1/4-inch circle (i.e., one grid point in each direction).

By the way, if you are using a Hercules-compatible monochrome display, as I do, your circle will look like an ellipse. The Hercules monochrome standard has much higher resolution across the screen than vertically. The result is a rather warped aspect ratio on the screen. Instead of your grid points describing squares, they will seem to describe rectangles. When you print the drawing, however, the distortion will disappear. The only way to overcome this warping is to draw circles and squares with the help of grid snap (or at least by lining things up by eye with grid points). To put it simply, with a Hercules-type display if it looks like a circle or a square on the screen, it isn't.

Back to the picture at hand. After you've drawn the circle, switch the grid to 1/8 inch and draw a rectangle about 1/8 inch wide by 1/4 inch long. Next, select the polygon and draw the six-sided top piece for the traffic light. The top, flat section is 1/2 inch wide; the bottom is an inch wide. The whole top piece is 1/2 inch high.

Now that we have the pieces, you could individually select them and move them into position. Or, you could save yourself some trouble and let the computer do it for you. Set the grid to its finest setting, and move the pieces roughly into position. Group them all with a selector box, and use the Align middle tool to shift them into position. De-select the elements (click on an open area of the canvas), and then reselect any elements you need to send to the back layer with Send to back.

The line running horizontally across the top piece can either be drawn as a line, or you can draw a rectangle that fits in that area. See Figure 7.7. I used a rectangle because it gives me the opportunity to make it a different pattern than the rest of the top (even though I left it the same).

The three signals are a little trickier. The circle is merely a 1/2-inch circle, but the sunshade is a bit more complicated. It's drawn like this:

1. Draw an arc from the left side of the circle to somewhere slightly above the top of the circle. Set your grid to its finest increments. It's okay if the arc doesn't quite touch the side of the circle.
2. Select the arc and pull it away from the circle. Give it a plain white pattern. Copy the arc (Alt-C), and then flip the copy horizontally (under Modify). Put the two arcs together and top align them (Alignment).
3. Group the pair of arcs and copy them. Make the copy have a medium gray pattern and a "none" line.
4. Select the gray and white arc pairs. Align them middle and center. You should now have a gray semi-ellipse with a visible line (provided by the white arc pair at the bottom layer). Group them together. See Figure 7.8.
5. Move the circle over and above the sunshade. Align center. You can now select the circle and give it any pattern you like. Copy the whole set twice for the other lights. Group the elements in each together.
6. Move the completed lights into roughly the right distances apart. Group them all and select even spacing. Align center and group all three together.

Figure 7.7

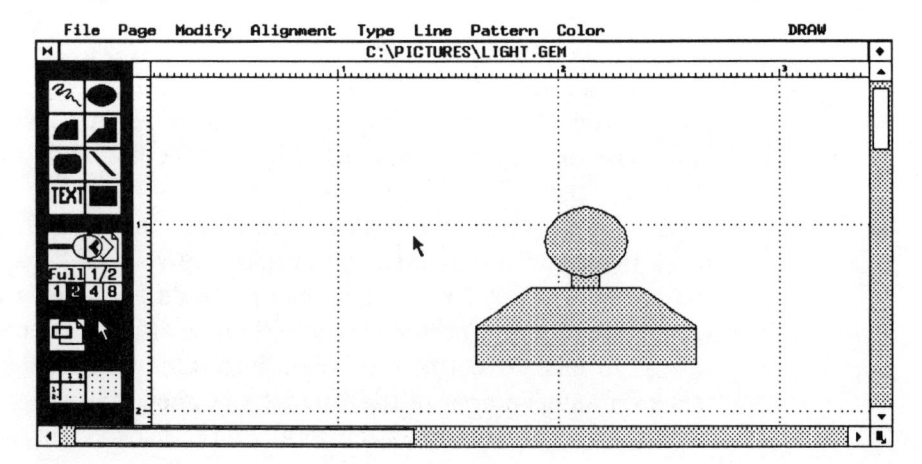

Figure 7.8

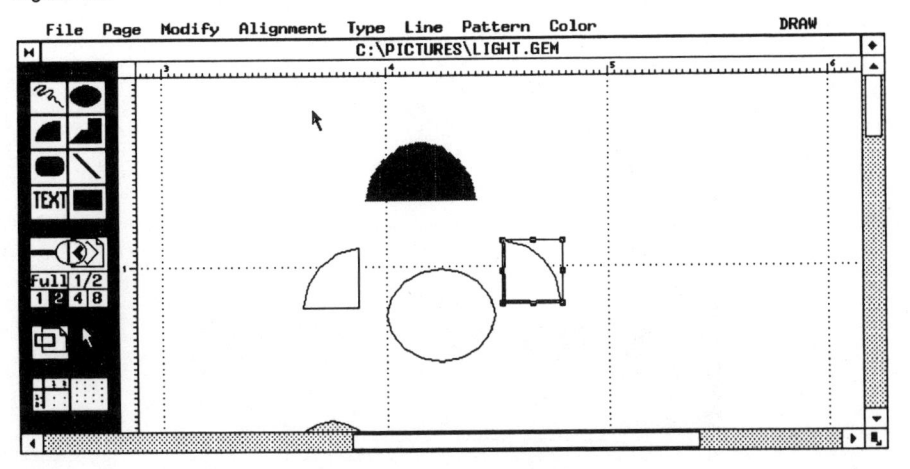

7. Draw a rectangle, the main body of the traffic light, over the lights and fill it with light gray. Send it behind the lights with Put in back. Group the lights and the rectangle together.
8. Move the main body of the light under the top piece until the two touch or slightly overlap.
9. Make sure all of the elements in the top piece are grouped. Now align the top piece and main body with Align center.

See how this works? You draw a part, group it, and copy it if need be. Then you align it with other parts, group, and keep building up the drawing.

DRAWING THE BOTTOM

The bottom part is really pretty simple too. Its top is just a light gray rectangle. Each side is a pair of duplicate arcs, aligned middle and center to superimpose exactly. One arc of the pair has a thin line and a "none" pattern. The other arc has no line but a white pattern. When I finished one side, I grouped them, copied the combined element, and then flipped it horizontally.

The bottom of the base is just a line, making the base hollow (no pattern). See Figure 7.9. The light gray pattern is supplied by a light gray rectangle, moved to the back layer. It doesn't appear beyond the arcs because their white fill pattern obscures the rectangle.

Figure 7.9

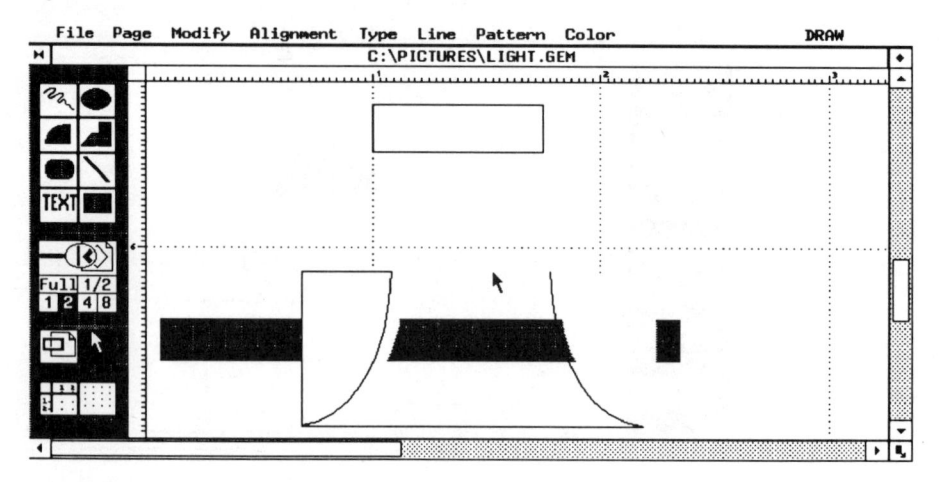

REVIEW

Okay, now you know how to:

- Use GEM Draw Plus's alignment features, whenever possible, to line things up.
- Use elements with no line but an opaque, white pattern to obscure parts of other elements. Sort of a reverse-logic erasure.
- Combine elements made of arcs that have lines but no pattern with copies that have patterns but not lines. This slightly roundabout method lets you combine arc shapes without the border lines for the fill patterns showing.

CLIP-ART

GEM Draw Plus comes with a library of graphics (not protected by copyright!) that you can use in any publication. A wonderful feature that offers a remarkably wide variety of graphics *that you don't have to draw*, this library can save you enormous amounts of time.

It's a good feature to imitate too. You can build your own library of drawings consisting of your own contributions and those of other GEM artists as well. This really begins to tap the power of GEM Draw Plus because once a thing is drawn it never needs to be drawn again.

If you have more technical needs, you can purchase the GEM Business Graphics Library. This contains all sorts of symbols:

- Electrical schematic symbols
- Flow charting symbols (computer programming)
- Control diagram symbols
- Organizational chart symbols

The Business Graphics Library also has a collection of borders, most of which can be modified for use with GEM WordChart. A README.DOC file tells you which ones can't be used with WordChart; these files (as of Library version 1.1) are: L210.GEM, P180W.GEM, P190W.GEM, P200.GEM, P210.GEM, P220.GEM, P230.GEM, and P240.GEM. I recommend getting the library, especially if you do much work with electrical schematics. With these symbols, you can whip together schematics in a lot less time than it takes by hand.

For the example drawing, we'll borrow some predrawn computer shapes for a simple technical illustration. We'll also show you how to draw call-outs, and we'll talk about the formal parts of an illustration (yes, there are conventions to this sort of thing).

PULLING IT TOGETHER

To create the clip-art technical illustration, we'll need a clean canvas (UNTITLED.GEM). If you already have a drawing on the canvas, click on New (File). One of GEM Draw Plus's idiosyncrasies is that you can't open a second file from UNTITLED.GEM. The easiest way around this is simply to draw a line, and then save the file as some new file name. *Don't* delete that line until you have brought over some clip-art; otherwise, GEM Draw Plus will discard the blank canvas when you open the clip-art file.

Use Open . . . (File) and go to the LIBRARY subdirectory. Find the BUSINESS subdirectory there and open it. Double click on the file named COMPUTER.GEM. If you can't find these subdirectories or the file, make sure you installed the GEM Draw Plus libraries from the Library disk.

Select the front view of the IBM PC (see Figure 7.10), the front view of the Olivetti/Xerox/AT&T computer, and the printer. Pull all three across to your almost blank canvas. Close the COMPUTER.GEM drawing after you have the clip-art across.

All we want from the Olivetti-type computer is the keyboard. Select the Olivetti and use Break group (Alignment) to break it down into component

Figure 7.10

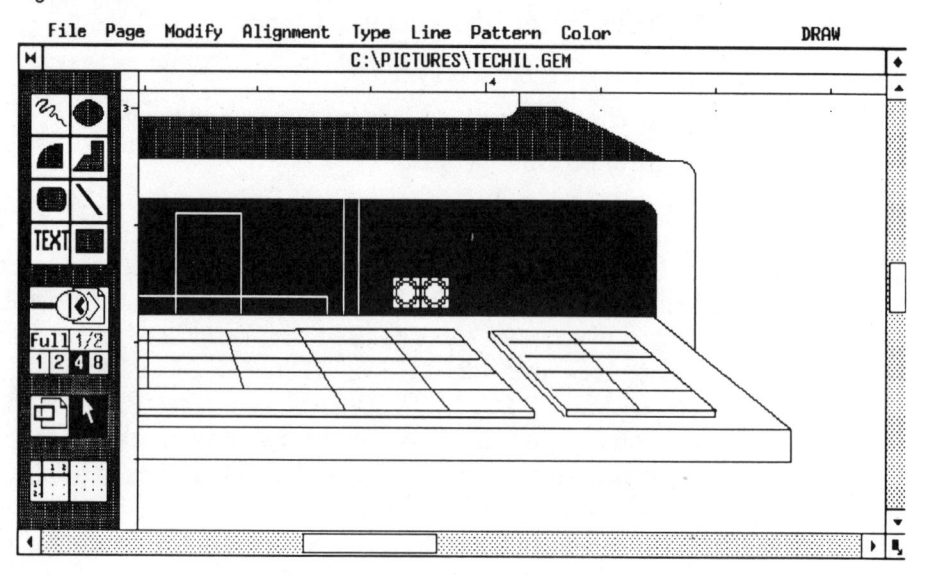

elements. Click on each of the nonkeyboard parts and Delete them (Modify). When you have a naked keyboard, group it and drag it in front of the PC. You might want to stretch the keyboard horizontally a bit to make it more of a match for the PC.

Select the PC and break it into its parts. We want to have a hard disk drive, not a floppy, on the right drive area. Use the control click technique to isolate the disk drive door lines, and then delete them.

Since hard drives usually have indicator lights, double click on the zoomer at 8:1 magnification, and put the panner rectangle over the right disk drive. Draw a couple of white rectangles, about 1/32 inch wide (set ruler increments to 1/32). The rectangles should be side by side. There we are: instant hard disk drive.

Get the panner again and go over to the white space just to the right of the PC. We need to draw a mouse. Nothing fancy about this mouse because it will be so small in the final illustration. Draw a polygon at roughly the same angles as the keyboard outline. Make the back about 1/16 inch wide, and the front 1/4 inch wide. Since you can't draw the buttons with grid snap on, turn Auto grid Off (Page). Draw the buttons as polys about half the length of the outer polygon, and then follow the side of the other polygon for the angle. The side toward the middle of the polygon is a straight line.

After you've drawn it, copy and Flip horizontal (Modify) for the other button. Get them aligned and group them with the larger polygon. The result is, at least, the suggestion of a mouse. See Figure 7.11.

Now use the zoomer and jump back to full view. Select the printer and drag it up to the right of the mouse. Note that our illustration is a bit too wide to fit in a standard book. The solution is simple: shrink it. But you must shrink your illustrations carefully, or more precisely, proportionally.

Use Select all (Modify) and select everything on the canvas. Group everything together. Now click on the lower right-hand extent box, and push to the left until the right-hand side is now at 3/4 of the size of the old group (GEM Draw Plus will leave the extent lines where they were as a reference for you). Push up until the vertical size is about 3/4 of the original. You can use the extent lines as a rough scaling measure whenever you shrink something. See Figure 7.12.

And there we have it: an almost no work illustration of a basic desktop publishing system, suitable for putting in a book about GEM. Except that it needs a little explanation. It isn't apparent from a drawing of the hardware exactly what kind of hardware it is. But that's okay because the drawing merely presents a concept; the supporting text adds definition to the concept.

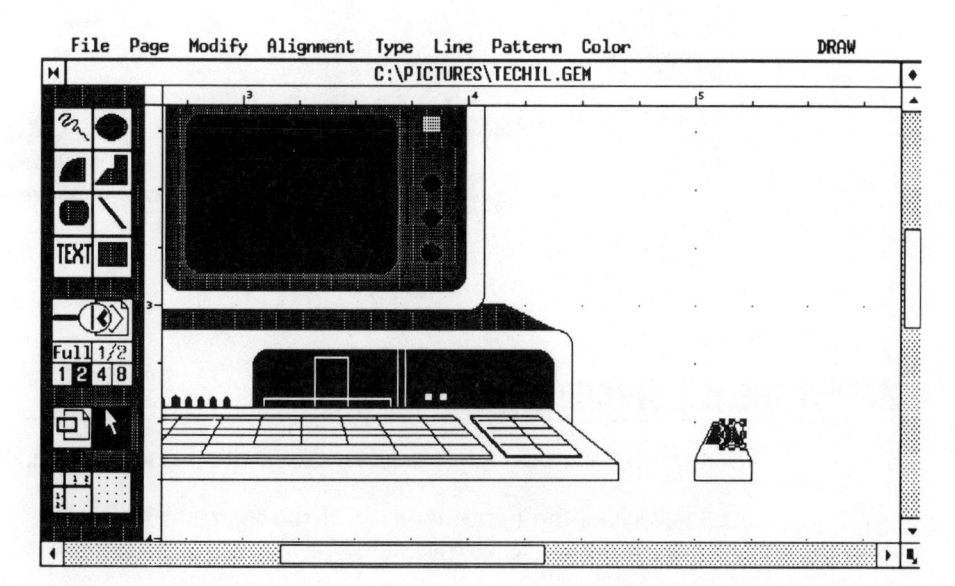

Figure 7.11

Figure 7.12

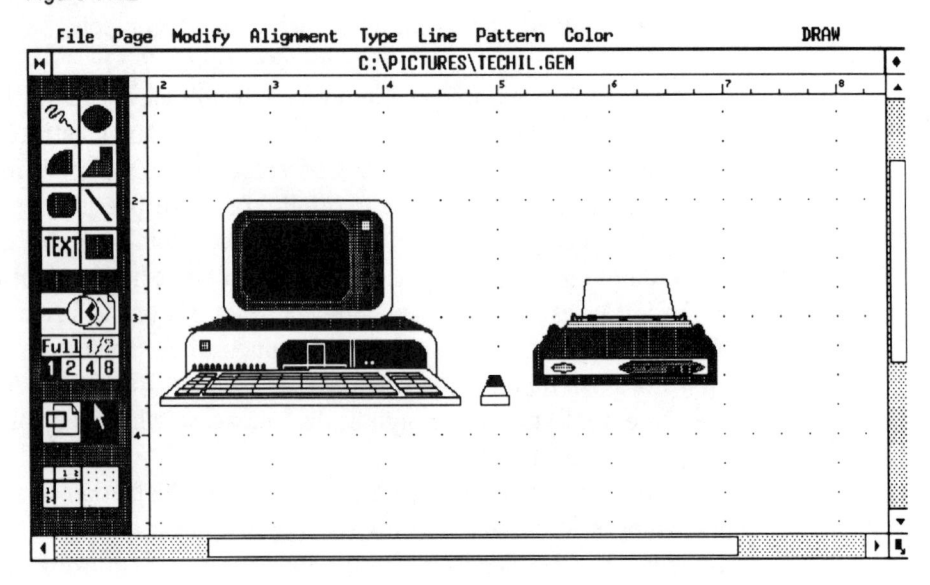

Figure 7.13

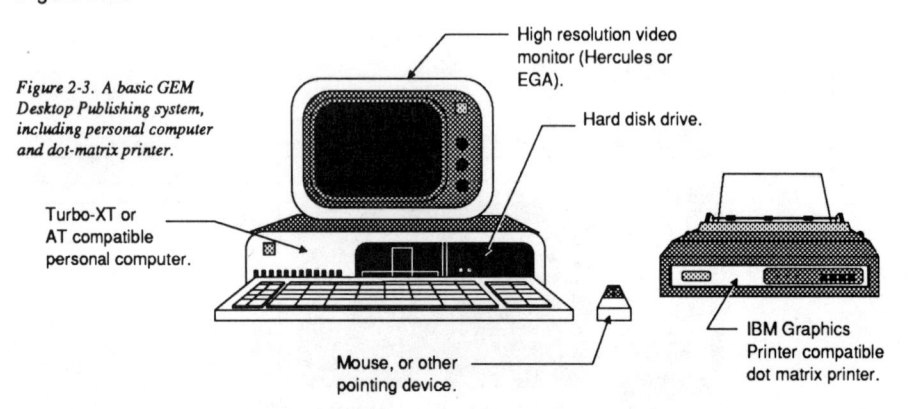

Figure 2-3. A basic GEM Desktop Publishing system, including personal computer and dot-matrix printer.

Turbo-XT or AT compatible personal computer.

High resolution video monitor (Hercules or EGA).

Hard disk drive.

Mouse, or other pointing device.

IBM Graphics Printer compatible dot matrix printer.

LABELING THE ILLUSTRATION

Figure 7.13 shows a caption off to the left that does two important things:

1. It provides the figure number (if the figure has one).
2. It explains just what the figure is.

The caption need not be hung out to the left; it could be below, above, or even to the right.

The call-outs and arrows point to the various important parts of the system that the reader should know about. For instance, it isn't just a computer; it's a Turbo-XT or AT-compatible computer. The call-out also defines our crude mouse drawing.

Call-outs are great devices because they stand alone to explain the parts of the illustration. Unfortunately, they also spread out all over the place, making the illustration larger. If you have big pages, fine. If you don't, or your figures fall within a column in a multiple-column format, you don't have all that width to play with.

Enter the second version, as illustrated in Figure 7.14. The title along the top is really the *caption* in the strictest sense of the word. The explanatory text below is the *legend*. We've reduced the space that the call-outs occupy by replacing the text with symbols. In this case, the symbols are merely black circles with white (color 0) text. The legend explains what the symbols mean.

Note that both drawings have arrows or pointing lines with white shadows. These let the reader's eye follow the line over a dark background. This

Figure 7.14

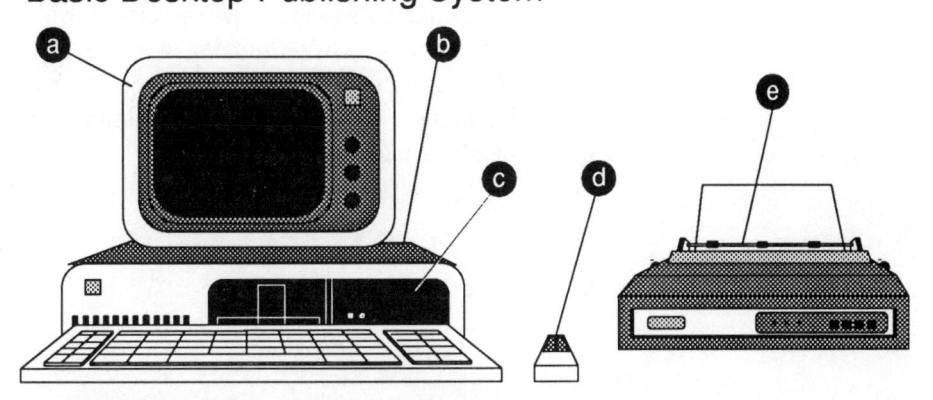

Basic Desktop Publishing System

The above illustration shows a complete desktop publishing workstation, including: (a) high resolution monitor, (b) PS/2, XT or AT compatible computer, (c) hard disk drive, (d) mouse or pointing device and (e) IBM Graphics Printer compatible dot matrix printer.

is easy to do: Just copy the line or arrow, zoom in with the zoomer, and take grid snap off. Move the copied line just under and behind the original. While the copy is selected, click on color 0. Use control click to grab the original line and move it to the foreground.

Arrowheads are done for you by bringing up the End styles menu. The left-hand arrowhead means that the arrow will appear at the starting point for the line. The right-hand arrow sets an arrowhead at the end point.

A WORD ABOUT SIZE

GEM 1st Word Plus can't size pictures; it can only import them. If you are using your drawings with GEM 1st Word Plus, therefore, make sure that the call-outs, captions, etc., all fit within the GEM 1st Word Plus margins. GEM Desktop Publisher can size and scale drawings. This is a tremendous capability, but be careful if you have text in your drawings. By reducing the graphic to fit the page, you may reduce the type beyond readability. Besides, it's unprofessional to have wildly varying type sizes in your illustrations—even if the differences are caused by scaling factors.

The rule of thumb is: If you have text in your illustrations, make the final size of those drawings as close as possible to the size you want them in the publication. This even applies if you're using Ventura Publisher. On the other hand, if you are using Ventura, you can leave the call-outs off the drawing and add them in the publishing program.

I think you're beginning to see just how powerful GEM Draw Plus really is. More importantly, I hope you're getting a sense of how much more powerful it can be if you are creative. As long as you think out your drawings before grabbing the mouse, you can overcome almost all of the apparent limitations in the drawing package.

CHAPTER 8

A New Dimension

TOOLING UP FOR 3-D	134
ISOMETRIC PROJECTIONS	134
SINGLE VANISHING POINT PERSPECTIVE	136
DUAL VANISHING POINT PERSPECTIVE	141
FINAL REVIEW	142

TOOLING UP FOR 3-D

GEM Draw Plus is an excellent two-dimensional drawing tool. So is a drafting board. In fact, the two are really almost identical in the kinds of tools you can use. There are straight line tools as well as tools for drawing boxes, circles, arcs, etc. It's really not too hard to see where the ideas for the drawing tools in GEM Draw Plus came from.

Any trained artist can use the same tools to draw three-dimensional and almost three-dimensional objects. So it stands to reason that the equivalent situation would be true with GEM Draw Plus. And it is true—almost. GEM Draw Plus falls short on complex arcs and curves. Every arc you make with GEM Draw Plus must describe 90 degrees. But, given that limitation, you can still draw remarkably good three-dimensional renderings with GEM Draw Plus.

Actually, we need to get our definitions straight when talking about three-dimensional art. It turns out that there are all sorts of ways to draw in 3-D. We'll talk about three of the most popular:

1. Isometric projection, which is three dimensional except that it doesn't take perspective into account at all.
2. Single vanishing point, which considers perspective but only in one direction.
3. Dual vanishing point, which provides the most realistic and also the most time-consuming drawings of the three.

ISOMETRIC PROJECTIONS

The three-dimensional box we did in the last chapter was an isometric projection. All sides were exactly to scale. The back of the box was drawn just as high as the front.

The box in the Figure 8.1 shows what's wrong with isometric projections. Notice how the back of the box looks too fat. This is a trick that your brain plays on you (you can't trust anyone). Your brain knows that since the back of the box is farther away than the front, it should be a little smaller all around. Only it isn't, so your brain figures it must actually be larger than the front. Only it isn't, so . . .

This interesting effect doesn't mean that isometric projections aren't useful. Actually most technical illustrations (and a lot of architectural drawings) are done this way. One way to make up for the lack of perspective is to change the view point. Figure 8.1 uses a dead-on isometric view. You can

Figure 8.1

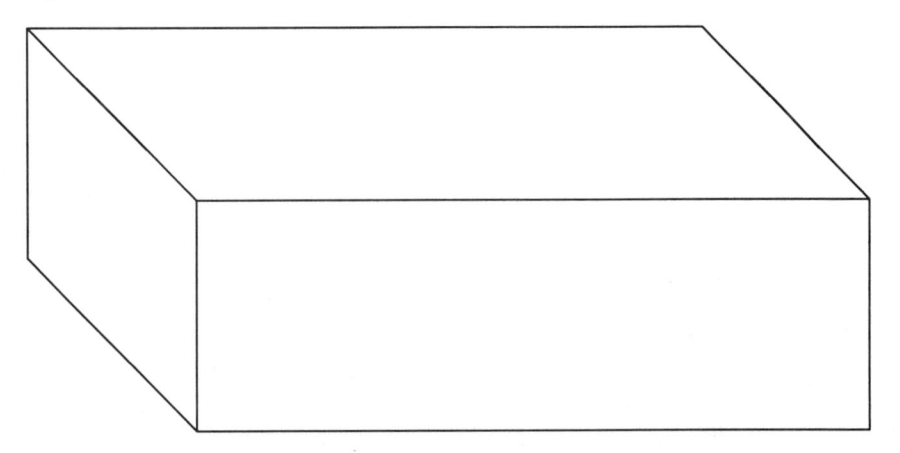

Figure 8.2

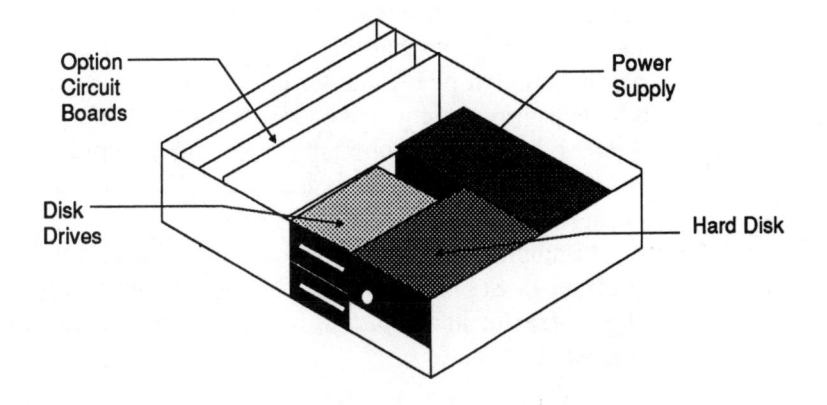

fool your brain a bit by moving the view point and setting all of the horizontal lines at an angle. Figure 8.2 is done this way. All of the vertical lines are truly vertical, but all of the horizontal lines are drawn at 30-degree angles. This minimizes the apparent distortion.

The problem with doing such a projection is that you don't have a protractor or triangle in GEM Draw Plus. But you can make them both.

MAKING A 30-DEGREE TRIANGLE AND A PROTRACTOR

Set the grid to 1/4-inch increments. Start a polygon at a point somewhere near the center of the canvas. Draw a line straight up for one inch, and then pull it to the right for 1¾ inches. Click and you have a 30-degree line. Now go due left until you are at a point one inch above and 1¾ inches to the right of the starting point. Click. Now draw a line back to the starting point.

The way you've drawn it, the triangle has two 30-degree sides. Rotate it and you'll get 60-degree sides. If the lines aren't exactly where you want them, use Flip horizontal or vertical.

Figure 8.2, illustrating the Frammis International Limited M.E.-II personal computer, was drawn as an isometric projection. All the horizontal lines were drawn against the 30-degree triangle. I also copied and vertically flipped the triangle, making it easy to draw polygons. You just move the two triangles together, and they provide background lines for the front and side polygons for all of the boxes. This is a nice projection for technical illustrations because it makes showing the interior of a widget very easy.

If you want to make a protractor with degree lines every 15 degrees, the easiest way is to start with the triangle you've already drawn. Copying and rotating the triangle gives you a 60-degree line. Align the 30- and 60-degree triangles so that they have a common origin point. Draw a line starting at the common point, and go up 3/4 of an inch and to the right 2¾ inches; 1/4-inch grid setting makes this easier. That's your 15-degree line. Start another line at the common point, and go up 2¾ inches and to the right 3/4 inch. That's the 75-degree line. The 45-degree line is just corner to corner within any of the inch grids.

Combine the lines, add a vertical and horizontal line, and you have your protractor. See Figure 8.3. It's a good idea to group these lines and tuck the protractor in a separate file. Then you can get the protractor whenever you want it.

SINGLE VANISHING POINT PERSPECTIVE

Figure 8.4 shows an even better way to convince your brain that the box really does have depth. The drawing to the right is another isometric projection. The drawing to the left is a box drawn in single vanishing point perspective.

Instead of lines drawn parallel at precise angles, the lines in the right-hand drawing run to a single point above and to the right of the drawing (although the point could just as easily have been below and to the left).

Figure 8.3

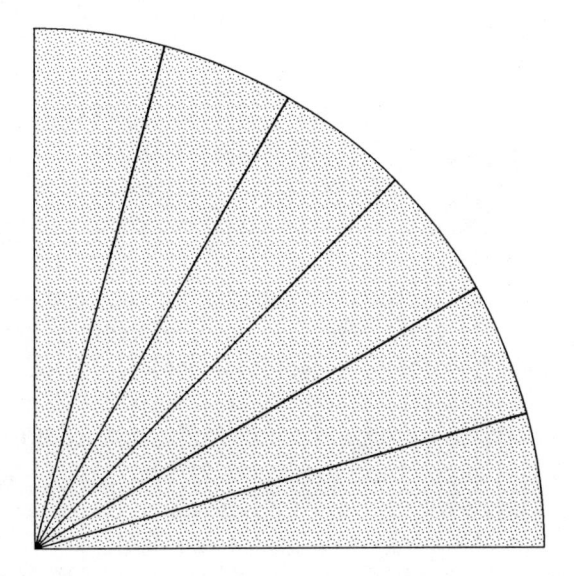

Figure 8.4

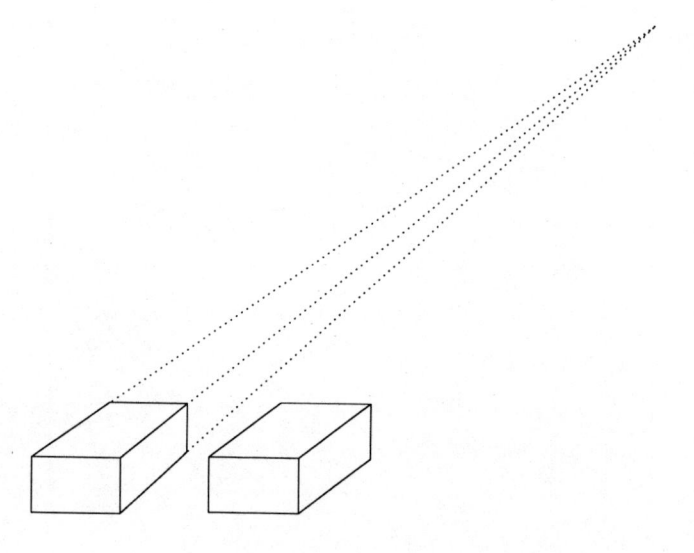

Such a point is called a *vanishing point*. Because the lines converge with distance, this provides the illusion of true perspective.

So far, everything we've done has worked well with grid snap, even at fairly coarse settings. Perspective views don't work quite that way, however, because they add an extra dimension to the grid. Now you not only have to worry about height and width, but depth as well. To make your task easier to manage, it's a good idea to draw your own additional grid lines.

Figure 8.5 shows a single vanishing point perspective grid. I just started at a point near the center of the canvas and drew radiating lines, each one intersecting at some even increment on the GEM Draw Plus grid.

The grid should also mark off depth in gradually decreasing increments (which provide the depth illusion). To do this, extend the horizontal line to the left until it's somewhere near the left edge of the canvas. Its left edge marks the *diagonal point*. Run a line from the diagonal point to the lower right edge of the gridwork. At every point where this diagonal line crosses a gridwork line, draw a horizontal line. These are your depth lines (the Z axis of your X, Y, Z grid if you like).

Group all of the lines. Then change them into dotted or dashed lines to make it easy to draw over the grid. When you've finished your drawing, you can either delete the grid or make it color 0 and send it to the back of the drawing.

Figure 8.6 was done against the grid. Notice how the doors, ceiling lights, and carpet all have lines that converge to the single vanishing point.

You can also use the vanishing point lines to generate shadows. The rectangle in Figure 8.7 illustrates this. The shadow is cast along the van-

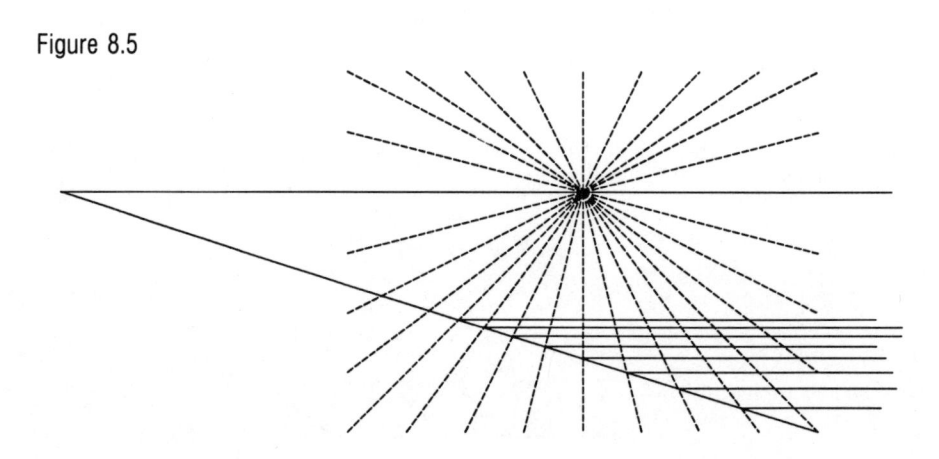

Figure 8.5

Figure 8.6

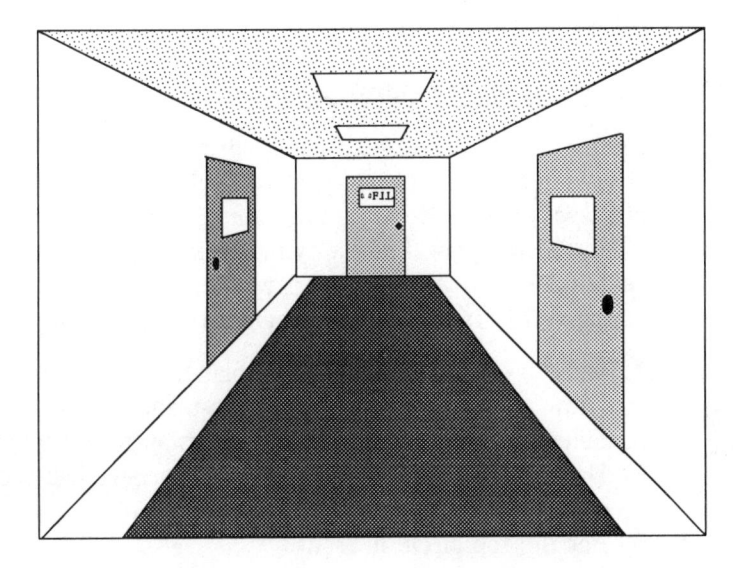

Figure 8.7

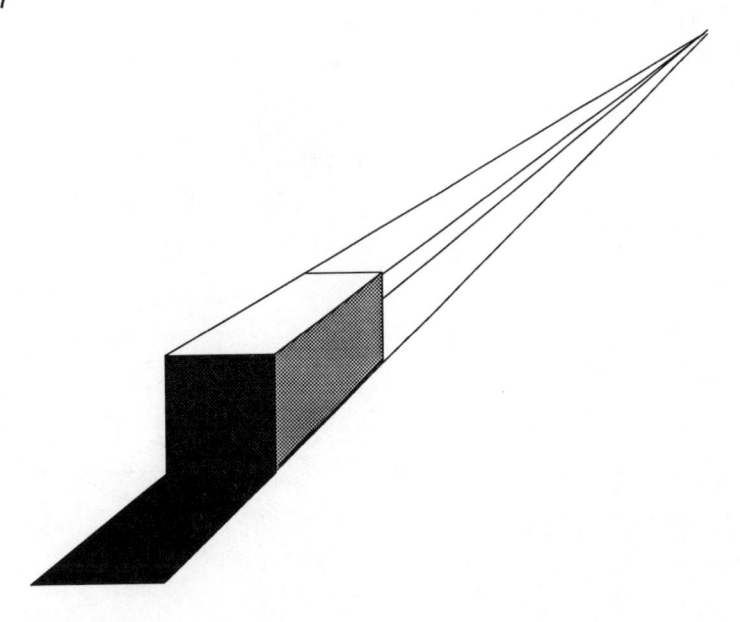

ishing point projection lines, with its length determined by the elevation of the light source.

DRAWING A CYLINDER IN SINGLE POINT PERSPECTIVE

Figure 8.8 shows a very handy grid for drawing circular and cylindrical shapes in single point perspective. Notice how each of the planes in the grid is drawn against the vanishing point lines.

In GEM Draw Plus, a cylinder is simply a combination of circles and rectangles. You need to overlay a few things to get a good cylinder. For instance, to draw a cylinder against this grid, you should:

1. Draw a circle against the top plane.
2. Draw a circle against the bottom plane.
3. Select both circles and pull them away from the grid.
4. Draw a rectangle, making sure its corners just touch the outside edges of the circles.
5. Put the top circle in front.
6. Copy the bottom circle. Make the copy have no lines.
7. Center and top align the circle copy with the bottom circle.

Figure 8.8

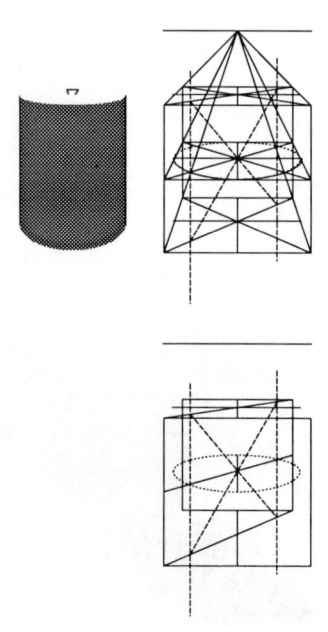

Now you have a cylinder. As long as the rectangle and the bottom circle copy have the same pattern, they will appear as one solid piece of the cylinder.

DUAL VANISHING POINT PERSPECTIVE

Not every drawing lends itself to single vanishing point perspective. For such cases, you can use dual vanishing point perspective. Like single point perspective, this is a lot simpler if you take the time to draw a grid (and remember, you only need to draw it once).

This time, you simply need a horizontal line running almost the width of the canvas and a vertical line somewhere toward the center. The ends of the horizontal line become the vanishing points.

To add the grid lines, run a series of lines from each vanishing point to even increments along the vertical line. To make it simple, I set the grid to 1/2 inch and just ran the lines up at each 1/2-inch snap point. When you're done, group the whole thing. You should make the lines dashed, dotted, etc., to make them easier to draw against.

Now when you draw, always make your lines parallel to the grid lines. Figure 8.9 shows a simple architectural shape drawn against the dual vanishing point grid. Notice that each side in the drawing is a polygon and that

Figure 8.9

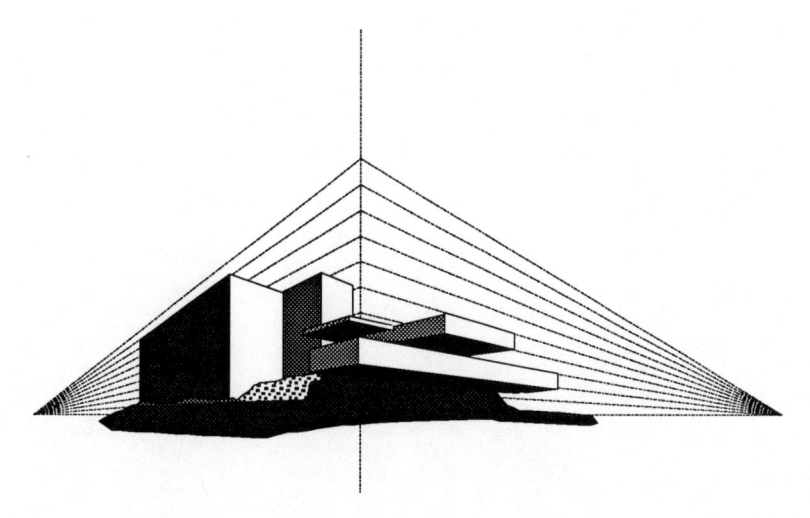

each polygon parallels the grid lines. The base is just random shapes generated with the freehand drawing tool.

FINAL REVIEW

When two-dimensional drawings just aren't good enough, remember the following:

- A straight-on isometric projection will accentuate the optical distortion. If you can, use one built on vertical lines and 30-degree angles.
- A single vanishing point perspective drawing can add the illusion of depth. This is really effective with long views receding into the distance.
- Dual vanishing point perspective adds realism. Keep in mind that horizontal lines must converge on one or the other vanishing point.

CHAPTER 9

GEM Graph

A POWERFUL PRESENTATION TOOL	144
STARTING UP	145
DATA ENTRY	145
GRAPHING: SCREEN TWO	148
PULL-DOWN MENU REFERENCE	152
GRAPHING WINDOW	157
THE MAP EDITOR	164

A POWERFUL PRESENTATION TOOL

GEM Graph is a treasure. It can turn rows and columns of figures into really lovely graphs so quickly that you'll be stunned. It's one of my favorite applications. You can either enter the numbers directly into Graph (it has a spreadsheet-like environment for this), or you can read data directly from SuperCalc, Visicalc, Lotus 1-2-3, dBase III+, or most word processors.

By the way, GEM Graph is the only GEM application that absolutely can't have more than two fonts on line at any given time. If you are purchasing additional fonts from either Specific Solutions or Bitstream, keep this two-font limitation in mind. Additional fonts are discussed in the Fonts chapter.

GEM Graph can automatically size your graphs. This is important if you're pulling graphs into GEM 1st Word Plus. You can size them to one-quarter, one-half, and full page sizes. You can also load the embellishing.

Not that Graph really needs GEM Draw Plus for embellishment. It has a staggering number of formatting options. Coupled with its ability to completely change from graph type to graph type in an instant, it is a powerful presentation tool indeed.

GEM Graph has two working windows instead of one. The first window, where you find yourself when you jump into Graph, provides a way of entering just text and data. The graphing window provides the graphics functions, including the graph type, line weights, fill patterns, and free-floating text. But you can't edit text or numbers entered in the original window while in the graphing window. A constitutional separation of graph and data, if you will.

Another unique thing about Graph, it's the only GEM application with no keyboard commands for menu or toolkit functions. There are a few commands for text editing and moving about in the data entry window, but that's all folks.

Graph is a difficult program to explain because books are, by nature, linear. One thing progresses to another, and so on. Graph doesn't work that way. Most menus are interrelated. I can only suggest that you use the following discussion as a general guide to what the menus and tools do, and then play around a bit with GEM Graph. The next chapter presents examples of several actual graphs and a step-by-step explanation of how they were created.

THE ORDER OF THINGS

You must follow a specific order of events when using Graph:

1. Enter the information you want to graph in the data area, or load the information from an outside source. This includes titles, row labels, and column labels.
2. Edit and modify the information until it's just what you want.
3. Select the type of graph you want. This will convert the information you entered into a graphic form and show it in the graphing window.
4. Add additional type, change shading or color, etc.

Of course, you can go back and forth between steps to tweak things up a bit. But these are the basic steps you'll follow to create a graph.

STARTING UP

GEM Graph has a decidedly un-GEM-like opening screen, looking more like a spreadsheet than a GEM program. There are a few familiar things: the typical top and bottom slider bars for moving around. And there's a full box and close box, really without much use since Graph can't have multiple windows. The top is occupied by an extensive menu bar, and the title bar lies under the menu bar. On opening, the title bar shows UNTITLED.GRF.

So much for the usual. The bulk of the screen holds the Graph Data Window. This has a place for a title, subtitle, and X and Y axis values and labels. The X axis labels are by row, and they are along the left of the screen. The Y axis values are labeled by column, and the labels run along the top of the spreadsheet area. See Figure 9.1.

DATA ENTRY

Even entering information is similar to spreadsheet techniques. The line that says "A1," right under the title bar, is the editing line. When you have the data window up on the screen, this is the line you'll use to enter all of your text and numbers. Where the text goes depends on the field or area you've clicked on. That area will reverse to white on black. For instance, click on the TITLE line. The editing line will suddenly hold 'TITLE. Note the apostrophe. As in many spreadsheet programs, the apostrophe denotes that what follows is text, not numbers.

By hitting the Escape key you can completely erase this, but remember to re-enter the apostrophe before typing in a title. The TITLE line holds the main title for the graph, while the SUBTITLE line holds (strangely enough) the subtitle.

Figure 9.1

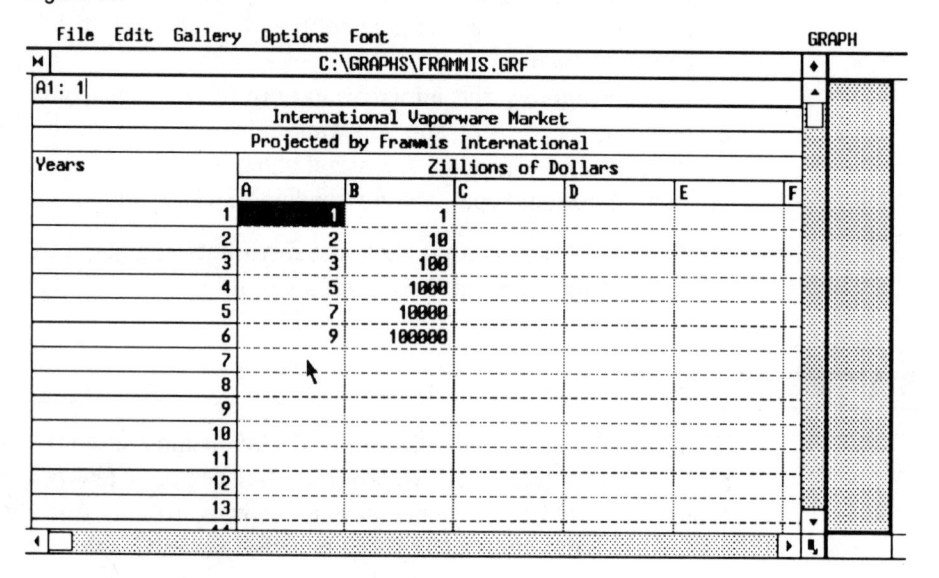

```
 File  Edit  Gallery  Options  Font                              GRAPH
                        C:\GRAPHS\FRAMMIS.GRF
 A1: 1
                    International Vaporware Market
                   Projected by Frammis International
 Years                          Zillions of Dollars
                 A        B        C        D        E      F
          1      1        1
          2      2       10
          3      3      100
          4      5     1000
          5      7    10000
          6      9   100000
          7
          8         ▸
          9
         10
         11
         12
         13
```

Click on the box that says X AXIS to enter an overall title for all X axis entries. Ditto for the Y axis. I always get confused about such things, so in case you're like me, just remember that the X axis is horizontal and the Y axis is vertical. The A, B, C, 1, 2, 3 hold individual labels for rows and columns. For instance, if you are putting a graph together for the sale of various types of melons over a period of years, the musk, water, cantaloupe, etc., entries would go in the 1, 2, 3 boxes. The years would go in the A, B, C boxes. Actually it doesn't make much difference because Graph can flip your data between the X and Y axes. We'll go over that in the pull-down menu section.

GETTING AROUND

There are basically two ways to get around in the data entry area:

1. Mousing. You can use the slider bars to move horizontally and vertically. You then click on the box you want to edit.
2. Keyboard shuffle. You guessed it: The arrow keys work like the cursor movement commands in most spreadsheet programs.

The keyboard cursor movement commands are:

Right arrow
Moves one box to the right. Hold it down to chug along continuously to the right.

Left arrow
Yep, one box to the left.

Up arrow
Climbs the data area, one box at a time. If held, it will zoom you all the way to the top.

Down arrow
Drops through the data area.

Tab
Scrolls the data area one screen to the right.

Shift-Tab
Scrolls one screen to the left.

PgDn
Scrolls down one screen.

PgUp
Scrolls up one screen.

Home
Jumps to block A1 in the data area.

End
Zips to the block in the last row, last column.

ENTERING AND EDITING

In addition to the various cursor movement commands, there is a set of editing commands. These help you enter or modify information on the editing line. To go from moving around the data area to the editing line, either click on the box or hit the Ins key.

Num Lock

When on, you can use the keypad for numerical entry. When off, you can use the keypad for cursor movement.

Right arrow

Moves the cursor along to the right of the text editing line.

Left arrow

Moves the cursor to the left across the text editing line.

Del

Deletes the character to the right of the cursor.

Backspace

Deletes the character to the left of the cursor.

Enter

Enters the information in the text editing line into the selected box.

That's really all there is to it.

GRAPHING: SCREEN TWO

Graphing is the fun part. Once all of your data is entered, you can select the graph type you want to use. We'll go over this selection process first, even though it is out of sequence with the rest of the pull-down menus, because it is the next logical step to building a graph.

GEM Graph has eight variations on five basic types of graphs, all of which are represented by icons that pull-down from the Gallery menu. See Figure 9.2. The five are pie chart, line graph, area graph, bar graph, and map chart.

PIE CHART

A very simple yet visually powerful type of chart. You've seen these a zillion times, in everything from newspapers to textbooks. Pie charts work well in showing basic size relationships between a few things. Just don't put in too

Figure 9.2

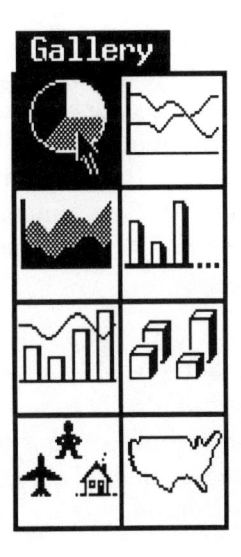

many sections; six is a good limit. Too many sections makes the chart too complex for a quick, single-glance-required-to-convey-the-message chart.

Graph can prepare all of the classic pie chart forms: sections shown as percentage, as a value, or just as a size relationship to the other slices. It can also "pop" a slice of the pie away for emphasis. Pie charts use only one column of values, which is always the extreme left X axis column. You can label the pie sections by using the X axis labels, 1, 2, 3, etc.

LINE GRAPH

Line graphs are useful for showing an ongoing process. An example might be the change in one or several things over periods of time, such as sales of product lines by quarter. Be careful with scaling. If you set your scale too high, variations along the lines will flatten. If the scale is too low, even a small variation will look like a major tremor. Graph does a fine job of automatically scaling your graph, and you should normally go with its decision.

Graph has an incredible number of options for line graphs. You can vary the scales, the axis, the grid markers, the line weights, and the way data points are displayed. Don't get too carried away, though; remember that the primary object is to convey information (unless you are in the illuminated manuscript business).

AREA GRAPH

This is a specialized sort of line graph, and it really requires the right kind of data to work effectively. If you have several lines, Graph will resort to trickery to prevent values in one layer from obscuring another. It "stacks" the values so that the next line back uses the previous graph as its baseline.

The area graph works best if all your lines show a steady growth, thereby minimizing the baseline jumping. It is most effective if you are trying to show both cumulative effect and several trends.

BAR GRAPH

Bar charts can be used like pie charts, comparing proportions for various things. They can also illustrate more complex relationships. For instance, they can compare proportions of variables within each bar, as well as comparisons between multiple bars and their parts. Graph can do all of the traditional bar graph types.

Clustered Bar Graphs

Things that bar graph bars measure are called independent variables. In clustered bar graphs, each independent variable gets its own bar and then all are clustered together. The clusters are grouped by dependent variables, which can be units of time, geographical areas, age groups, etc.

The clustered bar graph, like the pie chart, is a good choice for just comparing the relative size of the dependent variables. But unlike the pie chart, the clustered bar graph allows you to add dependent variables.

Stacked Bar Graph

This graph stacks the independent variables one atop the other, making it easy to show the proportions of things that go together to make up a complete something-or-other. GEM Graph makes no attempt to sort the stack by order of size; it merely graphs each value along the X axis as it finds it.

Vertical or Horizontal

Whether clustered or stacked, you can also decide on the orientation of the graph. Vertical is a typical, building-block type graph. Horizontal has the bars sprouting from the left side of the graph.

Horizontal bar graphs offer one big attraction: bar segments on their side are often long enough to hold labels. This means you can label them directly, without needing a key somewhere on the graph.

Whichever format you choose, don't throw in too many elements. If your reader must carefully pick out one element from the rest, you've goofed in making the graph. Remember that the whole idea of the graph is to make it easy for the reader to understand your point.

Bar and Line Graph

Reserve this one for comparisons and contrasts. All of the Y axis values are treated as if they are in a clustered vertical bar chart, except the extreme right column. This information is plotted as a line graph.

A bar and line graph can show the growth or decline of various things against a totally separate but related variable. For example, if you wanted to show the decline in population in various northern states versus the increase in population in the Sun Belt, you might want to choose the bar and line graph.

Three-Dimensional Bar Graph

Actually, this is just a jazzy clustered bar chart. Instead of the clustered bars standing beside each other, they're shown on a Z axis running off into the distance. To prevent a big bar from obscuring a smaller one behind it, the bars are shown at a three-quarter view. Graph puts the extreme left column of Y axis values in the front, with each row to the right one notch farther back.

Symbol Graph

Yet another bar graph. This one uses symbols, stacked one after the other, to form the bar. You can use symbols from the library that comes with Graph, or you can roll your own in GEM Draw Plus. As with standard bar charts, you can pick either vertical or horizontal bars.

The symbol graph is a great format for showing simple relationships. You've probably seen these used to show what percentage of the average wage goes into food, clothing, entertainment, etc. Graph will only plot one column for this type of chart (the one at the extreme left).

MAP CHARTS

Graph can make map charts for the U.S., including Alaska and Hawaii, and for Europe. Map charts come in two flavors: statistical and regional. Each type allows you to print values, percentages, and names by region.

Statistical Map Charts

These charts break map regions into groups based on their values. You assign regions with the Map Editor. You can select up to nine ranges, automatically calculated using the minimum and maximum values you entered. The default is five ranges.

The value groups can be independently shaded and colored. You can also display the regional names if you like.

Before editing, the U.S. map has each state as a separate region. The European map has each country as a separate region (unless the country is too small to display, such as Monaco).

Regional Map Chart

This type of chart shades and colors each region so that it contrasts with all of its neighbors. It will tag each region with a value or percentage.

PULL-DOWN MENU REFERENCE

The following sections explain the functions of all of the Graph menus.

FILE

This is the typical GEM application file management menu. A welcome piece of familiar turf. See Figure 9.3.

New

Trashes everything in the data and graphing windows. This gives you a clean working area. As always, Graph lets you change your mind or save your file before it goes ahead with this.

Open . . .

Pops the GEM file selector onto the screen. You use this to load .GRF files into Graph. All Graph files lead a dual life. The .GRF version is the one you load into Graph. The .GEM version is created to give Output something it can print, as well as to provide a way to import a graph into Draw Plus, 1st Word Plus, and Publisher (and any other application that recognizes the .GEM format).

Figure 9.3

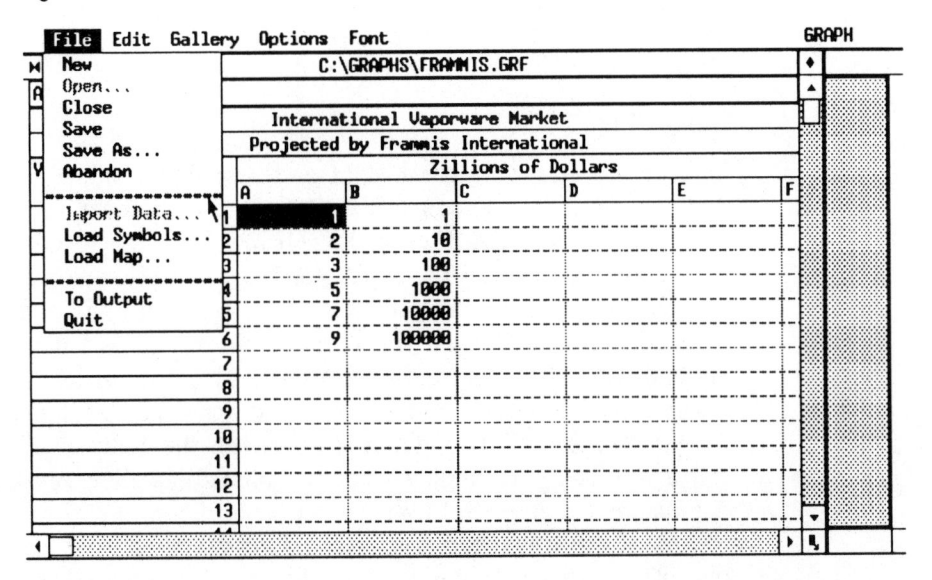

```
  File  Edit  Gallery  Options  Font                        GRAPH
┌─────────────┬─────────────────────────────────────────────────┐
│ New         │         C:\GRAPHS\FRAMMIS.GRF                   │
│ Open...     │                                                 │
│ Close       │                                                 │
│ Save        │        International Vaporware Market           │
│ Save As...  │       Projected by Frammis International        │
│ Abandon     │              Zillions of Dollars                │
│-------------│  A      B       C       D       E       F       │
│ Import Data.│  1      1                                       │
│ Load Symbols│  2     10                                       │
│ Load Map... │  3    100                                       │
│-------------│  5   1000                                       │
│ To Output   │  7  10000                                       │
│ Quit        │  9 100000                                       │
└─────────────┤                                                 │
              │ 7                                               │
              │ 8                                               │
              │ 9                                               │
              │10                                               │
              │11                                               │
              │12                                               │
              │13                                               │
              └─────────────────────────────────────────────────┘
```

Close

A GEM concept that really makes no sense in Graph. It closes the current data and graphing windows, leaving you to stare at a gray screen. Graph is still running, but with no active windows. If Graph could load two graphs simultaneously, this would make some sense, but . . .

If you click on Close by mistake, or you haven't saved your file, Graph will let you bow out gracefully.

Save

Saves any changes you've made to the Graph file. If you haven't assigned a name to your graph as yet (the title bar still shows UNTITLED.GRF), you can't use Save until you Save As . . . .

Save As . . .

Invokes the file selector so that you can assign a file name to your graph. All graph files must end in .GRF. You can use the file selector to wander between directories and drives until you find a likely home for the file.

Abandon

Dumps all changes you've made and reloads the last saved version. You'll be given a chance to reconsider this.

Import Data . . .

This only works with fresh data and graphing windows. Click on Import Data . . . and the file selector will appear with the wildest selection line you've ever seen. See Figure 9.4. GEM allows you to do DOS one better by setting multiple file filters. All you need to do is separate the file extents by commas, as was done with this file selector. It's set to search for .WKS files (Lotus), .DIF (Data Interchange Format, created by many spreadsheets), .CSV (Comma Separated Values, a common format used to exchange information between data base programs and used by SuperCalc), and .PRN (an ASCII file with fixed distances between the columns of figures).

If you like, you can add your own file extent filters. Just put in another comma, and then enter *.WHAtever.

All of the supported file formats load pretty cleanly except .PRN. This one places certain entirely reasonable requirements on the file:

- It can't have any blank values.
- Values must be separated by at least one space.
- A value and text must be separated by at least one space.
- If a value follows text, there must be at least two intervening spaces.
- Every line must end in a carriage return.

While Graph can import your information, that doesn't mean that everything will be exactly where you want it. You may need to move titles into the X or Y label areas. You can use the Cut and Paste commands for this.

Graph considers imported titles and labels in the data area as "missing data." Instead of plotting this as a zero, Graph won't plot it at all.

Load Symbols

Symbols can be created in GEM Draw Plus. To make a symbol, create the graphic; then put a rectangle around it. If you are making multiple symbols in the file, make them all the same size for consistency in your graphs.

Load Map . . .

Pops the file selector onto the screen so that you can pick either the U.S. map (USMAP.MAP) or the European map (EUROMAP.MAP). Unfortunately, you can't use Draw Plus to create a new map.

Figure 9.4

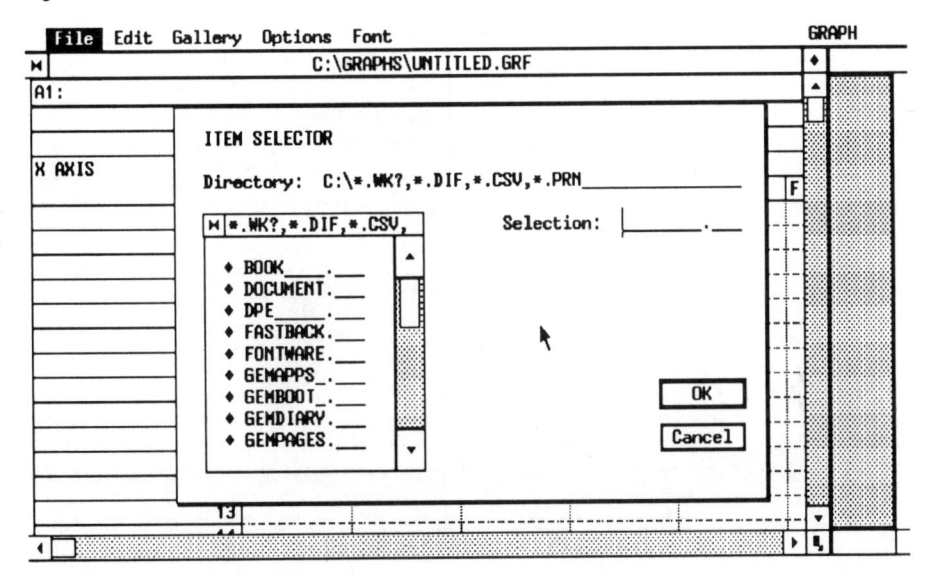

To Output . . .

In this case, Output serves a dual purpose. Primarily, it zips off to Output so that you can print the file. It also provides the way of making a .GEM version of your graph. This can be a bit clumsy if you're doing a number of graphs. Unless you use To Output . . . in each graph, you won't get a .GEM file that you can load into other applications.

Quit

Quit. And back to the Desktop.

EDIT

This menu has options that manipulate, move, or delete information in the data window. Delete is the exception to the rule, which has a limited function in the graphing window. See Figure 9.5.

Cut

Removes selected information from the data window, but hangs onto it in memory. Select another area and you can Paste it in.

Figure 9.5

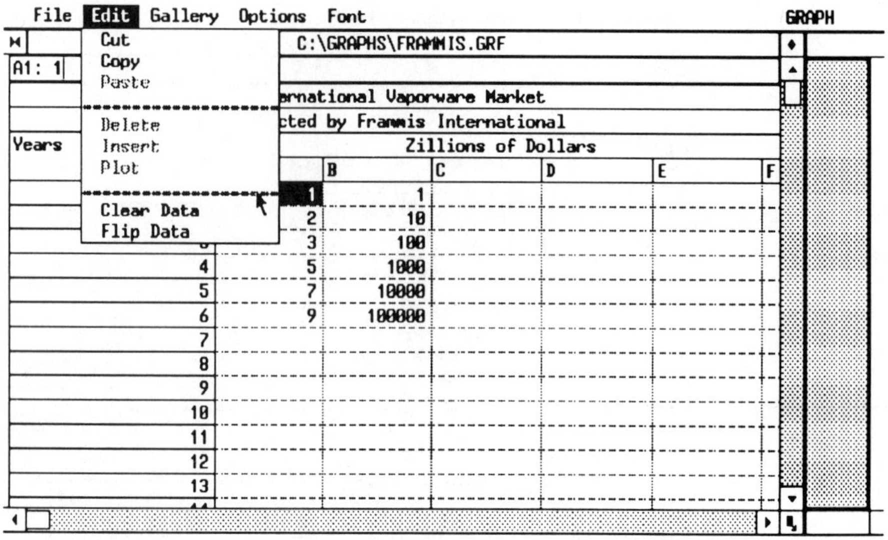

Copy

Puts a copy of the selected information into memory so that you can Paste it elsewhere.

Paste

Drops information in memory into the selected area.

Cut, Copy, and Paste can work with single blocks, multiple blocks, or complete rows or columns. To select a single block, double click on it. To select multiple blocks, click and hold. Drag the mouse around touching the blocks you want to select. To select one complete row or column, double click on the row or column label.

Delete

Deletes a selected row or column from the data window. Once deleted, you can't get it back. To select a row or column for deletion, select its row (X axis) or column (Y axis) label area; then Delete.

Insert

Inserts a row or column, depending on where the cursor is. If you've selected a row label (X axis), it will insert a row at that point. If you've selected a column label (Y axis), it'll insert a column at that point.

Plot

Lets you select rows or columns that Graph won't plot. Put the cursor in the row or column label area, and then select Don't Plot. The row or column in question will turn gray, denoting that it won't plot. If you decide later that you want it to plot, put the cursor in the label area again. The menu will now read Plot. Select this and the row or column will return to normal. This can be really useful when you pull data in from other programs, as it gives you a way of selecting what information you really want to plot.

Clear Data

You had better be sure you really want to do this. Selecting Clear Data erases all of the information in the working area. It will leave the row and column labels and titles intact.

Flip Data

This is fun. Click on Flip Data and the rows and columns switch positions. The extreme left column will become the top row, etc. It also switches the labels.

GRAPHING WINDOW

The remaining pull-down menus and the toolkit work only in the graphing window. The graphing window displays the graph, as Graph has created it, so that you can embellish at will. And you can embellish with gusto.

The graphing window has a toolkit that controls the color, fill pattern, and (where applicable) the line weights and data point markers. It also has a text editing tool that you can use to add free-floating text anywhere you like on the graph.

There are three active pull-down menus in the graphing window: Gallery, Options, and Font. Gallery allows you to change the basic graph style at will, playing "what-if-I-use-this-one?" Options directly affects the appearance of the graph. Font controls the type face, size, and style for labels, titles, keys, and free-floating text. See Figure 9.6. Don't worry if you select a size that is too big for the display area; Graph will gently inform you of the situation and refuse to change size.

TOOLKIT

The toolkit changes functions depending on which graph type is in use. Each section lists what graphs activate what tools.

Selector

Available for all graphs, the Selector provides a mouse pointer tool. Click on the parts of the graph that you want to select—typically bars, lines, symbols, areas, or text. Following the selection, extent boxes will appear roughly along the outline of the object.

You must select a part of the graph before you can use a tool to modify it; in the case of text, you must select before you can use the Font menu options.

Figure 9.6

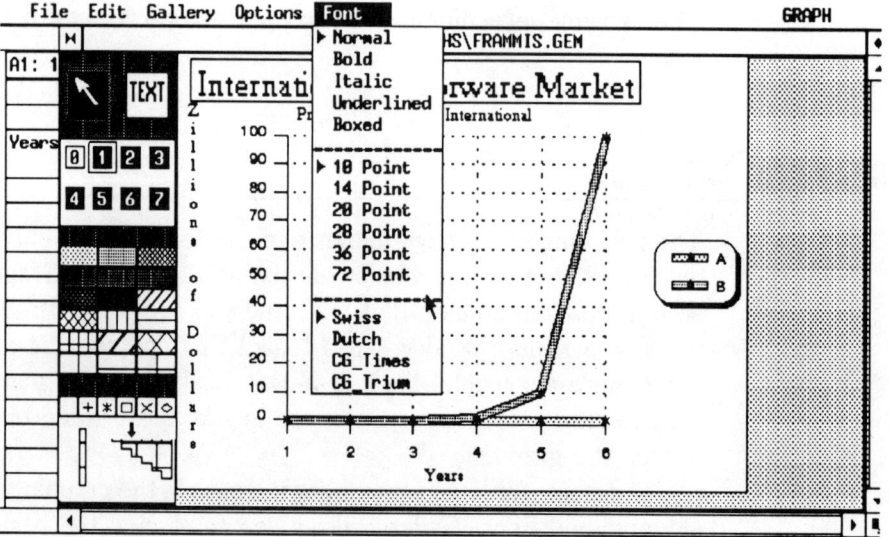

Text

A text editor that is available for all graphs, Text isn't nearly as flexible as the text tool in Draw Plus or Paint, but it's adequate. If you want to set a type face, size, or style, you do so before you select the text tool. You can only type or edit a single line each time you select this tool. When you hit Return, Graph simply cancels the editing mode and enters your text onto the graph.

If you want to add another line, just select Text again. You don't need to be too careful about positioning the second line because you can move it anywhere you want. Simply select it, put the mouse point over it, and then click and hold. You can now move the line anywhere on the surface of the graph.

If you want to edit an existing line, first select Text. Click on the line you want to edit. The text cursor will appear on the line, and you can move it right or left with the arrow keys. The Del key deletes to the right, while the backspace key deletes to the left.

Colors

This is available for all graphs. Select the object you want to change, and then click on the color you want. If you have a monochrome display, remember that color 0 is white. See Figure 9.7.

Fill Patterns

This is available for all but the symbol graphs. If you can select the object, you can change its fill pattern. Click on it to find if you can select the object. If you can, just click on the pattern you want.

Symbols

This is available only for the symbol graph. Click on the symbol bar you want to change, and then click on the symbol you want.

Data Points

This is available only for the line graph and the bar and line graph. Data points are the column values themselves, and their positions can be marked on line graphs. Your choices are none, box, plus, "X," square, and circle.

Click on the line to select it, and then click on the data point type you want. If you click on a data point itself, a double set of extent boxes will appear. If you click somewhere on the line, a single set will appear. Although

Figure 9.7

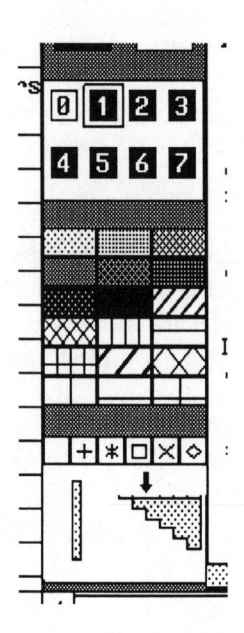

either one will work when selecting data point types, it's important to select the right one for the next section.

Line Weights

This is available only for the line graph and the bar and line graph. You must be careful to click on the line and not on a data point. You'll know you did it right if you get only one set of extent boxes falling directly on the line. Another way to select the line is to control-click on it.

You can now click and hold on the little down-pointing arrow on the line-weight selector. As you shift it left and right, the line-weight gauge will show the current weight. Release the arrow and the line weight will change.

OPTIONS

Preferences . . .

What this does depends on what sort of graph you've selected from the Gallery. In general, it asks if you want labels to display around the graph or in a keyed legend. You can also decide if you want values shown only on

Figure 9.8

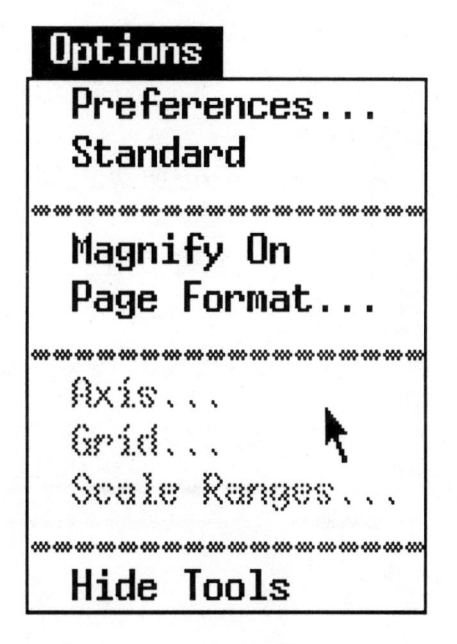

```
Options
  Preferences...
  Standard
  ~~~~~~~~~~~~~~~
  Magnify On
  Page Format...
  ~~~~~~~~~~~~~~~
  Axis...
  Grid...
  Scale Ranges...
  ~~~~~~~~~~~~~~~
  Hide Tools
```

the graph, as percentage labels, or as raw number labels. Some graph types lock this option out.

Enhanced or Standard

Enhanced provides a three-dimensional appearing graph. Standard is a simpler graph without graphic embellishments.

Magnify On/Magnify Off

When On, Graph zooms in on the graphing window. You can then maneuver about with the slider bars. Off is normal view. If you've selected a small size for the graph, such 1/4 page, you'll find this option inoperative.

Page Format

This one sets the overall size and orientation for the page. See Figure 9.9. There is the usual choice between portrait (vertical) and landscape (horizontal) formats.

Available page sizes are:

Figure 9.9

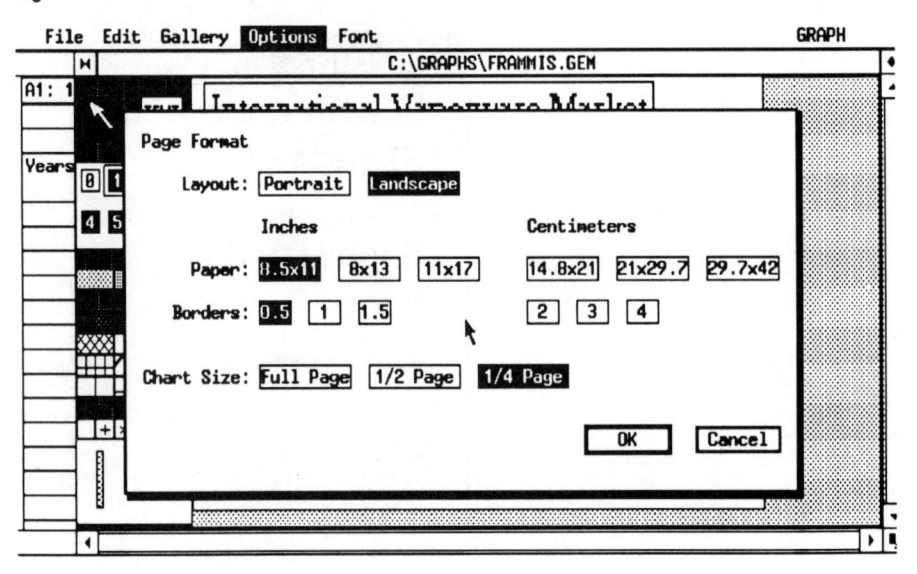

English	Metric
8.5x11	14.8x21
8x13	21x29.7
11x17	29.7x42

You can also set the width of the non-printing white border around the paper. Settings are:

English	Metric
0.5	2
1.0	3
1.5	4

Finally, you can decide how much of the page you want the graph to cover. Your choices are full page, 1/2 page, and 1/4 page. When using this program with GEM 1st Word Plus, stick to 1/2 or 1/4 page, with an 8.5x11-inch page (or 14.8x21 cm). This provides insurance that your graph will fit on the page. If you are loading the graph into Desktop Publisher or Ventura, you can pick any size you like. Both programs can scale the .GEM version of the graph to practically any similar size.

Axis . . .

Graph automatically decides how big the X and Y axes should be and what the step size between graph increments should be. See Figure 9.10. But maybe you want some other settings. The Axis option shuts down the auto pilot and gives you the controls (sort of). If you enter something that Graph just can't live with, it'll say so. It will also provide the range of values it will accept. Rather cheeky actually.

The X Axis Scale and Y Axis Scale boxes let you turn automatic off selectively for both axes. Reversed means they're on. Just click on either or both if you want to turn them off.

The Minimum option lets you set the smallest number that can appear on the axis. Maximum sets the biggest number. Step sets the number to skip between graph increments.

X Axis Crosses At: and Y Axis Crosses At: are fun. You can use them to move the axis lines around, even creating a cross-hair through the center of the graph if you like. This can be useful if you're trying to show values on either side of a baseline.

Grid . . .

This sets the grid display. You can choose from no display, dotted lines, dashed lines, or the ever-popular solid lines. Don't let the grid obscure the information in the graph.

Figure 9.10

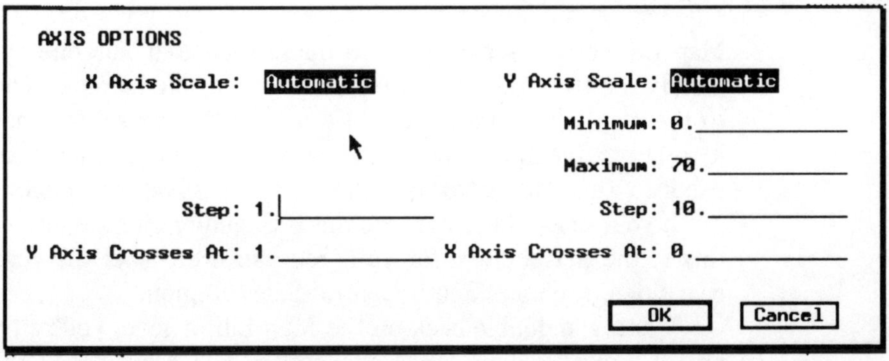

```
AXIS OPTIONS
        X Axis Scale: [Automatic]          Y Axis Scale: [Automatic]
                                                 Minimum: 0._____
                                                 Maximum: 70._____
                  Step: 1.|_____              Step: 10._____
    Y Axis Crosses At: 1._____       X Axis Crosses At: 0._____
                                                     [ OK ]  [Cancel]
```

Scale Ranges . . .

Valid only for statistical maps. On its own, Graph will set up five ranges of values based on the high and low data entries. If you want more or less than this, Scale Ranges . . . lets you select between one and nine ranges.

The Automatic box controls the size of the ranges. When on (reversed), the ranges are calculated for equal sizes. When off, click on it and you can grab the extent boxes on each range shown in the dialog. Just slide them up and down to adjust the size of each range.

Hide tools

Drops the toolkit from the display, letting you admire your graph in greater detail. This is especially useful when you've used Magnify On. Click on this again to regain the toolkit.

FONT

The Font pull-down menu controls the type face, style, and size. Graph and the Map Editor have the only Font menus in all of the GEM applications that offer Boxed. Boxed does what it says: It draws a box completely around the selected line of text.

Font works best if you type the text first, click on it, and then select the Font options you want. And by the way, despite what it says in the manual, Graph doesn't like additional fonts. There seems to be some sort of memory limitation that restricts Graph to just two fonts. If you purchase some additional fonts, you'll have to remove Swiss and Dutch from the CONFIG file; otherwise, your additional fonts will never appear in the menu.

THE MAP EDITOR

Map Editor is a separate GEM application that has one specific purpose: modify the two .MAP files that Graph uses. The hammer icon GEM assigns to the map editor marks it as a tool, and that's exactly what it is. You use it to rearrange and combine the various regions in each map. You can also use it to assign fill patterns, add text and symbols, and generally have a ball.

If your organization breaks the U.S. and/or Europe into various regions, this is the perfect tool for you. You can even label the regions with your own titles, such as "South Central Sales Region."

When you double click on the Map Editor icon, you're transported to a pretty typical looking GEM application. See Figure 9.11. The left side of

Figure 9.11

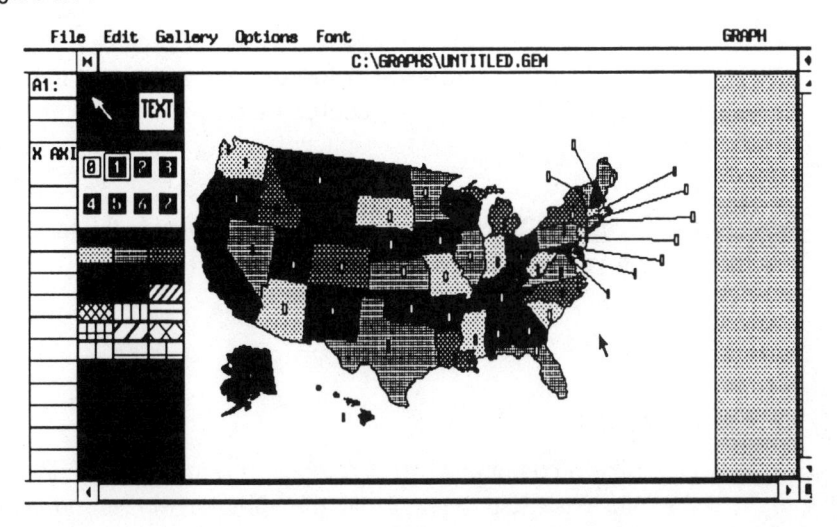

the screen has a toolkit, the top is bedecked with pull-down menus and the usual slider bars, and full and size boxes are present. The full and size boxes are largely decoration, as Map Editor can only edit one map at a time.

Being essentially a special-purpose tool, Map Editor doesn't have an elaborate set of pull-down menus. Still, you need to know what they do.

FILE

Open

Opens a map file. Unless you've used Save as . . . to create your own maps, you have two choices: EUROMAP.MAP and USMAP.MAP.

Save

Saves your changes back to the file. Don't do this unless you've used Save as . . . to set up a new map file with your own name. Otherwise, you'll overwrite the master map file.

Save as . . .

Use this to set up your own customer maps. Clicking on this option pops the files selector onto the screen. It's a good idea to keep your map files in the GRAFMAPS directory.

Abandon

Crumples up your changes and tosses them in the can. A good way of jumping back to the last saved version for another try. You'll get a chance to reconsider before Map Editor executes this.

Quit

Closes up and heads back to the GEM Desktop. Of course, Map Editor will remind you to save your file if you haven't done so.

EDIT

Make Region

Use this to combine several regions into one region. To select regions, use the shift-click technique. Hold the shift key down and click on each region you want to select. As long you hold the shift key, each new selected region will be appended to the set of already selected regions. Once the regions are selected, click on Make Region and they will all fuse into one region.

Break Region

If you want to break a composite region into all of its original component parts, this is your option. First select the region; then click on Break Region. You can't partially break a region. It will always revert to all of its original parts.

Delete

An indiscriminate killer. It will delete anything and everything currently selected: states, nations, map symbols, text boxes, whatever. Just select them, and click on Delete.

Undelete

This is available just in case you delete something you really want. But Undelete can only recall the last set of deleted items.

Hide text

Hide text hides all of the text areas on the map. To make them reappear, click on Show text.

Magnify On

Click on Magnify On to zoom in on the current map. Then you can tool around the map with the slider bars. See Figure 9.12. Click on Magnify Off when you want to return to normal view.

FONT

The Font menu lets you change the type style, size, and face for any text areas on the map. Just select the text areas, and then click on the Font option you want.

Toolkit

The Map Editor toolkit is pretty basic, with only one unique feature: the symbol palette. The top is the usual collection of colors. Select a region or a set of regions, and then select a color. The same technique works for the fill patterns. The symbol palette is interesting. Click and hold over the map symbol you want to use. Then just drag it onto the map and put it where you want it. Once on the map surface, the symbol is treated like any other movable object that you can select.

That's just about all there is to the Map Editor. If you drag a text box away from its native region, it will automatically become a call-out. Call-outs

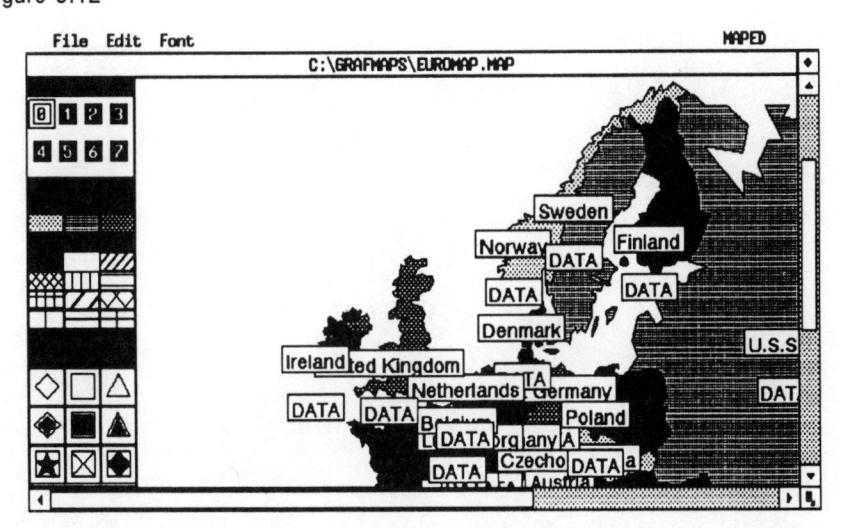

Figure 9.12

shoot out a line pointing to their habitat. The only other thing that you need to know is to keep the MAP.SYM file in the GRAFMAPS directory. It's not polite to hide the symbols from Graph.

CHAPTER 10
Advanced Graphing

TURNING YOUR CREATIVITY LOOSE	170
WHICH GRAPH?	170
PUTTING THE RULES TO USE	170

TURNING YOUR CREATIVITY LOOSE

Putting the reference chapter behind us, we forge ahead into the dark and unknown territory of graphing. Actually, graphing is fairly simple. There are a few well-proven and time-worn rules, and once you've mastered those, you can turn your creativity loose.

WHICH GRAPH?

If you're making a very simple comparison, such as the drop in Pittsburgh's population between 1975 and 1985, you don't need a graph at all. But if you're drawing a comparison between a variety of things or attempting to show a trend, you'll need graphs to get your point across.

The cardinal rules of graphing are (and you may recognize some of these from the previous chapter):

- Keep it simple. Don't try to make more than one point per graph.
- Bar charts and pie charts are easier to understand than line graphs. If you can make your point with a simple comparison, do it. If you need to show trends, keep the number of items in the graph to a minimum.
- If you have a lot of numerical information to present, break it into a logical progression of graphs, and back up each graph with supporting text. If you're doing a presentation, use WordChart to emphasize the point you're trying to make. If you're putting the information into a publication, make sure you have supporting paragraphs for your graphs. Research studies have shown that a combination of text and graphics is the most effective way to convey information.

PUTTING THE RULES TO USE

Let's say that you want to show the sales at Frammis International Limited by product. Simple, right? Frammis makes three major products: vaporware, clone computers, and radioactive lighting systems.

Because this is a simple comparison, you can use either a bar graph or pie chart. See Figures 10.1 and 10.2. The pie chart shows the three market segments, and I used Preferences to ask Graph for percentages. The labels were set to display with the slice. I popped the radioactive lighting product line out to emphasize its share.

Figure 10.1

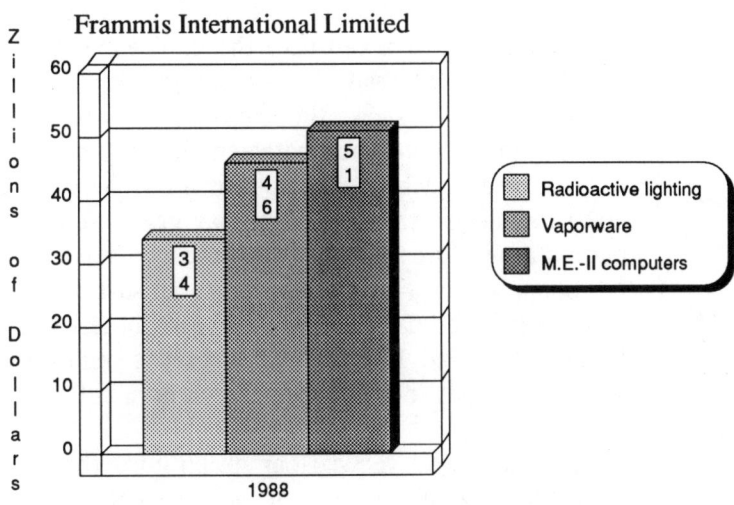

Sales by Product Line
Frammis International Limited

Zillions of Dollars

- Radioactive lighting
- Vaporware
- M.E.-II computers

1988: 34, 46, 51

Figure 10.2

Sales by Product Line
Frammis International Limited

Radioactive lighting 26%
Vaporware 35%
M.E.-II computers 39%

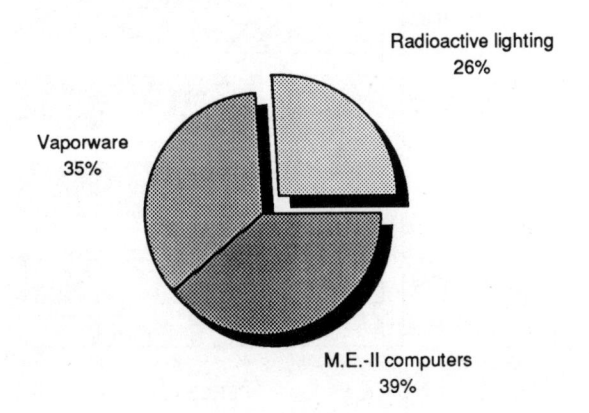

The bar graph took a little more work. With the bar graph, you know you have such goodies as X and Y axis names that you can assign. In this case, it was "Zillions of Dollars" and "1987." To give the graph a slightly different slant, I set Graph to display the actual values. I also reduced the scale with Axis to accentuate the differences between the bars. (You can get the same effect with the symbol graph.)

The pie chart shows the simplest relationships. Note that if there isn't a whole lot of difference between the size of your slices, your pie chart won't provide much visual emphasis. In such a case, go to a bar graph where you can collapse the scale. The bar graph allows you to qualify the information a bit more because it has the two axes.

Suppose you want to show the same sort of information but over a four-year period. You can now use either a clustered or stacked bar graph. See Figures 10.3 and 10.4. Both can provide multiple comparisons. Don't use the line graph yet, however; keep in mind that it's a little harder to comprehend.

The clustered vertical bar graph adds the yearly information. It also shows the growth or decline of each product line. The size of the bars allows the reader to visually compare the share of the total sales that went to each line.

Figure 10.3

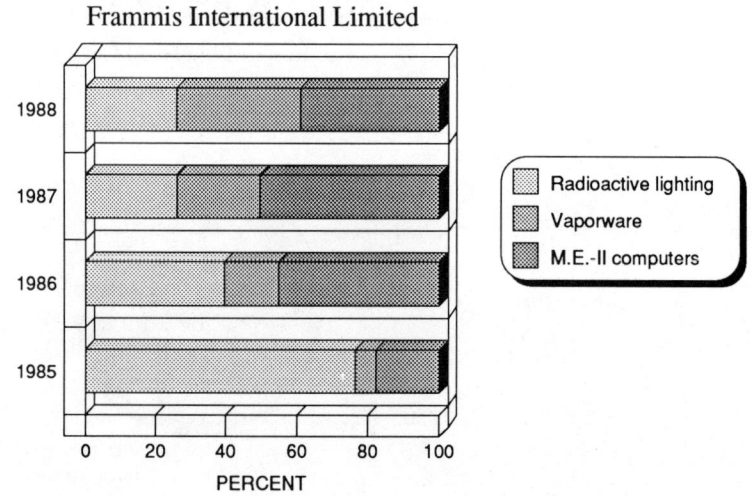

Sales by Product Line

Frammis International Limited

Figure 10.4

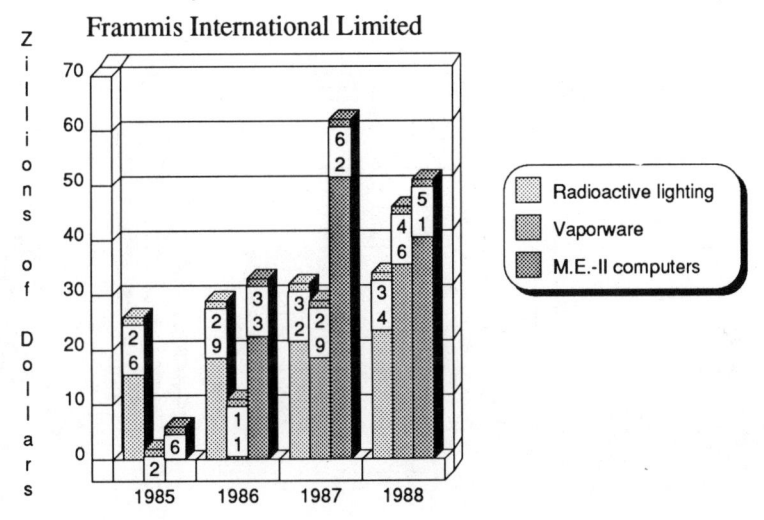

Sales by Product Line
Frammis International Limited

[Bar chart showing Zillions of Dollars on Y-axis (0-70) by year (1985-1988), with three product categories: Radioactive lighting, Vaporware, M.E.-II computers]

The horizontal stacked bar graph simply shows percentages. Notice how different the same information appears. In the vertical graph, it's easy to see that radioactive lighting is healthy but has a slower growth than vapor ware. In the horizontal graph, radioactive lighting appears to be sharply declining.

The three-dimensional bar graph in Figure 10.5 shows one of the things you have to watch. Notice that the middle set of bars (vaporware) is obscured by the front set. Also note that moving the rows around won't help. If your data causes this sort of thing to happen, don't make your reader try to sort it out.

Okay, suppose your real point is trends. To show trends most effectively, you'll need to resort to the line graph (Figure 10.6) and the area graph (Figure 10.7). The area graph shows the total sales and provides a visual comparison for market share. This is the one that you put in the annual report. Because of the cumulative effect of the graph, it's a bit difficult to see that clone computer sales are declining.

In the line graph we told Graph not to accumulate totals. This one clearly shows the true state of affairs; it's the one you show to the board of directors. The big dip makes it obvious that clone computers had a bad year in '88.

Figure 10.5

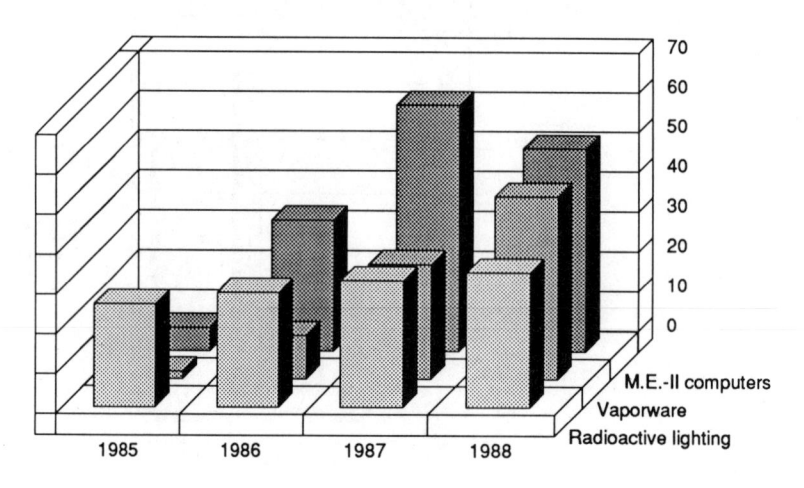

Sales by Product Line
Frammis International Limited

Figure 10.6

Sales by Product Line
Frammis International Limited

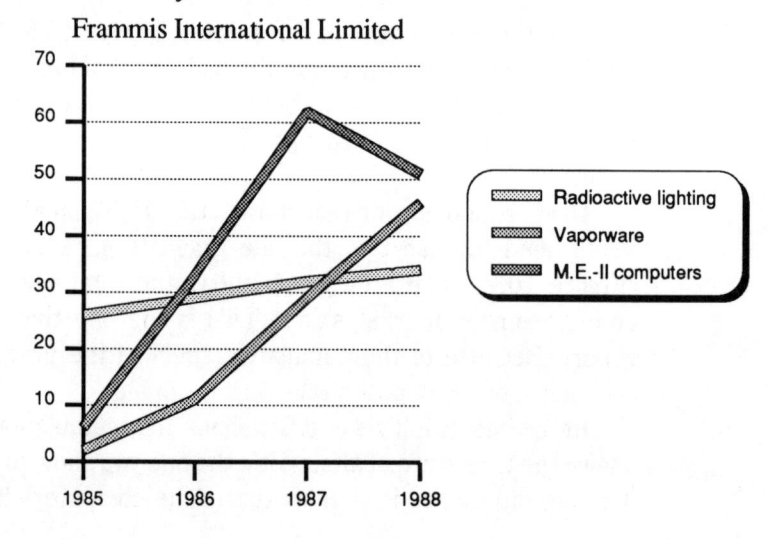

Figure 10.7

Sales by Product Line
Frammis International Limited

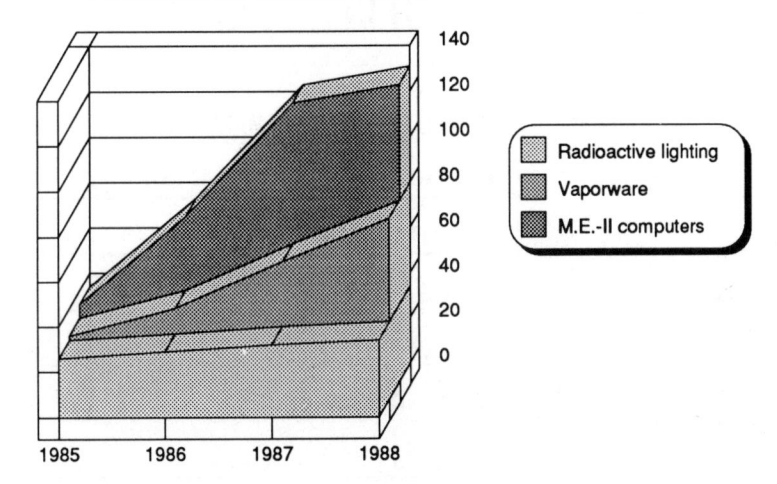

[Stacked area chart showing sales from 1985 to 1988 with three categories: Radioactive lighting, Vaporware, and M.E.-II computers. Y-axis ranges from 0 to 140.]

Think of the graph types as different tools with different functions. Choose the tool to match the job at hand. And be careful how you present the information: Choosing the wrong type of graph can obscure the facts—or make them altogether too clear.

CHAPTER 11

WordChart

A REAL PAGING PROGRAM?	177
THE CHARTING AREA	177
TOOLKIT	179
MENUS	182
WORDCHART	189
CHARTING YOUR COURSE	190
OUTLINES	195
DECIMAL TABS	195
BORDERING ON INSANITY	197
ENHANCING YOUR WORDCHARTS WITH GEM DRAW PLUS	197

A REAL PAGING PROGRAM?

I sometimes think WordChart was a dry run before attempting a real page-layout program. What WordChart really is, though, is a specialized and very sophisticated program for making single pages. Its primary uses are for making overhead projector charts and tables that you can drag into your publishing program. You can use WordChart to bang out a lot of professional-looking charts in a short amount of time.

One word of caution concerning fonts: more than two make WordChart a bit squirrely. Three fonts seem okay, but some of the tools come up with numbers in the place of legends. Four fonts is a disaster. You'll need to be judicious about what you load into the /GEMAPPS/FONTS directory (the chapter on fonts talks about how to shuffle fonts).

On opening, WordChart looks different from most other GEM applications. See Figure 11.1. The drawing area is smaller and the toolbox area stretches to cover one-quarter of the screen. There's no full box and no way to shrink or move the application around the screen (which is really okay because it wouldn't make much sense to do that anyway).

THE CHARTING AREA

Like most GEM applications, WordChart's functions are so interwoven that it's difficult to know just where to begin. We'll start with the charting area

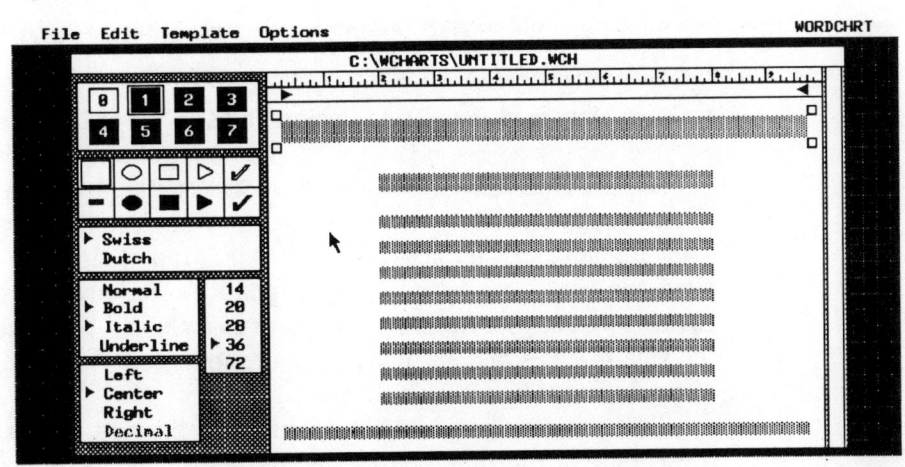

Figure 11.1

simply because a lot of the menu selections don't make sense unless you know what goes on here.

The basic idea behind WordChart is to let you type text into various canned formats. This lets you concentrate on the content of the charts while WordChart does all of the drudge work. You can have two basic types of charts, and therefore two different charting areas.

Portrait is a chart that is higher than it is wide (a standard 8.5x11-inch piece of paper). Landscape, on the other hand, creates a chart wider than high (a standard piece of paper turned on its side). Your choice depends largely on how you like to plop your charts on the overhead projector. If you are using paper charts, such as seminar materials that match overhead transparencies, you'll likely want to use portrait. Portrait charts also are easier to bind.

For the moment, we don't care what kind of charting area you have on the screen. We just want to go over WordChart's basic parts. The gray areas are *text fields*. Text fields are part of a larger text division called *zones*. Zones are the basic formatting areas on the chart. You can change the format for each zone, but you can't change the format for a single field within a zone.

You can tell how big a zone is by clicking the mouse pointer on one of its fields. WordChart will display extents around the zone, marking its borders. WordChart will also place the cursor in the field you've selected. Exactly where the cursor goes depends on the format of the zone, i.e.:

- Left justified, ragged right
- Centered, ragged right and left
- Right justified, ragged left
- Decimal aligned (similar to decimal tabs in a word processor).

As you type text into the field, it will continue to fill the field until it reaches capacity. Sorry, no hyphenation. When the field fills, it will extend itself for another line and your text will wrap. This goes on until you've filled the zone with text, at which point WordChart will pop up a menu advising you of your options. These are to make the type size smaller, make the side margins bigger, or make the zone larger. We'll cover how to do all of those things later.

Text editing is primitive but adequate for the task. Each arrow key moves the cursor in the direction of the arrow. No big surprises there. Delete erases the character to the right of the cursor; backspace deletes the character to the left. Strangely enough, WordChart also has creeping Word-Starism. That just goes to prove, by the way, that you can't keep an excellent program down. You can use the following WordStar commands:

Control-S	Cursor left
Control-D	Cursor right
Control-X	Cursor down
Control-E	Cursor up
Control-Y	Delete line
Control-N	Insert line

In fact, WordChart has keyboard commands for most of the menu functions. These are really handy, but I wouldn't recommend worrying about them until you get some practice with the program. For your convenience, a complete listing of the keyboard commands appears later in this chapter.

Those two black triangles on the ruler line are the margin markers. Click and hold on them, and you can shove them back and forth over the ruler. Only the margins for the selected zone will change.

The slider bar to the right is a familiar sight. In portrait mode, you'll need to use the slider bar to zip up and down the chart.

TOOLKIT

Color Palette

The top of the toolkit (see Figure 11.2) has the color palette. If you don't have a color monitor, and you want to output to a color printer, you can still click on colors 1 through 7 to assign them to parts of your word chart.

The trick is finding out just what color number prints what color on your printer. Try each one and write down the result.

Bullets, Numbers, and Letters

You can add hanging bullets, numbers, or letters to fields within any of the text zones. If you choose numbers or letters, WordChart automatically increments them for each text field in the zone. This is great for outlines, numbered lists, etc.

To select a bullet, number format, or letter format, follow this procedure:

1. Click on the zone you want to use. Its extents will appear to tell you that it is selected.

Figure 11.2

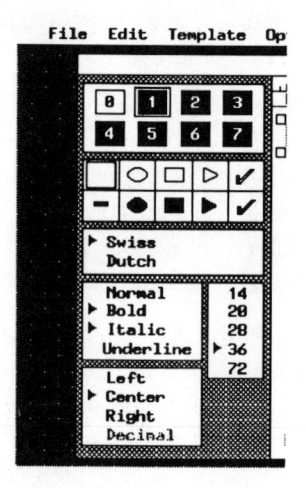

2. Click on the format you want. WordChart will automatically apply it to all of the fields.

Ah, but you say you don't want that many fields in your list? And you certainly don't want blank fields with only their bare bullets showing. Simple. Just click on the blank extra fields to put the cursor on them. When the cursor is in position in each one, blow it away with a Delete Row command (it's under the Edit menu).

If you are wondering where the numbers and letters selector is, click on Numbers & Letters under the Options menu. It will magically take the place of the bullets selector. If you want to go back to the bullets, click on Bullets (under Options).

Swiss, Dutch, and Other Flavors

Sounds like chocolate, doesn't it? We'll go into a big, heavy discussion of these fonts in the first Desktop Publisher chapter. For right now, you need to know that readability studies show no difference between people's ability to read well-designed serif (Dutch) and sans-serif (Swiss) fonts. Typographers may argue that serif type is easier to read for large amounts of text, but that certainly isn't the situation with charts. Bottom line: both Dutch and Swiss are highly legible and you can choose either one insofar as readability is concerned.

So why pick one over the other? Swiss is *the* business type font. Some experts feel that it may be the most popular typeface in use today. It looks clean, official, and high-tech. It also works well when combined with serif types, though I'm not recommending you wildly mix Swiss and Dutch in your charts.

Dutch was originally designed for use in newspapers. Because it is more compact than Swiss (yet just as readable), pick Dutch if fitting text on a line is your charting problem. It's also a bit friendlier than the more formal Swiss.

If you are using fonts other than these two, be careful. Make sure you pick something readable, not fancy. Bitstream Charter is a great choice (and a really nice all-purpose font). Any of the fonts designed as book faces will work well: Palatino, Bookman, Century Schoolbook, etc. Stay away from University Roman, Cloister, and other display faces.

Click on either available font, and the zone that's currently selected will switch to that type face. You can't mix the faces on a line, but you have too much taste to want to do that anyway. The little black pointer shows you the type face that's currently in use.

Normal, Bold, Italic, and Underline

Except for Underline, all of these affect the entire selected zone. Underline doesn't affect any hanging numbers or letters for the zone. You can combine these to your heart's content, but again, you can't mix them in a zone. And that would be handy.

Just click on the one(s) you want. The black triangles indicate which are active.

Point Size

If you have a Hercules-type monochrome or an EGA color system, you can get 14 point as your smallest type size. CGA color systems just don't have enough resolution for 14 point type in WordChart because WordChart doesn't have a zoom feature.

Again, whatever size you select will affect the whole zone. If you select a size that's too big for the zone, WordChart will dig in its heels and refuse to do it. It will also tell you why, so that you can select a smaller size, get rid of a row or two, or stretch the zone to accommodate the bigger type.

What type size you pick depends on what kind of chart you are making. You probably want to avoid using 14 point in overheads for two reasons:

1. No one towards the back of the room will be able to read it.
2. If you've gone to 14 point, you're likely trying to cram too much information onto a single overhead. That's bad chart design. You want to communicate, not overwhelm.

You can use 14 point for printed or copied visuals. Not only will these be readable, but done in much bigger type they might be overwhelming. We'll look at some examples in the design part of the chapter.

Left, Center, Right, Decimal

These left justify, center, right justify, or decimal align all of the text in the zone. If you have hanging bullets, letters, or numbers, anything but left will look silly. Decimal can only be used with figures, and will align the numbers in each of the zone's fields with the decimal points.

MENUS

WordChart has four menus: File, Edit, Template, and Options.

FILE

Like all GEM applications, WordChart has a file management pull-down menu. See Figure 11.3. This lets you save files and load previously created charts. You can also throw away all changes since the last save in case you decide you don't like the results.

Figure 11.3

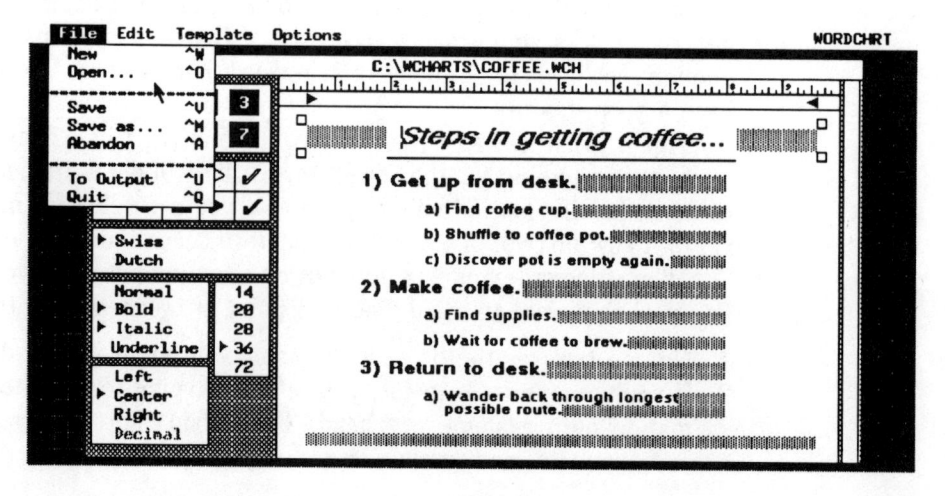

New

Clears whatever is on the charting area, but retains the current WordChart format. GEM gives you the option of bailing out if you haven't saved your file.

Open . . .

Calls up the file selector so that you can bring a WordChart file in. All WordChart files end in .WCH. WordChart allows only one file open at a time. There is no way to copy portions of an existing WordChart into the charting area.

Save

Saves your chart to the file shown on the title bar. This works only if you've previously used Save as . . . to assign a name other than UNTITLED to the file.

Save as . . .

Opens the file selector so that you can assign a file name to the chart and save it. Since you can move from directory to directory or drive to drive with the selector, you can put the file anywhere you like.

Abandon

Throws away any changes you've made since the chart was last saved (if ever). WordChart will reload the last saved version of the chart. As insurance against accidents, you'll get a chance to change your mind before WordChart actually abandons the changes.

To Output

Jumps off to the Output application so that you can print your chart to a printer, plotter, or the screen. If you haven't saved your file, you'll get a chance to (GEM can only print whatever has been saved to a file).

Quit

Closes up shop and heads back to the GEM Desktop.

EDIT

The Edit menu gives you some control over the format of the chart, including a way to load and delete borders. See Figure 11.4.

Figure 11.4

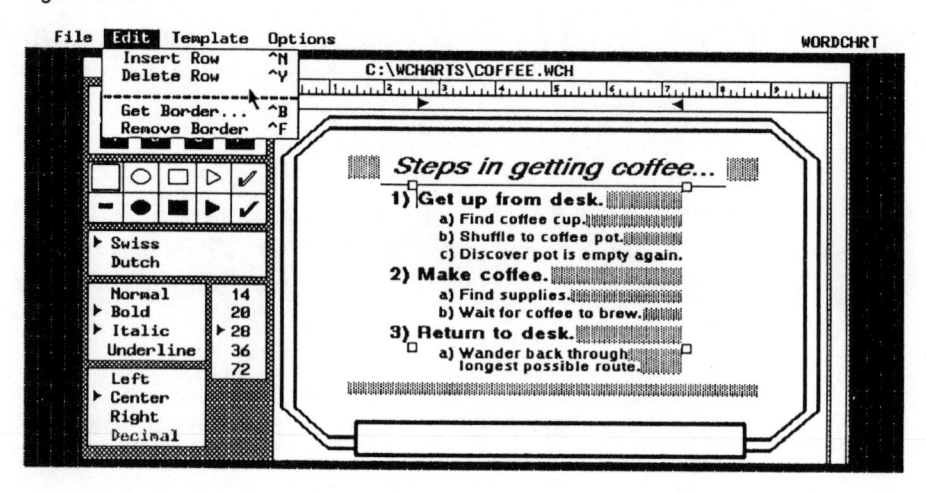

Insert Row

Adds a field above the field holding the cursor. The new field is a copy of the one below. For instance, if the field below is part of a group of fields in a zone, the new field joins that zone. If the field below is the only field in a zone, the new field has its own zone.

Delete Row

Deletes the field in which you've placed the cursor.

Get Border . . .

You can use this to load a border into your charting area. It's a good idea to do this before adding text because some borders require you to change your margins (so as to make more room for the border).

We'll go over borders later in detail, but these are really just special GEM Draw Plus drawings. You get a set with WordChart and another set that can be adapted for WordChart with the GEM Draw Business Library. You can also create your own.

Remove Border

If you have a border that you don't want in your chart, this will get rid of it. You can then load a new border, if you like.

TEMPLATE

Templates are predefined formats for each WordChart. These are the basic designs that you must start with to build your charts. See Figure 11.5. Although WordChart does not allow you to create your own templates, you do have fairly extensive format editing capability. Once you modify a template, you can save the modifications to the *template gallery*. Or, if you save a file with the modifications, you can load the modified template from that file.

Use Template From . . .

Loads a template, including all the customizing you've done, from a WordChart file. This is your way of reusing modified templates without disturbing the original template gallery.

Remember Template

Be careful with this one; it will permanently replace the template in the gallery with the one in your WordChart, including all modifications you've made. Since this is permanent, you'd better be really sure that you want to make the replacement—especially since you can load customized templates from an ordinary WordChart file.

Figure 11.5

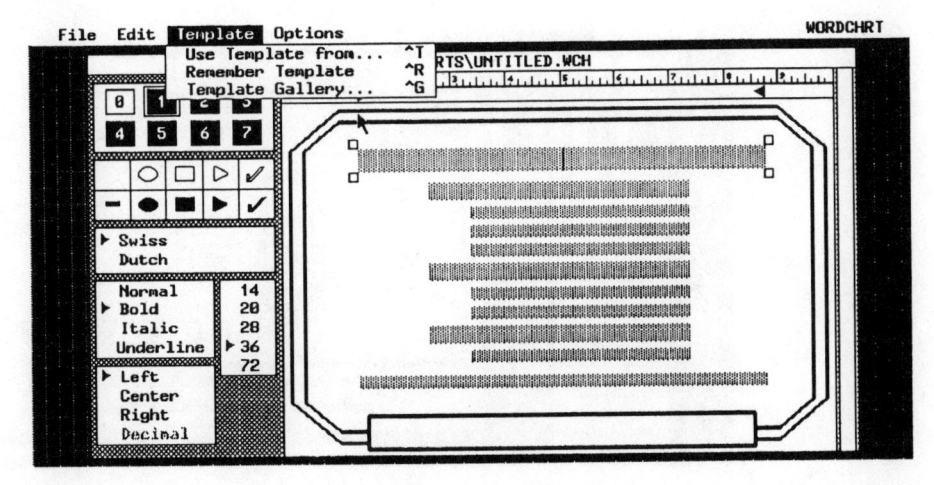

Template Gallery . . .

Calls up the template gallery. Click on the one you like and your chart will use that format. See Figure 11.6.

OPTIONS

This is the main control menu for WordChart, and it's really almost an extension of the Toolkit. You can change the parts of the Toolkit that display, modify the size of zones (or sets of zones), or change and enhance the appearance of your chart.

Portrait

Creates an 8.5x11-inch chart.

Landscape

Creates an 11x8.5-inch chart (think of it as a piece of paper turned sideways).

Lines & Boxes . . .

Adds rules above and/or below, or completely around all the fields in a zone. For ruling lines above and below, you can set them either to run the entire length of the field or just run the length of the text in the field. Both boxes and rules have four line weight selections, ranging from the standard GEM

Figure 11.6

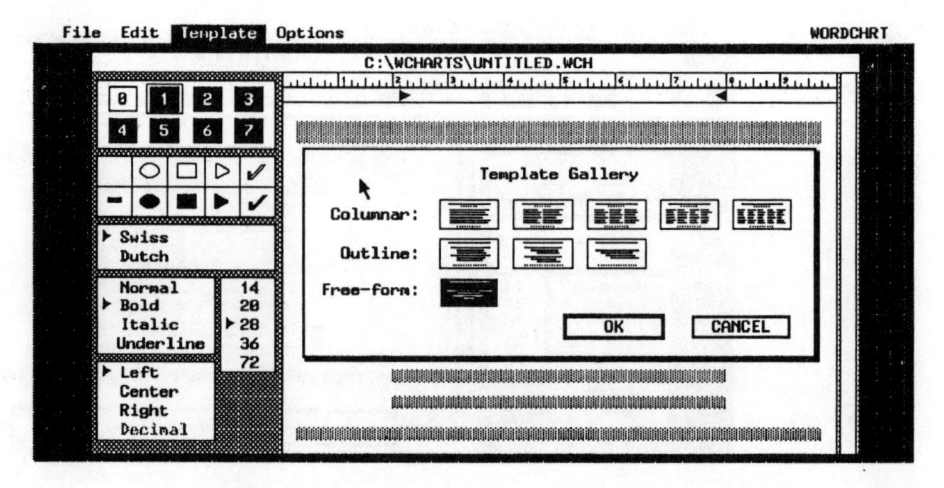

hairline to a 3/32 of an inch line. (Sorry metric fans, but GEM WordChart runs strictly in English units.) See Figure 11.7.

Numbers & Letters/Bullets

Toggles the Toolkit to display either the bullets or numbers and letters selectors.

Zone Markers/Toolkit

Toggles the Toolkit or the zone markers display. Zone markers let you expand or compress the vertical area of a zone. Sometimes, such as in free-form templates where every line is a zone, WordChart will lump several zones together into one zone marker area.

Zone markers have triangular extents, one at the top and one at the bottom. Sometimes they touch the extents on the next zone to form a diamond. See Figure 11.8. To move a single extent up or down, click and hold and then slide it up or down. To move two touching extents together (diamond), hold down the shift key while you select and move the extents.

Shortcuts . . .

Brings up a help menu to remind you of the most commonly used keyboard commands. See Figure 11.9.

Figure 11.7

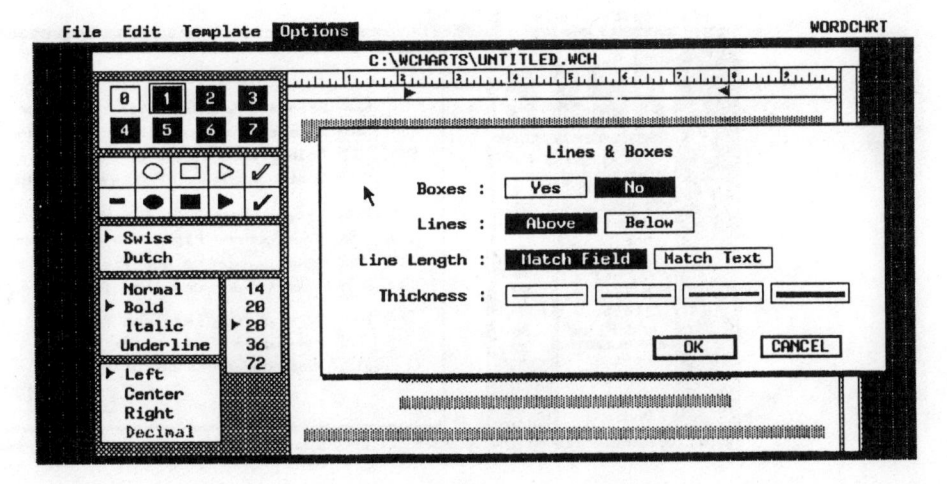

Figure 11.8

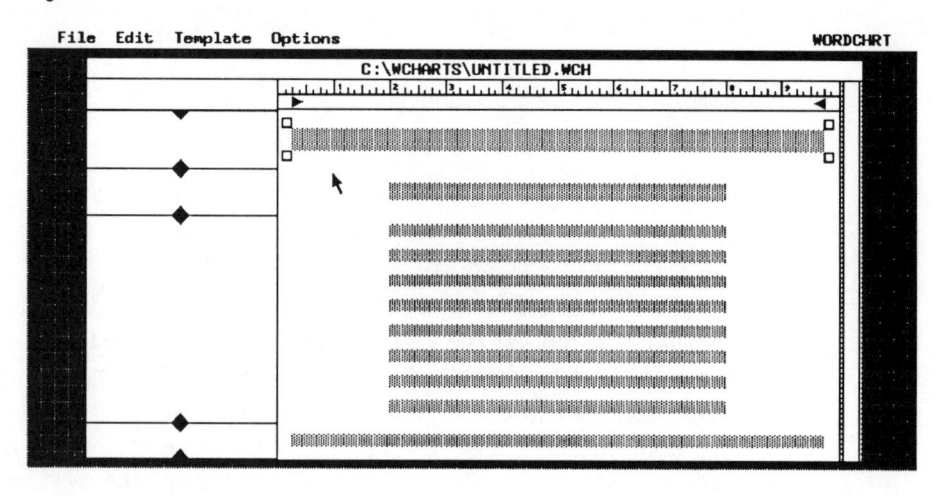

Figure 11.9

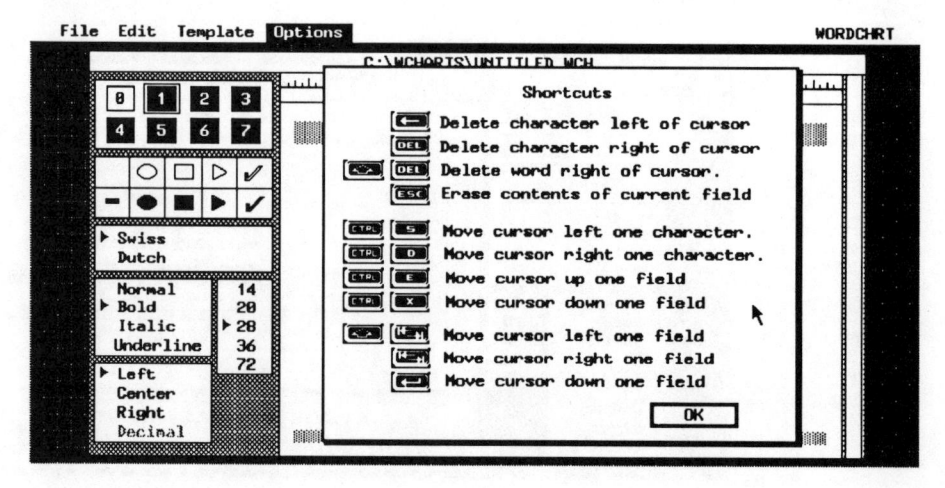

WORDCHART

This will let you select any Desktop accessories you may have, such as Diary, the Calculator, Clock, or SnapShot.

KEYBOARD COMMAND SEQUENCES

Like all of the later-release GEM applications, WordChart is well endowed with keyboard commands. If you take the time to learn them, you'll discover that you rarely need to resort to the pull-down menus. Many of the WordChart keyboard commands are standard throughout the later applications, such as GEM Draw Plus, GEM Graph, and GEM Desktop Publisher.

Cursor Movement

Cursor right	Control-D	Right arrow
Cursor left	Control-S	Left arrow
Cursor up	Control-E	Up arrow
Cursor down	Control-X	Down arrow
Cursor left one field	Tab	
Cursor right one field	Shift-Tab	
Cursor down one field	Return	

Deletion

Delete character right	Del
Delete character left	Backspace
Delete word right	Shift-Del
Delete field contents	Escape
Delete field	Control-Y

File Handling

New file	Control-W
Open file	Control-O
Save file	Control-V
Save file as . . .	Control-M
Abandon changes	Control-A
Go to Output	Control-U
Quit WordChart	Control-Q

Formatting

Insert row (field)	Control-N
Get a border	Control-B
Remove a border	Control-D
Use a template from . . .	Control-T
Remember a template	Control-R
Template gallery	Control-G
Portrait charting area	Control-P
Landscape charting area	Control-L
Lines & Boxes selector	Control-Z
Bullets/Numbers & Letters	Control-K
Zone markers/toolkit	Control-J
Shortcuts help menu	Control-C

CHARTING YOUR COURSE

WordCharts, whether for use in a publication or as overhead transparencies, should all follow one basic design rule: Keep it simple and uncluttered. In one respect, WordChart helps you do this. It just doesn't have a big enough text buffer to allow you to fill a page with 14 point type. So even if your boss wants to put the entire King James Bible on a single sheet, you're off the hook. The program just won't let you cram a page full of text.

A good way to think about design is to consider that each chart should convey one—and only one—idea. It's okay to remind your viewer of a number of important points, but the single point you want the chart to get across should stand out. For instance, let's say you are giving a seminar on desktop publishing. You want to list the four main reasons for using desktop publishing techniques. Later in the presentation you'll discuss each in detail, accentuating each point as you present it. See Figure 11.10.

Figures 11.11, 11.12, 11.13, and 11.14 illustrate a really simple way to do this. Of course, you'll have other overheads scattered in between these that will support your discussion of each point, but I've lumped all of them together so you see how they work.

All five charts were created with the free-form template in the Landscape mode. This template is great for series charts because each main text field is also a separate zone. This means that you can modify each one individually. I modified the top to be 28 point Dutch italic, centered. This makes a nice

WordChart 191

Figure 11.10

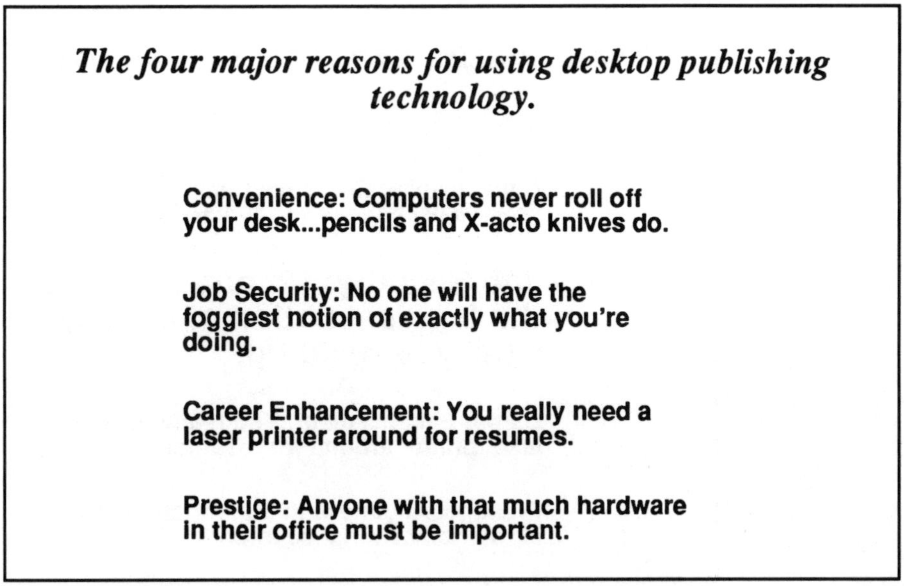

The four major reasons for using desktop publishing technology.

Convenience: Computers never roll off your desk...pencils and X-acto knives do.

Job Security: No one will have the foggiest notion of exactly what you're doing.

Career Enhancement: You really need a laser printer around for resumes.

Prestige: Anyone with that much hardware in their office must be important.

Figure 11.11

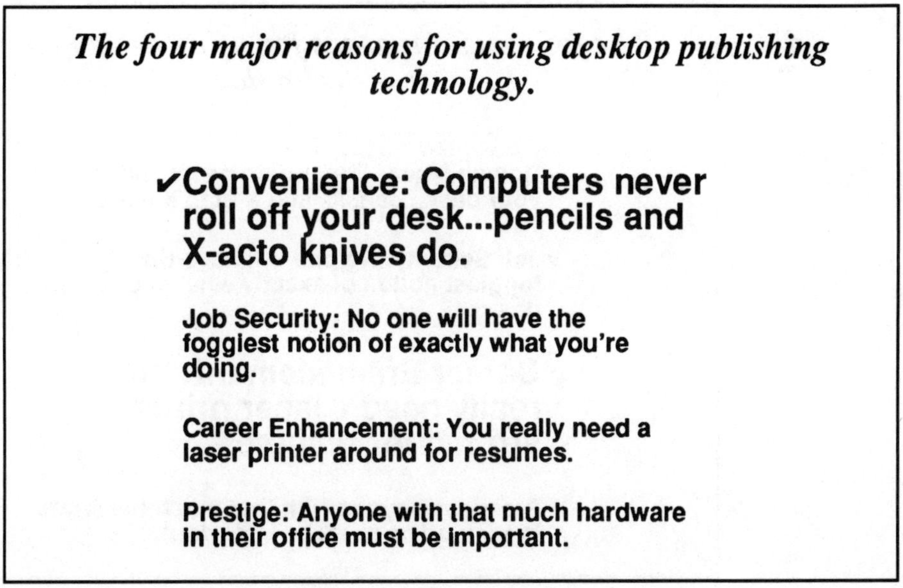

The four major reasons for using desktop publishing technology.

✔**Convenience: Computers never roll off your desk...pencils and X-acto knives do.**

Job Security: No one will have the foggiest notion of exactly what you're doing.

Career Enhancement: You really need a laser printer around for resumes.

Prestige: Anyone with that much hardware in their office must be important.

Figure 11.12

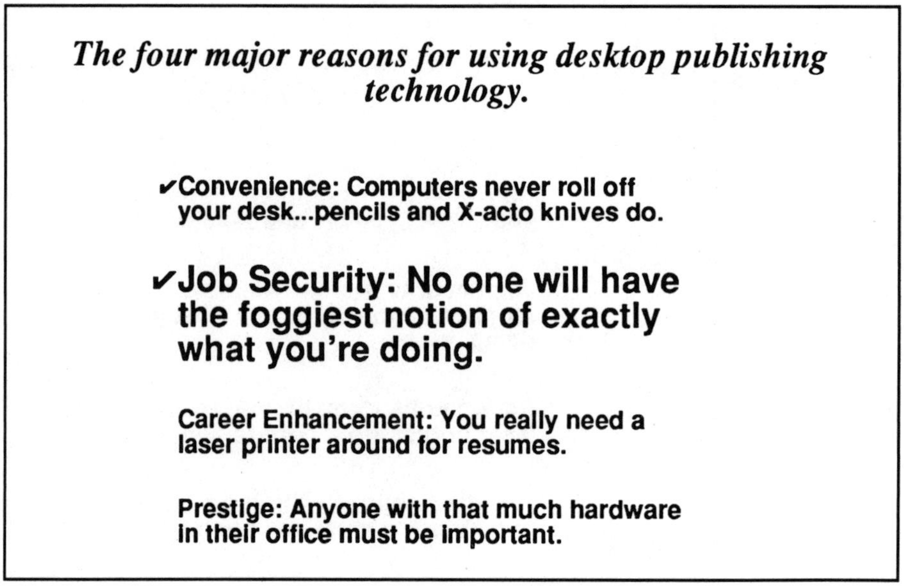

The four major reasons for using desktop publishing technology.

✔Convenience: Computers never roll off your desk...pencils and X-acto knives do.

✔Job Security: No one will have the foggiest notion of exactly what you're doing.

Career Enhancement: You really need a laser printer around for resumes.

Prestige: Anyone with that much hardware in their office must be important.

Figure 11.13

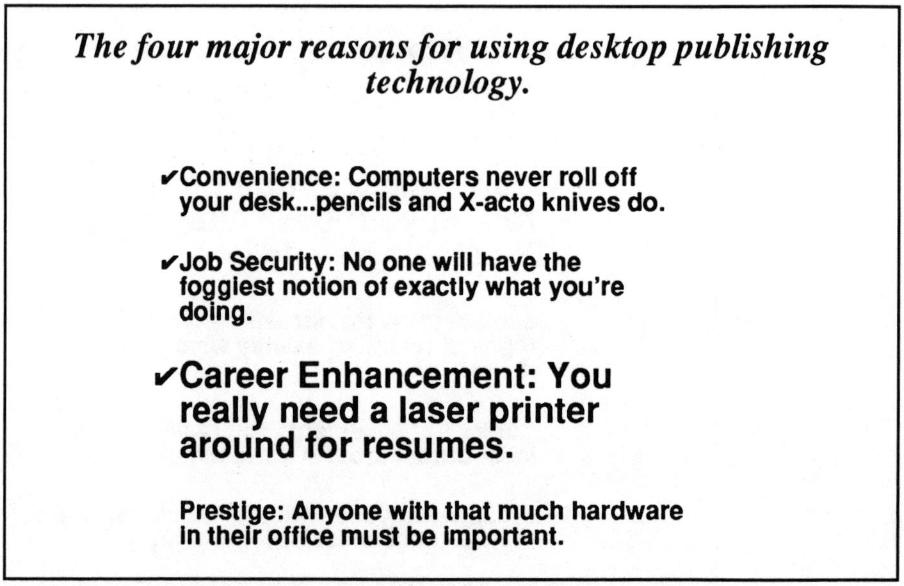

The four major reasons for using desktop publishing technology.

✔Convenience: Computers never roll off your desk...pencils and X-acto knives do.

✔Job Security: No one will have the foggiest notion of exactly what you're doing.

✔Career Enhancement: You really need a laser printer around for resumes.

Prestige: Anyone with that much hardware in their office must be important.

Figure 11.14

> *The four major reasons for using desktop publishing technology.*
>
> ✔ **Convenience:** Computers never roll off your desk...pencils and X-acto knives do.
>
> ✔ **Job Security:** No one will have the foggiest notion of exactly what you're doing.
>
> ✔ **Career Enhancement:** You really need a laser printer around for resumes.
>
> ✔ **Prestige: Anyone with that much hardware in their office must be important.**

visible heading. I also deleted a couple of the fields from the main text area, forcing a little more white space between the text fields.

The idea behind the first chart is to introduce the four main reasons for desktop publishing. As a result, each reason is given equal weight in the list. The following charts introduce a detailed discussion on each reason. The reason under discussion is highlighted with 28 instead of 20 point Swiss bold type. It's left justified to give it more of a "list" look and to line up with the check marks. The check marks indicate that the topic is under discussion, or has been discussed (for those who wake up in the middle of the presentation).

Having overheads like this sprinkled through your presentation will provide structure. It also will provide a graphic reinforcement for each point you are trying to make.

SIDE-BY-SIDE

Two-column charts are handy for comparisons, definitions, and the like. Figure 11.15 compares the language of Pittsburgh, PA (my hometown) with standard English. For this chart, I chose two-column Landscape. This pro-

Figure 11.15

A primer to the native dialect of Pittsburgh

Pittsburghese	*English*
Are yiens 'goin ta S'Liberty or Picksburg?	*Are you going to East Liberty or Pittsburgh?*
You're sooo ignorent!	*You lack social graces.*
Ya wanna go out or what?	*Would you like to go on a date with me?*
Gimme a pund of chipped-chopped-ham and a pund of jumbo.	*I would like to buy a pound of baked ham and a pound of bologna.*
Didja see the Stillers?	*Did you watch the Steelers game on television?*
Hey! What'sup?	*What is going on here?*
Looka da guy in da Full Cleveland.	*Look at the man in the bright green leisure suit.*

vides enough width for a fair amount of text and the two-column format needed to show "Pittsburghese" and the English translation.

Even though there is a fair amount of verbiage on the chart, it is still not overly crowded (although this is about as much text as I'd dare use). Because the chart is intended to show a group of examples for the viewers to read, this much text is acceptable. If the chart were supposed to present a set of important ideas instead of examples, however, this would have been a lousy design.

Because each column has its own elements, I chose italic for the right column to provide a visual contrast between the two. Using Dutch not only renders the kind of informality I want but also let's me get more text on a line.

OUTLINES

WordChart has three outline templates, ranging from a two-level to a four-level outline. Because each level is a zone, you can apply independent numbering to each. For example, Figure 11.16 shows a two-level outline format. Note how the large type steps are numbered 1), 2), etc., while the substeps are lettered a), b), c).

Outline charts are great for listing procedures. The example chart shows the basic steps one must master in getting coffee in a typical office environment. It could just as easily be steps in removing fuel rods from a nuclear reactor, or the agenda for a seminar.

DECIMAL TABS

WordChart has a lovely decimal tabbing feature for charts with columns of figures. Decimal tabbing lines up each set of figures in a column by the decimal point, instead of left, right, or center alignment.

Figure 11.16

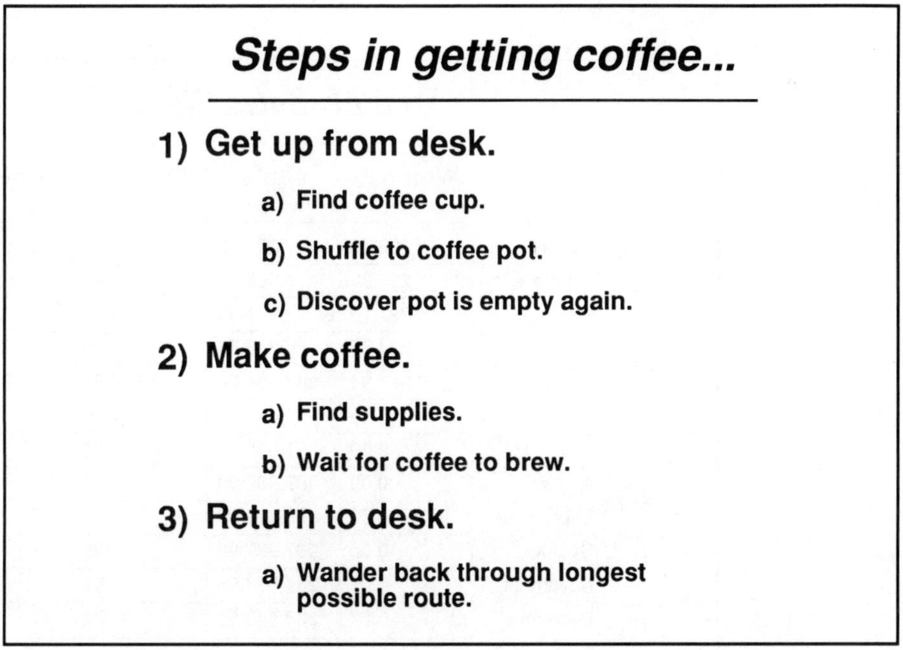

Steps in getting coffee...

1) **Get up from desk.**
   - a) Find coffee cup.
   - b) Shuffle to coffee pot.
   - c) Discover pot is empty again.

2) **Make coffee.**
   - a) Find supplies.
   - b) Wait for coffee to brew.

3) **Return to desk.**
   - a) Wander back through longest possible route.

Figure 11.17

Monthly Sales Figures

	Wombats	Stuff	Gadgets	Junque
January	123.45	234.45	1.34	11,111.23
February	234.33	1,000.99	99.22	1,234.23
March	987.76	1.99	100,000.12	234.44
April	234.87	2345.88	2.98	1,234.98
May	10,987.98	867,554.34	2,567.88	222.22
June	0.00	987.99	1.00	.23
July	0.00	11,634.78	1.00	.22
August	0.00	987,987.00	.99	111.11
September	0.00	89,876.00	1.01	19.23
October	0.00	987,987.98	.98	2.98
November	-0.01	234,567.98	.97	1.00
December	-0.03	234,543.00	1.02	99.99

Figure 11.18

Monthly Sales Figures

	Wombats	Stuff	Gadgets	**Junque**
January	123.45	234.45	1.34	**11,111.23**
February	234.33	1,000.99	99.22	**1,234.23**
March	987.76	1.99	100,000.12	**234.44**
April	234.87	2345.88	2.98	**1,234.98**
May	10,987.98	867,554.34	2,567.88	**222.22**
June	0.00	987.99	1.00	**.23**
July	0.00	11,634.78	1.00	**.22**
August	0.00	987,987.00	.99	**111.11**
September	0.00	89,876.00	1.01	**19.23**
October	0.00	987,987.98	.98	**2.98**
November	-0.01	234,567.98	.97	**1.00**
December	-0.03	234,543.00	1.02	**99.99**

Figure 11.17 shows a complete year's sales in four product lines. This is an awful lot of information in one chart, but it might be acceptable if it is going into a written report. If you are presenting something like this at a meeting, though, you might want to highlight each row in separate charts, such as shown in Figure 11.18. That keeps the audience from drowning in an ocean of figures (remember the rule: one idea per chart).

Note that all the figures are aligned to the decimal points. You could also do this with right alignment if you will always have two decimal places. If the number of decimal places varies, however, decimal alignment will still line things up for you.

Also notice the boxes around the figures. They provide a sort of grid work that makes it easier to follow rows and columns of figures.

BORDERING ON INSANITY

GEM WordChart has about a zillion borders, many of them with quite interesting designs. Figure 11.19 presents some representative examples of these borders in reduced form.

Have a care with these borders. You don't want the border to overpower the chart. After all, the idea is to get the message across, not distract the audience with the border. For presentations and the like, stick to simple borders. The first example shows one of these.

Figures 11.20, 11.21, and 11.22 show how borders can help you create all sorts of things. Figure 11.21 is a custom-made certificate for attendees of a training class. If your company or organization runs classes, now you can print certificates on demand. Figure 11.22 is a menu of daily specials, using the cutting board outline border. WordChart and the free-form template make it a snap to put in the specials and the prices.

Oh, and remember to load your borders *first*. If you type in the text first, you may not find enough room left for the border.

ENHANCING YOUR WORDCHARTS WITH GEM DRAW PLUS

You can use GEM Draw Plus to create borders and add graphics to WordCharts you've already created. First we'll cover making borders because you need to understand how GEM WordChart actually prints files before you can see how GEM Draw Plus comes into play.

198 GEM Desktop Publisher

Figure 11.19

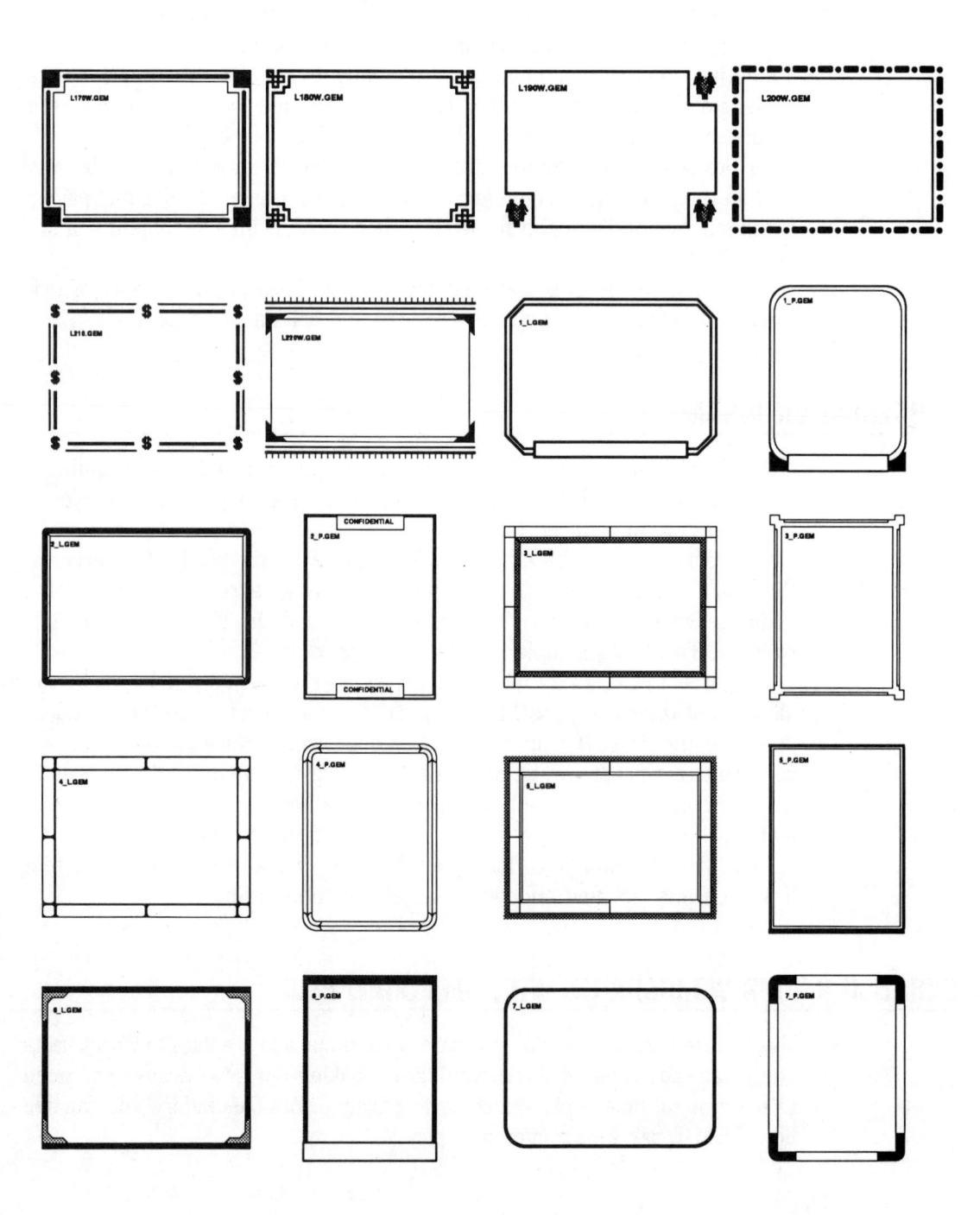

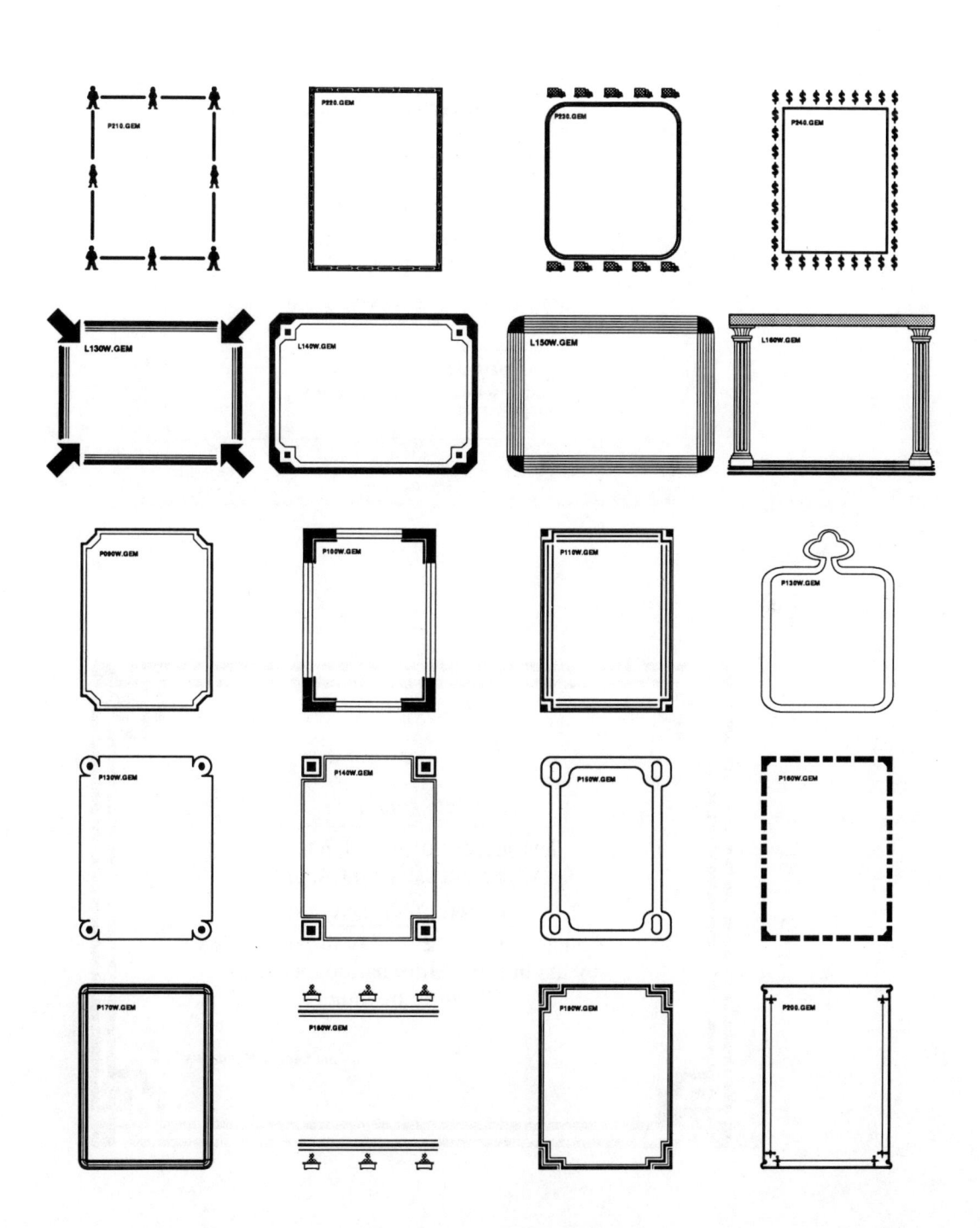

WordChart

Figure 11.20

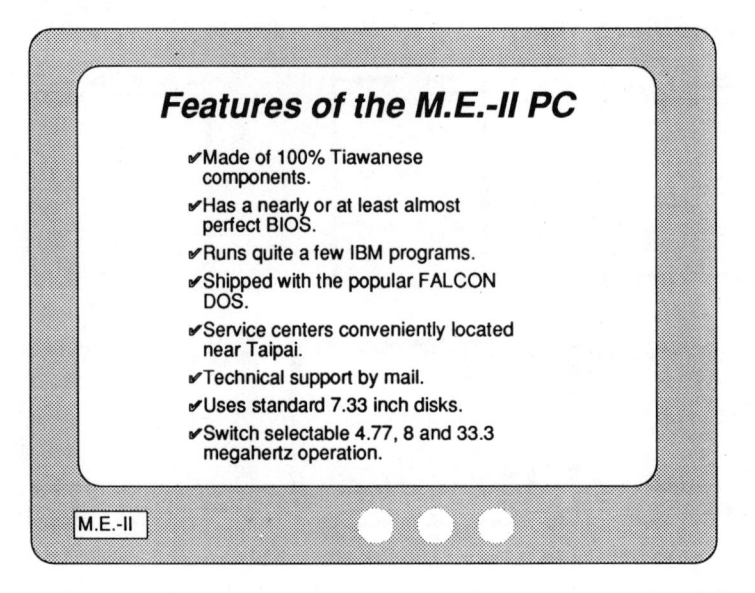

Features of the M.E.-II PC

- Made of 100% Tiawanese components.
- Has a nearly or at least almost perfect BIOS.
- Runs quite a few IBM programs.
- Shipped with the popular FALCON DOS.
- Service centers conveniently located near Taipai.
- Technical support by mail.
- Uses standard 7.33 inch disks.
- Switch selectable 4.77, 8 and 33.3 megahertz operation.

M.E.-II

Figure 11.21

This is to certify that

Buffalo Foonman

has successfully completed a comprehensive course in

Customer Obfuscation

conducted on the 22'nd day of April, 1988 by the Frammis International Limited Training Institute

"Sic Gloria Mendacity"

Figure 11.22

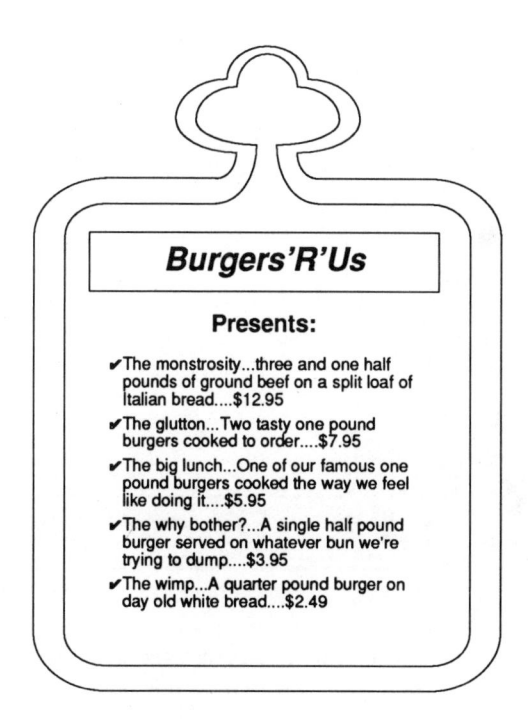

Burgers'R'Us

Presents:

- The monstrosity...three and one half pounds of ground beef on a split loaf of Italian bread....$12.95
- The glutton...Two tasty one pound burgers cooked to order....$7.95
- The big lunch...One of our famous one pound burgers cooked the way we feel like doing it....$5.95
- The why bother?...A single half pound burger served on whatever bun we're trying to dump....$3.95
- The wimp...A quarter pound burger on day old white bread....$2.49

Borders are really just GEM drawings with space left in the middle for text. There are two requirements for borders:

1. Don't make them too complex. If they take up too much memory, WordChart will just refuse to load them.
2. The text area must have a locator rectangle to define where the text is supposed to go within the border.

Figure 11.23 shows a locator rectangle in a border (note the extents give away its location). The locator rectangle must be set as color 0, and it must be moved to the back of the drawing with Put in back. That's really all there is to it.

Now, an explanation of how GEM Draw Plus relates to WordChart. When you tell WordChart to save your file, it also makes up a .GEM version of the chart. This can be loaded into GEM Draw Plus just like any other .GEM file. You can then add graphics, move things around, etc. There is one thing to watch, however. If you go back to WordChart and load that same .WCH

Figure 11.23

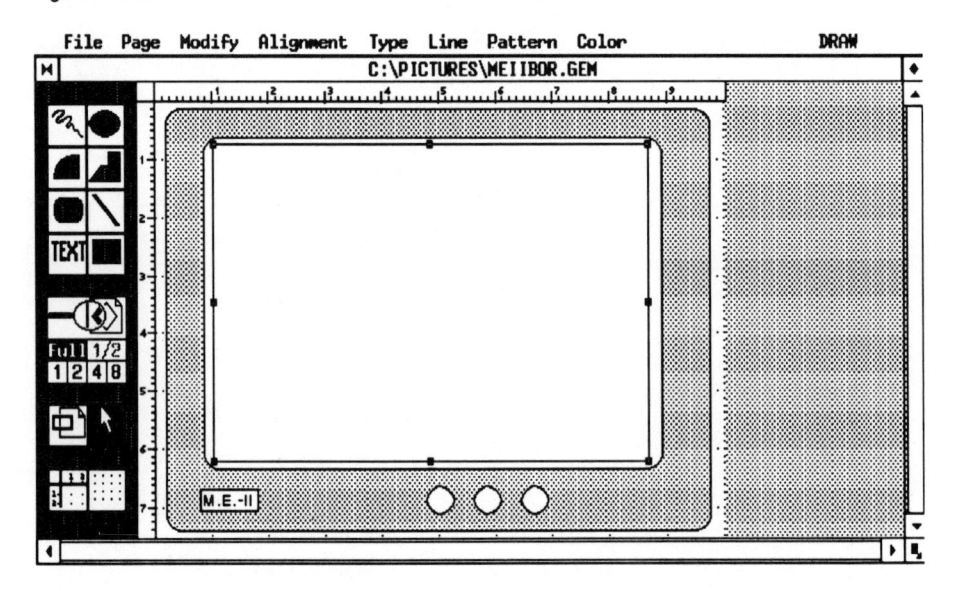

file, when you save it WordChart will overwrite the .GEM file you modified. To prevent this from happening, rename the .GEM file.

If you are going to use the borders that come with the GEM Draw Business Library, you'll need to modify them before WordChart can use them. First, you'll need to delete the nice fat file name that was placed in the drawing. The idea behind the file name is that if you Output it to the printer or the screen, the file name will be visible on the drawing. Second, you'll need to add the color 0 locator rectangle and move it to the back.

Borders with file names beginning with "P" are in the /LIBRARY/BORDERS/PORTRAIT directory. Borders with file names beginning with "L" are in the /LIBRARY/BORDERS/LANDSCAP directory. Both directories come with the GEM Draw Business Library from Digital Research. The file names beginning with "L_" or "P_" are found in the /BORDERS directory and are installed with WordChart.

Happy charting!

CHAPTER 12

GEM Write, the Original GEM Word Processor

PLUSES AND MINUSES	204
GETTING STARTED	205
MOUSE TECHNIQUES	207
PULL-DOWN MENUS	208
USING THE RULER	218
INSERT	219
SECRETS WITHIN	219
DOT-DOT COMMANDS	222

PLUSES AND MINUSES

GEM Write was the first GEM word processor and was designed to handle most mundane word processing tasks. That doesn't mean, however, that you should sneer at it. It was easy to use, had enough power to do most word processing assignments, and could integrate text and graphics. Its major drawbacks were: 1) no integrated spelling checker, 2) no mailing list program, and 3) no ability to handle multiple files.

I talk about GEM Write in the past tense because Digital Research tells me they won't be packaging and selling it anymore. But that doesn't mean you might not get a brand-new package from someone like AMSTRAD.

Actually, GEM Write wasn't a Digital Research product (but then, neither is GEM 1st Word Plus). Write was based on LifeTree Software's Volkswriter Deluxe. Sorry Volkswriter fans, the commands you know won't work.

Something you may not know: GEM Write will respond to nearly all of the WordStar command set. Don't bother looking in the manual; the WordStar similarity isn't documented anywhere. I discovered it because WordStar was second nature to me. I would just punch in WordStar commands from habit without realizing I was in GEM Write. To my surprise, the commands worked.

Because GEM Write integrates text and graphics, you can use it as a simple desktop publishing program. It's great for reports, proposals, and the like. Its limitations for publishing are:

- Single column output only.

- No graphics scaling or cropping; graphics must be created at the proper size.

- Only one laser font: Courier. This is a fixed-width font that looks like 10-pitch daisywheel output.

For many jobs, the above limitations aren't a problem. And the font limitation, in particular, is offset a bit because you can access bold, italic, and underline attributes.

GEM Write is a true what-you-see-is-what-you-get word processor. This applies to all of its functions. You can see the font attributes (bold, italic, etc.). Graphics display exactly as they will appear when printed. The only exception is justified text, which still appears as ragged right on the screen. In addition to standard text editing features, GEM Write provides a few embedded page formatting commands: the "dot-dot" commands. You just type ".." at the beginning of a new line, followed by the proper command, and you can call up a bevy of features:

- Force page breaks
- Comments that won't print
- Running headers and footers
- Reset page numbers
- Stop printing at a given page
- Send control sequence to the printer
- Include graphics file (although it's easier to let GEM Write do this one for you).

An important point to remember: GEM Write uses its own document format, with its own control codes. But it also has a nondocument mode that allows you to load ASCII files (such as program listings). Since most word processors also have an ASCII file mode, this gives you a way to move other word processor files into GEM Write. The nondocument mode also works quite well with the .ASC files created by GEM Desktop Publisher.

GETTING STARTED

You can open GEM Write in one of two ways:

1. Double click on the Write Icon. This will open GEM Write and display a blank page.
2. Double click on an associated Write file (by default these have a .DOC extension). I've used the Configure application . . . dialog box under Options (available at the Desktop) to add more extensions. Just put the mouse cursor on the first blank line beside Document types: and click. Use the tab key to go to the next entry line.

   I've found the following additional extensions useful: DOC, WRT, TXT, and ASC. These cover most of the document types I use with GEM Write. The .WRT extension is one I've used to keep from confusing GEM Write files with files from other word processors. Microsoft Word and Multimate use .DOC. The .TXT and .ASC extensions cover the usual ASCII file conventions. The .ME file is for those inevitable READ.ME files that accompany software.

When you open GEM Write for the very first time, it asks for your name and system configuration. Your name (or whatever you enter on this line) will appear when you pull GEM Write Info down. Click on the disk drive combinations that apply to your computer, and then click on OK (or press Return).

GEM Write has one of the best mouse interfaces available in a PC word processor. If you are familiar with a nonmouse-based word processor, you'll love how easy GEM Write is to use. Note that there is both a mouse pointer and a text cursor. They move independently, though you can position the text pointer with the mouse pointer.

TOPOGRAPHY

When you enter GEM Write, you'll find the usual screen full of goodies. The center of the screen is the work area. See Figure 12.1. In it you'll see either the veritable (and frightening) blank page or the beginning of the file you've opened. If you load a non-GEM Write and non-ASCII file (such as a WordStar document file), you'll find that may of the characters are something other than letters. Abandon ship if this occurs. You'll need to convert that file to ASCII before you can use it (consult your word processor manual or local computer guru).

The status line proclaims that you're on line 1 of page 1. The current document title is displayed in the center of the title bar. The text cursor is at column 1, and the mouse pointer can be practically anywhere.

Figure 12.1

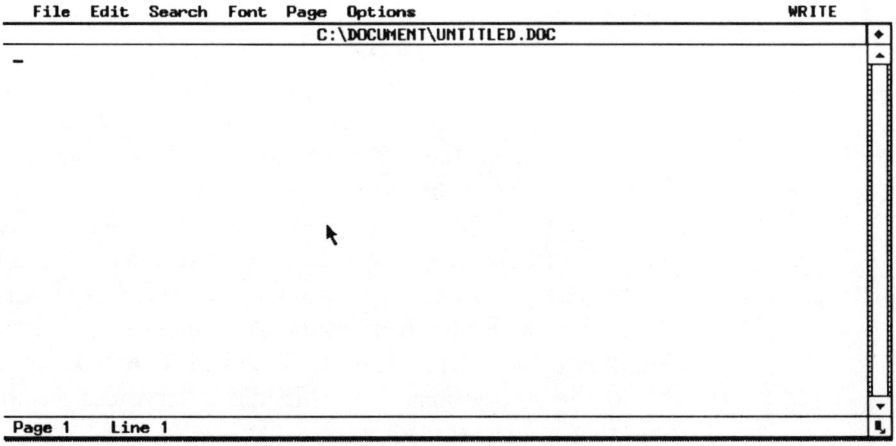

Note the slider in the scroll bar to the right. As your file gets bigger, the slider will get proportionately smaller until it reaches a minimum size. Don't worry, the minimum size is easy to grab and slide. You can use the slider to move forward and backward through your file.

Like all GEM applications, the size box and full box are available at the right. These are practically useless in Write, however, because you can have only one document open at any given time.

MOUSE TECHNIQUES

GEM Write has two mouse techniques that you'll use with text. One involves positioning the text cursor with the mouse cursor. Point the mouse pointer where you want the text cursor to be and click. The second technique involves "swiping," and you use that to select text. Put the mouse pointer at the beginning of the text you want to select, and then click and hold. Drag the mouse cursor to the right (and down if you like) to select text. As text is selected, it will reverse to white on black. See Figure 12.2.

There is a somewhat tricky way to select one complete line. Put the mouse pointer to that little bit of space at the left of the beginning of the line. Now click and hold for a moment. If all goes well, the line will reverse. See Figure 12.3. I have trouble with this one, but I must admit practice helps.

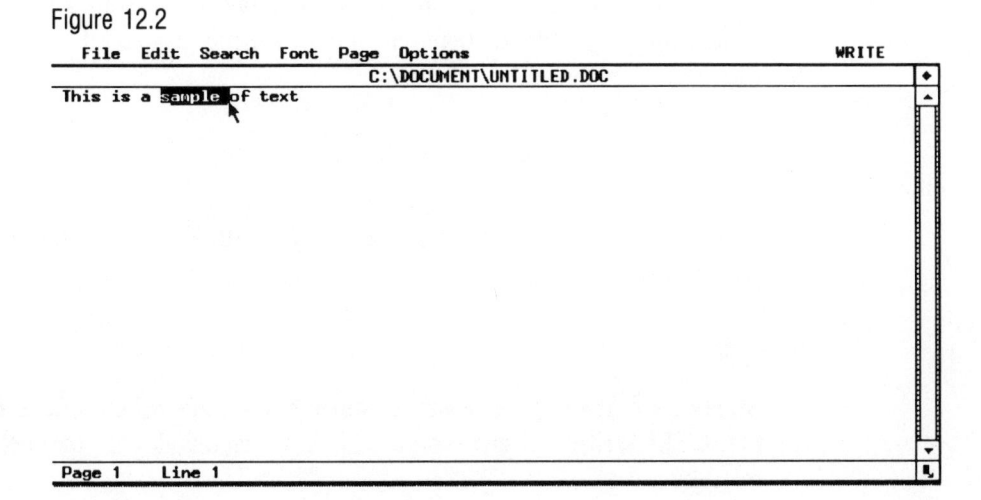

Figure 12.2

Figure 12.3

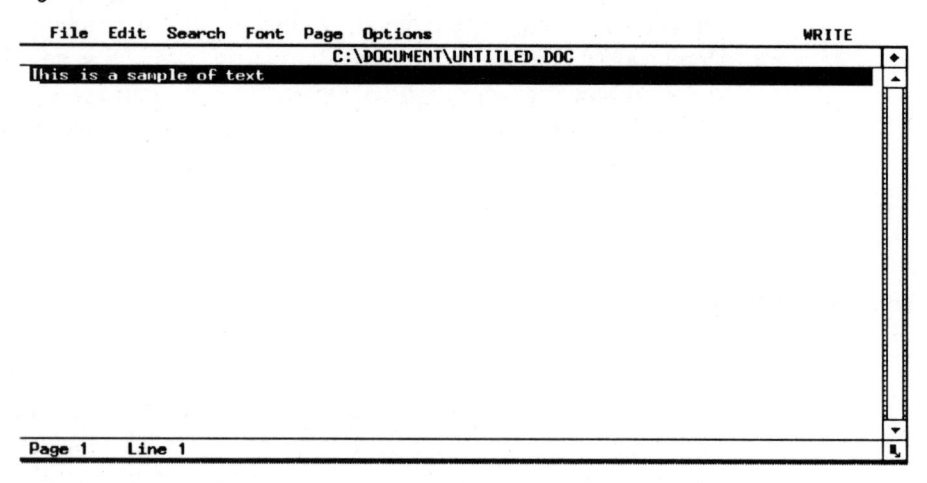

```
 File   Edit  Search  Font  Page  Options                          WRITE
                             C:\DOCUMENT\UNTITLED.DOC
 This is a sample of text




 Page 1    Line 1
```

PULL-DOWN MENUS

GEM Write was a very early PC word processor to use pull-down menus, and it uses them well. You can run almost all of the word processing functions from the pull-downs, and never need to learn the keyboard control codes.

The following listing briefly describes the functions and dialog boxes in the pull-down menus. By the way, you'll find that the pull-down menus list any keyboard commands. The diamond means the Alt key, the caret translates as the Control key, and the arrow pointing up refers to the shift key. Following the description of the pull-down menus, you'll find a table of all the control codes.

FILE

As the name implies, this menu deals with all of the file-handling functions. See Figure 12.4.

New

Starts over. It provides a way to get a blank page when you're done with a file. GEM Write will give you a chance to reconsider if you click on this by mistake.

Figure 12.4

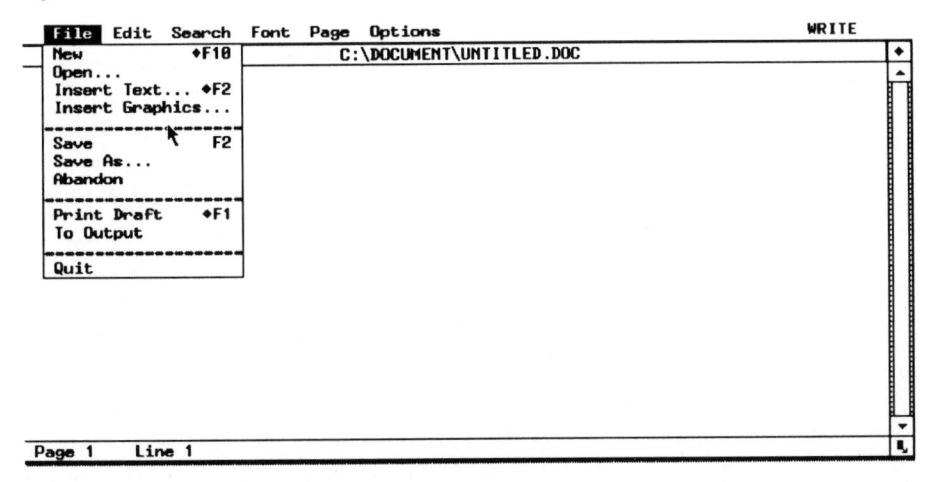

```
 File  Edit  Search  Font  Page  Options                           WRITE
 New         ♦F10              C:\DOCUMENT\UNTITLED.DOC
 Open...
 Insert Text... ♦F2
 Insert Graphics...
 ------------------
 Save          F2
 Save As...
 Abandon
 ------------------
 Print Draft  ♦F1
 To Output
 ------------------
 Quit

 Page 1    Line 1
```

Open

Calls up the GEM file selector so you can open a file. Again, if you haven't saved the file you were working on, GEM Write gives you a chance to cancel and save your file.

You can use the file selector to open any file, even a .COM or .EXE file (don't do that, though; it will likely cause the computer to have a minor seizure). To change the file type from the default .DOC, click on the line with the directory and file mask (the *.DOC). You can now type in any directory, file mask, or file name if you want to be that specific.

Insert Text . . .

Do this after you've placed the cursor where you want to drop in the text file. Once you've selected the text file, it will plop down wherever the text cursor is.

Insert Graphics . . .

This is the one that separates GEM Write from nearly every other word processor. Place the cursor on the line you want the graphic to start on; then select this option. The GEM file selector will appear, allowing you to find and select the graphic you want to include.

GEM Write can only read files with the .GEM extension. When inserting a GEM Paint file, don't reference the .IMG file. Instead, GEM Paint makes a separate .GEM file, which has nothing in it but points to the proper image file.

Graphics will always come in at the size and position they appear in the graphic file. If something is two inches high and in the middle of the drawing or painting canvas, it will arrive as a two-inch graphic centered between the margins.

If you want to erase a graphic, first use Turn Graphics Off under Page. Now select the entire graphic area with the mouse, including the ..GEM line and the lines in gray (or beginning with a dot). Delete them as you would text. You can't put text on any line that contains a graphic (actually you can, but it won't print). A graphic always takes up at least one complete line (margin to margin). You must also watch out for page breaks. You can split a graphic over two pages if it falls on a break.

You can move the graphic down to the next page by inserting lines above it or using the ..PAGE command (explained in the dot-dot command section).

Save

Saves the file. If you haven't selected a file name, GEM will ask you for one.

Save As . . .

You can save your current file to another file name. If you have any selected text, it will be saved to the file name you specify. This gives you a way to mark off sections of your document and save them to separate files.

Abandon

Drops everything and brings back the last saved version of the file (if any). A welcome function if you, like I, sometimes really mess things up.

Print Draft

A very handy printing option. Clicking on this will print the document as fast as your printer can go. You won't get text attributes like bold and italic—nor any pictures—but you will get headers, footers, and the like.

Print Draft starts printing at the current text cursor position. If you don't want to print your entire file, put the cursor on the starting point you want. You can type a ..END command at the beginning of a line just beyond the point you want printing to stop. You can also stop it by pressing Escape, but that isn't as accurate.

To Output

This one gives you three choices. Behind choice number one, Write zips off to the Output application. A version of your file with an .OUT extension will be loaded into the Output List. If you have Output set for Auto display, the file will begin to print.

Behind choice number two, GEM Write will set up an output (.OUT) file, but won't exit to the Output application. This will let you print the document later.

Choice number three allows you to back out gracefully if you triggered To Output by accident.

Quit

Back to the Desktop. If you haven't saved your file, GEM Write will give you one last chance.

EDIT

These are all text editing or block functions. See Figure 12.5.

Insert Line

Inserts one blank line at the current cursor position.

Figure 12.5

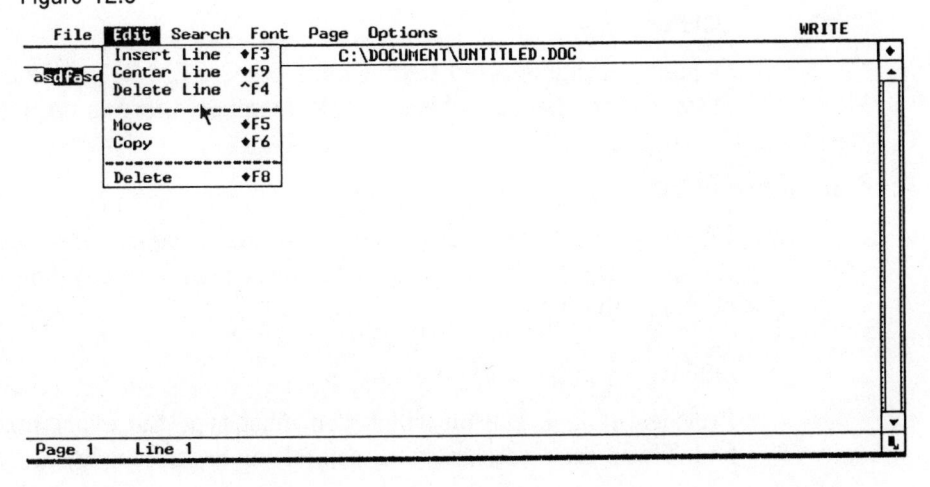

Delete Line

Deletes the line that the text cursor is on. As there is no undelete, don't do this frivolously.

Center Line

Centers the text on the line that the text cursor is on. Text will center between the right and left ruler margins.

Move

Works with selected text only. After you select Move, the mouse pointer will change shape and become an "I-beam." If you use GEM Desktop Publisher or Ventura Publisher, you've seen the I-beam before.

Position the I-beam at the point you want the selected text to move to, and then click. If you hold the mouse button down, the I-beam turns into a vertical bar. You can position this vertical bar anywhere on the screen, and when you release the mouse button, this becomes the Move point.

If you use the slider bar to move to the place where you want to position the text, you'll cancel the Move function. Once the mouse pointer changes from the I-beam, Move is turned off. What you need to do is select the text, move to the place you want it, and then call up the Move function.

Copy

Basically the same as Move, except that the selected text stays where it is and a copy of the selected text is inserted at the I-beam position.

Delete

Obliterates the selected text. Unlike other GEM delete functions, this one gives you no chance to back out. Remember, there is no undelete.

SEARCH AND REPLACE

Like any good word processor, GEM Write has search and replace functions. It can also jump to any page (document mode) or any line (nondocument mode) in the file.

Find

Provides a blank line on which you must type the exact text you want to find. This means watching your capital and lower-case letters. As Find jumps through the file, the slider bar at the right of the screen gives you a quick gauge of where you are. Note that it will jump back to the beginning of the file after it reaches the end, and then start the search all over.

Find can also look around for control characters. Just enter the control character in the find string. Commonly used control characters in GEM Write are:

Control-T	End of paragraph
Control-R	Beginning and end of bold
Control-]	Beginning and end of italic
Control-_	Beginning and end of underscore

Replace

Similar to Find, except that you can specify text to replace whatever you find. Again, you must be exact in your use of upper and lower case.

The Replace all option (see Figure 12.6) selects whether GEM should replace all occurrences that match the find text or just the first. If you do these one at a time, GEM Write works like this: The first time it finds the text, it puts the cursor at the text beginning and stops. Selecting Replace Next makes it replace the text. The next time you select Replace Next, it finds the next occurrence of text and replaces it without pausing.

Like Find, Replace can also use control characters. For instance, you can make Bob into **Bob**. For the replacement text, just enter a Control-R before and after Bob.

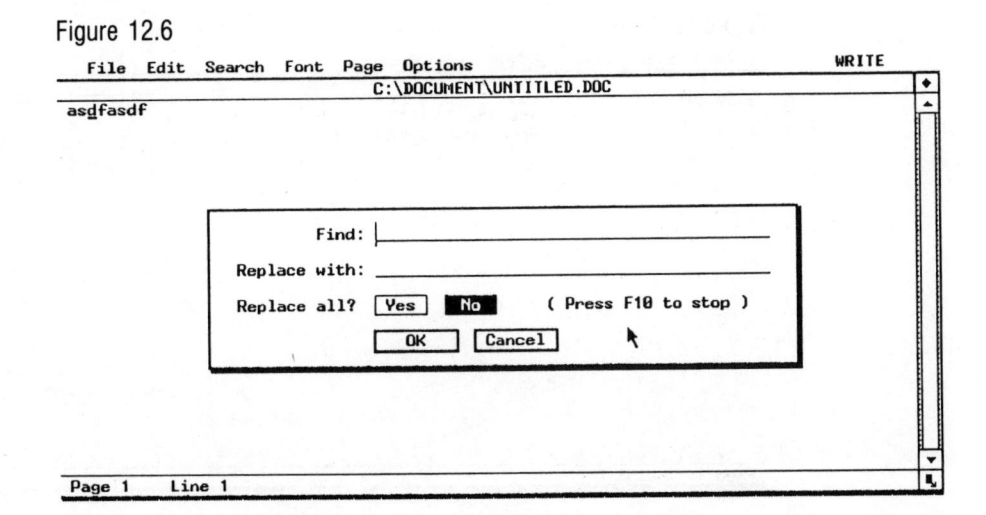

Figure 12.6

Find Next

Go to the next occurrence of the text.

Replace Next

Replace the next occurrence of the text.

Go To . . .

No, it's not where you think. It's go to a specific page (or line in the nondocument mode).

FONT

These really need very little explanation. Just select the text with the mouse (it reverses), and then click on the font you want. See Figure 12.7. Normal undoes all other fonts. If you enter the keyboard command for a font attribute, remember that you must enter it again where you want the attribute to end. If you don't, it will run to the end of the paragraph (which always cancels font attributes).

PAGE

Page controls miscellaneous options.

Figure 12.7

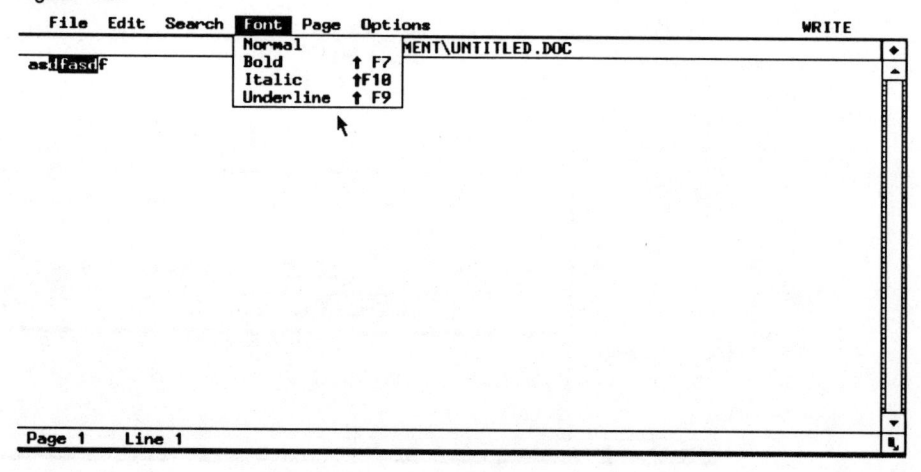

Turn Graphics OFF/ON

OFF shows graphics files as a gray area. Why bother? It takes GEM Write a while to write graphics to the screen, which can be quite disturbing when you're intent on editing text. This is a toggle, meaning it switches between on and off each time it's selected.

Turn Auto-Reformat OFF/ON

Another toggle. When OFF, GEM Write won't automatically even up the lines if you add copy to a paragraph. It will, however, still wrap to the next line automatically. When ON, GEM Write will automatically balance paragraph lines.

Turn Insert Mode OFF/ON

Toggles between a flashing underline cursor that writes over anything in its path (OFF) and a flashing bar that pushes text along as you type (ON). Regardless of how you set this, it will always eventually—and mysteriously—turn itself off.

Show Ruler

Pops the tab and margin ruler onto the top of the text area or removes it.

Set Tabs & Margins

Temporarily pops the ruler on, allowing you to set tabs and margins. OK saves your changes; Cancel doesn't.

FORMAT

Set the document format before you do anything else. Do this first because formats are easier to set than to re-do. Setting the document format the way you want it initially can save you considerable reformatting time later. If you're loading an ASCII file, setting to nondocument mode before you edit can save you from abandoning your changes and reloading the file.

GEM Write has its own end of paragraph marker. If GEM Write is in document mode, and the file you load doesn't have Control-T's marking the ends of paragraphs, it will turn the entire document into one big glob of text.

Set the document format as follows:

Document mode

On if you are creating or editing a GEM Write document. Off for an ASCII file. See Figure 12.8.

Pagination

On if you want your document broken into pages; off if you are creating an ASCII file such as a source code for a program.

Justification

I suggest you set this off. Since GEM Write doesn't have a hyphenation utility, the justified text may have wide spaces between words. On the other hand, if you are typing 65 characters to a line (normal for letters), the lack of hyphenation won't be much of a liability and justified text won't look too bad.

Line spacing

A great and easy way to double and triple space on demand. Set to one for normal spacing. Set to two or three if you are typing a draft to be edited (providing lots of room for comments between lines).

Page length

Normally no need to reset this. A setting of 66 is standard for most printers. You can, however, set it any way you like.

Figure 12.8

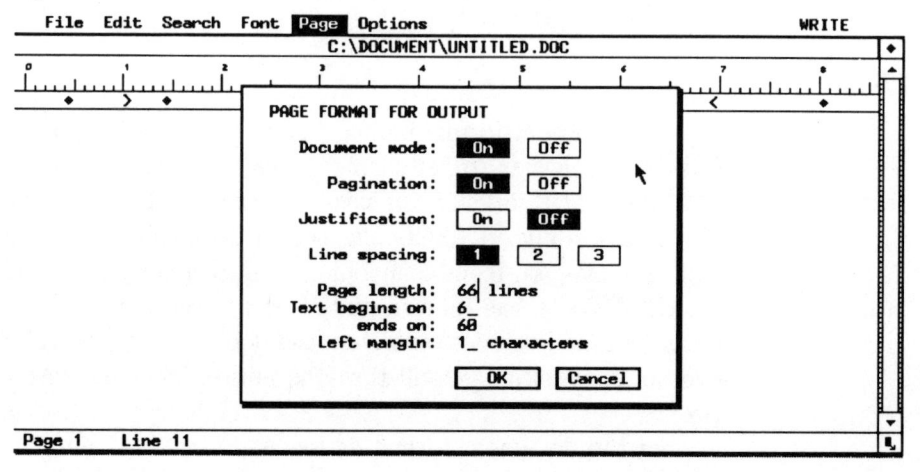

Text begins on . . .

The number of lines skipped from the top. The default setting skips six lines (one inch) from the top. You might want to increase this if you are using letterhead stationery.

Text ends on . . .

The number of lines skipped at the bottom. The default gives you six lines (one inch).

Left margin

This setting won't show in the on-screen ruler. It measures from the position of the first character, not the left edge of the paper (you do, of course, set the right margin with the ruler). The default of 10 gives you a left margin that is a bit over 1½ inches, which is fine for most printouts.

Click on OK when you're done setting the format. Then when you save your GEM Write file, GEM Write will create a companion file with an .INF extension. This companion file contains the default information set through the Format menu, the dialog box, and the ruler.

OPTIONS

Short Cuts . . .

A quick pop-up guide to the standard keyboard control characters used in GEM Write.

Set Preferences . . .

This one is important: It sets defaults for the program. Turn Graphics ON/OFF and Turn Auto-Reformat ON/OFF are the same as the selections under Page. This sets the state they'll be in when you start GEM Write. See Figure 12.9.

Create *.BAK files ON/OFF automatically turns the previously saved version of your file into a backup (.BAK extension) when you save a file. Don't do this if you have a floppy-based system because you'll eat up double the disk space with text files.

Delete *.OUT files ON/OFF automatically deletes your output files after printing through Output. This makes it impossible to go back to Output later for another print unless you first go to GEM Write and make one. It does save on disk space, however, if you have a floppy-based system. The

Figure 12.9

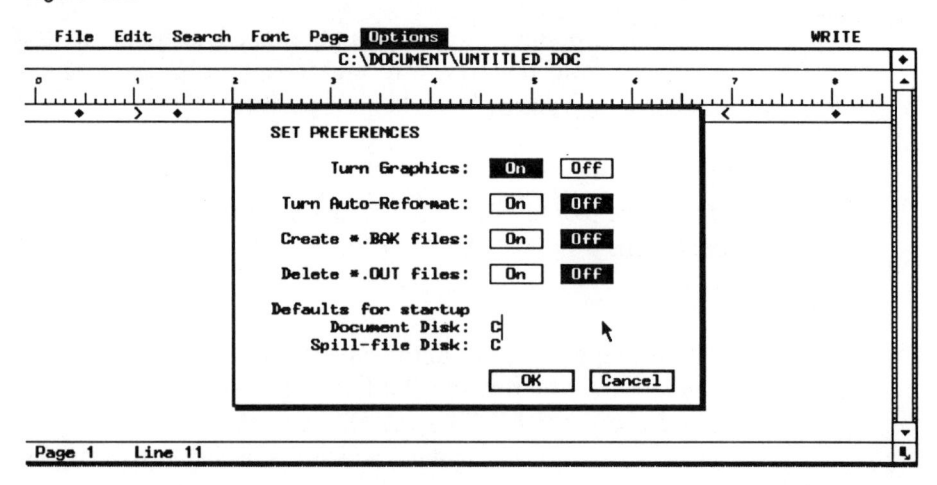

```
 File   Edit   Search   Font   Page  Options                              WRITE
                        C:\DOCUMENT\UNTITLED.DOC
```

            SET PREFERENCES
                Turn Graphics: [On] [OFF]
              Turn Auto-Reformat: [On] [OFF]
              Create *.BAK files: [On] [OFF]
              Delete *.OUT files: [On] [OFF]
              Defaults for startup
                  Document Disk: C
                  Spill-file Disk: C
                                    [OK] [Cancel]

    Page 1   Line 11

Document Disk is where GEM Write will go for documents. You should select your hard drive letter if you have one.

Likewise, set Spill-file Disk for your hard drive if you can. When a file gets so large that GEM Write can't hold it in memory, it shuffles some of it off to disk.

USING THE RULER

Aside from the Format . . . dialog box, you do most GEM Write page formatting with the ruler. Personally, I like this. You can see what you've done, where the margins are, and where tabs are set. You can also use the ruler to format such niceties as hanging indents. By the way, metric lovers, GEM Write stodgily refuses to budge from the English system. It's inches or nothing. See Figure 12.10.

When you put the mouse pointer into the ruler area, it changes into a hand with a pointing finger. This cute little visual aid means you can now change ruler settings. Margins slide right or left and are marked with greater than and less than signs. Tabs are diamonds, and they can be turned off and on. To move a margin, put the mouse pointer over it and click and hold. You can now slide it back and forth. Release it when you have it in position. Setting and unsetting a tab is as simple as positioning the mouse pointer and clicking.

Figure 12.10

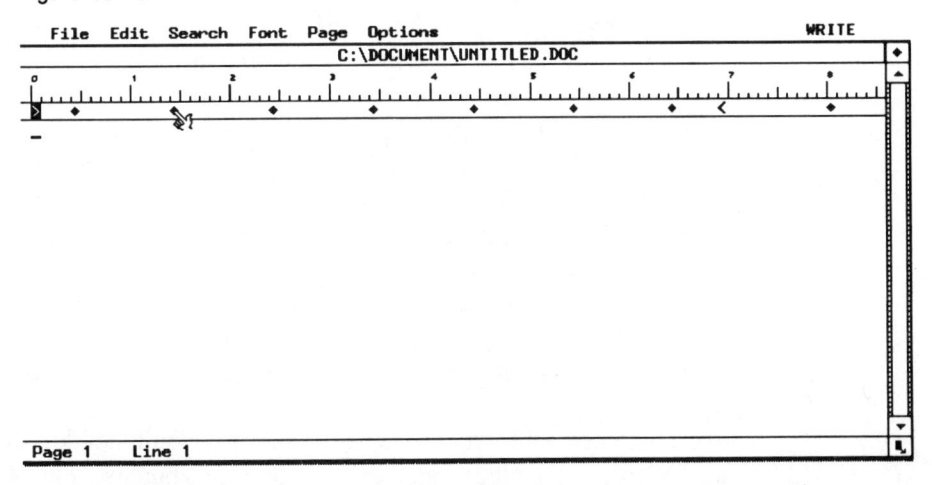

```
File  Edit  Search  Font  Page  Options                              WRITE
                           C:\DOCUMENT\UNTITLED.DOC
```

Page 1   Line 1

The black band on the ruler marks the current cursor position. I like to have the ruler on while I type, chiefly because of this band and the visible tab settings. Line and page figures are visible on the status line at the bottom of the screen.

INSERT

Something many of us find different in GEM Write: It defaults to insert off. This means that when you go to add text to a document, it overwrites any existing text as you type. Most word processors default to insert on. You can turn insert on, but GEM Write will turn it off when you least expect it. It's obstinate about this. It does, however, give a visual indication of what mode it's in. A flashing underline cursor means insert is off. A flashing vertical bar cursor means that it's on.

Still, being an old WordStar freak (where insert stays where you set it), I find myself caught off guard occasionally when using GEM Write. You can toggle insert on and off either with the Ins key or by clicking on Turn Insert Mode On under the Page pull-down menu. Either way, it will eventually turn itself off.

SECRETS WITHIN

If you press Control-F3, GEM Write displays the control characters embedded in your file. Not only can you see the control characters, but you can delete them. If you find GEM Write behaving oddly, it usually means that a control character crept into your file. You can root it out with this option. The only drawback to operating in this mode is that you can't select text.

You can also enter control characters directly in your text. You might have occasion to do this, especially if you're using GEM Write to create text for a GEM publishing package. Publishing packages, because they usually use proportionally spaced type fonts, do odd and terrible things to tables. Most word processors throw in spaces when you press the Tab key. If you put your tables together with these pseudo-tabs, they will look like they suffered through an earthquake when loaded into the publishing package. You can minimize such distortions by using real tab characters instead of spaces to line up columns. GEM Write displays a real tab as a little clock face.

To embed a control character in the file, you'll need to know its decimal equivalent. I've included an ASCII table in this book so you can look up these equivalents. Tab, for instance, is decimal 9. To insert a character, follow this procedure:

1. Put the text cursor where you want the control character.
2. Hold down the Alt key.
3. Type in the decimal equivalent of the control code using the numeric keypad.
4. Release the Alt key.

THE WORDSTAR CONNECTION

If you're familiar with WordStar, you're going to love this. If not, you can go get a cup of coffee and skip this part.

Most WordStar commands work in GEM Write. A few do some very un-WordStar things, but as a rule all the cursor movement and deletion commands work as expected. Although none of the printer commands (prefaced by Control-P) work, the rest of the command set is fairly well represented. In the following section you'll find the native GEM Write command as well as the WordStar command if it works.

KEYBOARD COMMANDS

If you take the time to learn these commands, you'll be able to run GEM Write faster. If you already know the WordStar command set, browse through to see what works. You might want to make a copy of this list and keep it handy. To get a complete set of keyboard commands, you need to use a combination of both the GEM function key commands and the WordStar commands.

Function	GEM Write	WordStar
Cursor left	Left arrow	Control-D
Cursor right	Right arrow	Control-S
Cursor up	Up arrow	Control-E
Cursor down	Down arrow	Control-X
Cursor left one word	Control-left arrow	Control-A
Cursor right one word	Control-right arrow	Control-F
Cursor to beginning/end of line	F3	
Scroll up	PgUp	Control-R
Scroll down	PgDn	Control-C
Cursor to top of screen	Home	
Cursor to bottom of screen	End	
Cursor to top of file	Control-Home	Control-Q Control-R
Cursor to bottom of file	Control-End	Control-Q Control-C
Delete character	Del	Control-G
Delete word	F4	Control-T
Delete to end of line	Alt-F4	
Delete line	Control-F4	Control-Y
Insert line	Alt-F3	Control-N
Toggle insert mode	Ins	Control-V
Center line	Alt-F9	Control-O Control-C
Reformat paragraph	F8	Control-B
Find	Control-Q	Control-F
Replace	Control-Q	Control-A
Find again	F7	Control-L
Replace again	Alt-F7	Control-L
Go to page/line	Control-F7	
Start text selection	F5	
End text selection	F6	
Move selected text	Alt-F5	

Function	GEM Write	WordStar
Copy selected text	Alt-F6	
Delete selected text	Alt-F8	
Save file and stay in Write	F2	Control-K Control-S
Save file and exit document		Control-K Control-D
Abandon file		Control-K Control-Q
New file	Alt-F10	
Insert text in file	Alt-F2	
Begin/end bold face	Shift-F7	
Begin/end italic	Shift-F10	
Begin/end underline	Shift-F9	
Format dialog box	Control-F1	
Print draft	Alt-F1	

DOT-DOT COMMANDS

GEM Write uses embedded commands for advanced formatting. These are the "dot-dot" commands, so named because they are prefaced by two periods. Dot-dot commands don't really take up a line in your document, so they won't affect the way the document looks. The commands are always entered as: ..command. They must be at the beginning of a line to work.

Here are descriptions of GEM Write's dot-dot commands:

..CMD

Although a little complicated to use, this one can be a lifesaver at times. This command lets you send any control sequence you want to the printer. For instance, you can turn on near letter quality mode or select 12 pitch type. The catch is that you must enter the codes as their ASCII decimal equivalents (yes, those again). Enter these by holding down the Alt key and typing the decimal number on the keypad. Control codes will display as graphics characters (triangles, arrows, etc.). Check the table for the ASCII decimal set and your printer manual for its control codes.

Since I have a printer that emulates an IBM graphics printer (and since that is supported by GEM), we'll use the IBM graphics printer code set for an example. The code ..CMDAlt12Alt15 will advance the printer to the next sheet of paper and command it to print in condensed mode (17 characters to the inch). The Alt12 is the ASCII decimal equivalent for a form feed.

The Alt15 is the decimal equivalent for the "shift in" control character, which puts the printer in the condensed mode. Note that there are no spaces between the ..CMD, the Alt12, and the Alt15.

..END

Stops printing at this point. This works for both draft and Output printing.

..GEM

This is the command GEM Write embeds when you bring in a drawing or image. The number following the GEM is the number of lines your graphic will take up. Remember that the graphic is brought in at its exact size. If you reduce this number, it has the effect of cropping from the bottom up. Following the size is the drive, page, and file name that identifies the file.

..FOOT and ..HEAD

The controls running headers and footers. They are fairly sophisticated, allowing flush left, flush right, centered, and alternating left and right headers. You can also tell GEM Write what line to print the header or footer on.

The syntax (almost sounds like programming doesn't it?) is: ..HEAD (or FOOT) 11Xyour text. The 11 is a two-digit line number (e.g., 03 for 3). The X is a control character. The control characters are:

A Alternating flush right and flush left headers and footers. They switch back and forth on odd and even numbered pages.
R The header or footer is always flush right.
L The header or footer is always flush left.
C Centers the header or footer.

If you want to get fancy and put the page number in the header or footer, enter "##." GEM Write will check the current page number and substitute it for the double number signs.

If you want to get rid of a header or footer, just enter a command with only the line number. For instance, ..HEADER01 will blow away a header that was running on line one.

..PAGE

Forces a page break. This is very useful for keeping a graphic from breaking over a page (who wants half of a picture on one page and half on another?).

..PGNO

This one resets the page number. If you've broken a chapter into two files and the second file really starts with page 27, this command will fix the problem. Just enter: ..PGNO27 ..whatever.

In addition, you can type comments that won't print. For example, you can leave yourself reminders, dates for revisions, etc. Just type whatever you want after the dot-dot. Of course, if you type a genuine dot-dot command, it will execute.

CHAPTER

13

GEM 1st Word Plus: Professional Editing Power for GEM

A TOOL FOR WORDSMITHS?	226
IN THE FOYER	227
INTO THE FILE	228
PULL-DOWN MENUS	231
SPELLING	245
GRAPHICS	247
HELP	249
KEYBOARD COMMANDS	250

A TOOL FOR WORDSMITHS?

Whew! Was I glad to see this one. Let's face it, as cute as GEM Write was, it was not a tool for wordsmiths. I tried and tried to use it, but I'd always give up and go to a more feature-packed program that had an integrated spelling checker. As a result, most of this book was originally written with WordStar Professional 4.0. I had to give up the smoother integration with GEM and mouse support to get the job done.

Then along came 1st Word Plus, and life suddenly got a lot easier.

A word of caution here: 1st Word Plus is a serviceable word processor, quite capable of handling almost any word processing task. In its original release, however, it is not as powerful as some of the leading contenders in the word processing market. But it's not nearly as expensive either. I decided to put it to the test by using it to finish this book. It never let me down. Moreover, its ability to have multiple files open *and* on the screen has been a tremendous help.

Some things that release 2.0 can't do:

- It cannot do multiple columns (such as in a newspaper) on-screen. There is a multiple-column mode in the mailmerge package, but it's a bit cumbersome to use.

- It can't control true, proportionally spaced type fonts. Forget about using Swiss, Dutch, Charter, or University Roman. 1st Word Plus can access only the Courier font in your laser printer. It *can*, though, do weird and wonderful things with the Courier font. (If you are a PostScript whiz, you can access other fonts by changing your printer's default font from Courier to something else. This is satisfactory, however, only if you stay away from justified text, as 1st Word Plus doesn't know about proportional spacing).

- It doesn't have a built-in thesaurus. To me this is a minor annoyance, but maybe you really like that feature. It also doesn't have macro capability, which I really do find annoying. If you are using your word processor to provide text for your desktop publishing package, then you'll want to be able to call up the formatting codes with a couple of keystrokes.

If these features are critical to you, find another word processor. On the other hand, nothing short of WordPerfect can provide the kind of graphics integration that you get with 1st Word Plus. Even WordPerfect doesn't provide such a what-you-see-is-what-you-get environment.

This chapter covers the commands and dialogs of the word processor itself. (Because this is a book on publishing and presentation graphics, I won't cover use of the mailmerge feature.) The following chapter discusses how to use 1st Word Plus to handle many day-to-day publishing problems without resorting to a publishing package.

IN THE FOYER

When you open 1st Word Plus, you find yourself in a no open file area. The program will offer to open a file for you, but for now just cancel that.

Think of this area as a foyer, from which you can enter all sorts of rooms. The set of characters in the center of the screen is the complete set of GEM characters, including special symbols. See Figure 13.1. The rectangles along the bottom and right correspond to the set of function keys (bottom) and special keyboard keys (right). Tap them with the mouse and they do exactly what you'd expect. Of course, you need to be in a document to see anything happen. The same goes for the character set. Tap any of those characters and 1st Word Plus will type that character.

If you know people who have a disability that prevents them from using a keyboard, tell them about 1st Word Plus. If they can move a mouse and click the left button, they can do nearly every word processing task with 1st Word Plus. They can type, change type attributes, and access dialogs all with the mouse. The only things that require keyboard entry crop up when a dialog has a text entry line.

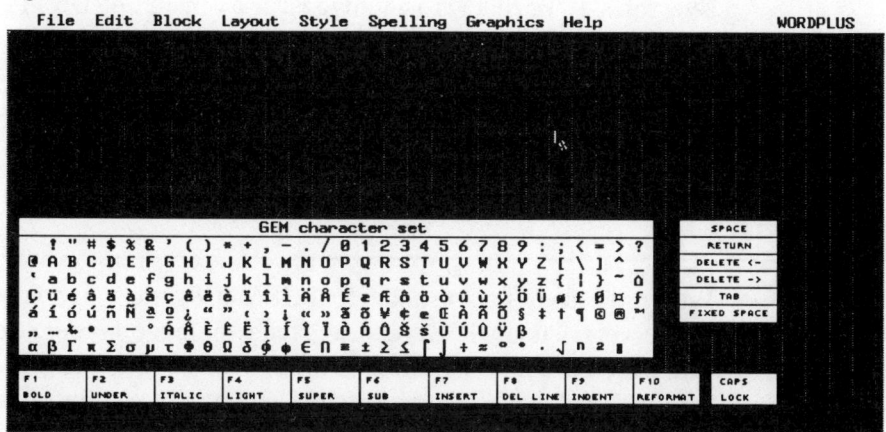

Figure 13.1

Tapping on special characters is an easy way to enter them into your text. 1st Word Plus doesn't require that you memorize the ASCII decimal counterpart for special characters. Instead, you can just pick them off the listing. Of course, die-hard coders can still access the special characters with the decimal equivalents.

At this level, most of the possibilities from any of the drop-down menus are locked out. But one important selection is available only from this point; you can't get at it from within a file. Under the Edit pull-down you'll notice a dialog marked Set Spill File. If you have a hard disk drive, setting a spill file will allow 1st Word Plus to use temporary files to hold text beyond what memory can hold. If you don't use a spill file, you won't be able to add any more text when memory fills.

You can do a few more things at this point:

- You can load the spelling dictionary. If you do this now, it will be available for use in your files. The dictionary is under the Spelling pull-down.
- You can check the Help pull-down. Actually, the Help pull-down is of minimal help, but you can play with it if you like. One interesting feature is Extra Help. If you toggle this one, 1st Word Plus will drive you bats by putting up a help window for every command you issue.
- You can load a file. This is called Open... under the File menu, and it brings up the familiar file item selector.
- You can go to Output. This is also under the File menu. You must close all open files before you can pop off to the Output application.

At this point, let's just open a file. Use Open... to pull up the files selector. 1st Word Plus will suggest a file name of UNTITLED.DOC. You can avoid this by entering whatever file name you like on the selection line. If it's a new file name, 1st Word Plus will nicely tell you that it will create a new file with that name if you like. Saying OK creates the file and opens with a blank text area.

INTO THE FILE

1st Word Plus has some additional GEM gadgets. The tall, skinny rectangle to the very left of the screen is called the page border. See Figure 13.3. The page border has a number of functions. Click the mouse anywhere in that area and you'll get a horizontal line with a number. That sets a forced page break. The number denotes the new page number under the line.

Figure 13.2

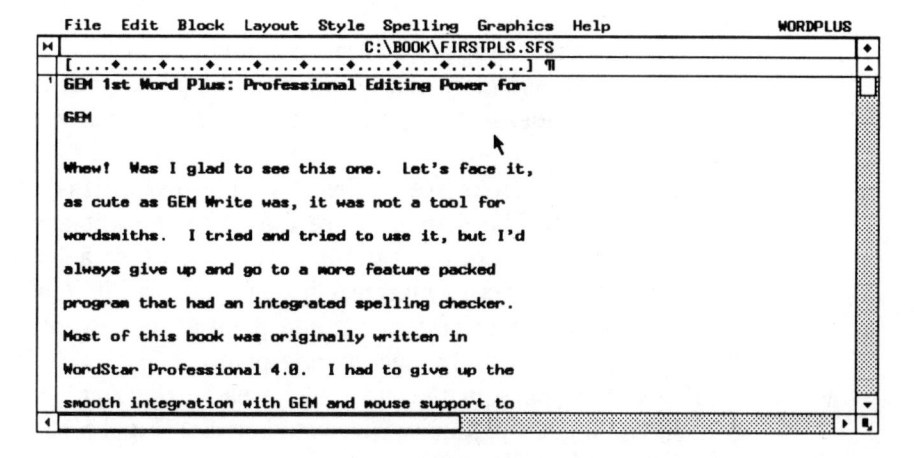

Figure 13.3

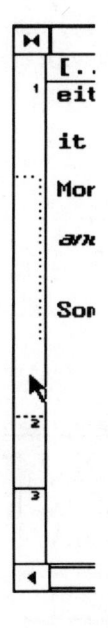

When 1st Word Plus inserts a page break on its own, it marks the break with a dashed vertical line. You can also add a conditional page. A conditional page means that if a page break should ever occur within a particular area, everything from the top of the conditional break section will jump to the next page. You can use this to protect tables, figures, and the like from being bisected by errant page breaks.

To set a conditional page area, click and pull in the extreme left area. The part that turns black marks the conditional page area. When it's the size you want, release the mouse button and the area will be marked by dotted lines.

The thing that looks like a ruler above the text area is just that: a ruler. See Figure 13.4. The diamonds are tabs, and the left and right brackets are margin settings. Click on a dot to set a tab; click on a diamond to remove one. If you want to move a margin, click and hold over it. You'll get a pointing finger cursor showing that you can now point at its new location. Releasing the mouse button sets the new margin point.

If you click once in the ruler bar area to the right of the paragraph symbol, you'll get the modify ruler window. See Figure 13.5. This lets you set all sorts of useful things:

- Under pitch, pica sets 10 characters to the inch, elite selects 12, condensed selects 17, and expanded selects six to the inch. Strangely enough, this also works with laser printers. You'll get various versions of Courier, with expanded print suitably sized for headings.

Figure 13.4

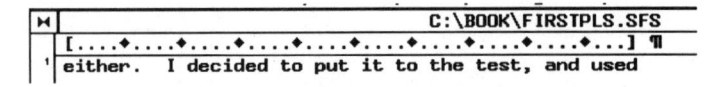

Figure 13.5

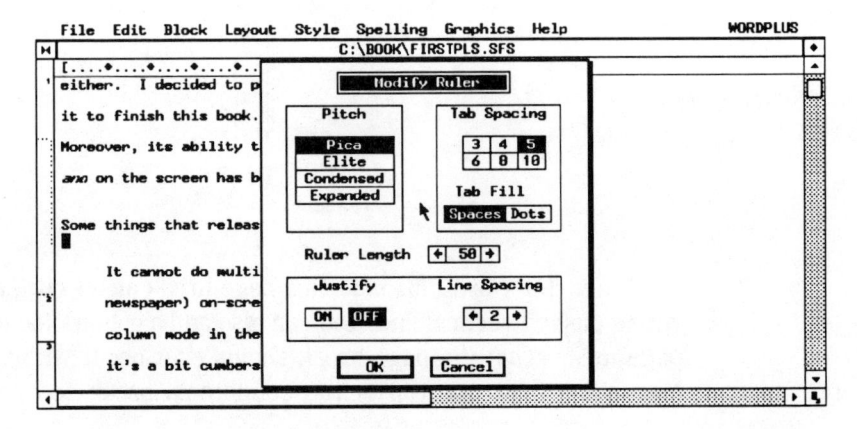

- Tab spacing lets you select the number of spaces between the automatically set tab stops. You can still set stops wherever you want, no matter what setting you choose here.
- Tab fill refers to the type of characters to use between tabs. Spaces simply pads spaces between each tab you enter, while dots uses periods as leaders.
- Ruler length provides another way of setting the ruler. Click on the right arrow to increase the length, the left arrow to decrease the length.
- Justify either turns right justification on or off. Watch this, as it doesn't do a really pretty job of justifying text (remember that 1st Word Plus doesn't know anything about proportional spacing).
- Line spacing sets the number of lines skipped between each line of text.

If you turn off the WP mode (check the explanation under the Edit pull-down), then the Modify Ruler window only sets the tab spacing and the ruler width.

PULL-DOWN MENUS

Being a proficient word processor, 1st Word Plus has quite a few commands. These are all available from the pull-down menus (as well as from keyboard control sequences, which are listed at the end of this chapter). Having all these commands available from the pull-down menus is a big help when you're learning the word processor, as they are grouped by function.

FILE

One of the richest file menus in a GEM program. See Figure 13.6. The File menu in 1st Word Plus offers the following selections:

Open . . .

Pops up the file selector so that you can open a file. 1st Word Plus allows four files open simultaneously, so you can just keep opening files until you reach the limit. Each additional file will get its own window, which you can size and position with the full box and mouse grabbing techniques.

Save and Close

Does just what it says. It closes only the active file window.

Figure 13.6

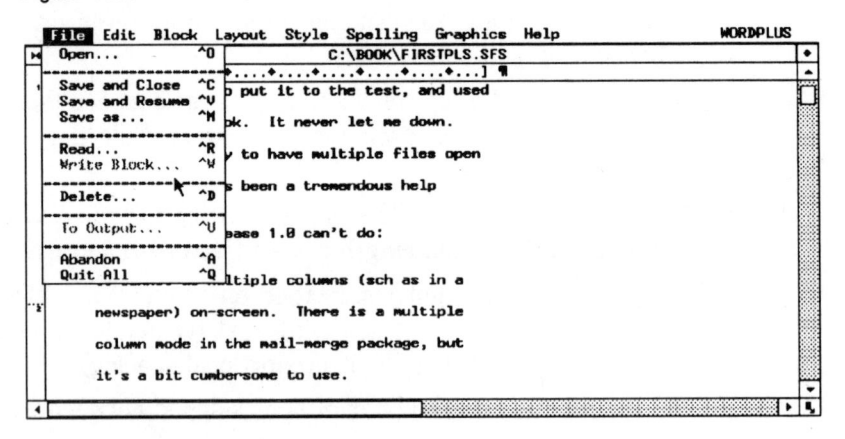

```
File  Edit  Block  Layout  Style  Spelling  Graphics  Help          WORDPLUS
 Open...            ^O           C:\BOOK\FIRSTPLS.SFS
                            ....+....+....+....+...] ¶
 Save and Close     ^C     put it to the test, and used
 Save and Resume    ^V     
 Save as...         ^M     k.  It never let me down.
 Read...            ^R     
 Write Block...     ^W     y to have multiple files open
                           
 Delete...          ^D     s been a tremendous help

 To Output...       ^U     ase 1.0 can't do:

 Abandon            ^A
 Quit All           ^Q     ltiple columns (sch as in a
         newspaper) on-screen. There is a multiple
         column mode in the mail-merge package, but
         it's a bit cumbersome to use.
```

Save and Resume

Lets you save a file without closing or even disturbing your current cursor position. You should make a habit of frequently saving just to protect yourself. Sometimes the power does drop out and . . . .

Save as . . .

Use this to assign a new file name to the file. You might want to rename a file if you are making a variation and don't want to disturb the original file.

Read . . .

This is a bit different. It will read the entire contents of another file into your current file. The other file will come in at the cursor position.

Write Block . . .

You use this to write a section of your working file off to a separate file. It works only if you have selected a block of text.

Delete . . .

The file you select will disappear from the disk.

To Output . . .

Available only when no files are currently open.

Abandon

Throws away all changes since the last time the file was saved and closes the file window. You'll get a chance to change your mind before Abandon does its thing.

Quit All

Bails out of all current file windows and drops back to the Desktop. Again, you'll get a chance to stop this before the command is actually executed.

EDIT

If a command didn't seem to fit anywhere else, it was given to the Edit Menu. See Figure 13.7. The following miscellaneous functions are still quite important.

Find . . .

The search command, but with a few eccentricities. For example, it won't accept an "@" for the first character. If you're searching for GEM Desktop Publisher or Ventura tags in the file, however, don't despair. You can substitute the wildcard character "?" for the "@."

I know of no good way to search for the end of a paragraph (a hard return). You can enter any graphics character or control code by holding down the Alt key and entering the decimal equivalent on the keypad.

Figure 13.7

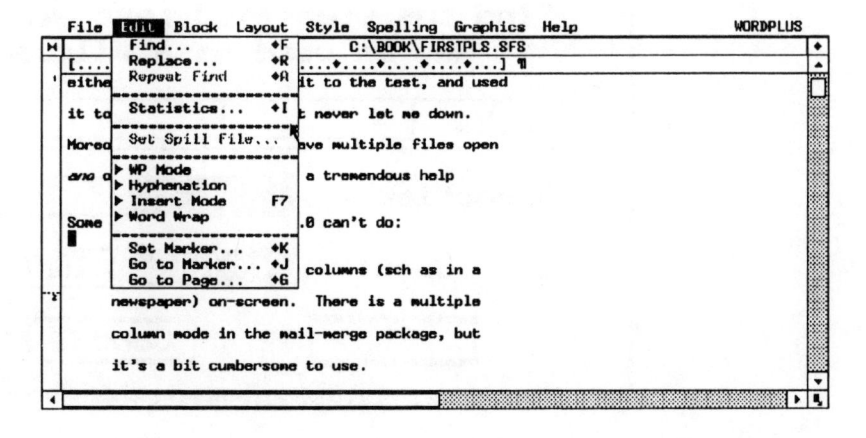

The other unique thing about Find . . . is the automatic direction change. The up and down arrows denote the direction of the search through the file from the current cursor position. See Figure 13.8. The idea is that if you searched for something down through the file, the cursor would then be at the bottom of the file. Given that, your next search path should be backwards, or up, through the file.

Case match and ignore is a toggle. It either requires an exact match to the case of the search pattern, or it will find any case combination of the search pattern letters.

Replace . . .

Search and Replace. See Figure 13.9. This time you enter both the text string that you want to find and the string that you want as a replacement. Scope governs how you want to handle the replacement. You can have it done to the first match or all matches. If you choose Query, then 1st Word Plus will ask your permission before it carries out each replacement.

Repeat Find

Repeats the last Find . . . or Replace.

Figure 13.8

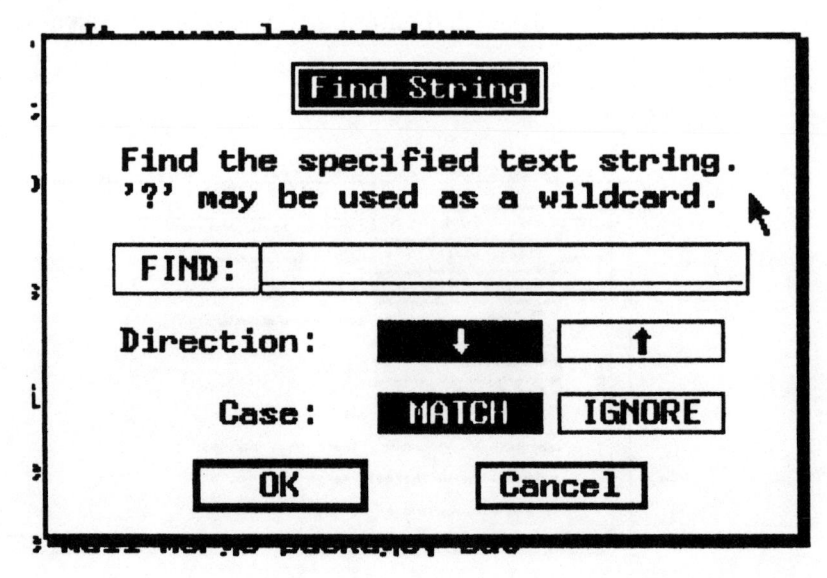

Figure 13.9

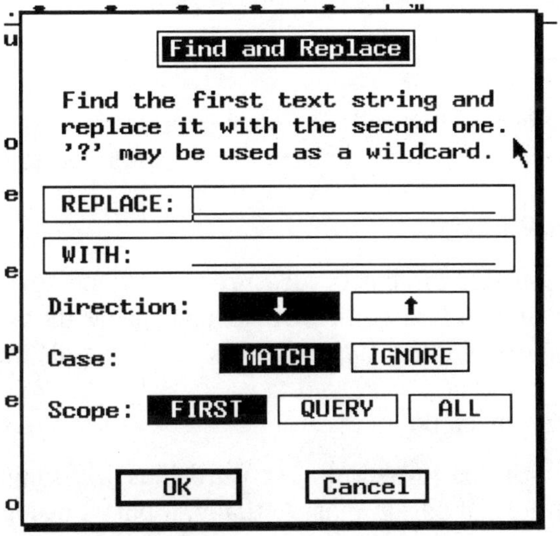

```
┌─────────────────────────────────┐
│        Find and Replace         │
│                                 │
│   Find the first text string and│
│   replace it with the second one.│
│   '?' may be used as a wildcard.│
│                                 │
│   REPLACE: [_____]  │
│                                 │
│   WITH:    [_____]  │
│                                 │
│   Direction:  [↓]    [↑]        │
│                                 │
│   Case:      [MATCH] [IGNORE]   │
│                                 │
│   Scope:  [FIRST] [QUERY] [ALL] │
│                                 │
│        [ OK ]     [Cancel]      │
└─────────────────────────────────┘
```

Figure 13.10

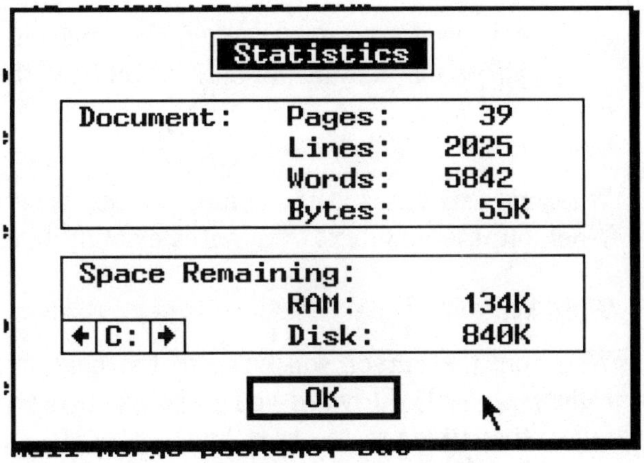

```
┌─────────────────────────────────┐
│           Statistics            │
│  ┌───────────────────────────┐  │
│  │ Document:  Pages:    39   │  │
│  │            Lines:  2025   │  │
│  │            Words:  5842   │  │
│  │            Bytes:   55K   │  │
│  └───────────────────────────┘  │
│  ┌───────────────────────────┐  │
│  │ Space Remaining:          │  │
│  │               RAM:  134K  │  │
│  │  ←[C:]→       Disk: 840K  │  │
│  └───────────────────────────┘  │
│            [  OK  ]             │
└─────────────────────────────────┘
```

Statistics . . .

Vital indeed. It lists the number of pages, lines, words, and bytes contained in the current working file. See Figure 13.10. You also get a look at the amount of RAM and disk space left, although you're really interested in the RAM space only if you haven't set a spill file.

Set Spill File

When no text files are open, you can tell 1st Word Plus to use the hard disk drive as virtual memory. This allows you to create very large text files.

WP Mode

Use this for most word processing and text editing. 1st Word Plus saves your file in a non-ASCII format, using its own internal codes for text formatting. It also appends a header to the file that contains layout information.

Hyphenation

With this turned on, 1st Word Plus will suggest hyphenation points as you reformat paragraphs. Actually, it puts a dialog box on the screen that allows you to OK its choice, move the hyphenation point right or left, skip hyphenation just this time, or cancel hyphenation altogether. If you have justification on and you turn Hyphenation off, the program will insert as many extra spaces as necessary between words to justify text. This could make your text look a bit stretched. If you have justification off, turning hyphenation off will force a more ragged right margin.

Hyphenation is available only if you have the WP mode on.

Insert Mode

When on, text typed at the cursor position is inserted into any existing text. When off, the new text overwrites existing text.

Word Wrap

When on, the cursor will wrap to the next line each time it reaches the right margin. If the word you were typing won't fit on the last line, it will follow the cursor to the next line.

Like Hyphenation, Word Wrap is available only if the WP mode is on.

Set Marker . . .

This produces a "mouseable" dialog that lets you set an invisible marker in your text. You can set up to four of these, just by clicking on the proper box (#1 through #4). Markers are not saved with the file.

Go to marker . . .

This one lets you jump the screen and cursor to any of the four markers. Of course, you must first set a marker before you can jump there.

Go to page . . .

Jumps to the top of the page you select in the dialog.

BLOCK

Block operations let you select a text string, ranging from a character to a file, and do any of the following to it: delete, copy, move, recall (if it previously had been deleted or copied), or append it to a clipboard area for later recall with perhaps other appended text. See Figure 13.11.

The easiest way to select a block is simply to drag the cursor over the rest of the block. The block will highlight when you release the mouse button. If the block is too big to fit on the screen, use the functions for Start and End.

The Block pull-down menu selections are:

Start

This defines the beginning point for a block.

Figure 13.11

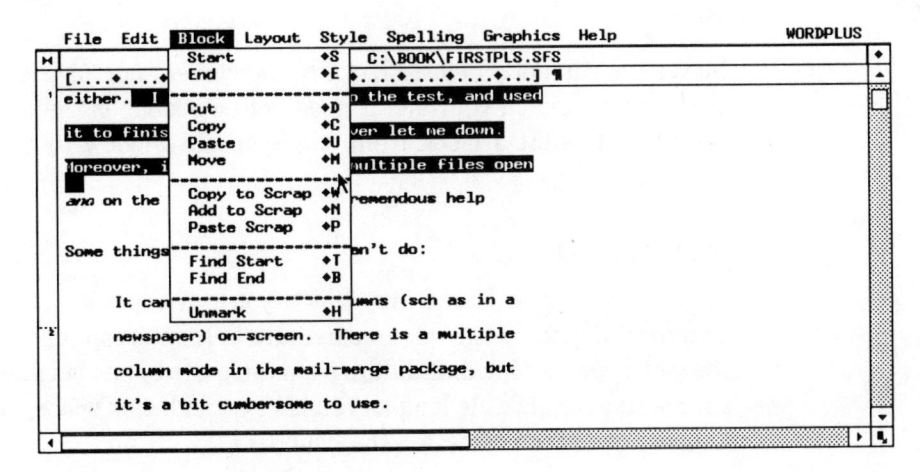

End

Defines the end point. When you define the end, the block will highlight to show you exactly what's marked.

Cut

Deletes the current block. This is available only if you have a marked block. Actually, the block is still held in the paste buffer, and the last deleted block can be recalled with a paste command.

Copy

Copies the current block to the paste buffer. You can pull as many copies of the block from the buffer as you like with the paste command, as long as you don't copy or delete another block.

Paste

Paste pulls the last copied or deleted block out of a memory buffer. You can define a block that is too big to fit in the buffer, and, should that happen, 1st Word Plus will warn you. You'll also get a warning if you are about to copy, move, or delete a block while there's currently something that was never recalled in the paste buffer.

The paste buffer provides a way of dealing with blocks that is universal to all open file windows. Anything in the paste buffer can be pasted in any or all open files, regardless of the file of origin.

Move

Moves the currently defined block to the current cursor position. The block can be anywhere in your file; it need not be visible on the screen. You can't use Move to shift a block from one open file window to another. Instead, use Cut or Copy.

Copy to Scrap

Scrap is a clipboard area into which you can copy something. Using this command deletes whatever is currently held in scrap and replaces it with the block you've copied. It differs from the paste buffer because the clipboard area is on your disk. As long as you have enough disk space, you can't define a block that is too large for the clipboard.

Add to Scrap

Because the clipboard area is really a disk file, you can easily append things to it. Add does just that. It adds the block without disturbing the current clipboard contents.

Paste Scrap

Reads the current contents of the clipboard into the currently open file window at the cursor position.

Find Start

Jumps the cursor and screen to the top of the currently selected block.

Find End

Jumps to the end of the currently selected block.

Unmark

Removes the block highlighting and the beginning and end points.

LAYOUT

These are functions that deal with formatting. Some provide advanced functions, such as running headers and footers or footnotes. See Figure 13.12.

Figure 13.12

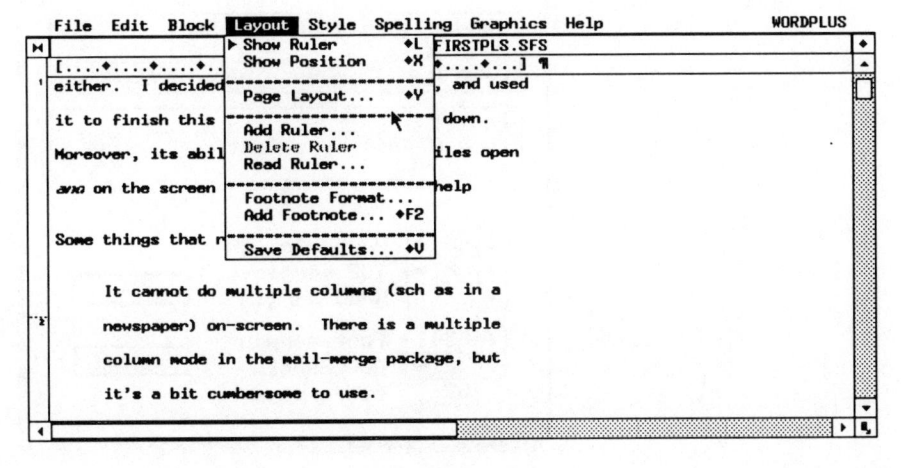

Show Ruler

Switches on the tab and margin ruler display.

Show Position

Puts the current page, line, and column that the cursor occupies in the ruler line, in place of the ruler.

Page Layout . . .

Produces the page layout form: a dialog for page formatting options. See Figure 13.13. The top three lines are for a running header. Left, right, and center refer to the points in the header where any typed text will appear. Things entered at left will always start at the left margin, while things entered at right will always end at the right margin. Centered information is always centered between the current margin settings.

   A number sign (#), entered on any of the header or footer lines, will cause 1st Word Plus to print the page number in that position.

   A couple of additional points: First, you can make 1st Word Plus alternate headers or even and odd pages (this option is available as you make up the file for output). For instance, you might want the page number always to

Figure 13.13

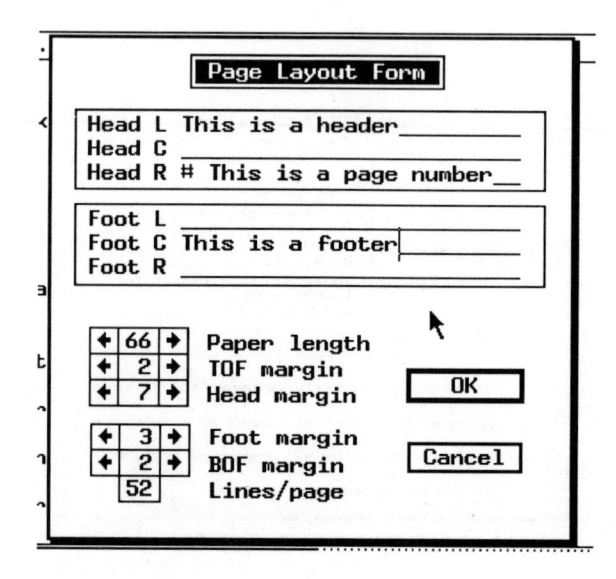

print on the top outside corner. And second, the pitch for headers and footers is always taken from the pitch at the top text line of the document itself.

Below the header lines are footer lines. These work exactly like the header lines, and they can be used to set footers that run on every page. 1st Word Plus puts the print page number symbol (#) under center as the default.

Paper length is the physical length of the page, measured in lines. No matter what pitch is set, 1st Word Plus considers there to be six lines to the vertical inch for these measurements.

The TOF margin sets the number of lines between the header line and the paper top. The head margin sets the number of lines from the header to the first text line. The header line is included in this number.

The foot margin is the number of lines from the last text line to the footer line. Again, the footer line is counted in this number. The BOF margin sets the number of lines from the physical bottom of the paper to the footer margin.

The lines per page indicator at the bottom simply reflects 66 (the length of a standard page) minus the number of lines you've allocated to the various top and bottom margins. This is only an indicator, and you can't change it directly with the mouse or keyboard.

Add Ruler . . .

Rulers let you change the margin and the pitch within your document. Rulers are added at the cursor position. When you select Add Ruler . . . , 1st Word Plus replies with the same ruler dialog you'd get by clicking on the open area of the ruler bar. The difference is that this ruler takes effect from the cursor position downwards through the document. If you insert another ruler below this one, the new ruler exerts its settings below its position, and so on.

As you run the cursor down through text with multiple rulers, you'll note that when the cursor reaches a new ruler's turf the ruler bar changes to reflect the new settings. Of course, that's a pretty clunky way to figure out where the ruler boundaries are.

If, however, you look at the page border area to the left of the screen (the same place you use to set page breaks), you'll notice a page number near the top of the column. Now just above that number is a small open white area below the close box. Click and hold there, and the page border shows a hashed line running up its middle. If a ruler is anywhere within the current screen area, that hashed line will point to its location with an arrowhead.

Delete Ruler

There's got to be a way to get rid of rulers, right? Well this is it. Put the cursor anywhere within a ruler's area of influence, and this option will trash the ruler.

Read Ruler . . .

This one reads the first ruler from any 1st Word Plus document into the current cursor position. You'll get the item selector for files to pick your file.

Footnote Format . . .

Yeah, how about that. Real footnotes, with superscripted numbers and everything. This dialog sets the format. See Figure 13.14. You can set the number of lines above the footnote rule to separate it from the main text. You can also specify the length of a separator rule (up to 160 spaces long). Finally, you can set the number of lines between the rule and the footnote text itself.

Add Footnote

This really is slick. Put the cursor at the point where you want to enter the footnote notation in your text. Pick this function, and you'll get a superscripted footnote number at that position. You'll also get a footnote window. See Figure 13.15.

Figure 13.14

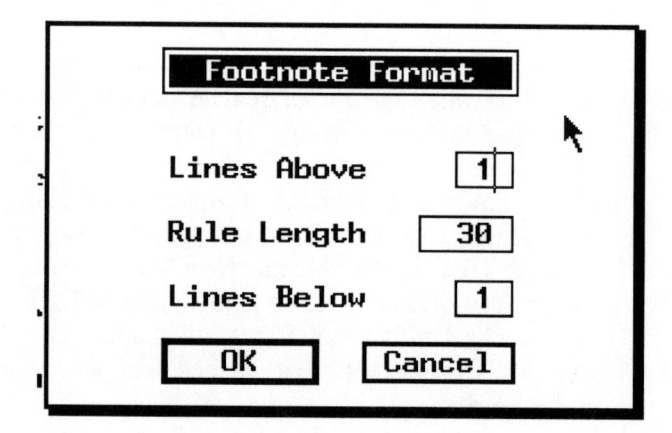

Figure 13.15

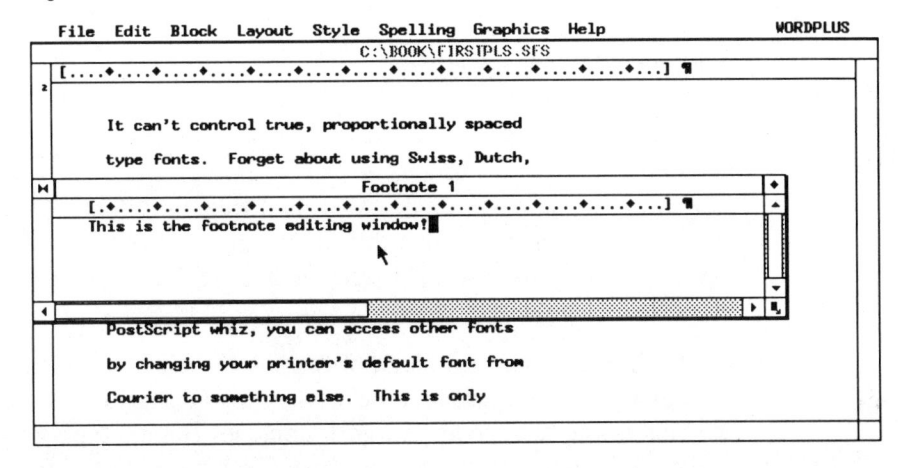

```
File  Edit  Block  Layout  Style  Spelling  Graphics  Help                WORDPLUS
                         C:\BOOK\FIRSTPLS.SFS
  [....♦....♦....♦....♦....♦....♦....♦....♦....♦....♦...] ¶
2
     It can't control true, proportionally spaced
     type fonts.  Forget about using Swiss, Dutch,
                          Footnote 1
  [.♦....♦....♦....♦....♦....♦....♦....♦....♦....♦....] ¶
     This is the footnote editing window!

                                  ▶


     PostScript whiz, you can access other fonts
     by changing your printer's default font from
     Courier to something else.  This is only
```

Enter text in the footnote window just as you would in any other file window. The ruler functions just like all other rulers and is fully adjustable. This lets you play around with the footnote formatting. Click on the close box in the footnote window to store the footnote.

If you want to edit the footnote later, double click on its superscripted notation in your text. This re-opens the footnote window. To remove the footnote, put the cursor on the notation and delete. As usual, the program will check to see if you really want to do that.

Footnotes always number in sequence, starting from one. If you add or remove footnotes, 1st Word Plus automatically renumbers the rest. You can't reset the footnote counter.

By the by, you'll notice that footnote entries carry a conditional page break. You can't delete this, but you can extend it or turn it into a full page break (just click on it).

Save Defaults

This saves all the following things as the general defaults:

- Ruler setting (taken from the current cursor position).
- Whether or not to use a spill file. Strange but true, you toggle the spill file off and on with no files open, but you must be within a file to save this setting.
- Layout settings.

- All of the start paths for the item selectors for text files, graphics files, and supplementary dictionaries.
- File window sizes and positions.

STYLE

Actually, they almost could have called this one "fonts." The first part of this menu lists all of the possible font attributes. See Figure 13.16. You can use any and virtually all of these for a given block of text. There are two ways to use them:

1. You can first select a block of text by the click and hold technique. The highlighted text will take on whatever font attributes you assign.
2. This is the change-as-you-go technique. Before typing text, select one or more font attributes. The text following the selection point will use these attributes until you turn them off. To turn off an attribute, just click on it again. You can tell if it's on by the little black arrowhead to its left.

The attributes described below affect lines and paragraphs.

Center

Centers the current line between the margins. It will also drop the cursor to the next line.

Figure 13.16

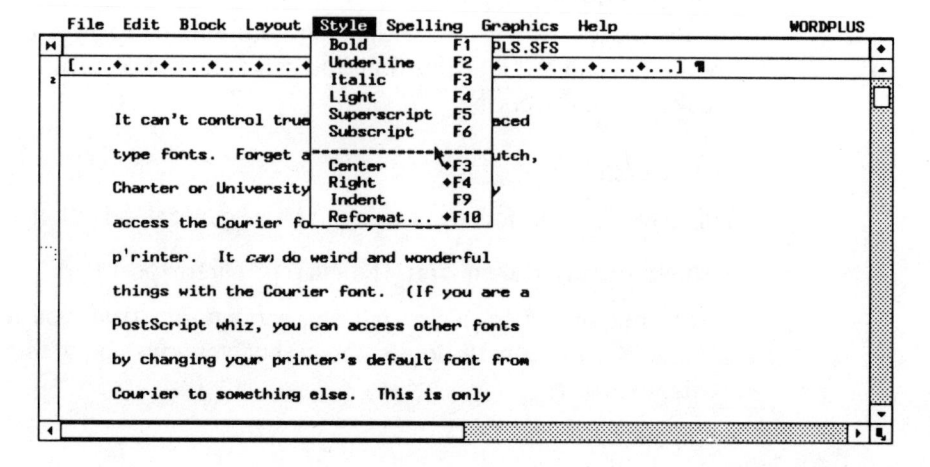

Right

Shoves the current line flush against the right margin.

Indent

This inserts a special sort of tab that acts like a temporary left margin for all following text. 1st Word Plus doesn't forget about these either; you can come back after saving and reopening the file and it will know about the indent. Use these to create hanging indents.

Reformat

Handy when you mess up a paragraph by adding or deleting text, this command forces paragraphs to conform to the current ruler settings. It comes up with a three-question dialog: Do you want to reformat a paragraph, the area covered by the current ruler, or the whole file?

SPELLING

At long last there's a GEM word processor with a good spelling checker. This one, however, is a bit eccentric. For example, you have to load the dictionary manually, the idea being that you shouldn't clutter up memory that can be used for text with a dictionary until you need it. Loading the dictionary, moreover, takes a while. See Figure 3.17.

Figure 13.17

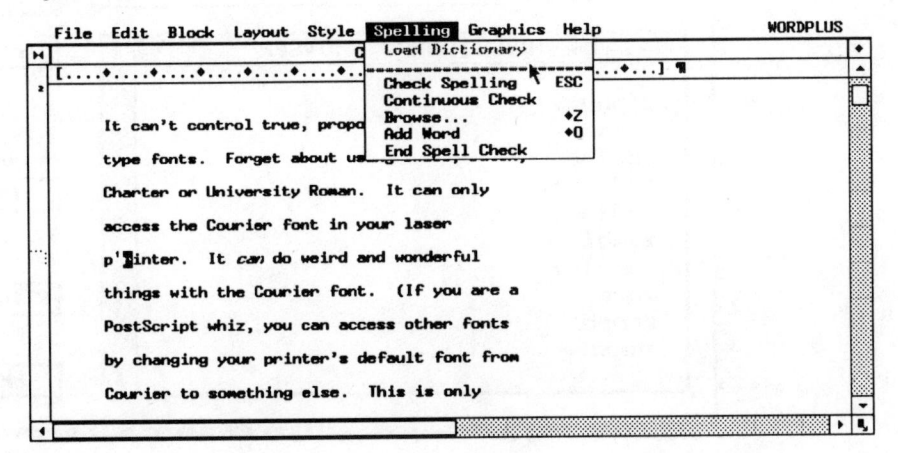

Load Dictionary

You guessed it. You will be asked if you want to use a supplementary dictionary—i.e., vocabularies specific to certain jobs and words you have added to the spelling checker.

Check Spelling

This launches the spelling checker. It will just keep going until it finds a word it doesn't recognize. There isn't much you can do to stop its quest until it finds a word. It always searches downward.

Continuous Check

You'll either love or hate this. Turn it on and 1st Word Plus will beep at you every time you make a typo or enter a word it doesn't recognize, such as a proper name. My current record for keeping this on is about three minutes.

Browse . . .

Select this and you'll get the dictionary browser dialog. See Figure 13.18. You can enter any word on the find line, and it will try to provide the proper area of the dictionary. That doesn't mean it will find the word, but at least you'll get to see the area the word would occupy if it were there.

Figure 13.18

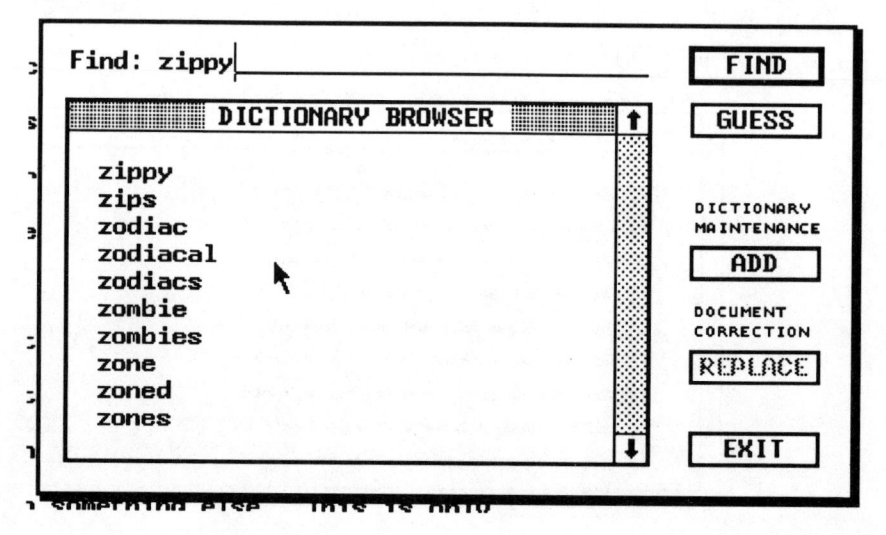

Among the other fun things you can do in Browse is play guessing games with the dictionary. If you can get a fairly close approximation of the word you are trying to spell onto the find line, the guess function will usually figure out what word you want. Don't use phonetics though; that doesn't work.

If the spelling checker jumps here during a check, it will usually suggest a proper spelling for the typo in the find line. Use Replace to replace the incorrect spelling in the file with the correct one.

Add

Another way to add a word to the dictionary. If the spelling checker stops on a properly spelled word and you want to add the word to the dictionary, just use this.

End Spell Check

This isn't quite what you might think. This doesn't stop a spelling check in progress. Rather, it unloads the dictionaries—main and supplementary—from memory.

If you commit a goof and put a misspelled word into your supplementary dictionary, no problem. The supplementary dictionary is just a text file that you can edit with 1st Word Plus. Since it's really just an ASCII file, don't turn WP on while you're in it.

If you want to add the supplementary dictionary to the main one, use the DICMERGE.APP utility that comes with 1st Word Plus. You'll find it in /GEMAPPS. This program creates a new dictionary (with a new name) by merging the supplement with the main dictionary.

GRAPHICS

1st Word Plus is one of the very few word processors that can merge text with graphics. See Figure 13.19. The next chapter talks about exploiting this powerful feature in various single-column publishing tasks. For now, we'll be content to cover the rules for using graphics.

You can load any graphics in the .GEM or .IMG format. There are a few catches to this, however, when you use scanned images (we'll cover those in a bit). The main thing to remember is that the graphics should be created in Draw Plus or Paint II at the actual size you want them to be in 1st Word Plus. 1st Word Plus can't size or scale graphics files.

The following paragraphs describe the functions in this menu.

Figure 13.19

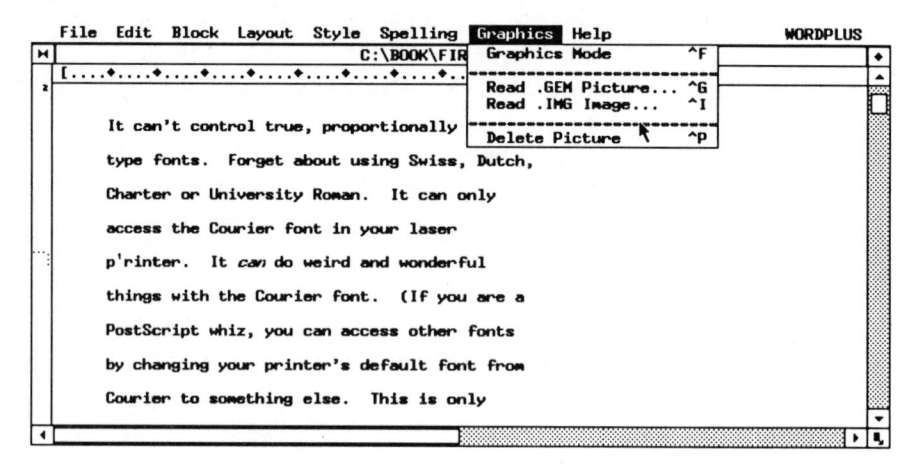

```
  File  Edit  Block  Layout  Style  Spelling  Graphics  Help              WORDPLUS
                              C:\BOOK\FIR    Graphics Mode       ^F
  [....+....+....+....+....+....+..           ─────────────────
                                               Read .GEM Picture... ^G
                                               Read .IMG Image...   ^I
       It can't control true, proportionally  ─────────────────
                                               Delete Picture       ^P
       type fonts.  Forget about using Swiss, Dutch,

       Charter or University Roman.  It can only

       access the Courier font in your laser

       p'rinter.  It can do weird and wonderful

       things with the Courier font.  (If you are a

       PostScript whiz, you can access other fonts

       by changing your printer's default font from

       Courier to something else.  This is only
```

Graphics Mode

With this option, you actually can see the graphic within the word processor. When off, you can see the dotted outline of the rectangular area the graphic will occupy. Being able to see the graphic is nice, but it can slow the screen down considerably.

Read .GEM Picture . . .

This opens the file item selector to pull in a .GEM Draw file. The file will arrive at the cursor location. While you can't size or scale, you can slide it sideways—at least until it hits the left margin. You can't run text beside a graphic (sorry).

Read .IMG Image . . .

Again, you are given a chance to pick a graphics file. This time it must have an .IMG extension. This works just fine for Paint II files. Scanned images are another matter. They have as much as four times the dot density of Paint II files. 1st Word Plus doesn't quite know what to make of this. As a result, you'll get pictures that are actually four times larger than they should be because 1st Word Plus simply expands the file until it has the same resolution as a Paint II file. You may also get a message saying that 1st Word Plus can't display such a big file.

Delete Picture

If you want to get rid of a picture, just put the cursor anywhere in its area and select this. You'll be asked if you're serious about doing this before the picture disappears from view.

HELP

This is a collection of miscellaneous help files you can use if you get stuck. They are cataloged in the menu for quick reference.

STORING FORMATS

A slick feature of 1st Word Plus is its ability to store canned formats by file extension. Format files are stored in the /GEMAPPS/FORMATS directory. A format file need not have text, just formatting information. If it does have text, that text is automatically loaded into the new file as well (which can be handy for things like memo headings).

Here's how it works: First, store a file in the /GEMAPPS/FORMATS directory with the ruler and layout settings that you will use as a standard format. Let's say that this is a file for memos. Call it FORMAT.MEM. Now, whenever you start a new file with the .MEM extension, 1st Word Plus will pull all the formatting information from /GEMAPPS/FORMATS/FORMAT.MEM and pre-load it into your new memo file. Pretty neat, eh?

USING CONVERT.APP

This is a very handy tool if you're bringing files from other word processors into 1st Word Plus. It is a bit odd in operation, however. First off, it's the only GEM application I've ever seen that introduces itself and then requires you to select RUN to actually run the program.

Operation is pretty trivial actually. The program opens with a file item selector, and you pick a file name to convert as well as a target file name to hold the converted text. That taken care of, you are then asked to select the format that the original file uses: GEM Write, Wordstart, or ASCII. See Figure 13.20.

Since almost any word processor can write ASCII files, you should be able to translate practically anything.

Figure 13.20

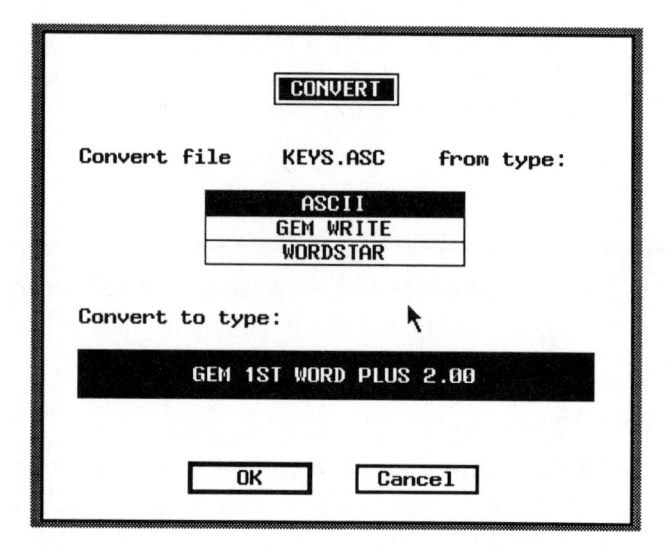

[Convert dialog box: Convert file KEYS.ASC from type: ASCII / GEM WRITE / WORDSTAR. Convert to type: GEM 1ST WORD PLUS 2.00. OK / Cancel]

KEYBOARD COMMANDS

Almost all 1st Word Plus functions can be accessed from the keyboard. In most cases, it's really more convenient to use the keyboard command than to pull down a menu. As with all GEM applications, the keyboard equivalents in 1st Word Plus are listed beside the pull-down menu selections. For your convenience, a complete list of keyboard equivalents (in alphabetical order by command) follows:

Command	Key
Abandon file	Control-A
Add block to scrap file	Alt-N
Add footnote	Alt-F2
Add word to dictionary	Alt-O
Beginning of line	Home
Bold	F1
Browse	Alt-Z
Center line	Alt-F3
Copy block to scrap file	Alt-W
Copy block	Alt-C
Cursor down	Down arrow
Cursor left	Left arrow
Cursor right	Right arrow

Cursor up	Up arrow
Cut block	Alt-D
Delete file	Control-D
Delete left	Backspace
Delete line	F8
Delete picture	Control-P
Delete under cursor	Delete
Delete word right	Alt-F8
End (block marker)	Alt-E
End of line	End
Find block end	Alt-B
Find start of block	Alt-T
Find	Alt-F
Go to marker number	Alt-J
Go to page/line	Alt-G
Graphics mode toggle	Control-F
Indent left margin	F9
Indent space (fixed)	Alt-F9
Insert/Overwrite toggle	F7
Italic	F3
Left one word	Control-left arrow
Light (gray) type	F4
Move block	Alt-M
Open file	Control-O
Page layout dialog	Alt-Y
Paste block in buffer	Alt-U
Paste scrap file	Alt-P
Quit all	Control-Q
Read .GEM picture file	Control-G
Read .IMG image file	Control-I
Read file	Control-R
Reformat paragraph	F10
Repeat find/replace	Alt-A
Replace	Alt-R
Right align line	Alt-F4
Right one word	Control-right arrow
Save and close file	Control-C
Save and resume	Control-V
Save defaults	Alt-V
Save file as	Control-M

Set marker number	Alt-K
Show position (not ruler)	Alt-X
Show ruler	Alt-L
Statistics (file/memory)	Alt-I
Subscript	F6
Superscript	F5
To Output	Control-U
Underline	F2
Unmark block	Alt-H
Write block to file	Control-W

CHAPTER 14

Publishing With 1st Word Plus

SPEAKING GRAPHICALLY	254
STATIONERY-ON-DEMAND	254
PUBLICATION DESIGN WITH 1ST WORD PLUS	255
DOING SOMETHING	256
SUMMING UP	259

SPEAKING GRAPHICALLY

GEM 1st Word Plus can be a very effective, simple publishing tool. It's great for technical papers, proposals, reports, letters, and memos.

At the risk of preaching, I want to emphasize a very important point: Keep your graphics small enough to be useful. Since they are brought in at actual size, make sure they fit the page without overwhelming it.

STATIONERY-ON-DEMAND

If you have your company or organization logo in either GEM Paint or GEM Draw Plus (preferably GEM Draw Plus because the resolution will be much greater), you can use GEM 1st Word Plus to place the logo at the top of your letters. Just position the logo at the top of the canvas, and align it with any accent lines, etc., so that it looks just like your present stationery. It must be the right size as well. See Figure 14.1.

In GEM 1st Word Plus, set the Page Layout dialog margins that control the top of the page to zero. Now go to the Graphics pull-down menu and turn the Graphics Mode on. Back at the Graphics menu, select Read .GEM Picture or Read .IMG Image and reel in the file. You can slide it left to right

Figure 14.1

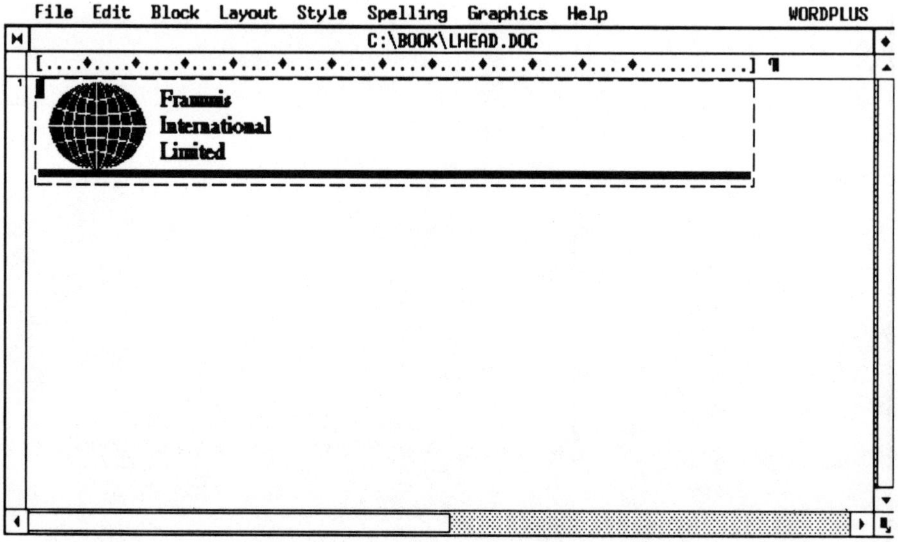

with the click and hold mouse technique. You might want to turn off the Graphics Mode after the file is in place, just to speed up screen redraw time.

You can also use the same trick for "second sheet" stationery. See Figure 14.2. If you want to print graphics at the very bottom of the page, reset the Page Layout bottom margins so that the last line prints on line 66. This will let you put the graphic right at the bottom of the page. While the results are impressive even with a dot-matrix printer, a laser printer can provide what appears to be genuine, pre-printed stationery.

PUBLICATION DESIGN WITH 1ST WORD PLUS

GEM 1st Word Plus can normally control just one font, either Courier on a laser printer or the default font for a dot-matrix printer. Let's say that you have a laser printer and are using Courier—a 10 pitch, fixed-space font. This means that you'll get 10 characters to the inch, or 65 characters to a normal 6.5-inch line.

You'll hear this again from me in the Desktop Publisher chapters, but it's important to present here as well. Present research regarding readability suggests that a line length of 55 to 70 characters is OK if the type face is clear and readable. Courier is definitely clear and readable. On the other

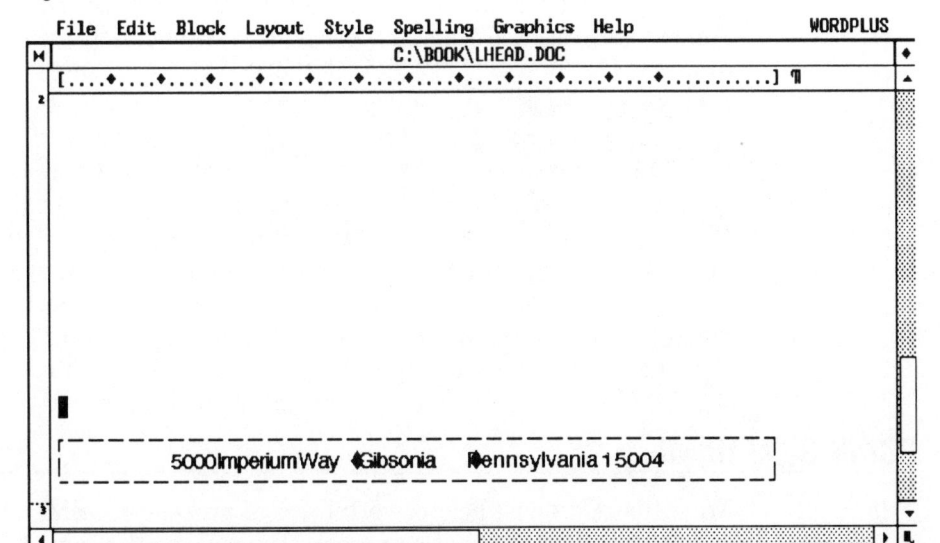

Figure 14.2

hand, a time-honored rule in typography is to make the line between 1.5 and two times the length of the lower-case alphabet (as printed in that type font and type size). I like time-honored rules myself. For longer documents, therefore, I'd recommend setting the line length approximately five to 5.5 inches. This provides readable lines, although it does leave you with rather wide margins.

To solve the margin problem, you can make the left margin "hang in." Simply drag the left margin marker on the ruler to somewhere between 1.5 and two inches. You can use that lovely white space to the left for headings and such. This will make them stand out from the text, and they'll be easy for your reader to find.

Or consider this as an alternative design: Bring both margins in to make a six-inch centered text space (1.25-inch margins). Headings can be centered, with one extra line above and two below each heading to make it stand out. I should note that centered formats are considered passe and artificial looking.

To make your headings even easier to find, you can make them bold or bold italic. If you want distinct visual differences between two levels of headings, make one bold italic and the other level bold. You can also use all capitals for the most important headings, though studies have shown that words in all capitals are harder to read.

Font attributes also can add emphasis to your text, but be careful. Like pepper, a little is fine, but too much ruins the effect. The fonts won't stand out if you use them continually.

If you really want to get fancy, you can use GEM Draw Plus or GEM Paint to generate the type for the headings. Although this requires a separate graphics file for each heading, if the document is short enough—or you confine your efforts to major headings—the task won't be too tedious. Use the same technique if you want to add horizontal rules to your document. After all, you can insert the same rule file as many times as you want.

Running headers and footers either can be generated by GEM 1st Word Plus or you can use graphics. This is the same technique used in making stationery. Reset the starting line for printing to one, and if you are using a graphic footer reset the last line to 66. If page numbers are important to your document, use either the GEM 1st Word Plus header or footer entry lines under Page Layout to generate these (graphics can't help with page numbers).

DOING SOMETHING

To demonstrate just how powerful a page processor GEM 1st Word Plus is, we'll do a couple pages of a proposal. You can use the same basic techniques to create other types of documents as well. For the basic format, we'll set the margins at two inches to the left (20 characters) and seven inches (70 characters) right. This provides a five-inch, or 50-character, line which is quite readable. It also provides a nice wide left margin in which to hang the headings.

A proposal should have running headers and footers. 1st Word Plus can alternate headers and footers between right and left pages. This means that you can put the page number on the outside, bottom edge of every page. If you're wondering where the toggle for alternating headers is hidden, you'll find it in the dialog that pops up when you set up an output file.

The headers should offer information like the title of the proposal and your company or organization's name. Again, since you can alternate headings, you can pick what goes on the right or left.

Next I'll add the company logo by using Read .GEM Picture to pull in the file. I'll skip a line and insert the proposal title. The title is in 20 point Dutch (Times Roman) type created in GEM Draw Plus and saved as a separate graphics file. I moved the type up to the very upper left corner of the drawing canvas so that it would position properly when brought into GEM 1st Word Plus. See Figure 14.3.

Figure 14.3

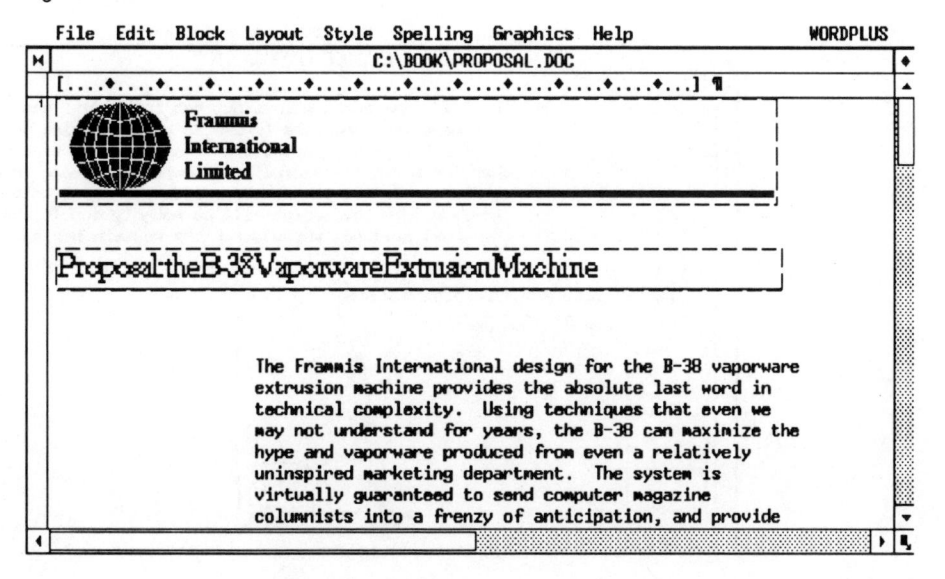

Figure 14.4

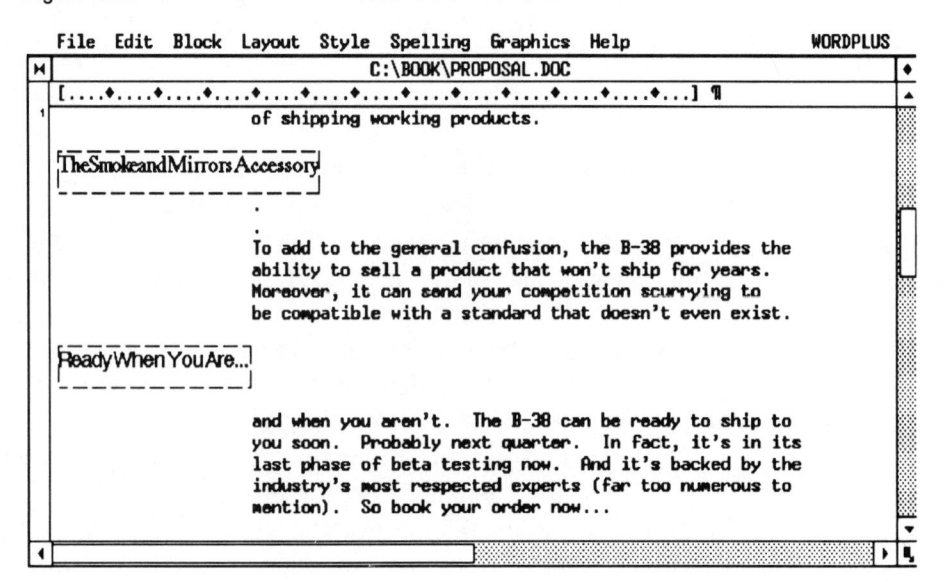

```
  File   Edit  Block  Layout  Style  Spelling  Graphics  Help                WORDPLUS
┌──────────────────────────────────────────────────────────────────────────────────┐
│ ⋈                         C:\BOOK\PROPOSAL.DOC                                 ● │
│   [....♦....♦....♦....♦....♦....♦....♦....♦....♦....♦...] ¶                   ▲ │
│ 1                     of shipping working products.                              │
│    ┌─ ─ ─ ─ ─ ─ ─ ─ ─ ─ ─ ─ ─┐                                                   │
│    │The Smoke and Mirrors Accessory│                                             │
│    └─ ─ ─ ─ ─ ─ ─ ─ ─ ─ ─ ─ ─┘                                                   │
│                          .                                                       │
│                       To add to the general confusion, the B-38 provides the     │
│                       ability to sell a product that won't ship for years.       │
│                       Moreover, it can send your competition scurrying to        │
│                       be compatible with a standard that doesn't even exist.     │
│    ┌─ ─ ─ ─ ─ ─ ─ ─ ─┐                                                           │
│    │Ready When You Are...│                                                       │
│    └─ ─ ─ ─ ─ ─ ─ ─ ─┘                                                           │
│                       and when you aren't. The B-38 can be ready to ship to      │
│                       you soon. Probably next quarter. In fact, it's in its      │
│                       last phase of beta testing now. And it's backed by the     │
│                       industry's most respected experts (far too numerous to     │
│                       mention). So book your order now...                      ▼ │
│ ◄                                                                            ► ▮ │
└──────────────────────────────────────────────────────────────────────────────────┘
```

Figure 14.5

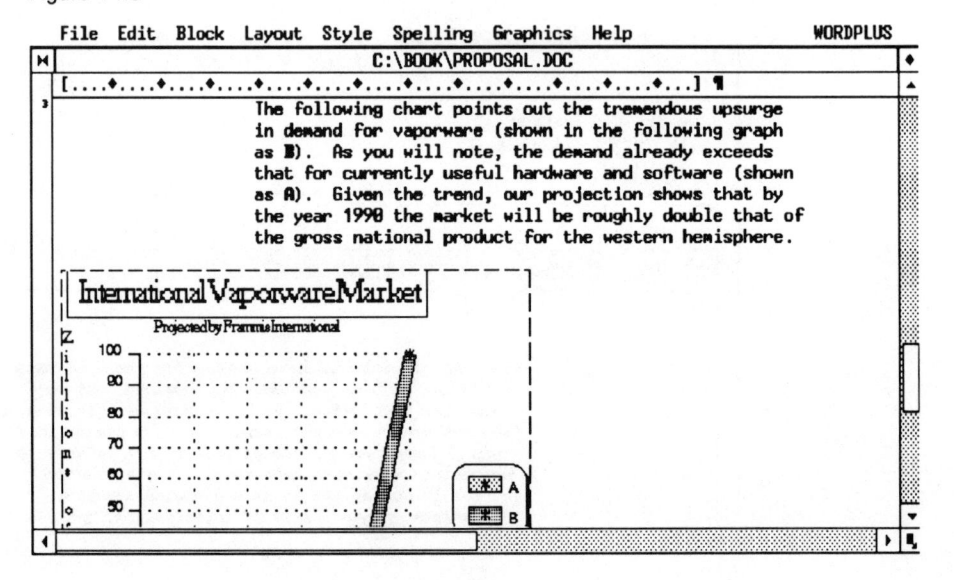

```
  File   Edit  Block  Layout  Style  Spelling  Graphics  Help                WORDPLUS
┌──────────────────────────────────────────────────────────────────────────────────┐
│ ⋈                         C:\BOOK\PROPOSAL.DOC                                 ● │
│   [....♦....♦....♦....♦....♦....♦....♦....♦....♦....♦...] ¶                   ▲ │
│ 3                    The following chart points out the tremendous upsurge       │
│                      in demand for vaporware (shown in the following graph       │
│                      as ■). As you will note, the demand already exceeds         │
│                      that for currently useful hardware and software (shown      │
│                      as ▦). Given the trend, our projection shows that by        │
│                      the year 1990 the market will be roughly double that of     │
│                      the gross national product for the western hemisphere.     │
│   ┌─ ─ ─ ─ ─ ─ ─ ─ ─ ─ ─ ─ ─ ─ ─ ─ ─ ─ ─ ─ ─┐                                    │
│   │    International Vaporware Market      │                                     │
│   │      Projected by Frammis International │                                    │
│   │ z                                      │                                     │
│   │ i 100 ·····················▓···········│                                     │
│   │ l  90 ·····················▓···········│                                     │
│   │ l  80 ·····················▓···········│                                     │
│   │ i                          ▓            │                                    │
│   │ o  70 ····················▓············│                                     │
│   │ n  60 ···················▓·············│    ┌────┐                           │
│   │    50 ··················▓··············│    │▓▓ A│                           │
│   │ o                                      │    │▦▦ B│                           │
│   └─ ─ ─ ─ ─ ─ ─ ─ ─ ─ ─ ─ ─ ─ ─ ─ ─ ─ ─ ─ ─┘    └────┘                         ▼│
│ ◄                                                                            ► ▮ │
└──────────────────────────────────────────────────────────────────────────────────┘
```

Skip two more lines and we're ready for text. The beauty of 1st Word Plus is that you have all the text editing convenience of a word processor along with the ability to add the graphics you need.

The subheading is brought in just like the main heading. It lives in its own GEM Draw Plus file. Being a smaller heading, it's in 14 point Dutch. Again, the type is positioned at the upper left corner of the GEM Draw Plus canvas. See Figure 14.4.

All pages following the main page have a running graphic header. This too is a GEM Draw Plus file, inserted at the beginning of each page. Don't put headers or other graphics (except for headings and subheadings) in place until you finish the publication. The rationale for this rule is that as you add or delete text, graphics will also move. As a consequence, you could be left with graphics split over pages—unless you use the conditional page markers.

The chart on the second page was created in GEM Graph, and the resulting .GEM file was loaded into GEM Draw Plus and centered in the canvas. The graph was created with the one-quarter page size selected to make sure it would fit the page. See Figure 14.5.

SUMMING UP

GEM 1st Word Plus, coupled with the other GEM applications, can handle many publishing jobs without requiring an additional page-layout program. I've given you a few examples of what you can do. Take it from here and play around with the program. The more creative you are, the more things you will discover you can do.

CHAPTER

15

GEM Desktop Publisher: The Basics

SIMPLY SUPERIOR	261
SYSTEM REQUIREMENTS	261
WHAT TO FEED DESKTOP PUBLISHER	262
OPENING UP	263
THE TOOLKIT	264
PULL-DOWN MENUS	268
ATTRIBUTES	273
PAGE NUMBERS	283
OPTIONS	289
KEYBOARD COMMANDS	294
EMBEDDED COMMANDS	298

SIMPLY SUPERIOR

GEM Desktop Publisher is the crown jewel of the GEM applications, and an electronic page-layout tool par excellence. It draws on all of the capabilities of the other applications, and it can combine them all. Desktop Publisher release 2.0 has capabilities that push it into the high end of desktop publishing. Yet it remains simple to use (thank goodness).

Desktop Publisher version 1.0 seemed like a baby Ventura Publisher. Desktop Publisher version 2.0 is not only more powerful, but it has taken on a character of its own. Compared with Ventura, Desktop Publisher is less automated but a lot more friendly. And less automated doesn't always mean less capable. In this case, it just means that doing a task in Desktop Publisher may take a step or two more than in Ventura. In addition, Desktop Publisher offers a few features that Ventura lacks.

This chapter discusses the controls, menus, and functions in Desktop Publisher. There's a lot to discuss. Where applicable, I'll also go over some general design principles that apply to using commands. I've designed this chapter to be a reference guide that you can read through to get an idea of what the commands do. In the future, when you need to look something up, you can find the information quickly in this chapter. The following chapter talks about publication design and provides examples of how to use the commands.

SYSTEM REQUIREMENTS

Most GEM applications will run on nearly any PC with enough memory to handle the job. Desktop Publisher demands at least a machine that has two floppy drives, a color graphics adapter (CGA card), and a minimum of 512 kilobytes of memory. In addition, you must have GEM/3 and you really should have 640 kilobytes of memory, a hard disk drive, a mouse, and at least standard EGA or Hercules-compatible graphics.

Desktop Publisher is a what-you-see-is-what-you-get page-layout program. In other words, it will display the text as closely as possible to the way it will appear on the printed page. Because this often means gobs of type on the screen, you'll need a sharp graphics system to read it. Believe me. I've used the program with a CGA-type color card, and it's just too much eye strain.

If you intend to run GEM Desktop Publisher on floppies, you'll need to limit the size of your publications. Desktop Publisher makes a printer file with a .GMP extension that can be very large indeed.

Memory is life's blood to Desktop Publisher. You can get by with a bit less than 640 kilobytes, but don't try. With 640 kilobytes you can keep the calculator/clock/print spooler accessory around and still have enough memory to see image files on the screen. With less memory, you may lose the ability to see image files, or you may not be able to load Desktop Publisher at all. DesqView users who don't have an EEMS-type memory board should forget running Desktop Publisher from DesqView.

WHAT TO FEED DESKTOP PUBLISHER

Desktop Publisher is fairly omnivorous; it can accept text files from the following word processors:

- GEM 1st Word Plus
- GEM Write
- WordStar (any U.S. version)
- WordPerfect
- Microsoft Word
- MultiMate
- IBM DCA files (such as Lotus Manuscript generates)
- ASCII text

Once you've loaded the text file in, Desktop Publisher will convert the text attribute control characters (along with some of the formatting), making an ASCII file of its own. While it does convert things like bold, italic, etc., you'll still need hard tabs to set up tables (it can't convert a series of spaces to tabs).

You can find the text file that Desktop Publisher makes by looking for the word processor file name but with an .ASC extension. It'll be in the same directory as the original text file. Desktop Publisher makes a file for each text file you load. The .ASC file will hold any changes you make with the Desktop Publisher editor, and the changes won't be written back to your word processor file.

Desktop Publisher can accept the following graphics files:

- GEM Draw Plus, GEM Graph, and GEM WordChart files with a .GEM extension.
- GEM Paint, SnapShot, Halo DPE, and scanned files with an .IMG extension.

If you have The Graphics Link from PC Quick-Art, you can also access files from practically any PC-based paint program. For all you scanner aficionados, The Graphics Link can preserve a 300x300-dot resolution when translating to GEM Paint format.

Now that you know what you can feed into Desktop Publisher, let's open it up.

OPENING UP

Desktop Publisher opens to a blank work area, set at normal view. See Figure 15.1. Think of the work area as a graphics studio in which you have a typesetter (which formats your copy), a stat camera (which sizes and scales illustrations), and some illustrating tools. You also have paste-up boards called "rectangles."

Rectangles are terribly important to Desktop Publisher. They provide frames for your text and graphics. If you keep this in mind as we go over the tools and menus, things will make a bit more sense.

The opening screen looks pretty much like other GEM applications, including the usual assortment of items:

- A menu bar along the top with five pull-down menus
- A toolkit to the left
- Slider bars (for moving around the paste-up board) along the right and bottom

Figure 15.1

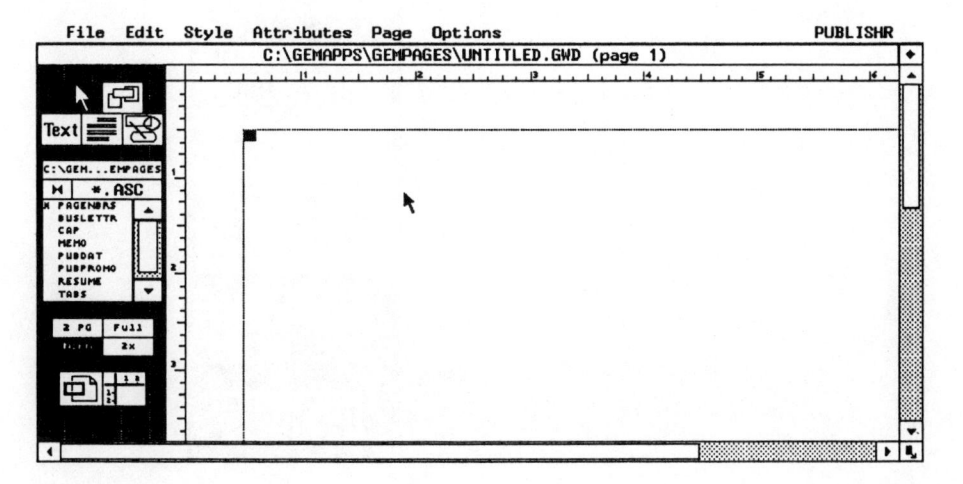

- A size box (for reducing the size of the application on screen) and a full box (for popping back to normal size). This GEM feature is virtually useless with Desktop Publisher because 1) you can have only one publication open at any given time, and 2) you want to see as much of the paste-up area as possible.

THE TOOLKIT

The Desktop Publisher toolkit changes the mode of operations. Once you have the formatting defined through the pull-down menus, you use the toolkit for nearly all of the actual layout work. The toolkit has three main parts: the five mode icons on top, the mini-selector in the middle, and the viewing tools at the bottom. See Figure 15.2.

THE MODE ICONS

Desktop Publisher has five major operating modes:

- Make rectangles
- Move and modify rectangles

Figure 15.2

- Assign and modify formatting tags
- Text editing
- Draw graphics and add call-outs

These are all accessible from the Toolkit, and you can tell which mode you're in by the icon that's reversed. The cursor will also take a distinct shape depending on the active mode.

Make Rectangles

This is always the first thing to do. You must make a base rectangle that really defines the left, right, top, and bottom margins. This base rectangle, when loaded with more text than a page will hold, automatically repeats from page to page.

An interesting feature of Desktop Publisher: While it automatically repeats your rectangles from page to page until the entire file is formatted, each of the rectangles remains independent of the others. For instance, you can make the rectangle on page two have a different number of columns without affecting any of the following rectangles.

To make a rectangle, position the mouse cursor at the point you want to be the upper left-hand corner. Click and hold; then drag the box that formed down and to the right until it reaches the size you want. Release the button and you'll have your rectangle.

A very nice feature is Desktop Publisher's ability to show either the current cursor position (both vertically and horizontally) or the size of the rectangle as you draw it. Both of these features can be toggled off and on, and they live in the Page menu.

Move and Modify Rectangles

This works much like the shape selector in GEM Draw Plus. Click on the rectangle you want to move or modify, and extent boxes will appear at each corner. Click and hold on the extent box, and you can expand or contract the size of the rectangle horizontally, vertically, or both directions at the same time. Click and hold on the rectangle itself, and the mouse pointer will turn into an open hand. You can now slide the rectangle around the screen.

You can use the shift-click technique to select multiple rectangles. You can also use the control-click technique to select one layer at a time down through overlapping rectangles.

Formatting Tags

Advanced page-layout programs provide a way to automate most of the formatting work, and that way is tags. Tags allow you to predefine formats for paragraphs. Then you just select a paragraph (by clicking on it) and click on the tag name. The selected paragraph takes on all of the formatting that you defined for the tag.

Tags in Desktop Publisher allow you to set the following formatting attributes:

1. Font, including type face, style, color, and size. Desktop Publisher 2.0's improved typography includes the ability to select any point size for PostScript printers.
2. Spacing (or, more properly, leading), including interline, interparagraph, and indent spacing. You can also set alignment (such as justified or ragged right), snap to the text grid, and even tracking. Tracking is a sophisticated typographic feature that lets you select how tightly the program should pack letters into words and words into a line.
3. Hyphenation. This is essential to a publishing package. Without hyphenation, it is impossible to produce good justified text. You can select among a variety of hyphenation routines for foreign languages as well as for English.
4. Tab positions, a completely different set for each tag. This is an enormous help when doing tabular work.

You can create tags at will by copying an existing tag's formatting settings to a new tag. This means you don't have to start each tag from scratch.

Text Editing

The Desktop Publisher text editor provides all the basic text editing tools you need to make final changes to a manuscript. Although not designed to create large volumes of text, it allows you to insert and delete text and to copy blocks of text from one point to another.

Graphics Editor

This mode allows you to draw rectangles, circles, rounded corner rectangles, and lines. Each drawing function is activated by clicking on the proper icon. The arrow-shaped icon at the top allows you to select objects you've drawn. You can then shuffle them about, stretch them, copy them, or delete them.

There are two attribute dialogs that work with the drawing tools: line attributes and fill attributes. Both live under the Attributes menu. Line attributes apply to all of the things that you draw. They set the line width and type (dotted, ending with arrows, etc.). Fill patterns affect everything but lines. They set color, shade, and whether the object is transparent or opaque; PostScript devices won't print transparent objects transparently.

MINI-SELECTOR

The mini-selector sits just under the five mode icons. What the mini-selector does really depends on the mode icon you're using.

Rectangle Modes. In the two rectangle modes, the mini-selector functions as a smaller version of the GEM file selector. The top shows the current directory. The file extension area shows the file type to which it's currently pointing. The mini-selector will point only to the file types for the word processor and graphics programs it knows about. You can set the word processor file extensions through the Options pull-down menu. Click on this area to cycle through the file extension list.

The close box lets you move to higher directory levels and eventually to a different disk drive. You can then enter a new subdirectory by clicking on it, or actually load a file by clicking on that. Remember, you must first select a rectangle to hold the text or graphics file before you can load the file.

Tag Mode. The mini-selector shows you the tag names for all of the tags you have predefined. These tags are all stored in a style sheet, and you can have as many style sheets as you like (each with its own set of tags).

To assign a tag to a paragraph or a set of paragraphs:

1. Click on the paragraph(s). Selected paragraphs display in reverse (white on black).
2. Click on the tag name in the mini-selector. You may need to use the mini-selector slider bar to find it if you have a fair number of tags.

That's all there is to it. It's sort of scary when I think about how easy it is. A few years ago, formatting type demanded a good deal of tedious file encoding. Now it's just point and click.

Text Mode

When you're editing text, the mini-selector displays the type attributes: bold, italic, underline, and normal. You merely click and hold at the start of the text you want to select, and then sweep the mouse over it. The text will reverse to show what is selected. Then click on the type attribute you want. Type attributes assigned this way override the tag settings.

You can also change type size and style with the Character option under the Style pull-down menu. We'll talk about exactly how Desktop Publisher does this at the end of the chapter.

VIEWING TOOLS

These let you change the screen magnification, adjust the position of the viewing area, and pop the rulers on and off.

Magnification sets how much of the page you can see on the screen. Norm shows a roughly one-to-one relationship between the screen and the final printed output. Actually, on my Hercules-compatible display the screen image is somewhat larger than the printed output.

2X zooms in for double the magnification. This is really handy for small type and very critical rectangle alignments. Full displays a full page, with all text greeked (a printer's term for text shown made up of any characters, in this case little x's). The 2 PG setting shows left and right pages side-by-side. Again, text is greeked.

If you are in Norm or 2X, you can easily move around the page with the panner. Just click on it, and the display will momentarily jump to full view. A rectangle will show the current viewing area; you can click and hold on that, and then shift it anywhere you like on the board.

The ruler icon toggles the side and top rulers on and off. To select either English or Metric units, use the Image Size option under the Page pull-down menu. No matter which measuring system you select, you can always switch to picas through Rulers in Inches, also under Page.

PULL-DOWN MENUS

Desktop Publisher has the richest set of pull-down menus among the GEM applications. That's a polite way of saying you have lots of things to set and diddle.

As we go through the typographic options, I'll give you some rules of thumb for setting them. These guidelines will give you a starting point when you design your pages.

FILE

The File menu offers the typical file-handling choices you've seen in all of the other GEM applications. See Figure 15.3.

Figure 15.3

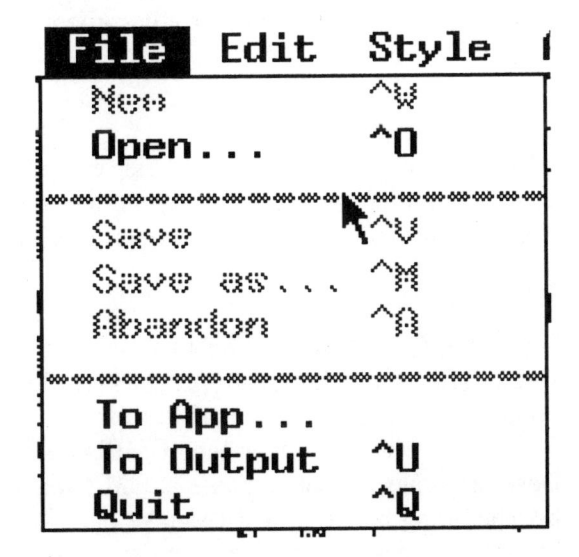

```
┌─────────────────────────────┐
│ File    Edit    Style       │
├─────────────────────────────┤
│  New           ^W           │
│  Open...       ^O           │
│ ··························· │
│  Save          ^V           │
│  Save as...    ^M           │
│  Abandon       ^A           │
│ ··························· │
│  To App...                  │
│  To Output     ^U           │
│  Quit          ^Q           │
└─────────────────────────────┘
```

New

Clears the paste-up board so that you can start another job. If you haven't saved your work, Desktop Publisher will give you a chance to do so.

Open . . .

Pops up the file selector so that you can pick a .GWD file to open. Files with .GWD extensions are Desktop Publisher document files; they point to the proper text, graphics, and style sheet files that make up a publication.

Save

Saves your work back to the file. Before you can do this, though, you must first assign a file name through the Save as . . . option. You can't save work to the UNTITLED.GWD file name that appears when no file is loaded.

Unless you set the program not to do it (via the Set Preferences dialog in the Options menu), Desktop Publisher will make up a print version of the file with a .GMP extension every time you save. This file can be rather large, resulting in long waits and lots of occupied disk space.

Save As . . .

This pops the file selector onto the screen so that you can assign a document file name to your publication. You can't save your document to the default name UNTITLED.GWD. Document files all end in .GWD. You can also use Save As . . . to make a copy of a document so that you can have variations on the same basic publication.

Abandon

Ooops button. If you want to get rid of your changes and call back the last saved version of the file, this is your way out. Desktop Publisher will give you a chance to cancel if you click on this by mistake.

To Output

Off to the Output application to print your file to the printer, plotter, or screen. (But don't run Desktop Publisher files on your plotter; it's a terrible thing to watch that mechanical arm draw every letter on the page.)

Output can print only the .GMP version of your file. If you've told Desktop Publisher not to make a .GMP version every time you save, you'll be wondering how to get it to make one. Turn the function back on in the Set Preferences dialog under Options. Now do a Save As . . . , and write the file back to its own name. As it writes the file you'll get the .GMP version, allowing you to go merrily off to Output.

To App . . .

This allows you to jump to another GEM application from Desktop Publisher. It is a one-way jump, however.

Quit

Back to the Desktop. Don't worry if you hit this by accident or forget to save your file. Desktop Publisher will give you a second chance.

EDIT

The Edit Menu provides text and graphics editing functions. You can use it to delete, copy, and move text and graphics. It can also select all of the text or graphics on a given page. See Figure 15.4.

Cut

This works with the "clipboard." Think of the clipboard as a place you can put one chunk of text and/or one set of graphics. Yes, you can put one of each in the clipboard. Once something is on the clipboard, you can paste it back into your publication as many times as you like.

Figure 15.4

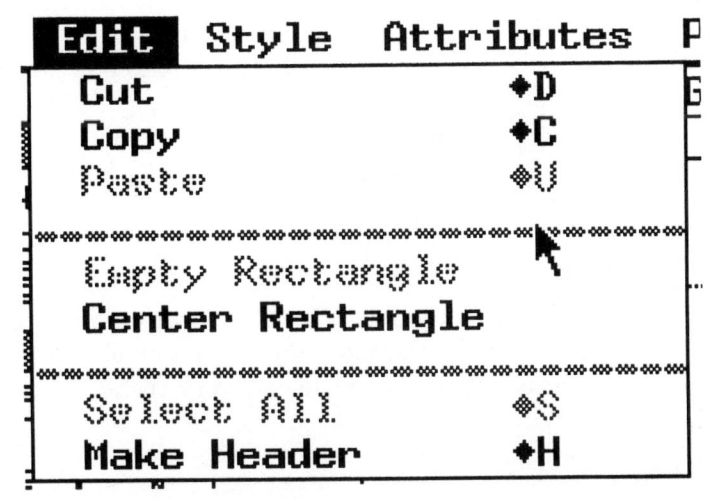

```
┌─────────────────────────────────────┐
│  Edit    Style    Attributes    P   │
│  Cut                      ◆D        │
│  Copy                     ◆C        │
│  Paste                    ◆U        │
│  ·································  │
│  Empty Rectangle                    │
│  Center Rectangle                   │
│  ·································  │
│  Select All               ◆S        │
│  Make Header              ◆H        │
└─────────────────────────────────────┘
```

Copy

Another clipboard function. Use the mouse to select the block of text that you want to copy to the clipboard. Note that Copy doesn't delete the selected text. To copy graphics, select as many rectangles on the page as you would like to put on the clipboard. Every selected rectangle will copy.

The clipboard is really a special subdirectory called /GEMAPPS/CLIPBOARD. The text and graphics placed on the clipboard go into files in /GEMAPPS/CLIPBOARD. You can't append text blocks or rectangles from various Cuts and Copies. Instead, each Cut and Copy operation overwrites the last. You can have text and graphics both on the clipboard at the same time.

When pasting, make sure you're in the right mode. It's easy to paste text when you thought you were dropping in rectangles.

Paste

This one gets a copy of the text and/or graphics from the clipboard and stuffs it onto the current page. For text, it will drop in at the text cursor position. Rectangles pop into the exact position they occupied before being Cut or Copied. If you use Copy and then Paste them onto the same page that they originally came from, they will precisely overlay the original rectangles. You can select them and move them away from the originals.

Empty Rectangle

This will remove the contents of a rectangle. The command works equally well on a text or graphic file loaded into a rectangle.

Center Rectangle

Centers a selected rectangle on the page (centered, at least, between the right and left edges of the page).

Select All

This is fun to watch in text mode. Click on Select All and Desktop Publisher selects every paragraph in every rectangle on the page. In either of the rectangle modes, it will select every rectangle on the current page.

STYLE

The Style Menu controls the style sheets. See Figure 15.5. All of your tags are saved in a collection called a style sheet. Each style sheet is an individual file with an extension of .STL. That makes it very handy because you can load a style sheet file into any document. Once you have defined a standard style, you can apply it to many documents.

Get Style Sheet . . .

Pulls up the file item selector so that you can assign a style sheet to the publication you have open.

Save Style Sheet . . .

Available only if you've made changes to your style sheet. Saves the changes back to the style sheet file.

Figure 15.5

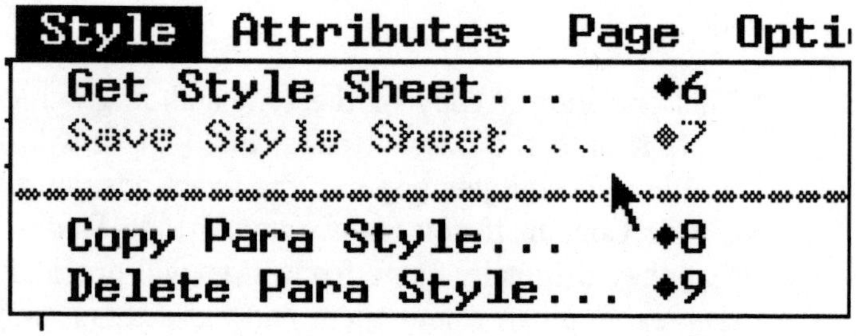

```
┌──────────────────────────────────────────┐
│ Style  Attributes   Page   Opti│
│   Get Style Sheet...    ♦6     │
│   Save Style Sheet...   ♦7     │
│ ────────────────────────────── │
│   Copy Para Style...    ♦8     │
│   Delete Para Style...  ♦9     │
└──────────────────────────────────────────┘
```

Copy Para Style . . .

Copies all of the formatting characteristics from one tag to another tag. See Figure 15.6. This makes it easier to create new tags since you can keep the formatting commands you want from other tags.

Delete Para Style

Deletes a tag from the style sheet.

ATTRIBUTES

The Attributes Menu controls the appearance of things, from paragraph tags to rectangles and the graphics created in Desktop Publisher. See Figure 15.7. The following sections discuss the dialogs in groups, according to what they affect.

TEXT ATTRIBUTES

These apply to paragraph tags. The Character dialog also applies to text that you've selected with the mouse.

Character

This is the typographic dialog. It controls type font, style, size, and color. See Figure 15.8. The fonts that are available depend on the type of printer and what fonts you've loaded into GEM/3 through the Bitstream Font Loader.

Figure 15.6

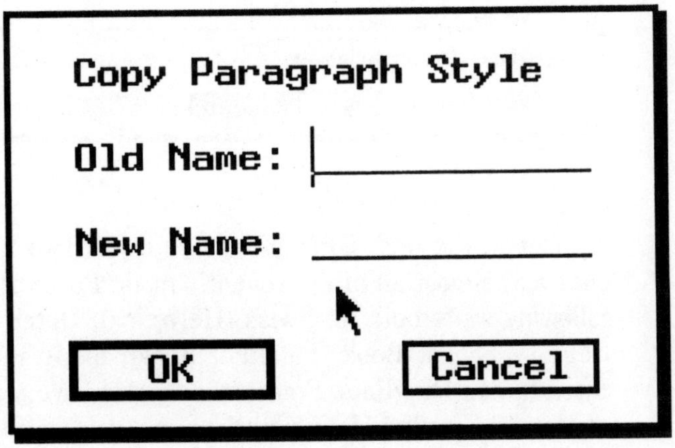

Figure 15.7

```
Attributes   Page    Options
  Character...         ◆1
  Paragraph...         ◆2
  Hyphenation...
  Paragraph Tabs...    ◆3
  Rectangle...         ◆4
  ─────────────────────────
  Line Attributes...
  Fill Attributes...
  ─────────────────────────
  Page Numbers...      ◆5
```

Figure 15.8

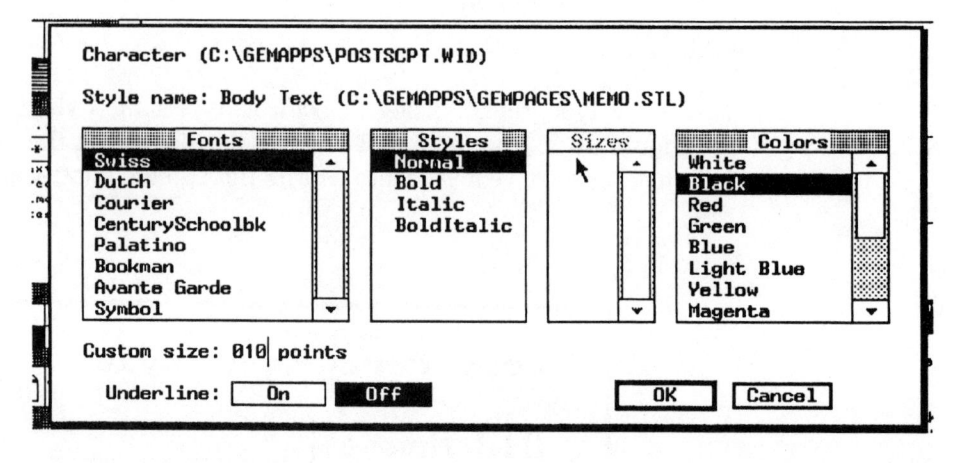

```
Character (C:\GEMAPPS\POSTSCPT.WID)
Style name: Body Text (C:\GEMAPPS\GEMPAGES\MEMO.STL)

    Fonts              Styles         Sizes         Colors
  Swiss              Normal                       White
  Dutch              Bold                         Black
  Courier            Italic                       Red
  CenturySchoolbk    BoldItalic                   Green
  Palatino                                        Blue
  Bookman                                         Light Blue
  Avante Garde                                    Yellow
  Symbol                                          Magenta

Custom size: 010 points
Underline:  [ On ]  [ Off ]              [ OK ]  [ Cancel ]
```

Out of the box, GEM comes with just two fonts: Swiss and Dutch. In contrast, almost all of the recently made PostScript printers come with the following fonts built in: Swiss (Helvetica), Dutch (Times Roman), Courier, Century School Book, Palatino, Bookman, Avant Garde, Zaph Chancery, Symbol, and DingBats. Some models also have a pseudo-condensed version of Helvetica called Helvetica Narrow.

Desktop Publisher knows about these and has built-in width tables for these fonts. Because a width table can hold only eight fonts, you'll find the total set of fonts divided into the POSTSCPT.WID and PSTSCPT2.WID. width tables. Desktop Publisher, however, has screen fonts only for Swiss, Dutch, and any screen fonts that you've generated with the Bitstream font loader. If you pick a PostScript font other than Swiss or Dutch, you'll get the proper spacing on-screen, but GEM/3 will use the Swiss Screen Font.

The PostScript driver is truly universal. With it you can drive Linotronic, Itek, and AM PostScript-based typesetters as well as laser printers.

Type style again depends on what's available with the font. For most faces, you have a choice of normal (roman), bold, italic, and bold italic. You can also combine underlining with any of the these. Some Bitstream fonts don't have the complete range, however. For example, Helvetica Light doesn't have a bold version. Headline fonts, such as University Roman, usually have no additional styles.

Size is also dependent on the fonts you've created. If you haven't created any additional sizes, then you have the usual assortment of GEM sizes: 7, 10, 14, 18, 20, 28, 36, and 72 points. (Remember, 72 points equals an inch). PostScript allows any point size up to 255 points.

Color is useful only if you have a color printer. If you are going to run an offset lithography job with two or more colors, these colors are no help at all. Color offset printing requires a separate negative for each color used. That means you must have a separate layer for each ink color and the various layers must be in absolutely precise alignment. Unfortunately, Desktop Publisher can't print each color separately.

If you are setting up masters for a multicolor printing job, get some tissue paper and tape it over the master pages you get from your laser printer. Circle all of the type to be printed in color, and then mark the color beside the circle. The folks at the print shop can do the rest.

Color 0 is a special case. This provides white type—called "reversing" type—which will show up nicely against a black or very dark gray rectangle.

Paragraph

This dialog box controls spacing between lines and paragraphs, as well as left and right indents. See Figure 15.9. You can access this dialog, which sets the spacing for tags, only in paragraph mode. To move from option to option, you can use the left and right arrow keys or the mouse. The tab key will also advance to the next option, while shift-tab backs up one option. The Escape key completely erases the option setting.

Figure 15.9

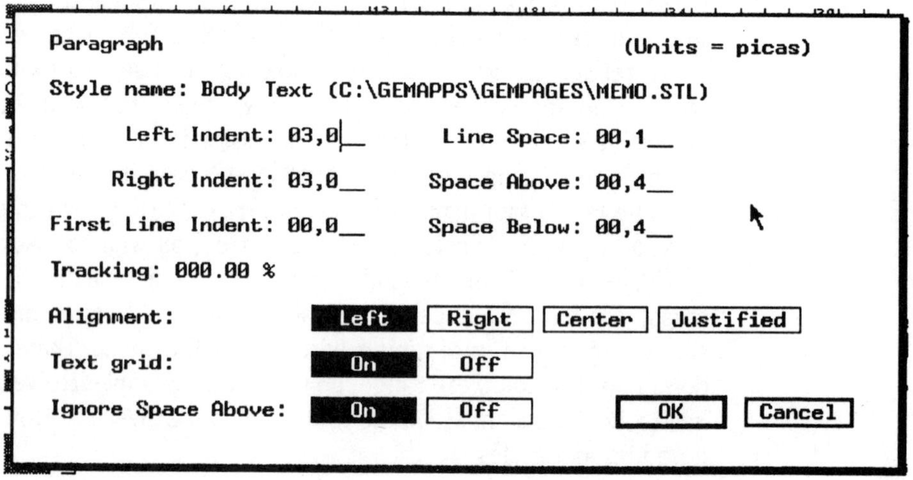

```
Paragraph                                           (Units = picas)
Style name: Body Text (C:\GEMAPPS\GEMPAGES\MEMO.STL)
        Left Indent: 03,0__      Line Space: 00,1__
       Right Indent: 03,0__     Space Above: 00,4__
  First Line Indent: 00,0__     Space Below: 00,4__
           Tracking: 000.00 %
          Alignment:     [ Left ] [ Right ] [ Center ] [ Justified ]
          Text grid:     [ On ]   [ Off ]
  Ignore Space Above:    [ On ]   [ Off ]        [ OK ]   [ Cancel ]
```

To begin, let's deal with Line Space. The spacing between lines is called "leading." Printer's lingo is filled with terms that go back to the days when type was set by hand. This is one of those terms, and it dates back to the time when lines were spaced with strips of metal having a high lead content.

Leading makes the type easier to read by adding a little extra white space between the lines. The longer the line, the more leading you should add. If your line is 39 characters wide, one point should do nicely. But if your line is 50 characters or more, two points would be better.

The choice of leading also depends on the type face you are using. Swiss has a high "X" height (that is, the height of a lower-case letter is rather tall compared to other type faces of the same size, including Dutch). Due to the height of its lower-case letters, setting Swiss without enough leading will make for crammed looking type.

Space Above and Space Below control the amount of extra space above and below paragraphs. In Desktop Publisher, any number of characters (even just one) followed by a carriage return/line feed (you get these by pressing Return) is a paragraph. Because you usually have more than one paragraph in your text, the spacing between paragraphs is actually the sum of Space Above and Space Below.

If you don't set these controls, there won't be any extra space at all between your paragraphs. Aside from looking odd, your text will be difficult to read. As a general rule, set the Space Above and Space Below for body text at half the size of your body type. Ten point type means Space Above set to five points and Space Below set to five. You can add or subtract a point or two from both to get a more open or compact look.

When setting up a tag for a heading or subheading, you'll want to add a bit more space above and below. For instance, for a 14 point subheading you could set Space Above: 12 points/Space Below: 9 points.

Left Indent sets a left margin measured from the left edge of the rectangle holding the text. Right Indent sets a right margin measured from the right edge of the rectangle. The combination of the two sets the length of your line. Note that if you put text in a rectangle smaller than the base rectangle for the page, you'll get shorter lines.

Just how long your lines should be is partly a function of the type face, partly the type size, and partly the amount of leading. An old typographer's rule is to set your lines between 39 and 52 characters wide. You can set longer lines, but be careful. If you set a huge mass of text in wide lines, the text will become terribly difficult to read. If you have very long lines, you might want to make Line Space three points.

First Line Indent sets an indent for the first line of every paragraph assigned that tag. Keep these indents small. A good general setting is one pica. Of course, you don't have to use any indent at all.

Tracking is a typographic function that sets the amount of spacing between both the letters and the words. Desktop Publisher accepts tracking from +50 to −50 percent, with the plus side spreading things apart and the minus side tightening the spacing.

Tracking can be useful in two ways. Opening text up a little bit can sometimes make it easier to read. And opening it up drastically or tightening up the space is great for special effects.

You'll normally pick alignments of either left or justified. Left is actually more commonly called "ragged right." The left side of the column is aligned flush, but the right side isn't aligned. Justified aligns both sides of the column.

Don't use justified unless you activate hyphenation. To justify text, Desktop Publisher sometimes must stretch the spacing between words and between letters. Hyphenation allows the program to break words so that excessive space is not needed to make the lines even.

Right aligned text is sometimes useful in advertising, although it's a bit difficult to read. Automatic centering is handy, especially for centered headings.

Text grid aligns columns of text. It applies to the Body Text tag as well as to any tag that has the same type size as Body Text. The grid normally overrides the settings for Space Above and Space Below. If you select Text grid Off, the Space Above and Space Below settings reign unchallenged.

Ignore Space Above applies to a tag that falls at the top of a page, such as a heading. In this case, you might not want the insertion of additional space above. Select On and you won't get the additional space if the paragraph is at the top of the page.

Hyphenation

This dialog lets you select the hyphenation algorithm, by language, that you want to use. See Figure 15.10. When you select an algorithm, it's applied to the text for that tag throughout the document. This is kind of neat to watch, as it takes so little time to hyphenate all those words.

Don't try to justify text without hyphenation. If you do, Desktop Publisher will add too much space between words, and you'll see what typographers call rivers of white. These are winding bands of white space that flow down through your page.

Paragraph Tabs

This can be reached only in the paragraph mode. Each tag can have its own set of tab stops. Tabs are measured from the left edge of the rectangle. See Figure 15.11.

When setting tabs, keep in mind that Desktop Publisher sorts your settings in ascending order. If you set tab 1: at nine picas and tab 2: at six

Figure 15.10

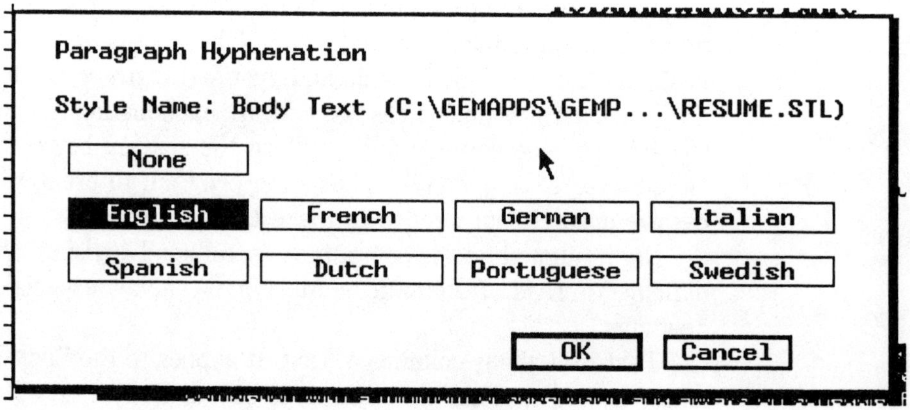

```
Paragraph Hyphenation
Style Name: Body Text (C:\GEMAPPS\GEMP...\RESUME.STL)

    [  None  ]

    [ English ]  [ French ]  [ German ]  [ Italian ]
    [ Spanish ]  [ Dutch  ]  [ Portuguese ] [ Swedish ]

                              [  OK  ]  [ Cancel ]
```

Figure 15.11

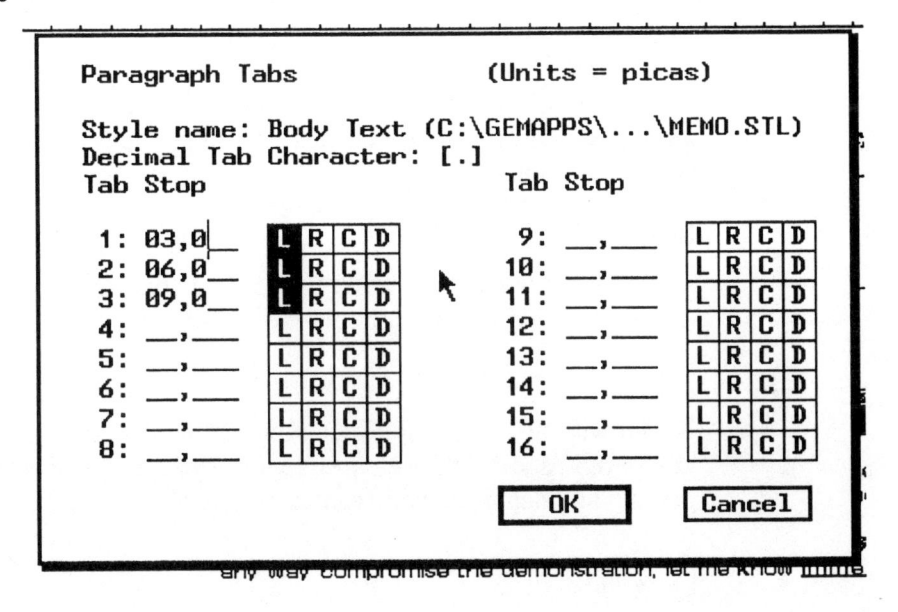

```
┌─────────────────────────────────────────────────────┐
│  Paragraph Tabs              (Units = picas)        │
│                                                     │
│  Style name: Body Text (C:\GEMAPPS\...\MEMO.STL)    │
│  Decimal Tab Character: [.]                         │
│  Tab Stop                    Tab Stop               │
│                                                     │
│   1: 03,0__  [L] R C D       9: __,__  L R C D      │
│   2: 06,0__  [L] R C D      10: __,__  L R C D      │
│   3: 09,0__  [L] R C D      11: __,__  L R C D      │
│   4: __,__    L  R C D      12: __,__  L R C D      │
│   5: __,__    L  R C D      13: __,__  L R C D      │
│   6: __,__    L  R C D      14: __,__  L R C D      │
│   7: __,__    L  R C D      15: __,__  L R C D      │
│   8: __,__    L  R C D      16: __,__  L R C D      │
│                                                     │
│                             [  OK  ]   [ Cancel ]   │
└─────────────────────────────────────────────────────┘
```

picas, Desktop Publisher will shuffle them to tab 1: at six picas and tab 2: at nine picas.

Tabs come in four flavors:

L: Left justified. The text begins at the tab stop.

R: Right justified. The text slides over to end at the tab stop.

C: Centered. The text shifts around to center at the tab stop.

D: Decimal. The decimal point in a figure aligns at the tab stops. This is great when working with columns of figures.

Tabs in Desktop Publisher are just that, the genuine tab character. If your word processor throws in a number of spaces when you hit the tab key, you have a good deal of reformatting to do when you load a table into Desktop Publisher.

RECTANGLE AND GRAPHIC ATTRIBUTES

These affect base rectangles (both graphic and text) and the shapes and lines created in the graphics mode.

Rectangle

Rectangle is active only when Desktop Publisher is in either of the rectangle modes and a rectangle is selected.

The Graphics Rectangle dialog box lets you pick the background color and screen pattern for rectangles. It also provides cropping or scaling controls. See Figure 15.12.

Color

Again, this is useful only if you have both a color monitor and a color output device. Click on the background color you want.

Pattern

Useful with any printing device. You can choose from white, one of seven gray levels, and black. Be careful with dense grays, however; you will lose graphic line definition and type against them.

Figure 15.12

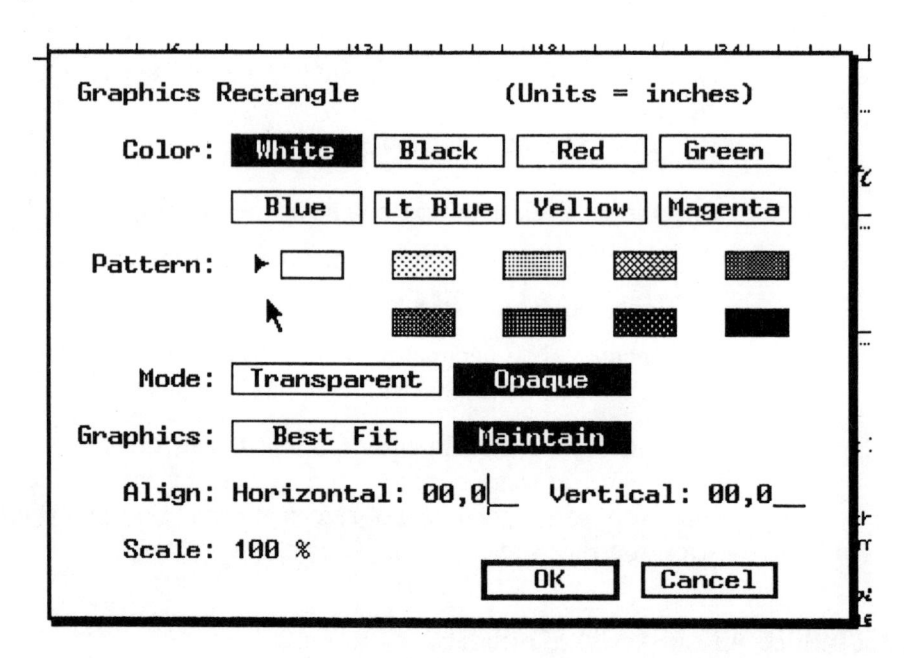

Mode

Transparent allows anything underneath the rectangle, such as text or another graphics rectangle, to show through. Opaque is what it says, nothing shows through.

When you select transparent, text no longer wraps around the rectangle. It flows under it instead. Why would anyone want to do this? Well, let's say that you want to run text around an irregular object, not just its rectangle. To do this, first make the graphic rectangle transparent. Then draw individual rectangles, one line deep, to push the text away from the picture. Don't worry that these smaller rectangles obscure the picture; we'll fix that.

After all of the small rectangles are drawn, use control-click to select through the mess and get the graphics rectangle. Delete it, and then undelete it. Presto! The picture is now on top and clearly visible.

Graphics

Graphics selects whether a .GEM or .IMG file is shown scaled to fit the rectangle (Best Fit), or should be custom scaled (Maintain). If you choose Maintain, you can select the percentage of reduction or enlargement. This is just like having an electronic stat camera.

Selecting Maintain also lets you play with the Align settings. Use these if the image is larger than the rectangle (which can happen if you are scaling the image), and you want only a certain section to show. Horizontal shifts the image to the left by the specified amount. Vertical shifts the image down by the specified amount.

LINE ATTRIBUTES

This dialog affects lines and all of the shapes you can draw in the graphics mode. See Figure 15.13.

Color

This one's pretty obvious if you have a color monitor. Those with monochrome viewing can still select black or white.

Type

You can choose from solid, dotted, hashed, or dotted-hashed lines. The custom line weight setting works only with solid lines.

Figure 15.13

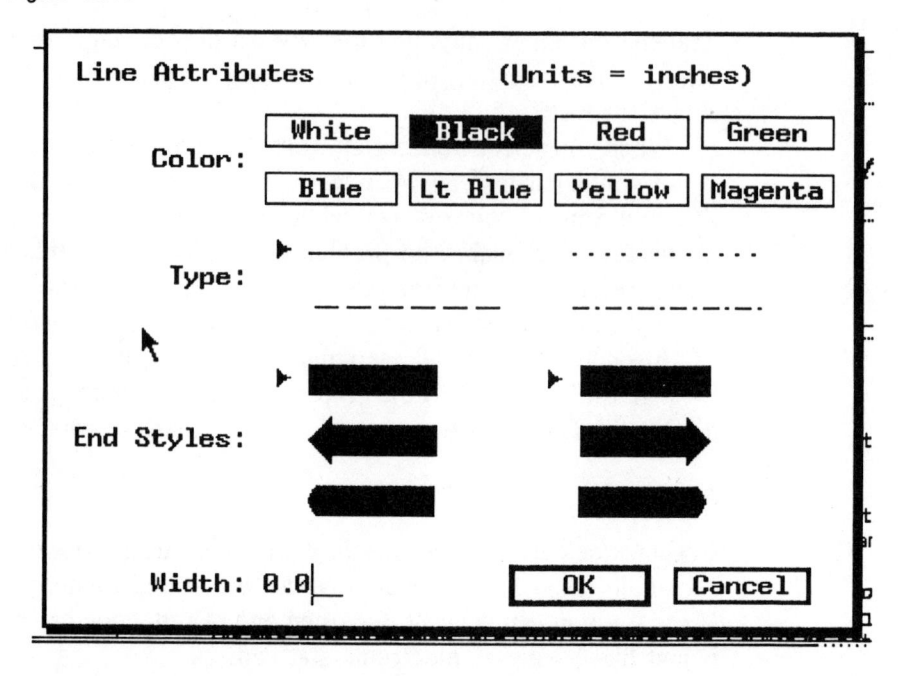

End Styles

This only applies to lines; you can't set the end styles for shapes. You can choose from round, square, or arrow-equipped ends.

The selector follows the mystifying convention of all GEM line end style selectors: the left side refers to the starting point of the line while the right side refers to the end point. Got it?

Width

This allows you to specify a custom line weight up to one-half inch. It also proportionally fattens arrowheads if you've selected them.

FILL ATTRIBUTES

This dialog affects the innards of any selected shape. See Figure 15.14.

Color

Yes, you can set the inside color of the shape separately from the line color.

Figure 15.14

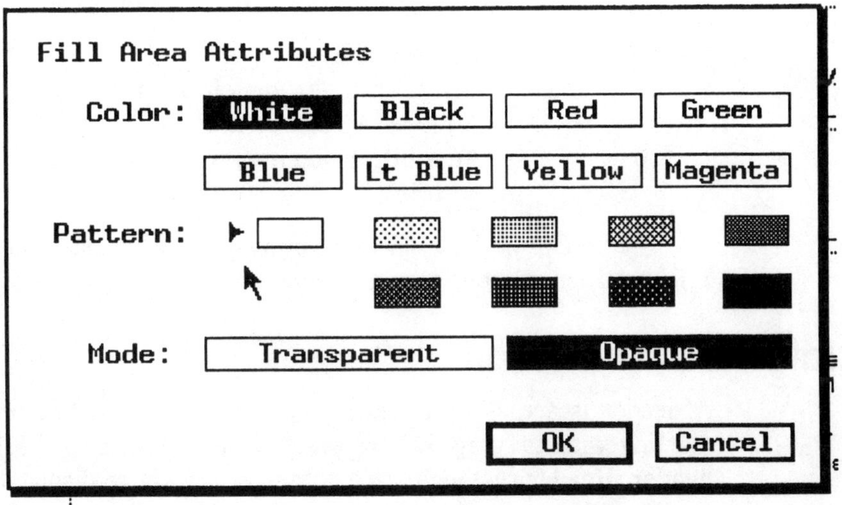

[Dialog box: Fill Area Attributes — Color: White (selected), Black, Red, Green, Blue, Lt Blue, Yellow, Magenta. Pattern: various fill patterns. Mode: Transparent, Opaque (selected). OK, Cancel buttons.]

Pattern

Allows you to fill the shape with any of the available screen densities.

Mode

Transparent allows whatever is behind the graphic to show through, while Opaque lets the graphic obscure what's behind it. These attributes can be very, very useful. Suppose that you want some gray text. Simply draw a box (graphics mode) that covers the text. Select white for the color and a light screen for the fill pattern, and then flip on Transparent. The only things that occlude the text below the graphic are the white dots of the screen, which in turn screen the text itself.

PAGE NUMBERS

Desktop Publisher lets you choose to number your pages with arabic numerals, lower-case letters, upper-case letters, lower-case roman numerals, or upper-case roman numerals.

Page numbering itself is done through a GEM Draw Plus file that is made into a header. GEM Desktop Publisher comes with several page number files. You can find these in the /PAGENBRS directory. Each of the example files has a coded name, and the decoding rules are:

PN	Page number
C, R, or L	Centered, right, or left aligned number
07	A file seven inches wide
00n	An arbitrary number assigned to each file in the series.

The coding is there so that you can tell what each file is, but you can rename them without any ill effects.

PLACING HEADERS IN A DOCUMENT

A header is actually a repeating rectangle. It repeats from page to page, starting with the page where you first elevated it to the lofty position of header. Header rectangles are automatically set to display their .GEM contents at 100 percent (not Best Fit). Position matters not, however, and you can use the Make Header command to make headers, footers, or frames that repeat through the center of each page.

To make a header, select the rectangle and click on Make Header in the Edit pull-down menu. And remember, it repeats only on subsequent pages.

MAKING A HEADER IN GEM DRAW PLUS

A header file consists of a background rectangle, text (including page numbering codes), and graphics (such as rules, logos, etc.). The background rectangle is the rearmost object in the file. It should have a solid white pattern and a "none" line. The background rectangle can be wider than the text or graphics it holds, but it can't be smaller.

Text can be anything you like, but it must fit in the rectangle. If you want to number pages or throw in dates automatically, there are codes that you can embed into the text. The codes are:

Code	Result
<$dateFUSA>	January 25, 1989
<$dateLUSA>	01/25/1989
<$dateMUSA>	01/25/89
<$dateSUSA>	1/25/89
<$dateFEUR>	25 January, 1989

<$dateLEUR>	25/01/1989
<$dateMEUR>	25/01/89
<$dateSEUR>	25/1/89
<$lastpage>	n (where n is the last page with the header)
<$page>	n (where n is the current page number)
<$time12L>	3:26 p.m.
<$time12U>	3:26 P.M.
<$time24>	15:26

As your taste dictates, you should either left align, center, or right align your text in the background rectangle.

As for graphics, they can be anything you like. The only necessity is that they fit inside the background rectangle.

THE PAGE NUMBERING DIALOG

Once you've embedded the <$page> in your header file (or just called up one of the ones provided with GEM Desktop Publisher), you can use this dialog. The top five selection boxes let you pick the page numbering format. See Figure 15.15. This page #: allows you to set the starting number for the current page. Legal page numbers range from 1 to 99.

Figure 15.15

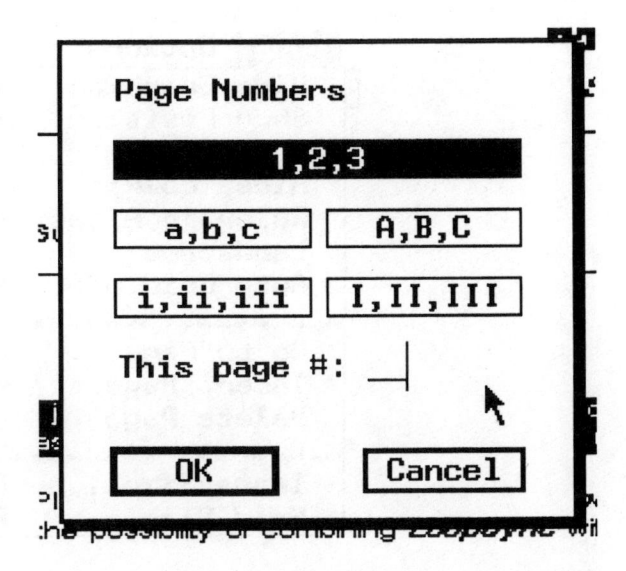

PAGE

The Page pull-down menu consists of a motley collection of options, each of which affects the page in some way. See Figure 15.16. They are all working tools that you'll constantly use during layout.

Hide Graphics

Depending on your computer, it can take a while to redraw graphics on the screen. Click on this option and Desktop Publisher will fill the graphics rectangles with gray instead of the picture. This really speeds up screen redraws.

Desktop Publisher also shows the file name for the contents in each rectangle. This is handy, too, because it allows you to see what file is where (in case you're like me and may want to modify a particular graphic but can't remember the file name). Click on this again to redisplay the graphics.

Show Position

I love this command. When it's turned on, the current position of the mouse cursor is displayed. This is measured from the top and from the left of the page. Click again to turn the function off. Two things to note: 1) Desktop Publisher must be in either the select rectangle or make rectangle mode

Figure 15.16

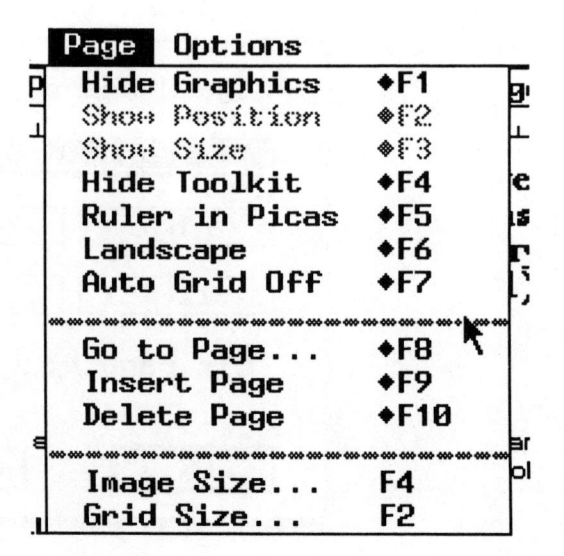

```
Page   Options
  Hide Graphics    ◆F1
  Show Position    ◆F2
  Show Size        ◆F3
  Hide Toolkit     ◆F4
  Ruler in Picas   ◆F5
  Landscape        ◆F6
  Auto Grid Off    ◆F7
  ─────────────────────
  Go to Page...    ◆F8
  Insert Page      ◆F9
  Delete Page      ◆F10
  ─────────────────────
  Image Size...    F4
  Grid Size...     F2
```

for this to work, and 2) by turning on this command, you automatically turn Show Size off.

The upper right number is the distance from the left of the page, shown in whatever units you're currently using. The lower left number is the distance from the top of the page.

Show Size

Works only in the select rectangle or make rectangle modes. When Show Size is on, Desktop Publisher displays the size of the rectangle you're drawing or modifying. In the select mode, you need to click on an extent box to get the rectangle size.

The top right number is the width of the rectangle in the currently selected units. The bottom left number is the rectangle height.

Hide Toolkit

Drops the toolkit at the left completely off the screen. This gives you that extra viewing area you sometimes need. Since toolkit functions are available through keyboard commands, you can continue to run this way. All the keyboard commands are listed following the description of pull-down menus.

Rulers in Inches or Picas or Centimeters

Switches the measuring units between inches and picas. If you are using metric pages (set with Image Size), this switches between picas and centimeters.

Portrait or Landscape

Portrait, the default, is the way you normally look at a page. Landscape is a page turned on its side. Landscape provides some interesting design opportunities. For example, it makes it easy to put illustrations beside columns of text. And Landscape pages can be bound either at the side or top. If, moreover, you put two text rectangles on the page (one on the right and one on the left), folding the result will give you an 8½x5½-inch pamphlet. Just click to change from one page type to the other. But be sure to do this before you start adding rectangles.

Auto Grid On or Off

Desktop Publisher has an invisible grid, similar to the grids in GEM Draw Plus or GEM Paint. The distance between grid points is set with the Grid Size . . . option.

When the grid is on, rectangles will snap to the grid points both as you draw them and as you move them. This lets you line things up with precision, and it makes grid-based layout possible. Grid-based layout, an extension of the grid design methods used by graphic designers, is covered in the following chapter.

If you turn the grid off, you can slide things anywhere you like. You can also draw rectangles of any size.

Go to Page . . .

Pops up a little dialog box that asks what page you'd really like to see. Just enter the page number and click on OK.

If you can't remember how many pages are in your publication file, and you want to get to the last page—no problem. Enter a page number higher than your document could possibly have (such as 378).

Insert Page

Inserts a blank page before the one currently on the screen. The blank page will then display. No text or graphics will be lost on any subsequent pages.

Delete Page

Removes the page currently on the screen. This won't delete any text from the publication, but it will push the text off to the next page. Any graphics rectangles on the deleted page will also disappear.

Image Size . . .

Sets the page size and whether to use English or metric units of measure. See Figure 15.17. Don't worry; picas are available in both systems. Desktop Publisher supports the following page sizes:

English	*Metric*
8x10 inches	17x25.7 centimeters (A4)
8x13 inches	25.7x38 centimeters (A3)

Why 8x10 inches when your laser printer takes 8½x11-inch paper? Imaging area. For example, the Apple LaserWriter can't image in from the paper edge for about one-half inch on all sides. Check your laser printer; it might do better than this.

The larger page size will work even if your printer doesn't support it. Output can split large paper sizes into 8½x11-inch chunks so that you can paste them together.

Figure 15.17

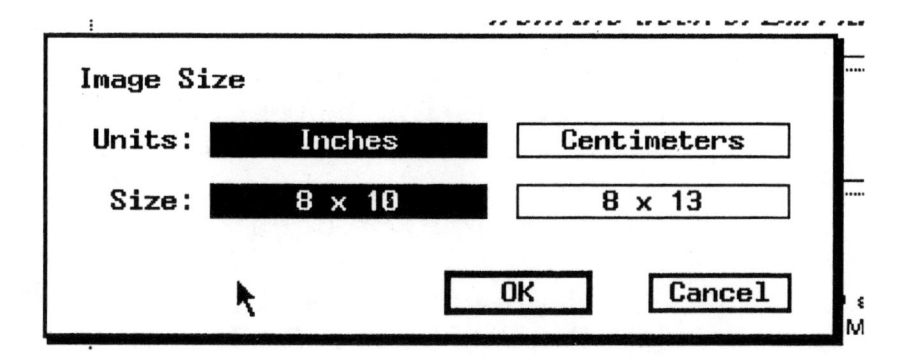

[Image Size dialog: Units: Inches / Centimeters; Size: 8 x 10 / 8 x 13; OK / Cancel]

Grid Size . . .

Sets the distance between the grid points on the invisible page grid. You can set them in inches, centimeters, or picas. The following increments are available:

Picas	Inches	Centimeters
12	1	3
6	1/2	2
3	1/4	1
2	1/8	1/2
1	1/16	1/5
1/2	1/32	1/10

Note that the increments from one scale to another are not equivalent. Picas allows a setting of two inches (12 picas). Centimeters allows you to set the grid down to a millimeter.

OPTIONS

You won't be in Options nearly as often as the other pull-down menus. Options sets up defaults, copies your Desktop Publisher files, and provides a couple of keyboard command help screens. See Figure 15.18. Don't try to copy Desktop Publisher documents with the GEM Desktop or the DOS copy command. A document file has pointers to text, style, and graphics files. When Desktop Publisher copies a document, it copies all related files and resets the file pointers.

Figure 15.18

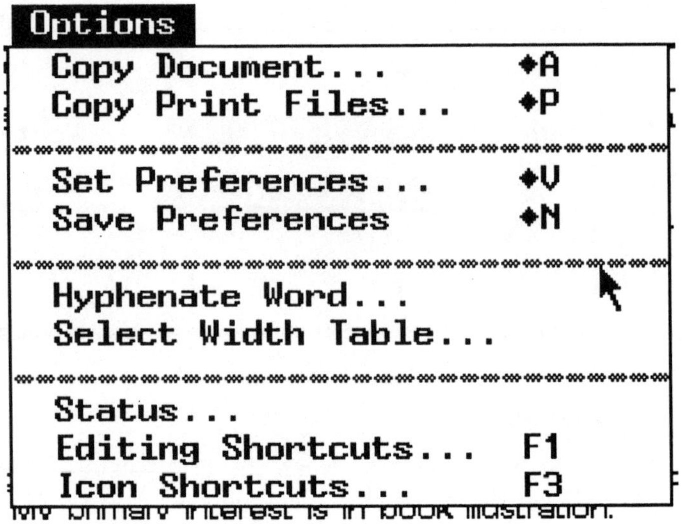

```
Options
 Copy Document...          ♦A
 Copy Print Files...       ♦P
 ~~~~~~~~~~~~~~~~~~~~~~~~~~~~
 Set Preferences...        ♦V
 Save Preferences          ♦N
 ~~~~~~~~~~~~~~~~~~~~~~~~~~~~
 Hyphenate Word...
 Select Width Table...
 ~~~~~~~~~~~~~~~~~~~~~~~~~~~~
 Status...
 Editing Shortcuts...      F1
 Icon Shortcuts...         F3
```

COPY DOCUMENT . . .

Use this whenever you want to copy a document, whether for backups or just to move the document to another directory. You can copy any .GWD file; it need not be the one currently loaded in Desktop Publisher. Copy Document . . . is a tad tricky to use, however. Before you can copy the .GWD file, you need to pick the copy destination.

The destination is whatever disk drive and directory are currently showing on the mini-selector (in the toolkit at the left of the screen). Desktop Publisher must be in either the make rectangle or select rectangle mode to display the mini-selector. It doesn't matter what file extension the mini-selector is showing.

After you set the mini-selector for the disk drive and directory that will receive the copy, click on Copy document . . . . A typical GEM file selector will pop up on the screen. Use the selector to move around directories and drives until you find the file you want to copy. See Figure 15.19.

If you want to retrieve a backup you've made with Copy Document . . . , you'll need to use it again to move the backup from the floppy to your hard drive. This time, set the mini-selector to point to the hard drive working area you use (probably GEMPAGES, since that's the Desktop Publisher default menu). Use the file selector in Copy Document . . . to click on the floppy disk backup.

Figure 15.19

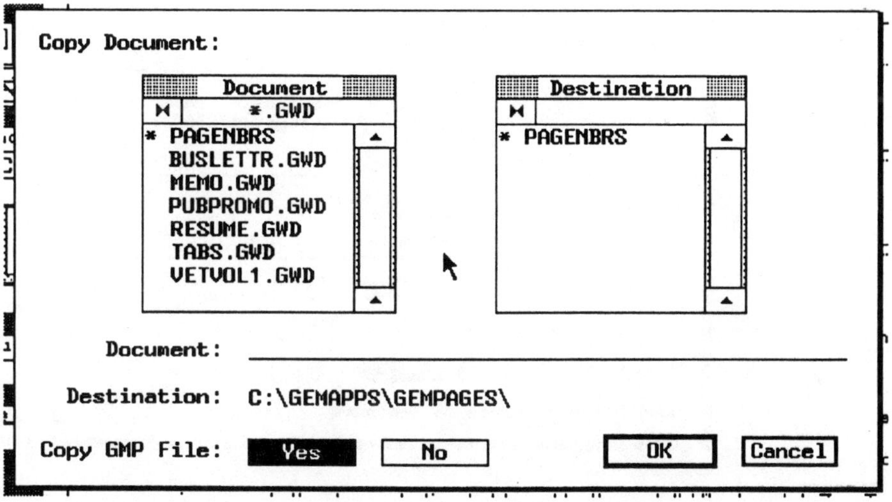

```
Copy Document:
            Document              Destination
         *.GWD
         * PAGENBRS              * PAGENBRS
           BUSLETTR.GWD
           MEMO.GWD
           PUBPROMO.GWD
           RESUME.GWD
           TABS.GWD
           VETVOL1.GWD

    Document: _____
    Destination: C:\GEMAPPS\GEMPAGES\
    Copy GMP File:  [Yes]  [No]        [OK]  [Cancel]
```

Copy Document . . . won't let you copy a file to the same directory it's already in. It will let you copy a .GWD file and its retinue over a previous copy, as long as the source and destination directories are different.

COPY PRINT FILES

You really don't need to use this one unless your publication has paint files. All the text and graphics from .GEM files end up in the printer file for the publication. But .IMG files from either a scanner or GEM Paint aren't in the .GMP files. Instead, the .GMP file points to those files and loads them when it's time to print their contents.

If your publication has .IMG files, use this. It will drag the .IMG files along so it can find the copies of the .IMG files at print time.

This option works just like Copy Document . . . . You point to the destination with the mini-selector before clicking on Copy Print Files.

SET PREFERENCES

This sets defaults for Desktop Publisher. See Figure 15.20. The word processing file extensions selector sets the text file extensions that appear in the mini-selector. This is the only way to change the mini-selector extensions.

GEM Desktop Publisher 2.0 can translate a number of word processor files, including GEM 1st Word Plus. It can even properly translate formatting,

Figure 15.20

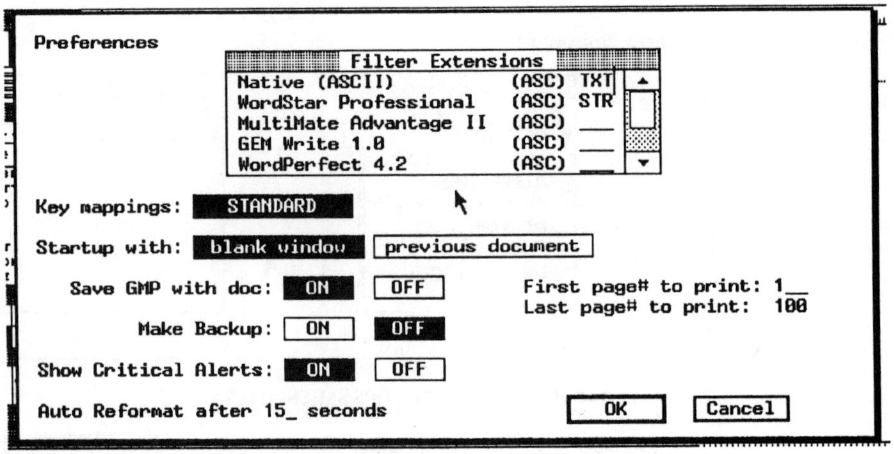

```
Preferences
                    Filter Extensions
          Native (ASCII)         (ASC) TXT
          WordStar Professional  (ASC) STR
          MultiMate Advantage II (ASC) ___
          GEM Write 1.0          (ASC) ___
          WordPerfect 4.2        (ASC) ___

Key mappings:   STANDARD
Startup with:   blank window    previous document
   Save GMP with doc:  ON   OFF     First page# to print: 1__
                                    Last page# to print:  100
        Make Backup:  ON   OFF
  Show Critical Alerts:  ON   OFF
  Auto Reformat after 15_ seconds        OK    Cancel
```

such as bold, italic, etc., from some word processors. Supported word processors include WordStar (any version including 5.0), Multimate Advantage II, GEM Write 1.0, GEM 1st Word Plus, WordPerfect 4.2 (but not 5.0), and Microsoft Word (any version). It can also translate an RFT/DCA format file.

If you don't have any of the supported word processors, despair not. Desktop Publisher can also read ASCII files.

Watch out for the .DOC extension. Nearly every other word processor on the market uses this one, including Microsoft Word, Multimate, and GEM 1st Word Plus.

Key mappings

This refers to keyboard mapping files (covered later in this chapter). Such files allow you to redefine the Desktop Publisher commands to approximate your word processor command set.

Startup with

Sets Desktop Publisher either to open with a blank layout board or automatically load the last document you were working on. Whatever is handiest for you.

Save GMP with doc

A wonderful improvement. Version 1.0 drove you bonkers with larger files because it would stop to make up a printer file every time you saved. You can toggle this off to keep it from writing the printer file until you're done. Just remember to toggle it on before your final save.

Make Backup

This is handy if you're attempting to run Desktop Publisher from floppy disks because not making a backup file conserves disk space. As one who really doesn't trust computers, however, I like to have backup files.

Show Critical Alerts

If you turn this off, Desktop Publisher won't show you alert messages such as "Word too long for line."

Auto Reformat

Sets the number of seconds Desktop Publisher will wait for you to hit a key before it reformats the text. This works only with the text-editing mode. If you want to drive someone crazy, set it to zero. Desktop Publisher will reformat after practically every character entry.

First page to print/Last page to print

Use this to specify the start and stop page for the printer (.GMP) file.

SAVE PREFERENCES

Saves the settings you've made in the Set Preferences dialog box. You may not always want to do this, especially if you've just reset the text file extensions to load in a file with an oddball name.

Hyphenate Word . . .

Desktop Publisher uses a hyphenation algorithm. This is a section of software that uses rules to hyphenate words. Unfortunately, English doesn't always play by the rules. Sometimes following the rules produces weird results. To compensate for this, you can enter words in the exception dictionary, which contains words that are exceptions to the rules. See Figure 15.21.

Desktop Publisher will then follow your hyphen placements in these words. If you don't want hyphens in a word at all, just enter the word without hyphens in the exception dictionary.

Figure 15.21

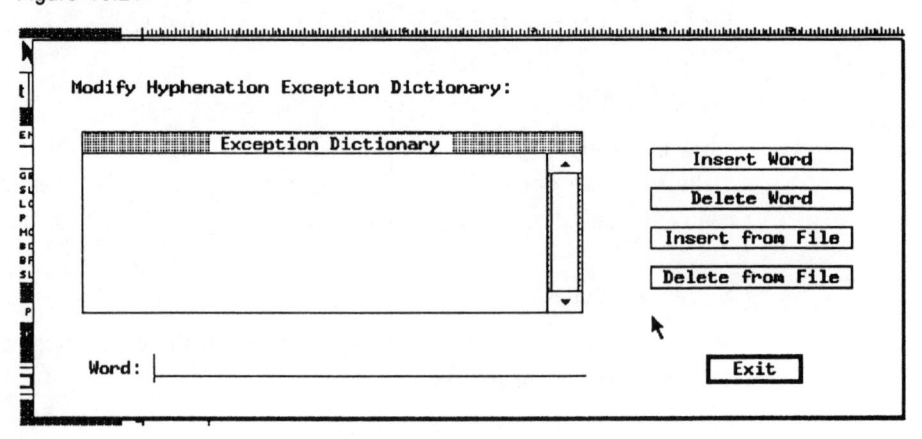

```
Modify Hyphenation Exception Dictionary:

    ┌─────── Exception Dictionary ───────┐    ┌─────────────────┐
    │                                    │    │   Insert Word   │
    │                                    │    ├─────────────────┤
    │                                    │    │   Delete Word   │
    │                                    │    ├─────────────────┤
    │                                    │    │ Insert from File│
    │                                    │    ├─────────────────┤
    │                                    │    │ Delete from File│
    └────────────────────────────────────┘    └─────────────────┘

    Word: |                                          |    ┌──────┐
                                                          │ Exit │
                                                          └──────┘
```

Status

This is a lovely thing. It tells you how much room is taken up by files, graphic elements, etc. Maximums are 64 files, 100 pages, 256 rectangles, 32 paragraph styles. See Figure 15.22.

Editing Shortcuts

This is the help screen that has the Desktop Publisher keyboard commands for editing.

Icon Shortcuts

Another help screen that lists the keyboard commands corresponding to the icon functions.

KEYBOARD COMMANDS

The following is a complete list of Desktop Publisher keyboard commands. You might want to keep this list handy at your desk. Of course, if you redefine the keyboard commands, this list won't be of much help.

Miscellaneous Commands

Character Up	Up arrow
Character Down	Down arrow
Character Left	Left arrow

Figure 15.22

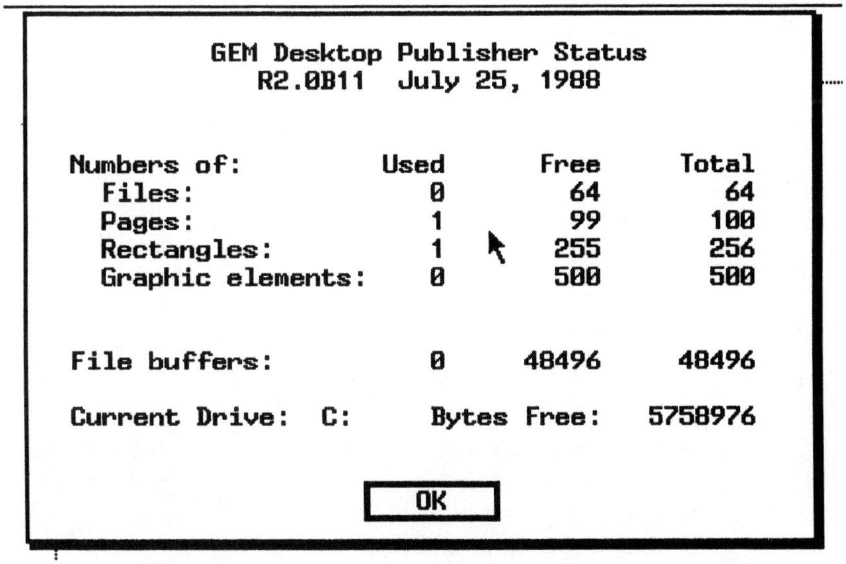

```
          GEM Desktop Publisher Status
            R2.0B11   July 25, 1988


   Numbers of:         Used       Free       Total
      Files:            0          64         64
      Pages:            1          99        100
      Rectangles:       1         255        256
      Graphic elements: 0         500        500


   File buffers:        0       48496      48496

   Current Drive:  C:    Bytes Free:      5758976

                      [   OK   ]
```

Character Right	Right arrow
Create Rectangle Mode	Shift-F2
Cursor to Beginning or End of Line	Control-Z
Delete Character Left	Control-H
Delete Character Right	Delete
Delete Word	Control-T
Delete Line	Control-Y
Down Arrow	Alt-X
Full Page View	Shift-F6
Left Arrow	Alt-E
Mini-Selector Close Box	Control-F9
Mini-Selector Path	Control-F10
Mini-Selector Line #1	Control-F1
Mini-Selector Line #2	Control-F2
Mini-Selector Line #3	Control-F3
Mini-Selector Line #4	Control-F4
Mini-Selector Line #5	Control-F5
Mini-Selector Line #6	Control-F6
Mini-Selector Line #7	Control-F7

Mini-Selector Line #8	Control-F8
Next Page	PgDn
Next Word	Control-right arrow
Normal View	Shift-F7
Page Bottom	End
Page Top	Home
Panner	Shift-F9
Paragraph Mode	Shift-F4
Previous Word	Control-left arrow
Previous Page	PgUp
Right Arrow	Alt-F
Rulers	Shift-F10
Select Rectangle Mode	Shift-F1
Slider Bar Up	Alt-Q
Slider Bar Down	Alt-Z
Slider Bar Left	Alt-R
Slider Bar Right	Alt-G
Soft (discretionary) Hyphen	Alt-dash
Text Mode	Shift-F3
Two-Page View	Shift-F5
Two-to-One view	Shift-F8
Up Arrow	Alt-W

File Menu

New	Control-W
Open	Control-O
Save	Control-V
Save As	Control-M
Abandon	Control-A
To Output	Control-U
Quit	Control-Q

Edit Menu

Cut	Alt-D
Copy	Alt-C
Paste	Alt-U
Select All	Alt-S
Make Header	Alt-H

Style Menu

Get Style Sheet	Alt-6
Save Style Sheet	Alt-7
Copy Para Style	Alt-8
Delete Para Style	Alt-9

Attributes

Character	Alt-1
Paragraph	Alt-2
Paragraph Tabs	Alt-3
Rectangle	Alt-4
Page Numbers	Alt-5

Page Menu

Hide Graphics	Alt-F1
Show Position	Alt-F2
Show Size	Alt-F3
Hide Toolkit	Alt-F4
Ruler in Whatever	Alt-F5
Landscape/Portrait	Alt-F6
Auto Grid	Alt-F7
Go to Page	Alt-F8
Insert Page	Alt-F9
Delete Page	Alt-F10
Image Size	F4
Grid Size	F2

Options Menu

Copy Document	Alt-A
Copy Print Files	Alt-P
Set Preferences	Alt-V
Save Preferences	Alt-N
Editing Shortcuts	F1
Icon Shortcuts	F3

EMBEDDED COMMANDS

You can do a good deal of formatting work in your word processor by typing the Desktop Publisher codes into your text. There are two types of embedded codes: 1) "at-commands," and 2) "angle bracket commands."

At-commands refer to tags you've defined in a style sheet. They are always placed at the beginning of a paragraph, and they always follow the syntax:

@TAGNAME = Your paragraph . . .

Angle bracket commands, so named because they open and close with angle brackets, can be stuck anywhere at all in your text file. They control fonts, and a few of them can cause Desktop Publisher to have a coronary if misused. For this reason, the manual lists these commands as "For Publisher use only." But I figure you can be trusted, right?

AT COMMANDS

At commands give you a way of tagging paragraphs in your word processor. If you misspell a tag name, don't worry. Desktop Publisher will simply add it to the tag list in the mini-selector. But since the tag doesn't have any defined formatting, it will use the body text formatting. You can then use Delete Para Style to delete the wrong tag name and simultaneously reassign it to the proper tag name.

The at command must be placed at the beginning of the paragraph, with the @ in column one. There must be a space before and after the equals sign. Any untagged paragraphs will default to the body text tag.

If you want to put an actual @ in your text, enter it as @@. Doing that prevents both you and Desktop Publisher from getting confused.

ANGLE BRACKET COMMANDS

Angle bracket commands override the tag format and can be placed anywhere you like. You can use these commands to change type face, font, size, and color. The simpler commands—such as bold, italic, and underline—can be combined. Angle bracket commands use the following syntax:

This is some <turn something on> text in your <turn it back off> word processor.

If you botch a command, Desktop Publisher will usually just treat it like text—i.e., it will appear in your text in Desktop Publisher. If you enter the wrong type face, type size, or type color codes, though, Desktop Publisher will reply with an internal error message. You may need to re-boot the computer if this happens and it could trash your text file. **Remember, you have been warned!**

The following list presents the Desktop Publisher angle bracket commands for type faces, fonts, sizes, and colors.

	Turn on command	*Turn off command*
Bold	<B>	<N>
Italic	<I>	<N>
Underline	<U>	<N>
Bold italic	<BI>	<N>
Bold italic underline	<BIU>	<N>
Swiss	<F2>	<FN>
Dutch	<F14>	<FN>
7 point	<FNS84>	<FNSN>
10 point	<FNS120>	<FNSN>
14 point	<FNS168>	<FNSN>
20 point	<FNS240>	<FNSN>
28 point	<FNS336>	<FNSN>
36 point	<FNS432>	<FNSN>
72 point	<FNS864>	<FNSN>
White	<FNNSNC0>	<FNNSNCN>
Black	<FNNSNC1>	<FNNSNCN>
Red	<FNNSNC2>	<FNNSNCN>
Green	<FNNSNC3>	<FNNSNCN>
Blue	<FNNSNC4>	<FNNSNCN>
Light Blue	<FNNSNC5>	<FNNSNCN>
Yellow	<FNNSNC6>	<FNNSNCN>
Magenta	<FNNSNC7>	<FNNSNCN>

I listed only the Swiss and Dutch fonts codes, but it's possible to turn on any resident font in GEM. Ask the company that produced the font for its code number.

KEYBOARD MAPPING

You can define practically any set of keyboard commands you like for Desktop Publisher. It reads its keyboard commands from a file called STAN-

DARD.KYS resident in the /GEMAPPS directory. Any file with a .KYS extension can be read as the keyboard command list. It will appear as an additional selection in the Set Preferences dialog box.

Simple right? Now all you need to do is write the keyboard mapping file. Actually, it isn't too bad. Simply make a copy of the STANDARD.KYS file, and edit it for your new keyboard file.

The column on the left is the hexadecimal code for the control code. The center column explains what the code does, and the right column is the code itself. Neither the description nor the actual code at the right has anything to do with the actual function of the code; they're just around for your benefit. The code is read from the hexadecimal number and is assigned to the function by its position in the file. For instance, line 13 is always Save File. For that reason, **don't add or delete any lines in the file.**

You can reassign any of the commands as long as you keep this in mind: The command must be one hexadecimal number. For instance, the WordStar command to save a file is Control-K Control-S. That's a no-no here because it is a pair of hexadecimal values. Be careful not to repeat codes either.

Enjoy!

CHAPTER

16

Desktop Publisher: Advanced Techniques

A FEATURE-LADEN PACKAGE	302
TASTE IN TYPOGRAPHY	302
A FEW RULES FOR SINGLE-COLUMN MATERIAL	304
MULTI-COLUMN WORK	307
BROCHURE: HANGING GRAPHICS ON THE GRID	315
SUMMING UP	319

A FEATURE-LADEN PACKAGE

This chapter really is appropriate to any of the popular desktop publishing packages—e.g., Ventura Publisher, Office Publisher—but it concentrates on the set of features in GEM Desktop Publisher, which, by the way, is not a shabby set of features. In fact, with GEM Draw Plus installed, you can do just about anything that the more expensive packages can do. One exception is super- and subscripts; GEM Desktop Publisher can't shift individual characters above or below the baseline.

TASTE IN TYPOGRAPHY

Although GEM Desktop Publisher can now hold up to eight type styles, don't use eight in one document. Two is plenty. You can use one type style for body text and one for contrasting headings. Using more type styles in a single document tends to look amateurish.

In typography, some faces are designed for readability while others are for effect. All three of the fonts that come with GEM/3 are highly readable.

Helvetica (Swiss) is unquestionably the most popular sans-serif type. It may be the most popular typeface period. It can be used all by itself for almost any job. You can use it in larger sizes in bold or italic for headings.

Times Roman (Dutch) was originally designed for news print, and as such it wears well as a laser printer type. Aside from being easy to read, it is extremely "tight." That is, you can fit a lot of Dutch type on a line. If you want contrasting headings, you can use Swiss with the Dutch text.

The Charter font that comes with your GEM/3 Fontware is a dandy body text font. It's crisp and easy to read, even when printed with a laser printer. In fact, Charter was designed to be highly legible when printed at laser printer resolution. Again, you can use Swiss for the headings, but be sure to pick Swiss bold or italic. Charter's heavier stroke can overwhelm regular Swiss.

In addition to these fonts, Bitstream makes a wide variety of downloadable faces, including type especially designed for headlines and displays. The following is an annotated list of commonly used Bitstream typefaces. Remember to choose your typeface(s) carefully.

Avant Garde

Designed in 1970, Avant Garde was inspired by the hand-lettered title font of *Avant Garde* magazine. Avant Garde is not quite as readable as Helvetica or Univers (other san-serif type styles), and you should avoid using it in situations involving long, dense copy such as books and magazines.

Century Schoolbook

Use this face when you really want clarity and easy-to-read text. Century Schoolbook was designed for textbooks, but it can work well for almost any application.

Courier

Courier is a fixed-width font, just like the Courier you get from a typewriter. Aside from mimicking daisywheel output, you can use it for such things as representations of computer displays. (Frankly though, you can do a much better job of computer displays in GEM Paint II).

Futura

Another sans-serif font. Bitstream has Futura in all sorts of weights and even offers a book face version. Futura has a smaller "X-height" than Helvetica (X-height is the height of a lower-case letter such as an "x," hence the name). For this reason, it's a bit harder to read than Helvetica. Given that, I would avoid dense or long copy in Futura, but it does make a dandy headings face.

Galliard

Galliard is a modern adaptation of a 16th century typeface. It has an almost script-like italic that is pure elegance. Unfortunately, the italic's fine, angled strokes suffer rather badly in laser printing. As a typeset font, though, Galliard is great for newsletters, brochures, and the like.

Garamond

Another modern version of a 16th century face, Garamond has a more readable italic than Galliard and survives laser printing fairly well. A good choice for documents with a great deal of copy.

Korinna

This one's really neat. It has a very individual character, reminiscent of Art Nouveau design. Yet it remains very readable. A good face for a very distinctive look.

Souvenir

A very friendly looking, highly readable font. Use Souvenir to set a more informal tone.

Zaph Calligraphic

Otherwise known as Palatino, this is a modern face with a heritage in historic type design. It is an almost universally appropriate face. Although the letters fuzz-up quite a bit when set by a laser printer, typeset Zaph Calligraphic/Palatino offers letter forms that you can really appreciate.

Zaph Humanist

One of my all-time favorites. This is a sans-serif font that makes up for serifs by varying the stroke weight in the letters. The result is a face that almost implies serifs yet retains a very clean, modern look. Unfortunately, the subtleties of the face are diminished when set by a laser printer.

Headlines 1

This is a set of display fonts. You use these to draw attention to short bits of copy, such as in advertising pieces. University Roman—one of the faces in the set—is also very nice for certificates, invitations, and the like.

While not exhaustive, I hope this list helps you a bit in deciding what faces you might want to use.

When designing with type, remember that while type should convey a mood, it should also be largely invisible. The typography should never distract the reader. It should normally be like soft background music. Occasionally, you may want to use it like a drum roll. But let's face it, nobody really wants to sit through a continuous drum solo.

A FEW RULES FOR SINGLE-COLUMN MATERIAL

If you're doing technical manuals, proposals, reports, and the like with GEM Desktop Publisher, you'll find single-column layout to be a very workable design. Single-column design requires, however, that you be very careful not to make the document difficult to read. The following guidelines are intended to help you accomplish this.

HORIZONTAL WHITE SPACE

I hope some department heads and other managerial types read the following paragraphs. I've seen more people make this mistake, and when said people are managers it's sometimes really tough to get to them to acknowledge the error of their ways.

Don't try to cram all of the information in this hemisphere onto a single page. Adding white space makes your text more readable. Really, paper is pretty cheap stuff.

One engineering manager I know has access to a laser printer. He carefully sets aside a half-inch margin on each side of the page, and then pours in as much 10-point Swiss type as the page will hold. Each page literally looks black. Reading this stuff necessitates a conscious effort. And these are important documents, such as multi-million dollar proposals!

Rule of thumb: A line should be somewhere between 39 and 52 characters. If you have a fair number of headings, bulleted items, and other things to break up the left side of the text, you can push line length to

Figure 16.1

maybe 70 characters. Go ahead, let the rest of the page be white. It makes the type stand out as well as making the page more friendly and open.

By the way, it's equally frustrating to try to read something that's too ragged on the left. I've seen documents that were set up with about a half dozen different hanging indents. Each was intended to convey a particular meaning. Sort of typographic semaphore. The person who designed these documents really thought that he was helping the reader, but the results were almost too distracting to read.

So where do you put white space? In single-column work, you'll usually want to open up the left side of the page with the additional white space. You can start headings and notational material out there to make them easy to find. They really stand out when not surrounded by text.

You can use Desktop Publisher's left indent function to handle the left margin for all body copy tags. When calculating where to set the indent, remember that Desktop Publisher provides page imaging areas that are eight inches by 10 inches. You cannot reduce the half-inch margins at top and bottom or the quarter-inch margins at each side.

If your text column is five inches wide, just set the indent to three inches (or 18 picas). If you are widening the left and right margins, of course, you must account for that extra amount as well.

VERTICAL WHITE SPACE

Don't cram your lines together either. The longer the line, the more vertical white space you should have between lines. Use one or two points leading (line spacing) for lines of medium length. For those lines approaching 70 characters, however, you'll need at least two points of extra line spacing.

Another way to open up your document is to add a little extra space between paragraphs. GEM Desktop Publisher has commands for space above and space below paragraphs. Normally, you set this command to different values for headings. You usually want more space above a heading than below it. For body text, set the values small and equal. Just a bit of extra space will greatly improve the appearance of your piece.

CENTERING

Try to avoid centering. Centering looks terribly artificial. You want your document to look natural, as if it just seems to flow in a logical way. Centering forces the reader's eye to keep jumping to an arbitrary midpoint. That becomes tiring.

MULTI-COLUMN WORK

Did you ever wish that there were some relatively simple way to design good-looking documents? Many professionals use a method called grid-based design. Grid-based design consists of first creating a column grid to hang the work against, and then tacking the text and graphics on the grid.

Why bother with grids? They do two things for you: 1) They provide consistency to your page design, and 2) they simplify the layout task by providing guidelines for placement of text and graphics.

Desktop Publisher helps the process by automatically popping columns onto the screen. Actually, you can use the columns to free flow text if you like, but this makes a very static, and therefore rather boring, design.

THE NEWSLETTER

To illustrate some design principles, we'll set up a three-column newsletter format for 8½x11-inch paper. Desktop Publisher can easily build a three-column background grid, but we won't use one for text. See Figure 16.2. Instead, we'll make individual column and banner rectangles. This will let us continue articles from page to page, or force an article to jump from column to column without going back to the top of the base frame.

To begin with, crank up Desktop Publisher and set the rulers to picas, in one-pica increments. Draw a page frame with a three-pica (half-inch) margin all around. We'll use this base rectangle just to help position the column and banner rectangles. When we're done, we'll delete the base rectangle.

First, draw a base rectangle wide box at the top to hold the newsletter banner. Make it about nine picas deep, running the entire width of the base page rectangle.

OK, now for the real type columns. Turn on the show size option, and reset the grid to half-pica increments. Give yourself a little white space under the banner area. Then, starting at the left edge of the column frame, pull a rectangle down and to the right. It should be 13½ picas (13 picas, six points) wide and as deep as the base page rectangle.

Now, use the select rectangle icon and select the box you've just drawn. Use copy and paste to make another rectangle. Drag the new rectangle over to the right side of the base page frame, and line it up with the top of the left side rectangle. Paste one more rectangle, and drag it into the middle.

To get the middle rectangle aligned, you'll need to zoom in to normal view and turn the grid off. Wiggle the middle rectangle around between the two existing columns until there is an evenly sized gutter on both sides. Make sure all three rectangles are aligned at the top.

Now you have three single-column rectangles with which to work. See Figure 16.3. Click on the gutter space between the three columns to select the base rectangle, and then delete it.

What we've done is to trade some of the automated features in Desktop Publisher for flexibility. If you save this file just as it is, you'll have the basis for all your newsletters. Since it has no base frame, no frame will repeat from page to page. You simply select the three single-column rectangles, copy them, and then paste them into each newsletter page as needed. For subsequent pages, which don't have a banner, remember to stretch your three type columns to full height.

POURING INTO THE GRID

First, pull in a banner into the top banner rectangle. What, you don't have

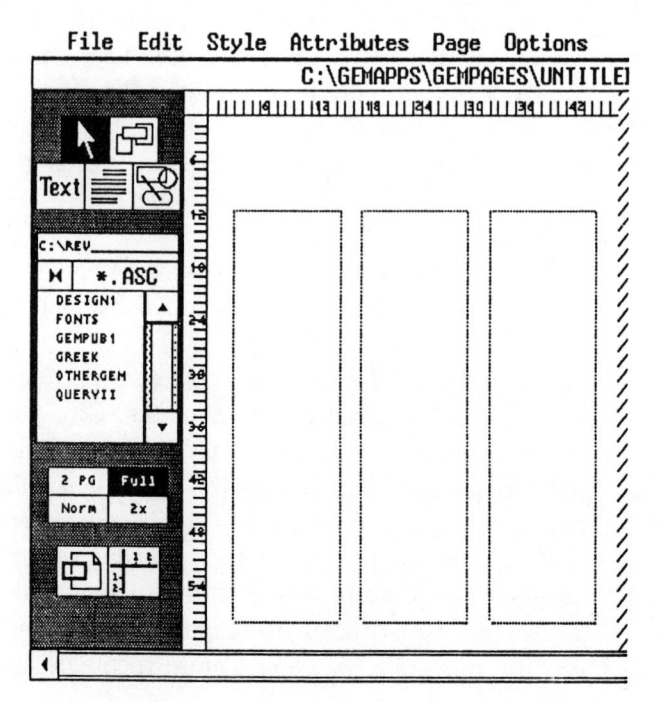

Figure 16.2

Figure 16.3

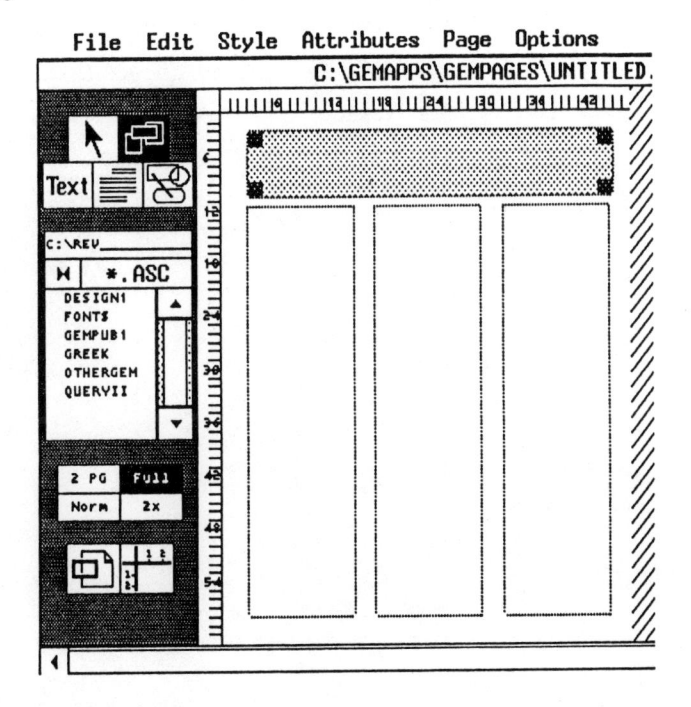

a banner? This is a great time to practice making one. Play around with ideas in GEM Draw Plus, GEM Paint, or any of the GEM-compatible graphics packages. Remember that you don't need to get the size exactly right in the graphics program, just the right proportions. Desktop Publisher will stretch the graphic to fill the box.

Now for the first article in the newsletter. We want this article to cover the top halves of the middle and right columns. To do this, just draw a new rectangle that size over the top halves of the columns. See Figure 16.4. Use the Rectangle dialog and specify two columns. When you load an article (any text file will do for practice), the text will flow to fill the two columns. See Figure 16.5.

Suppose your file is bigger than the space in the rectangle. Great! On some subsequent page you can draw a text rectangle and just select the file again. The additional text will automatically spill into that area. Then just go back to the text rectangle on page one, and, at the end of the last line,

Figure 16.4

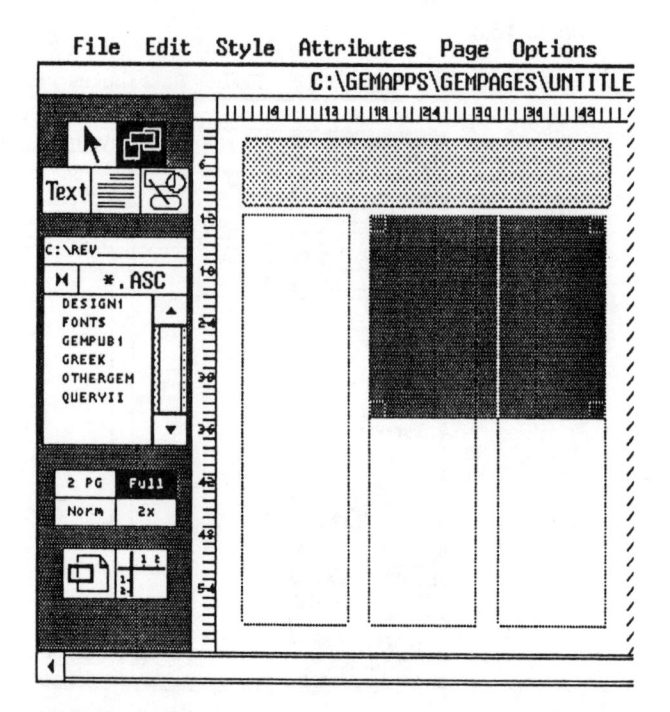

Figure 16.5

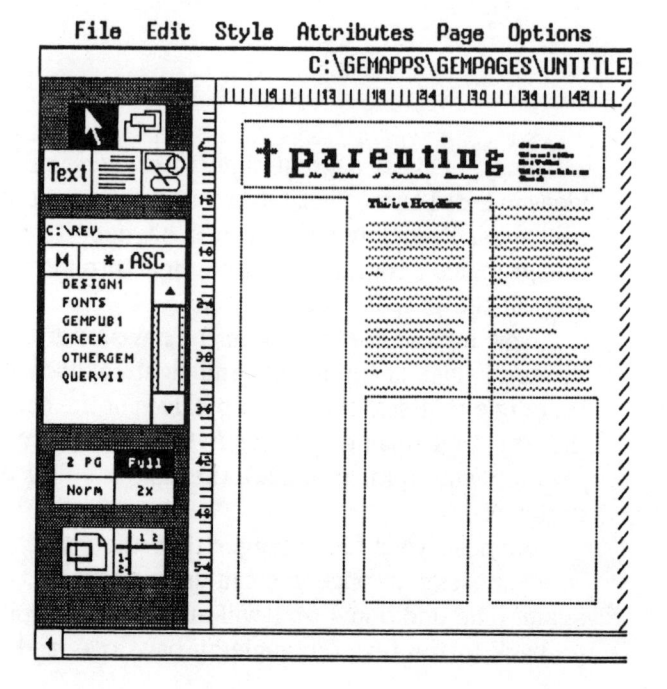

Figure 16.6

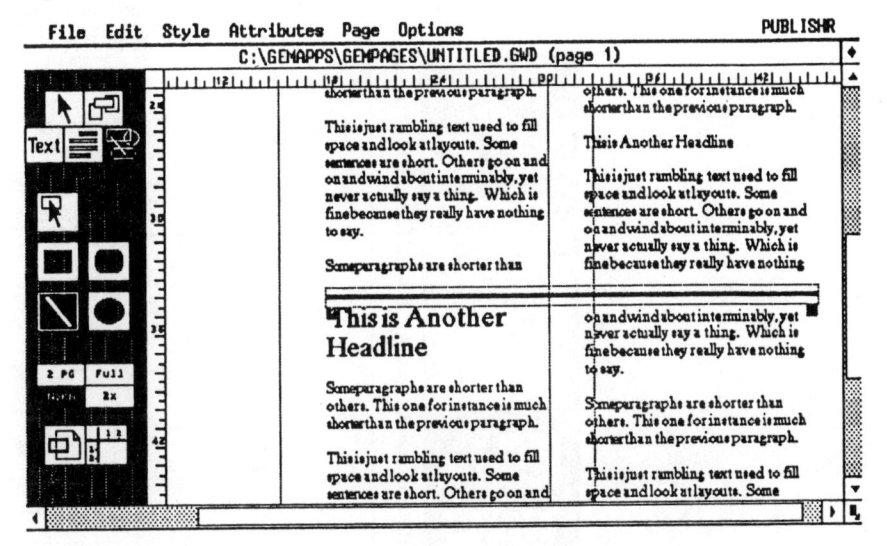

type in "cont'd on page whatever." You'll likely want to put that in italics and within parentheses.

As for type, I've selected 10 point Dutch for my body text and 14 point Dutch bold for the headings. I didn't touch the leading or interparagraph spacing; Desktop Publisher's defaults looked just fine.

Figure 16.6 shows another two-column text rectangle, added under the first. This one was done just like the first, right down to the two-column format. To emphasize the separation between the two articles, I added a horizontal rule (drawn in the graphics mode with the line tool). I set the line width to three points.

Once the rule is in place, you can pour article two into the second text box. As before, you can continue this article, if necessary, anywhere else in the newsletter. See Figure 16.7.

In the left column, I ran a listing of events that would interest the newsletter audience. To do this, I just poured the listing directly into that column. No fancy stuff this time. To make the events stand out, I assigned them to a new "Events" tag using 14 point Dutch italic type. See Figure 16.8.

To help the reader find things in the newsletter, I added a table of contents in a small column-wide text rectangle at the bottom of the column.

Figure 16.7

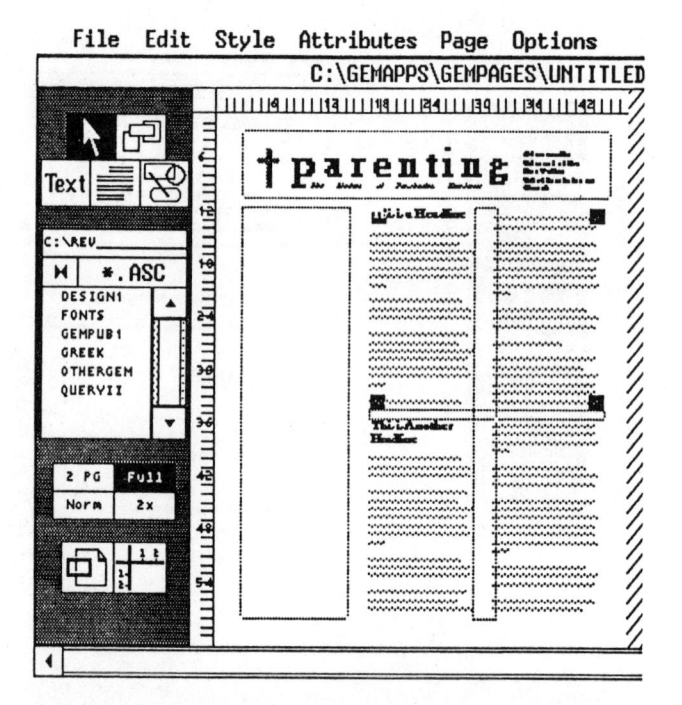

Figure 16.8

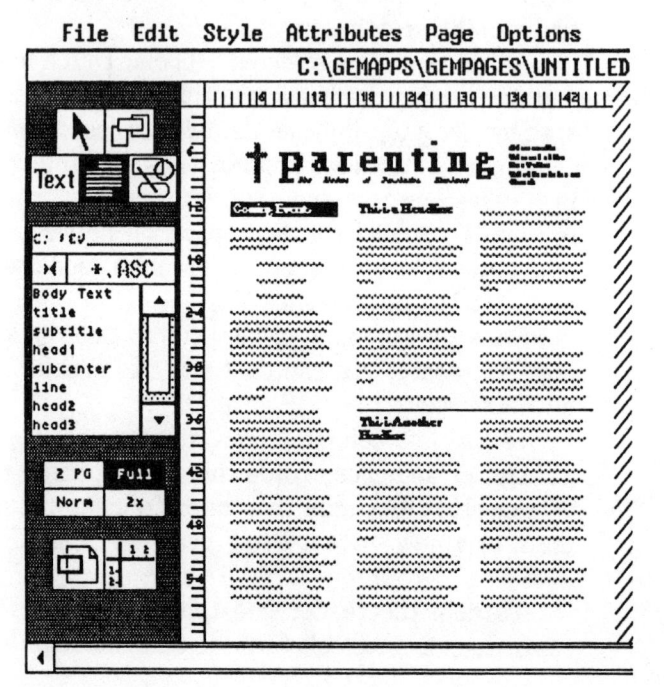

Figure 16.9

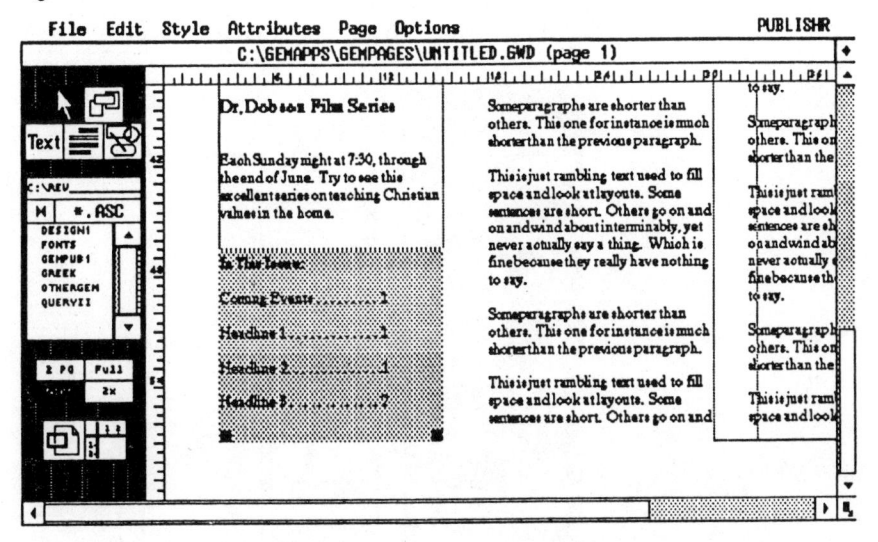

To call attention to the rectangle, I used the Rectangle dialog to add the lightest of the background screens. Remember to switch the color from white to black or you'll never see it. See Figure 16.9.

Note that I added leaders between the articles and features and the page numbers. This requires a little explaining. The page numbers were all moved into their position at the right of the box by setting a nine-pica tab. I then used Desktop Publisher's text editor and typed in a space followed by a period over and over until the number jumped down a line. When I then backspaced one space, I had my leader.

By the way, don't try to create leaders by just typing a series of periods with no spaces between them. Desktop Publisher sees this string as one long word and forces some bizarre-looking word spacing. By adding spaces between the periods, you make the program throw in word spaces throughout the leader.

One final touch. I wanted to set off the left-hand information (events and table of contents) from the articles. To do this, I needed a vertical rule. Now Desktop Publisher will automatically put in vertical rules between columns that it creates. But in order to do a spiffier job, I created my own columns. So I needed to create my own rule. See Figure 16.10.

The vertical rule is another line drawn with the graphic mode. This one was also set to three points. Not really too complex, once you get the general

Figure 16.10

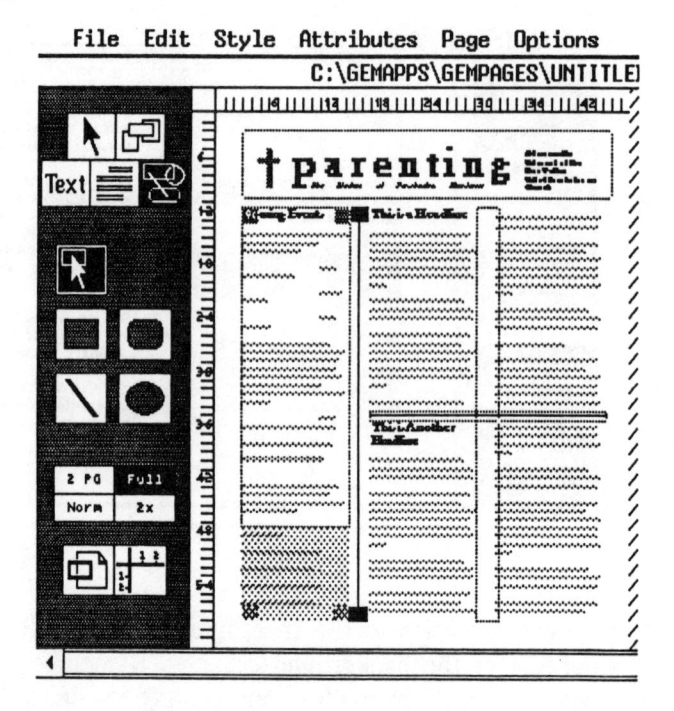

idea behind what's going on. In fact, once you get onto the techniques that you need to really unleash Publisher, you'll be amazed at what you can do.

The design principles that we applied are pretty basic, and you can carry them over into other projects. Just remember to:

- Build a column grid. If you are drawing your own column rectangles, you aren't limited by the number of columns.
- Use horizontal rules to separate different subjects.
- Use vertical rules to separate different types of things (e.g., text from sidebar from editorial comments, etc.).

Occasionally, you can use a background screen to call attention to something, but be careful with this. Text is harder to read against a screen. You can also use white type in a black rectangle.

Also beware of tombstoning. Tombstoning is the unnatural urge to align headlines in different columns like headstones in a well-ordered graveyard. Note in the example that headlines are aligned in columns one and two. That's okay, but don't do it all over the place.

You may have noticed that we haven't touched on the subject of graphics at all. That's exactly why we included the following section.

BROCHURE: HANGING GRAPHICS ON THE GRID

True grid-based design uses rows as well as columns. Rows break the columns into blocks, and blocks become the spaces where you place graphics. You can span several blocks or fractions of blocks. The idea is to give you some structure on which to hang everything.

If you want to build a true grid system to use as a template for text and graphics, instead of just a column grid, you can easily do that as well. The first thing we need to do is set up the basic grid. Let's say, for example, that you want to do an advertising piece in a two-column format.

You can use Desktop Publisher's two-column feature to flow text from column to column. But if you will be pouring text from different files into your document, you won't want to do this. For this example, we'll say that we want separate column rectangles for each column.

The easiest way to create a true grid is by using **GEM Draw Plus**. Figure 16.11 shows a true grid, drawn with one-inch squares. The gaps between the squares are one-quarter inch. Drawing the grid was a simple matter of drawing one, setting snap to increments of one-quarter inch, and then copying and positioning the squares until it was done. No sweat.

Once all of the squares were drawn, I merely selected and grouped them all, and then pulled them out until they filled the page. I kept the resolution to one-quarter inch while I did this.

The GEM drawing now becomes a four-column grid template. You can use this with a two- or four-column layout. Using it with a two-column layout helps you create graphics rectangles in half-column wide documents.

When in Desktop Publisher, just draw a base frame with the usual margins. Then load the grid template GEM drawing into the base frame. Note that gaps between the squares are now closer to one pica (one-sixth of an inch). Since the gaps were a quarter-inch wide in the GEM drawing, which is now loaded into a rectangle somewhat smaller than 8½x11 inches, the gaps are smaller as well.

Don't worry about the funny checkerboard pattern on your page. It's only there to help with positioning. It can be deleted when everything is in position. It can also be easily copied and pasted onto additional pages.

Now it's a simple matter to draw the text columns. Each column rectangle is two squares wide and as deep as the base rectangle. After drawing

316 GEM Desktop Publisher

Figure 16.11

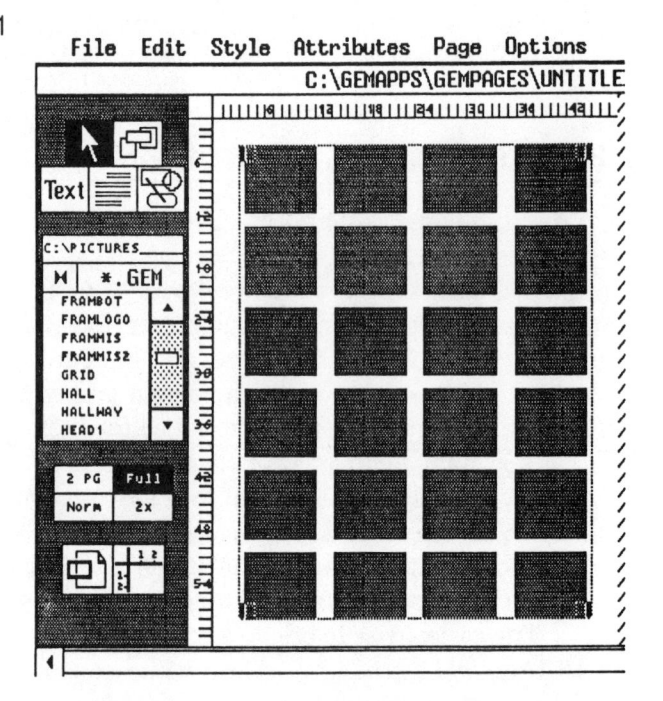

Figure 16.12

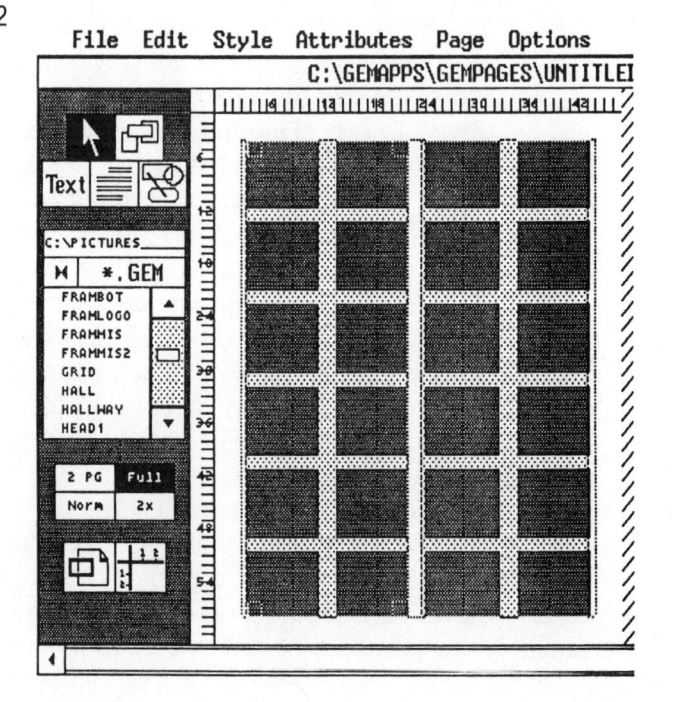

Figure 16.13

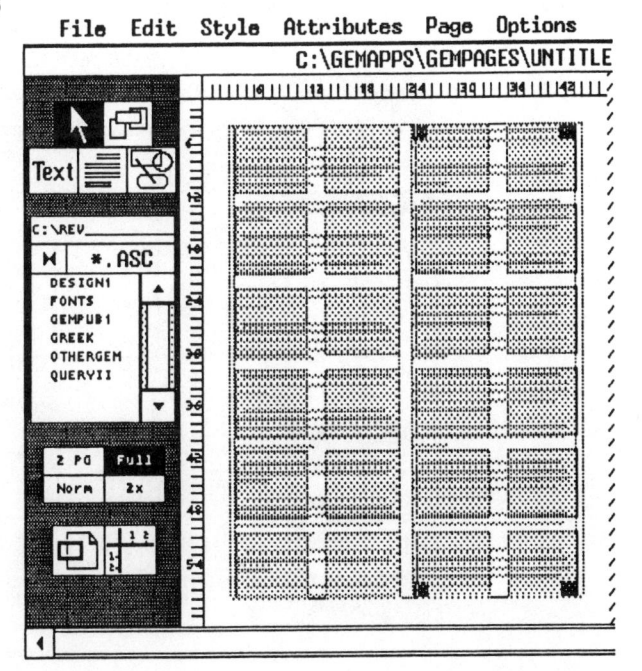

Figure 16.14

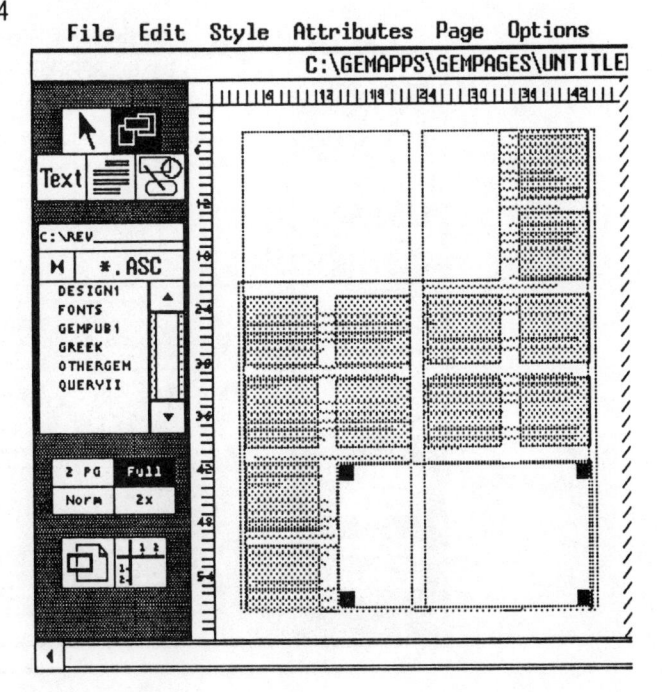

Figure 16.15

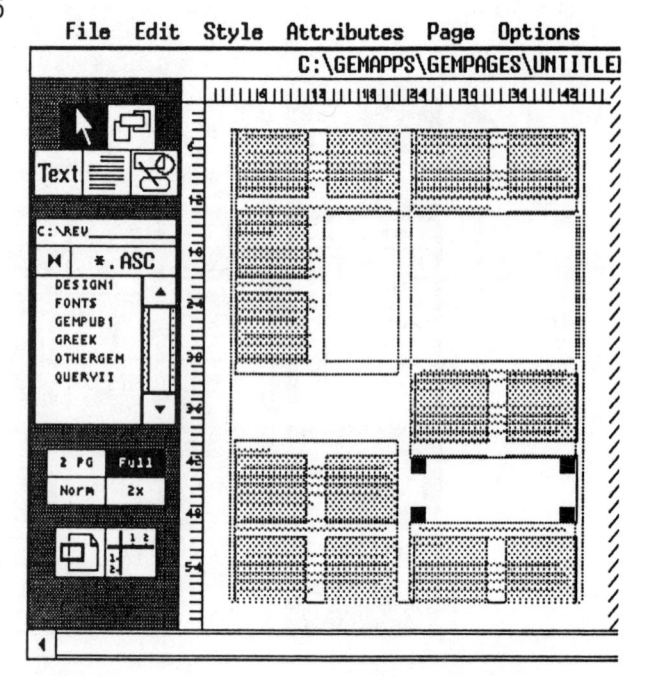

Figure 16.16

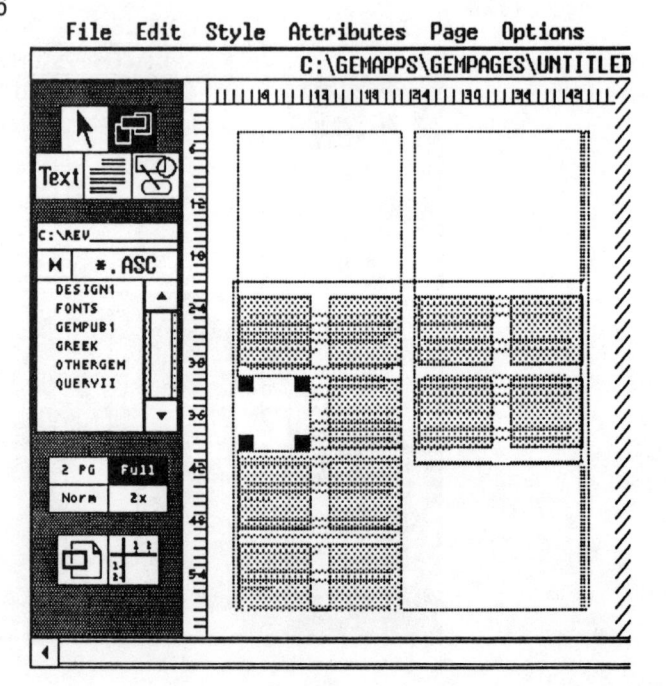

the rectangles, make sure that you go into the rectangle dialog and set each as transparent. See Figure 16.12.

After loading text into both columns (any text will do for the exercise), we can start to have fun. Keeping in mind that things should look somewhat balanced when we're done, start drawing graphics frames. The background grid squares serve as your template. Figures 16.13, 16.14, 16.15, and 16.16 show what kinds of things can be done.

If you have graphics rectangles fairly close together, you'll notice Desktop Publisher trying to squeeze some text between them. Just add a few little rectangles to close up the gaps.

SUMMING UP

Depending on how "griddy" you want to get, you can create either column grids or a row/column grid template. Both give you outstanding flexibility in positioning multiple text and graphics files in Desktop Publisher. When you get used to the techniques, you'll find that you can bang out really complex layouts with a minimum of hassle. And that, after all, is what desktop publishing is supposed to be about.

CHAPTER

17

Other GEM Applications

WIDER HORIZONS	321
OFFICE PUBLISHER	321
VENTURA PUBLISHER	325
SUPERBASE	332
MASTERPLAN	334

WIDER HORIZONS

Up to this point, you've seen only GEM applications from Digital Research. Well, there are quite a few more applications. This chapter highlights four GEM applications from other software publishers that I find very useful: Office Publisher, Ventura Publisher, SuperBase, and MasterPlan. The first two are both quite powerful publishing packages, each one having its own advantages and shortcomings. I'll try to describe them so that you can see their strengths and weaknesses. SuperBase and MasterPlan can be quite valuable for database and spreadsheet work, respectively.

OFFICE PUBLISHER

I want to talk about Office Publisher first because it's the one with which people are generally least familiar. That's a shame, because this is a dandy package. As far as I know, it's the only package with its roots firmly in the soil of traditional typesetting. See Figure 17.1.

Back before the time of WYSIWYG publishing packages, there were typesetting codes. Practically every typesetter manufacturer had a particular code set, and those of us who actually typeset whole books with our word

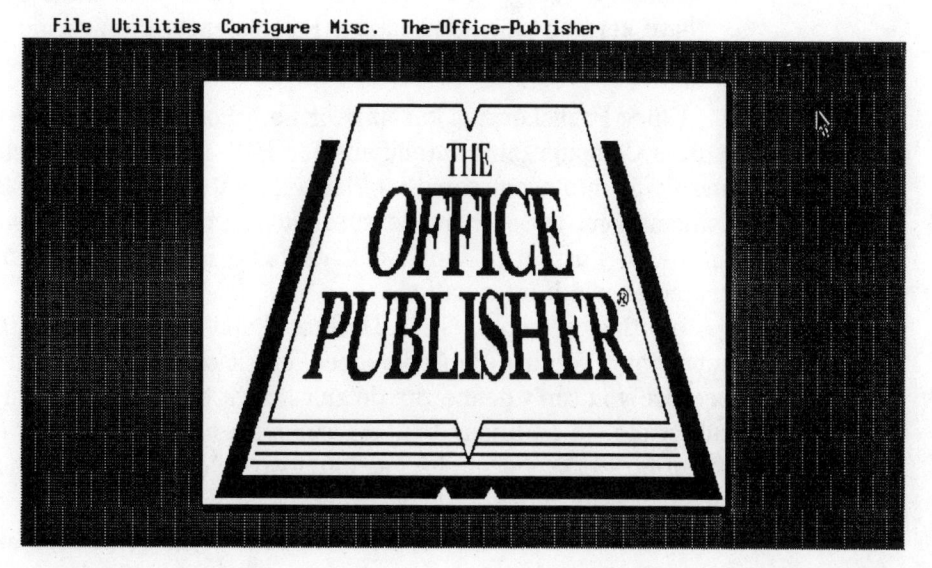

Figure 17.1

processors did so by embedding the manufacturers' codes into our text. Tedium to the max. And all the while we were doing that, everyone kept mumbling, "If we only had some way of seeing this before we set the type."

Office Publisher, an excellent high-end publishing package that provides almost everything a professional could want in typographic control, is really a set of visual tools built around one of the richest typesetting coding sets: CORA. Although Ventura Publisher also uses a coding set to format text, the Ventura set is not nearly as flexible as CORA.

Maybe you don't want to deal with codes. You just want to wiggle the mouse pointer over the page and format text with your tags. Fine, Office Publisher provides a very flexible tag system. It allows you to assign tags to anything from a single character to a whole page. It also lets you do more with coding than any other true WYSIWYG package. That gives you a really handy way to preformat pages while you're creating the text.

Office Publisher was designed for professional graphic designers and typographers. If typography is your life, Office Publisher is your tool. Consider its kerning capabilities. Kerning is an old typographic term (its roots go all the way back to Latin) that refers to adjusting space between letters to get a more pleasing and readable appearance. You can kern it two ways:

1. Track kerning adjusts the spaces between all the letters in a given block of text. Ventura, Desktop Publisher, and Office Publisher can do this.
2. Pleasing looking spacing also depends on the width and shape of each character. To get the most readable type, you'll want your program to have kerning pair information. For instance, the spacing between "wa" should be different than between "ma."

Office Publisher has kerning for both PostScript and HP fonts (because it uses Compugraphic Intellifonts for HP) and takes both character width and shape into account with a "look-up" table of more than 200 letter pair combinations. In contrast, Ventura Publisher has built-in kerning that works only with PostScript fonts, and its table is built by looking only at the character width information.

Another example. GEM Desktop Publisher doesn't support super- or subscripts. Ventura Publisher does, but it doesn't allow you much latitude because you can't define the default height or type size of superscripts and subscripts. In addition, Ventura supports just one level of each. In some scientific work you might get into two level super- or subscripts (super-superscripts as it were). Office Publisher has two-level super- and subscripts, and it lets you define the default size and height for each tag.

If a typographer tells you that desktop publishing systems can't do high quality typography, tell him or her about this program. Office Publisher can compete with the best typesetting systems. See Figure 17.2.

In the following chapter on non-GEM based programs that you can use with GEM, you'll find a discussion of a program called NewFont. NewFont can generate special-effect PostScript fonts for Ventura Publisher. With it, for example, you can create fonts skewed either forward or backward, screened fonts, outline fonts, and fonts printed with drop shadowing. But Office Publisher can do many of the same things with its typography menus. Better yet, you don't need to build special fonts for these effects because Office Publisher can do its magic with any existing font.

Okay, it's a whiz at type. So what else can it do? Office Publisher has a very competent text editor, offering such wonders as global search and replace. Although it falls short of being a complete word processor, it boasts the best built-in editor I've seen in a publishing package. It's also the only publishing editor that can actually show you embedded formatting codes and allow you to delete them.

Office Publisher has an internal graphics editor that's really a mini-paint program you can use to edit at the pixel level on high-density scanned images. Figure 17.3 shows the graphics editor in its pixel-poking mode. You also have a fully adjustable set of line and box drawing tools.

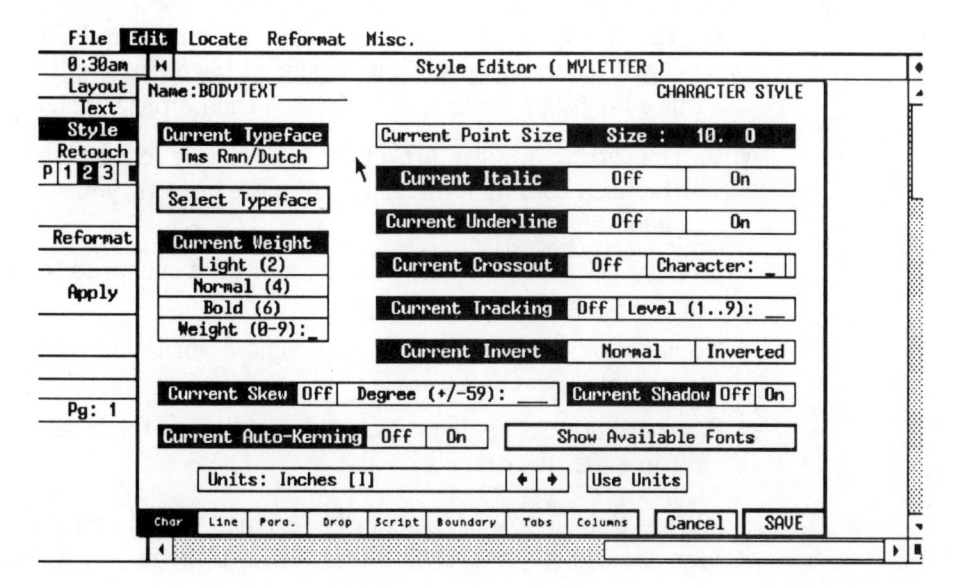

Figure 17.2

Figure 17.3

FORMS AND OTHER GOODIES

Have you ever thought about how much printing and publishing work deals with forms? Think of all the forms your company or organization uses. Office Publisher was designed to help you create these forms. It is, as far as I know, the only desktop publishing program running on PC-compatible computers with functions specifically designed for forms creation.

Office Publisher features are almost too numerous to list. A few highlights:

- Variable zoom. You can preset the zoom levels to whatever you find comfortable on your monitor. Aside from the presets, you always have access to infinitely variable zoom.
- Floating rulers. I really like not having rulers anchored to the top and left of the screen.
- No need for chapter files. You can build a document up to 30,000 pages in one file.
- Password protection. Now you really don't want the boss snooping in your resume file, do you?

Office Publisher was specifically designed to run under GEM/3. In fact, it even puts its Compugraphic Intellifonts right in the /GEMSYS/FONTS directory where other GEM programs can access them. How's that for well mannered?

A FEW DRAWBACKS

Elegance does have its price: Office Publisher is slooow! You should have an 80386-based computer to run this program. Although the new version is much faster, you'll need a fair amount of computing horsepower to do anything serious (especially when using the text editor). And you'll need between six and eight megabytes of free space on your hard drive to load the program.

Office Publisher is limited to bit mapped graphics. You can't bring in files from GEM Draw Plus or any CAD package. You also can't read encapsulated PostScript files. This is a serious consideration, and you'll need to think carefully about your graphics requirements before selecting Office Publisher.

One other thing. This program takes a while to learn. Ventura Publisher is tough, but this one is quite a bit tougher. On the plus side, it does have built-in, context sensitive help.

SUMMATION

If you are a graphics or publishing professional, you should really consider Office Publisher. It's especially appropriate if you use a lot of paint file graphics, have long documents, or you need powerful formatting capabilities. See Figure 17.4. If you use graphics from a draw or CAD program, however, or you don't have a computer with a fast 80386 processor, then it's not the program you should choose.

VENTURA PUBLISHER

Ventura Publisher—the most popular professional publishing package in the GEM environment—is a workhorse, packed with power and capability. Its popularity is a big plus because it means the program is quite well supported. There are plenty of books available, as well as companies offering Ventura training. There are also major users groups (e.g., Ventura Users of North America, 20 Glen Elm Avenue, Toronto, Ontario, Canada M47 1T7), and most major cities have a chapter of a Ventura users group.

Because Ventura is so popular, you can buy a wide range of add-on utilities for it. For instance, the NewFont program mentioned in the preceding discussion is specifically a Ventura utility. If there's a feature that

Figure 17.4

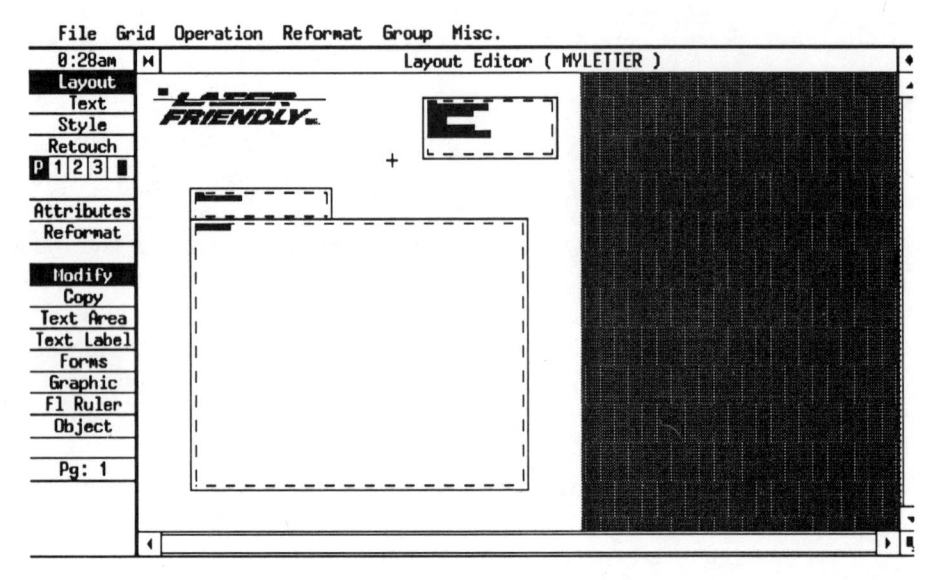

Ventura doesn't have or something you don't like about the program, you stand a pretty good chance of being able to purchase your way around the problem.

Finally, Ventura's popularity means that type and graphics vendors are likely to understand what you need. And, of course, knowing how to use Ventura looks pretty good on a resume....

A POWERFUL PACKAGE

Ventura 1.1 will run quite nicely under GEM/3, but Ventura 2.0 won't. Even without the professional extension, Ventura 2.0 requires too much memory to run under the Desktop.

Ventura has become the benchmark for PC-based publishing programs, and it is undoubtedly your best choice for a general-purpose, professional, GEM-based publishing package. Although it doesn't have quite the typographic or tagging flexibility of Office Publisher, it has more than adequate power in both areas. With the addition of its professional extension, Ventura competes very well with such expensive packages as Interleaf.

Ventura really excels in graphics capabilities. See Figure 17.5. It can import graphics from just about every major paint, scanner, draw, and CAD package. It can even use graphics created on the Macintosh or under Mi-

Figure 17.5

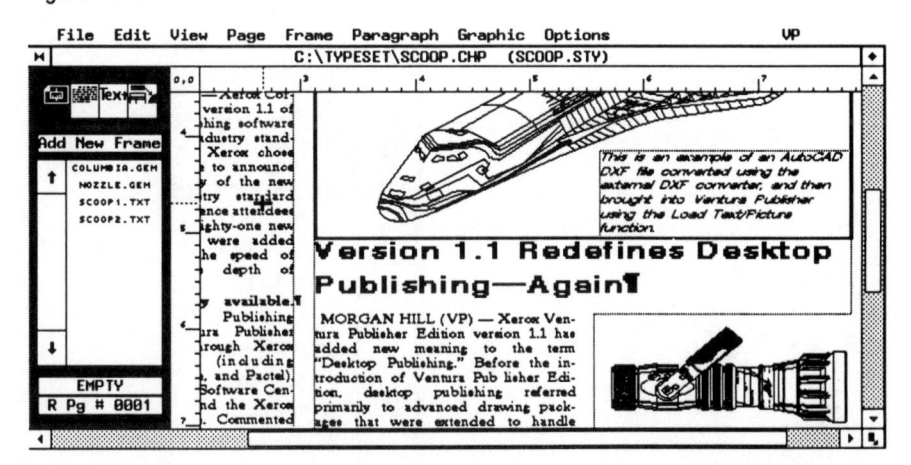

crosoft Windows. Ventura is so flexible that you'll discover you no longer worry about the lack of standards in the PC world. Ventura is the great integrator.

Ventura 2.0 is slower than the previous versions. I wouldn't try to handle serious documents with anything less than an 80286-equipped computer. Still, Ventura is many times zippier than Office Publisher.

OF MICE AND MODES

Ventura is the height of mode/function software design. Functions are logically grouped under four modes of operation. See Figure 17.6. You can't access a function unless you're in the proper mode. This can be maddening at first, as you find yourself pulling down menus only to discover that a function is locked out (shown in gray). Once you learn what functions go with what modes, however, you actually begin to appreciate the organization scheme.

Ventura's four modes are Frame, Tags, Text, and Graphics.

Frame

You use this for creating or editing frames within the document. Ventura will automatically provide you with a base frame for the page. This holds your main text. If you want to bring in graphics or multiple text files, you need to create additional frames.

Figure 17.6

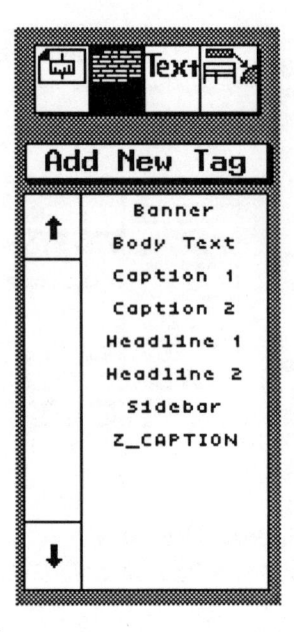

```
┌─────────────────┐
│ [icons] Text    │
├─────────────────┤
│  Add New Tag    │
├─────────────────┤
│ ↑    Banner     │
│    Body Text    │
│    Caption 1    │
│    Caption 2    │
│    Headline 1   │
│    Headline 2   │
│    Sidebar      │
│    Z_CAPTION    │
│                 │
│ ↓               │
└─────────────────┘
```

The program will automatically generate various special frames for you, such as frames for captions or headers and footers. You can also specify repeating frames—i.e., frames that show up in the same position on multiple pages.

Frame editing includes borders, number of columns, width of gutters, and even the background shade. You can also reverse the frame and print white letters on a black background. Frames can be moved, stretched, copied, or deleted at whim.

A frame's position is normally anchored to wherever you've placed it on a given page. Since Ventura allows you to anchor frames to text, however, the frames will follow the text as you change the layout. You'll really appreciate this feature as your copy and graphics go through several revisions.

Tags

Ventura Publisher was the first WYSIWYG publishing program to use tags. As in Desktop Publisher, a tag sets the formatting for a paragraph. Ventura allows you to select multiple paragraphs (using the shift-click mouse technique) and assign a tag to all of them.

Tags can do all sorts of things beyond just assigning type fonts and spacing. You can have paragraphs that are automatically numbered, or you can design hanging indents or specify bulleted text. You can even automatically turn the first letter of a paragraph into a large, dropped capital. Ventura 2.0 lets you rotate type in 90-degree increments.

Should you want to change the format of something smaller than a paragraph, you can do that too. You merely sweep over the text with your mouse while in the text editing mode.

Text

The text mode has a primitive editor. You can use it to add, delete, or copy text. You can also select text to change fonts or diddle the text's position from the baseline. But that's about it. You don't want to write large amounts of copy with the editor; its purpose is to make minor changes.

You do use the text mode for a few special things. Ventura has several kinds of hidden text, used for index and footnote entries. The locations of these are shown by a tiny degree symbol in the text. Such text is accessible through menu selections in the text mode.

Graphics

Ventura has a sort of mini-version of GEM Draw Plus built in. You can create primitive graphics such as rectangles, circles, and lines, but its main function is to add call-outs and keys to illustrations. This insures that your keys and call-outs are all the same size and font. Such consistency is quite a difficult task if you add call-outs with your graphics programs, as you often size and scale graphics when they're brought into the publishing package. It's also impossible to make type from a draw package match type from a paint package.

Graphics attach themselves to whatever frame has been selected. If you need to move or remove a frame, the call-outs and graphic symbols follow it. See Figure 17.7.

If you need indexes, tables of contents, or tables of illustrations, Ventura can build these on command. Indexes are built from hidden text codes, while tables are built in a hierarchy of tags you select.

CHAPTERS AND PUBLICATIONS

Ventura breaks large documents, such as books and technical manuals, into chapters. Version 1.1 can handle about half a megabyte in text for a given

Figure 17.7

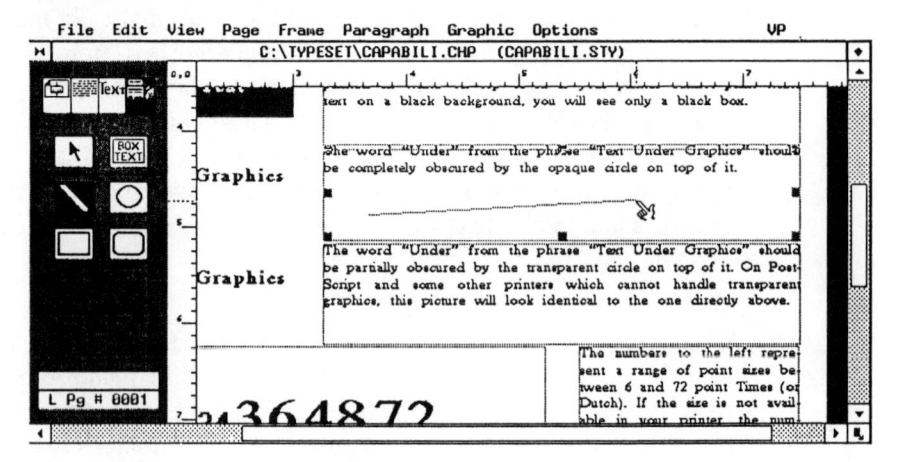

chapter (if you have a computer with 640 kilobytes of memory). You can have up to 128 files attached to that chapter, including the housekeeping files created by Ventura itself. Ventura 2.0 can handle even larger chapters if you have gobs of extended memory in your computer.

You string chapters together to form a publication. The same dialog that you use to create publications (the multi-chapter option) also allows you to copy chapters or publications. That's real handy given that you can have a zillion files spread out over one or more hard drives. Ventura keeps track of where they are, and copies them all off to whatever drive and subdirectories you like (it even sorts files by type into different subdirectories).

TYPOGRAPHICS

Ventura 2.0 has very competent typographic controls. Kerning, tracking, baseline position, etc., are all available. The professional extension provides carding and feathering (another old typographic term, this one meaning vertical justification). You can make certain that your text fills a given area if you so desire. See Figure 17.8.

Ventura has always been the best PC WYSIWYG program for dealing with mathematical symbols and formulas. The professional extension has a vastly capable formula writing language. If you've ever struggled trying to typeset formulas, you really owe it to yourself to see Ventura in action.

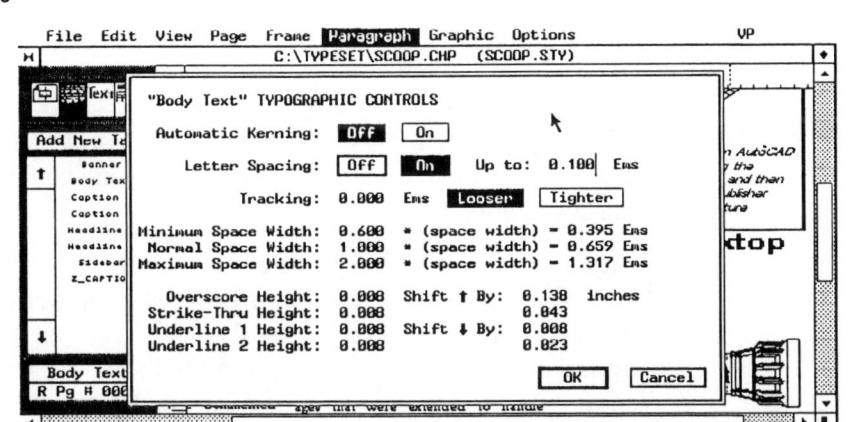

Figure 17.8

TEXT FILES AND CODING

I like the way Ventura deals with text files. Once you load text from your word processor into Ventura, the publishing package begins to throw in its native codes. That's unavoidable. Since Ventura leaves the text in the basic format your word processor uses, however, you can edit the file on your word processor's terms. GEM Desktop Publisher and Office Publisher, on the other hand, make a pure ASCII copy of the file and then add their own codes to the ASCII version, thus making further file editing with your word processor a bit troublesome.

By the way, Ventura can also translate files from one format to another. If you find that you really must translate a Multimate file to Microsoft Word format, just load the file into Ventura and then write it out in Word format.

Surprisingly, Ventura can directly translate a great deal of the text formatting from your word processor. Things like bold, underline, etc., translate cleanly. If you want to take care of more of the formatting in your word processor, you can add codes from Ventura's native code set. This is, incidentally, nearly the same code set that GEM Desktop Publisher adopted.

Ventura codes are pure ASCII, and therefore they can be embedded by any word processor. They open with a less than sign, and close with a greater than sign. For instance: <B> means bold face type.

You can also tag paragraphs with your word processor. Tags precede the paragraph text and always begin in column 1 with an at sign (@). A typical tag might look like this:

@BULLET =

followed by the text of the paragraph.

DRAWBACKS

There aren't many drawbacks to Ventura, but you should consider a couple of important points:

1. Ventura is a professional package. If you don't need all of that power and complexity, don't buy it. GEM Desktop Publisher can crank out very nice newsletters, brochures, and the like. Why put yourself through a long learning curve if GEM Desktop Publisher can do the job for you?
2. Ventura was designed to automate layouts for repetitive formats. If you do a great deal of free-form layouts, you might want to consider Office Publisher. Not that you can't do free-form layouts with Ventura, but they are a bit more difficult.

SUPERBASE

Like many GEM applications, SuperBase Personal originally came from Europe (the U.K. to be exact). See Figure 17.9.

SuperBase is a relational database system running under the GEM environment. If you do catalogs, multiple-page price lists, or large directories, SuperBase can be as handy as your desktop publishing program. Because

Figure 17.9

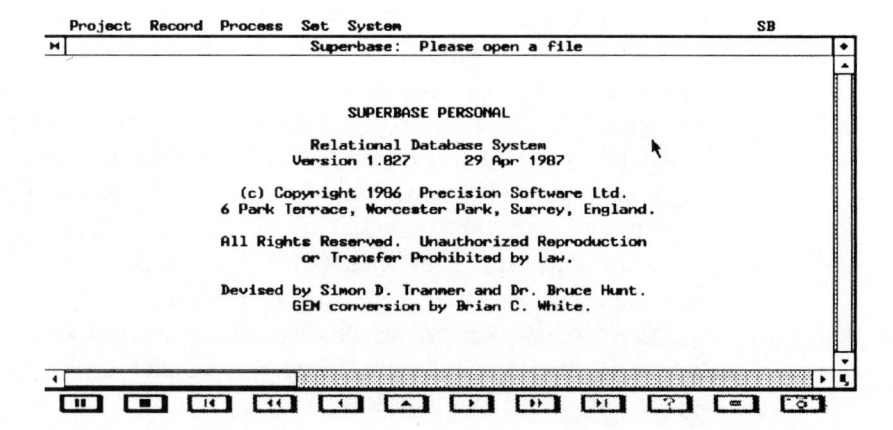

SuperBase can display external text and graphics files, you can also use it to organize your writing and artwork.

DATABASE PUBLISHING

Database publishing is perhaps the most dramatic example of how computers can cut down on the drudgery of publishing. Almost every organization publishes a list of some sort. It might be a price list or a phone list of members. All such lists change from time to time. Sometimes they have numeric data, like prices, which occasionally go up (or even more occasionally go down). Usually it takes so much effort to publish these things that there isn't any extra time or interest left to make them look professionally done.

SuperBase and any of the GEM publishing programs can change that. Best of all, once you decide to put the information into a database package, that's the last time you'll need to struggle with the job. From then on, the computer will have most of the information, and all you must do is edit or append.

For example, let's take a look at a church directory. There are several kinds of information you may want to keep on hand: names, addresses, phone numbers, areas (if you divide your congregation into geographical areas), and groups or committees on which people serve.

You might want to put some of the information into a phone directory. You might want to use a separate set of information to generate a list of the appropriate people to see about particular functions. You might even want to send people lists of other church members who live in their neighborhood.

Figure 17.10 shows a typical data entry screen from SuperBase. Notice how easy this is: Just type in the information. You can then use SuperBase to sort and select the information you need for any of the publishing projects mentioned above, and print that information as an ASCII file.

SuperBase has excellent sorting and selecting features, including a unique LIKE command. You can ask for all last names beginning with Q, or in a range of P through T. You can even ask for all names with "art" somewhere in the names field.

SuperBase also has the ability to export the information to an ASCII file, which is marvelously handy since all of the GEM desktop publishing packages can read ASCII files. You can also select your own separator characters between information in fields (the types of information for each entry), and information in records (each entry itself). This can be a big help in

Figure 17.10

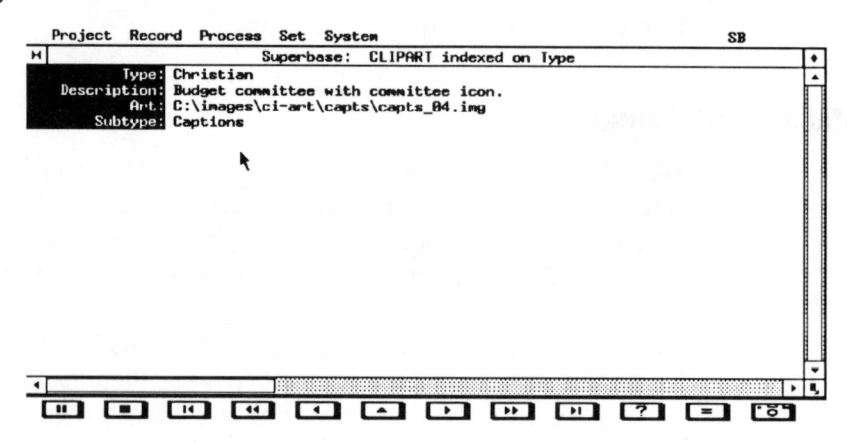

setting up tabular information, which is typical for directories, price sheets, etc.

The thing you'll like best about SuperBase is that it's so easy to use. I've used dBase III to create files for database publishing, and it along with other "high end" database programs work just fine. But nothing I've seen can touch the simplicity of SuperBase. After all, who wants to learn to be a database guru when you can get a program that does what you need without breaking your budget or taxing your mind?

THE GREAT ORGANIZER

SuperBase can also organize your GEM .IMG and word processor files for you. There are a couple of gotchas here, however. One is that your graphics files must be in GEM .IMG format. If you are buying clip art libraries from T/Maker, that's just what you want. See Figure 17.11. A second gotcha is that SuperBase can only display ASCII text files. If your word processor uses ASCII files you're okay, but most word processors don't use strictly ASCII files.

If you use SuperBase to organize art or text, you can set up all sorts of cross-reference fields. For instance, you might cross-reference clip art for Fourth of July or as Column Heads. Whatever suits your needs.

MASTERPLAN

A Lotus 1-2-3 (version 1A) compatible spreadsheet running in the GEM environment, MasterPlan has its own graphing capabilities, making it a mini-

Figure 17.11

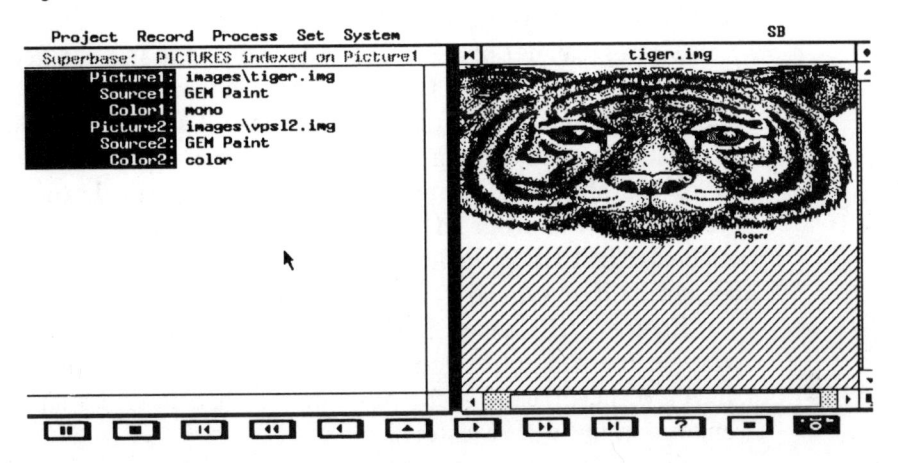

Figure 17.12

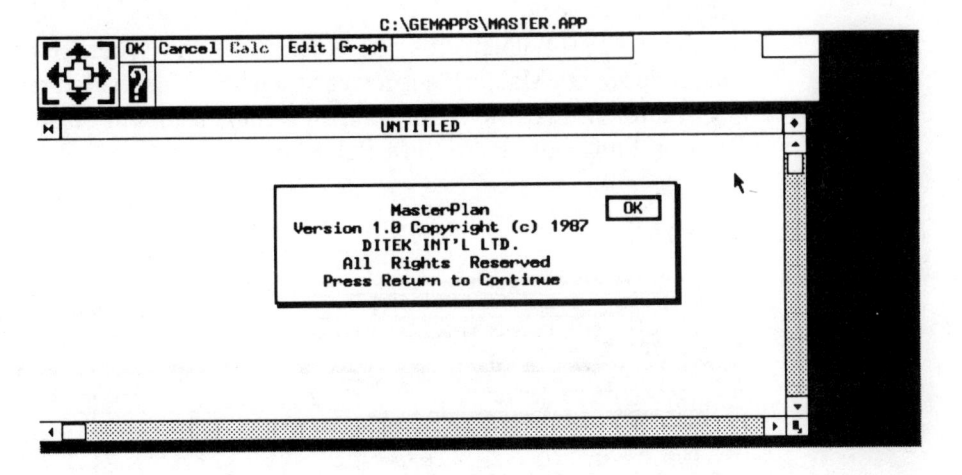

GEM Graph as well. If your publishing work requires tables of data and financial reporting, you may well find MasterPlan a valuable tool. See Figure 17.12.

John C. Dvorak, the well-known computer columnist, has a theory that spreadsheets cause you to think like an accountant. Even if you find this threat of creeping bean-counterism disconcerting, you may very well need a spreadsheet. Anyone who publishes financial data, for example, needs a way of organizing it. Since the most popular spreadsheet is Lotus 1-2-3, it would be nice if you could just read Lotus files.

MasterPlan not only can read Lotus files but also can keep track of your budget and even create .GEM type graphs from whatever data you want to plot. The graphs aren't quite as spiffy as GEM Graph can do. But if fancy is what you want, Graph can read files created by MasterPlan. I want to warn you about one thing concerning MasterPlan. It took me a while to learn to use the program. I actually had to sit and read (Gasp!) through the manual. Most GEM applications are nearly intuitive in the way they work, especially if you understand GEM. MasterPlan is different in that respect.

Figure 17.13 shows MasterPlan with some sample data loaded. Once you get the hang of it, you can really zip around the sheet with the mouse. If you've never used a spreadsheet that had mouse support, you'll really enjoy working with MasterPlan.

Since MasterPlan directly reads Lotus 1A compatible .WKS files, you don't have to worry about converting existing spreadsheet files. The only problem you may encounter is file size. MasterPlan doesn't know about expanded memory.

Figure 17.14 illustrates one example of the types of graphs that you can produce with MasterPlan. You can then load MasterPlan-generated graphs either into GEM Draw Plus for further embellishment or directly into GEM Desktop Publisher or Ventura Publisher.

Figure 17.13

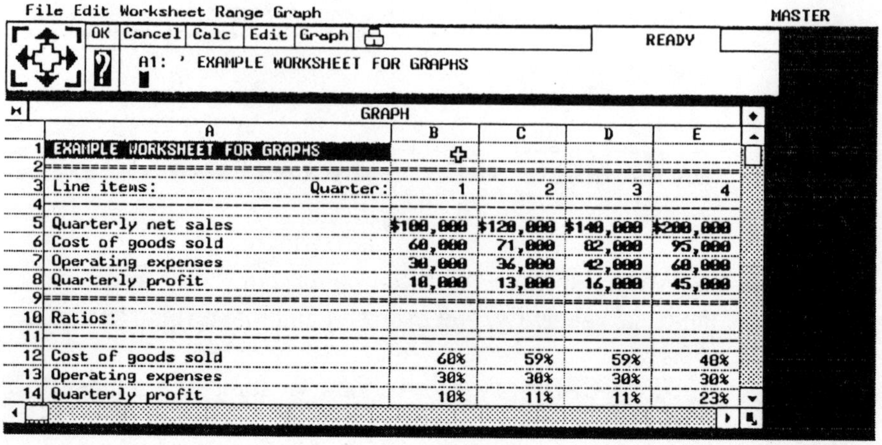

Figure 17.14

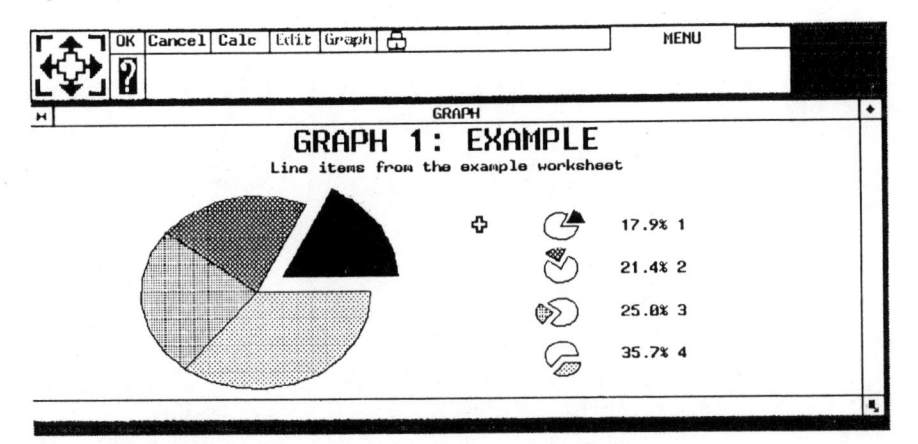

CHAPTER 18

Non-GEM Programs You Can Use

BEYOND GEM	339
HALO DPE	339
THE GRAPHICS LINK	341
PC QUICK-ART	342
T/MAKER	344
COREL	346
DESQVIEW	348

BEYOND GEM

In addition to the GEM applications, I've discovered a few other software packages that are invaluable to the GEM user. Among the best are HALO DPE, The Graphics Link, PC Quick-Art, T/Maker, Corel, and DesqView. I've found all of these packages tremendously helpful, and recommend them highly. The following sections cover each of these packages in detail.

HALO DPE

HALO DPE is an incredibly powerful paint program by Media Cybernetics that can write .IMG type files and, if you have an expanded memory card, edit graphics at a full 300 dots per inch (even scanned images).

Media Cybernetics actually bills this software as a desktop publishing package, and in the strictest sense of the word it is. You can use it to do a complete single-page layout (text and graphics). Although I find its page-layout capabilities a bit primitive for serious work, its graphics capabilities are a marvel. I don't normally gush, but I really love this package.

The one major drawback involves the required hardware. You can run HALO DPE at the same resolution as GEM Paint II without an expanded memory card. But if you want to do full-page graphics at 300 dots to the inch, you'd better add about two megabytes of random access memory.

ADVANCED DRAWING FEATURES

HALO DPE has all of the drawing capability of GEM Paint II, except for the latter's almost infinite selection of line weights. Instead, you are restricted to four very serviceable thicknesses. But HALO DPE offers, in addition to the features that Paint II has, a whole bag of tricks you won't find anywhere else.

Not only can HALO DPE draw smooth arcs of any degree, but it can also curve fit to any polygon you draw. It then allows you to modify and tweak the curve before casting it into pixels. Sort of an electronic french curve. See Figure 18.1.

It also can project a rectangle into a pseudo three-dimensional shape. That is, it will do automatic isometric projection, though not vanishing point. Still, this can be a really useful feature.

If you like to snap your lines to a visible grid (as in GEM Draw Plus), you'll feel right at home with HALO DPE. It offers quite a few more grid

Figure 18.1

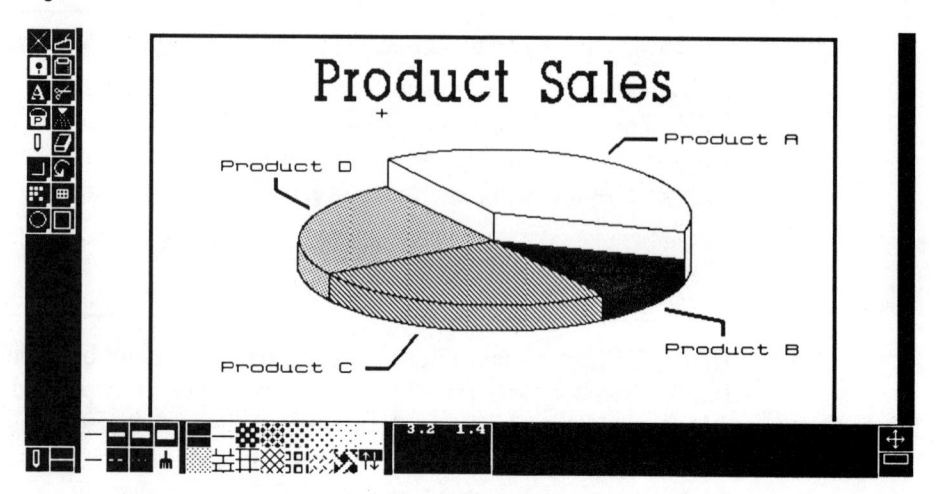

settings than GEM Draw Plus, and it allows you to use the grid function to automatically draw a grid pattern within a defined area.

Like GEM Paint II, HALO DPE makes it possible for you to edit pixels. But if you have an expanded memory board, you can edit with HALO DPE at much higher resolution. You can really smooth things out.

TYPOGRAPHICS

HALO DPE comes with a large collection of built-in bit image fonts. Unlike GEM Paint II's system font, you can choose from eight different but very computer-like fonts. You can also choose from a large library of type faces, including lookalikes for Palatino, Helvetica, Times Roman, Script, Gothic, Optima, Century Schoolbook, American Typewriter, Futura Bold, and a few I don't recognize.

A cautionary word. These are very nice for bit image fonts. But they aren't as sharp as PostScript fonts. If you look closely you'll see the rough edges.

All fonts can be commanded at fixed point sizes or stretched to any size you want. There are several drop shadowing options and underlining available for each type style. Best of all, you can tilt the baseline to run type at any angle you like. See Figure 18.2. You also can use HALO DPE's powerful type functions to generate headlines for any of the GEM graphics programs.

Editing is not wonderful, but adequate. You compose each line in an editing box before actually adding it to the page. While the line is in the

Figure 18.2

box, you can backspace and change your mind. The area the type will occupy is shown on the screen by a box that you can drag about at will. Once you hit Return to actually create the type, the box advances one line.

FILE CAPABILITIES

HALO DPE can actually read ASCII files and preserve whatever formatting you've done with your text editor, working really well in conjunction with GEM 1st Word Plus. As a result, HALO DPE is ideal for generating graphics of computer screens (valuable for those of you, like me, who document software). I just load a text file that looks like a screen after selecting one of the computer-like fonts. I then reverse the area around the text, and write that section off as a GEM .IMG file.

Which brings us to graphics files. HALO DPE can read only its own graphics file formats, but it can write .IMG and .TIF files. Because it can edit 300 dot per inch files, I use it to modify files I've scanned with GEM Scan. I use The Graphics Link to translate the .IMG files created by Scan to HALO DPE's .CUT format.

If you really need a first-rate graphics package or a package that can work with scanned line art and halftones, HALO DPE is your answer.

THE GRAPHICS LINK

Because it can translate almost any major bit image file type into almost any other major bit image file type (including .IMG), The Graphics Link is a nearly universal file translator for bit image graphics. In addition, it can scale graphics (up and down). Due to the lack of graphics standards in the PC world, The Graphics Link (a product of PC Quick-Art) is almost an essential tool for anyone who is truly serious about desktop publishing.

For example, let's say that you want to use files generated by a scanner that creates .PCX (PC Paint compatible) files. No problem: Just tell The Graphics Link that you want to translate them directly to .IMG files, and you can load them into GEM Desktop Publisher. Or you can translate them into .CUT files and load them into HALO DPE.

The Graphics Link is easy to use, prompting you along at every turn. It can read files from any drive or directory and write those files to any other drive or directory. Best of all, it is one of the fastest conversion utilities I've seen. Fast as it is, though, you'll still have time to get a cup of coffee when you're translating large, 300 dot per inch files (300 kilobytes and up).

The one thing that the program can't do is map colors from one graphics program to the next. Since color is really limited to use in presentation graphics, however, this shortcoming shouldn't pose much of a problem.

PC QUICK-ART

In addition to The Graphics Link, PC Quick-Art offers clip art packages in .PCX (PC Paint) format at a full 300 dots per inch. These are razor-sharp graphics that you'll especially appreciate if you have a laser printer. See Figure 18.3.

Now why would anyone want clip art? Well, if you are doing newsletter work, these things likely will make up the majority of your graphics. Consider the advantages: The artwork is already done, it covers topics you need for the newsletter, and it's even catalogued.

PC Quick-Art offers a wide variety of packages, including:

- Advertising Tools: Dingbats, decorative images, etc., designed for ads, newsletters, and so forth.
- USA & World Maps: A collection of all of the states with their counties outlined and all of the continents with outlines of the various countries.
- Activities & Events: Eye-catching headlines, birthday cakes, figures, etc., to add sparkle to newsletter announcements.
- Services & Merchandise: Pictures ranging from trucks to firemen.
- Holidays: Images related to all of the major American holidays.

Figure 18.3

- Food: Headlines and images of various foods.
- Cartoons: Ranging from amusing to utterly wacky.
- Computers: The most comprehensive collection of data processing images I've seen.
- Religion: Judaic-Christian images that can be used in bulletins, newsletters, and special publications.
- Business & Finance: All sorts of images of people, money, etc.

All of the artwork is high quality stuff, taken directly from the Scripps-Howard newspaper archives. It is all presented in 300 dot per inch format, which is one of those good news/bad news situations. The good news is that the high resolution makes for very sharp graphics. The bad news is that the images are too large to edit in GEM Paint II and that they will slow your laser printer down for a few minutes.

All graphics are shipped in .PCX format, which both Ventura Publisher and Office Publisher can read directly. A mini-version of The Graphics Link comes with the art, allowing you to translate the files to .IMG format. That will get them into Desktop Publisher.

Getting the images into 1st Word Plus, however, is a bit tricky. Since 1st Word Plus has no scaling capabilities, it will expand the size of the file by a factor of four. The reason for this has to do with the difference in resolution between GEM Paint II files and the PC Quick-Art files. 1st Word Plus figures that .IMG files should have 75 dots to the inch. As a result, it expands the 300 dot per inch files to four times their size to get 75 dots to the inch.

By the way, set aside some drive space when using PC Quick-Art. Loading one of these image packages takes up a couple of megabytes. To save space, you can also load them onto a set of multiple floppies.

T/MAKER

Another excellent clip art library, T/Maker's files are—with the exception of their encapsulated PostScript series—strictly 75 dots to the inch images. As a result, they can be edited directly by GEM Paint II. The one set that is in encapsulated PostScript form is for use with Ventura Publisher. These files always print at the ultimate resolution of the printer (over 2,500 dots to the inch on a Linotron 300).

Each set of T/Maker clip art has its own installation program and will install the graphics files on either floppies or your hard drive in the format you want. Like the PC Quick-Art packages, though, be prepared to sacrifice a couple of megabytes of space.

Another good news/bad news story. The good news with T/Maker packages is that they can be loaded easily into GEM Paint II and 1st Word Plus. They also print quickly. The bad news is that they are a bit jagged looking. Since most of these images are small, however, the jagged look is fairly inconsequential.

T/Maker art is designed to integrate well. For instance, the Christian Images package offers lots of newsletter column banners that all carry a somewhat standardized look. Along with the banners, you get plenty of graphic devices that can be moved and swapped between banners. See Figure 18.4.

T/Maker bit-mapped clip art packages come in various themes with completely different art in each package:

- Business Images: Over 1,000 images including abstract logo elements, national flags, office equipment, computers, map symbols, industrial symbols, etc.

Figure 18.4

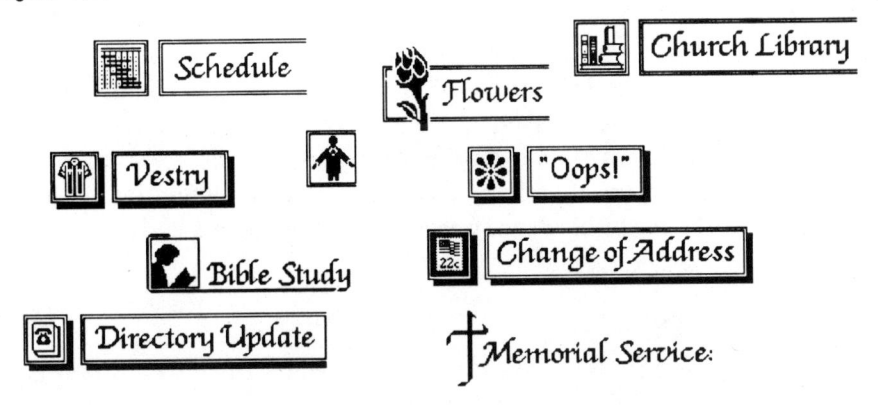

[Schedule] [Flowers] [Church Library] [Vestry] [figure icon] ["Oops!"] [Bible Study] [Change of Address] [Directory Update] [Memorial Service:]

- Personal Graphics: Famous people, cars, cartoons, dingbats, and so forth.
- Publications: A newsletter editor's dream. Borders, calendar elements, dingbats, cartoons, illuminated manuscript letters, desk items, column banners, maps, etc.
- Holiday Images: Borders and images for all of the major American holidays.
- Christian Images: A superb package. If you are publishing a church newsletter or work in an outreach function, you'll love this package. It has captions, church life images, holiday images, the most complete collection of Crosses I've ever seen, Old Testament images, images of Christ illustrating events in the Gospels, etc.

T/Maker also offers a general-purpose clip art package with encapsulated PostScript images. Encapsulated PostScript is a format that saves graphics in the PostScript page description language, along with a bit-mapped image that some programs can display on the screen. The only GEM-based publishing program that can use these images is Ventura Publisher. If you have Ventura, these images are well worth considering.

Because the graphics are in PostScript, they will print at the ultimate resolution of any PostScript-based printer. If you send one of these files to a Linotron 300, for instance, you'll get resolution better than 2,500 dots to the inch!

Be warned, though, stacking a bunch of these encapsulated PostScript images on a page can sloooow your printer to a crawl. Especially if the printer must do a lot of scaling.

COREL

Since we're on the subject of Ventura Publisher (or at least we were if you read the last section), Corel makes products especially for Ventura. A few, however, work equally well with Desktop Publisher.

Ventura is probably the most popular non-Digital Research GEM application. If you are a Ventura user, you'll find that there's a Corel product for just about every feature that Ventura lacks.

NewFont

NewFont is a PostScript font editor that works only with fonts for the PostScript page description language. You can take any PostScript font and modify it with one or a combination of the following effects:

- Outline
- Shadow
- Gray
- Tilt
- Rotate the baseline up to 45 degrees
- Stretch

You can also use NewFont to create outlined screen fonts for Ventura.

Headline

Headline is a very powerful PostScript special effects package. Since it creates encapsulated PostScript files, you can't load Headline with anything but Ventura, but outside of that limitation its capabilities are almost unlimited.

If you can imagine the effect, Headline can probably do it.

IK

This is a little memory-resident program that makes it easy to enter characters that don't appear on the keyboard. Such characters include symbols and foreign language characters from the Ventura International Character Set.

Styler

If you use Ventura 1.1, you know how annoying it is that you can't look at the contents of a style sheet. You have to open each tag individually to figure out what it does. Styler provides a report on all of the tags in any given style sheet.

Vpop

This is a pop-up utility (memory resident) that helps you add tag names and text attributes directly to your text files. As the attributes list and tag format for Ventura and Desktop Publisher are virtually identical, Vpop works equally well for both publishing environments.

Tabin

This is not a vaccine. When doing tables for any of the GEM-based publishing packages, you'll want real tabs (not spaces) separating the columns. Tabin will save you lots of tedious reformatting because it translates a string of spaces in an ASCII file to real tabs. If you are using GEM 1st Word Plus as a text tool for any of the publishing packages, Tabin can save you considerable grief.

Vcopy

This one is specifically designed for use with Ventura Publisher. It allows you to copy a chapter file and all of its related files. The advantage is that Vcopy saves you from opening Ventura and using its multiple chapter option to copy the files.

Psprint

You use this with any PostScript printer to convert an ASCII file to PostScript so that you can dump it onto the printer. You can do the same thing with GEM Output.

Timeout

If you have a really complicated PostScript page, PostScript may time out before the page is actually printed. I have had this happen a few times, and it is maddening. Timeout makes sure that it won't happen.

DESQVIEW

Hear me out on this one. DesqView is a sort of environment of its own, one that runs a level above GEM. What it allows you to do is switch between applications without closing them. If you have a fast enough computer, you can even run multiple applications at the same time. Sounds wonderful, huh? Well, given the right combination of hardware and software, it truly is.

To be quite fair to Digital Research, you can do similar things with the company's latest versions of Concurrent DOS '386 (for 80386-based computers) and Concurrent DOS XM. My fondness for DesqView is based on its ease of installation and use and the fact that it works with virtually anything. You can even switch between DOS, GEM, and Windows tasks.

Of course, all of these benefits have their penalties (why is that always true?). You need the right kind of memory board to make DesqView work. An EEMS type, otherwise known as expanded-extended memory, works best. Without this type of memory board, you can't run large tasks (like any of the GEM-based publishing programs).

PC Technologies makes a board called the RamRacer that provides just the sort of memory you need. It also has an 80286 microprocessor that kicks an XT computer into high gear. Costing a few hundred bucks, it offers a great way to make your XT, Leading Edge, or Compaq into a real tiger. You'll be amazed just how slick DesqView is with this board.

DesqView normally works by swapping the currently running task out of memory and loading the next task in. It does this every time you switch tasks. With a fast hard drive, this is quite tolerable. With an expanded memory card, it's almost instantaneous. In this case, it's just swapping between areas of memory. With an expanded-extended memory card, it doesn't really need to swap. Instead, it switches between tasks loaded concurrently in different areas of memory.

Another penalty is that you must be careful. DesqView will happily allow you to open the same file with multiple applications. This can have disastrous results. So what good is this program? Well, most of this book was written under DesqView. It allows me to pop between my word processor and the application that I'm writing about. If I want to see what something does, I just hit a couple of keys to jump into the GEM application, then hit a few more keys to go back to writing. I really wouldn't want to try writing a book like this without DesqView. Being able to zip around from the word processor to the subject at hand is an absolutely invaluable tool.

In a publishing environment, you can use DesqView to hop between GEM Draw Plus and GEM 1st Word Plus. If you need an illustration to go with the text, all you have to do is switch between tools.

ACCESSORIES

DesqView comes with a number of pop-up accessories that can run in expanded or expanded-extended memory. These accessories are:

Notepad

A memory-resident, WordStar-compatible word processor.

Calculator

The best calculator accessory I've seen. It even has a "tape" that appears on the screen.

Link

A communications package that can operate your modem in a background mode. It has Xmodem file transfer, supports electronic mail, and offers automatic log-in features for data services.

Datebook

An appointment book with complete calendar functions.

DIRECTORY OF MANUFACTURERS AND VENDORS

SOFTWARE

The following listing presents the contact information you need if you wish to obtain additional information about the software products described in this book. The listing is organized in alphabetical order by product name.

DesqView and DesqView Companions
Quarterdeck Office Systems
150 Pic Boulevard
Santa Monica, California 90405
(213) 392-9701

Fontware and Fontware Installation Kit
Bitstream, Inc.
215 First Street
Cambridge, Massachusetts 02142
(800) 522-3668 or (617) 497-7512

GEM/3 Desktop, GEM 1st Word Plus, GEM Desktop Publisher, GEM Diary, GEM Draw Plus, GEM Graph, GEM Paint II, GEM WordChart
Digital Research Inc.
70 Garden Court
Box DRI
Monterey, California 93949
(800) 443-4200 or (408) 649-3896

The Graphics Link and PC Quick-Art Libraries
PC Quick-Art, Inc.
394 S. Milledge Avenue, #252
Athens, Georgia 30606
(404) 543-1779

HALO DPE
Media Cybernetics
8484 Georgia Avenue
Silver Spring, Maryland 20910
(800) 992-HALO or (301) 495-3305

MasterPlan
ISD Marketing Inc.
P.O. Box 3070
Markham Industrial Park
Markham, Ontario
Canada L3R 6GA
(416) 479-1991

NewFont, 1k, Styler, Vpop, Tabin, Vcopy, Psprint, Timeout
Corel Systems Corp.
1600 Carling Avenue
Ottawa, Ontario
Canada K1Z 7M4
(613) 728-8200

Office Publisher
Laser Friendly
930 Benicia Avenue
Sunnyvale, California 94086
(408) 730-1921

SuperBase
Precision Software Inc.
8404 Sterling Street, Suite A
Irving, Texas 75063
(214) 929-4888

T/Maker Click Art Libraries
T/Maker
1973 Landings Drive
Mountainview, California 94043
(415) 962-0195

Ventura Publisher
Xerox Corporation
P.O. Box 24
Rochester, New York 14692
(800) TEAMXRX

HARDWARE

The following listing presents the contact information you need if you wish to obtain additional information about the hardware products described in this book. The listing is organized in alphabetical order by the manufacturer/vendor name.

Apple Computer, Inc.
20525 Mariani Avenue
Cupertino, California 95041
(408) 966-1010

Hewlett-Packard Corp.
11311 Chinden Boulevard
Boise, Idaho 83714
(208) 323-6000

IBM Corp.
Old Orchard Road
Armonk, New York 10504
(800) IBM-7257

Logitech
6505 Kaiser Drive
Fremont, California 94555
(800) 231-7717

Microsoft Corp.
16011 N.E. 36th Way
Redmond, Washington 98073
(800) 426-9400

Moniterm Corp.
5740 Green Circle Drive
Minnetonka, Minnesota 55343
(612) 935-4151

NEC Information Systems
1414 Massachusetts Avenue
Boxboro, Massachusetts 01719
(800) 343-4418

Wave Mate Incorporated
2341 205th Street
Suite 110
Torrance, California 90501
(213) 533-8190

Wyse Technology
3571 N. First Street
San Jose, California 95134
(800) GET-WYSE

Xerox Corp.
P.O. Box 24
Rochester, New York 14692
(800) 832-6969

GLOSSARY OF GEM TERMINOLOGY

Accessory: A memory-resident tool in GEM. In GEM/3, the accessories are located in the /GEMAPPS/GEMSYS directory.

Application: Any executable program within the GEM system.

Bit mapped: Graphics files where graphics are made of pixels rather than line and geometric elements. The .IMG files are bit mapped.

CGA: Color Graphics Adapter. A low-resolution color display standard that GEM uses in its monochrome mode to maximize resolution. Marginally useful with GEM.

Click: A mouse technique (executed by pressing the leftmost mouse button once) used to select an item.

Click and hold: A mouse technique (executed by pressing and holding the leftmost mouse button) used to grab an item.

Clip art: Non-copyrighted prepared artwork that you can add directly to documents or modify at will.

Close box: A box with a bow-tie shape at the upper left of any GEM application or the Desktop that causes the application, directory, or device to "close."

COM?: A designation for a serial port.

Control click: A mouse technique (executed by pressing and holding the Control key and then pressing the leftmost mouse button) used to select an item from among other items.

Desktop: A term describing the top level (systems operation level) of GEM.

Dialog: Any pop-up that prompts you for some sort of response. Pull-down menu items that activate dialogs always end in ellipses.

Disk drive: A mass storage device that uses removable 5.25-inch or 3.5-inch diskettes.

DOS: The disk operating system of the computer.

Dot-matrix printer: A printer that utilizes a head equipped with small, ballistic pins to strike the ribbon and produce dots.

Double click: A mouse technique (executed by rapidly pressing the leftmost mouse button twice) used to activate an item.

Driver pack: A disk or set of disks that allows you to install devices not shown on the GEM installation and modification menus.

EGA: Enhanced Graphics Adapter. A medium-resolution color display standard.

GEM: Graphics Environment Manager. A desktop environment for personal computers. The reason you bought this book.

File redirection: An output option that allows you to write the printer information to a file. Useful as an intermediate step in printing when you want to send the file over a network or send it via disk or modem to a typesetter.

Folder: A directory or subdirectory.

Font: A type face.

Full box: A box with a diamond at the upper right of any GEM application that causes a window to snap to full screen size.

Hard disk: A fixed mass-storage device that has many times the storage capacity of a floppy disk drive.

Hercules graphics: A medium-resolution monochrome graphics standard that is well suited for use with GEM.

Icon: A pictorial representation of an application and its related files.

Ink jet printer: A printer equipped with tiny ink sprayers that produce dot patterns on paper.

Laser printer: A printer that passes a laser over a sensitized drum (much like a television passes an electron beam over the face of a cathode ray tube) to produce high quality output.

Laser typesetter: A very high resolution printing device that prints directly on photosensitive paper.

LaserJet: A tradename for Hewlett-Packard laser printers. Many laser printers emulate the LaserJet, LaserJet+, or LaserJet II, and can be used with those GEM drivers.

LPT?: A designation for a parallel port.

Menu bar: A row of menu titles at the top of any GEM application or the Desktop. The menus drop down when activated.

Modem: A device used for sending and receiving computer files over telephone lines.

Mouse: A pointing device with one, two, or three buttons. GEM uses only the leftmost button.

Object oriented: A graphics package, such as Draw, that uses lines and geometric shapes instead of pixels. The .GEM files are object oriented.

Output: A special GEM application that allows you to output .GEM, .GMP, and .OUT files to a printer, monitor, plotter, or file.

Output list: A special file that lists multiple files to be loaded into Output.

Parallel port: One of the two types of communications ports on an IBM or compatible microcomputer. Wiring these is almost never a problem.

Pixel: Picture element. The smallest element in a bit-mapped graphics file.

Plotter: A device with a pen (or pens) attached to servo-driven mechanical arms.

Pointer: A graphics cursor attached to the mouse's movements. The pointer will change shape to indicate the current mode.

PostScript: A page description language, marketed by Adobe Systems, that is used in conjunction with laser printers and laser typesetters.

Pull-down menu: A GEM menu that drops from the menu bar when its title is activated.

RAM: Random Access Memory. Often defined as the available memory in the computer.

RAM disk: A pseudo disk drive created from normal or expanded memory. Used for very high speed access.

Scanner: A device that can digitize graphics and/or text. It is used to avoid retyping printed material into the computer or to convert photographs and line art into image files.

Serial port: One of two types of communications ports on an IBM or compatible computer. This method sends information one byte (character) at a time. Wiring can be a problem as there are various control, transmit, and receive wiring combinations.

Shift click: A mouse technique (executed by pressing and holding the shift key and then pressing the leftmost mouse button) used to select more than one item.

Size box: A box with a rectangle and arrow at the bottom right of applications that allows you to size the window.

Slider bars: Tools at the right of the Desktop and the right and bottom of applications that allow you to pan the screen.

Title bar: In an application, a bar just below the menu bar that holds the name of the currently open file.

VGA: A medium-to-high resolution color graphics standard popularized on the PS/2 computers. Very well suited to GEM.

Windows: A competitive desktop environment to GEM. Windows applications and their files are almost never compatible with GEM (and the reverse is also true).

WYSIWYG: What-you-see-is-what-you-get. A program where the display corresponds with the printed results.

ASCII CHART

Dec.	Char.	Dec.	Char.	Dec.	Char.	Dec.	Char.	Dec.	Char.
00	NUL	28	FS	56	8	84	T	112	p
01	SOH	29	GS	57	9	85	U	113	q
02	STX	30	RS	58	:	86	V	114	r
03	ETX	31	US	59	;	87	W	115	s
04	EOT	32	Space	60	<	88	X	116	t
05	ENQ	33	!	61	=	89	Y	117	u
06	ACK	34	"	62	>	90	Z	118	v
07	BEL	35	#	63	?	91	[	119	w
08	BS	36	$	64	@	92	\	120	x
09	HT	37	%	65	A	93	]	121	y
10	LF	38	&	66	B	94	^	122	z
11	VT	39	'	67	C	95	_	123	{
12	FF	40	(	68	D	96	`	124	|
13	CR	41	)	69	E	97	a	125	}
14	SO	42	*	70	F	98	b	126	~
15	SI	43	+	71	G	99	c	127	Delete
16	DLE	44	,	72	H	100	d		
17	DC1	45	-	73	I	101	e		
18	DC2	46	.	74	J	102	f		
19	DC3	47	/	75	K	103	g		
20	DC4	48	0	76	L	104	h		
21	NAK	49	1	77	M	105	i		
22	SYN	50	2	78	N	106	j		
23	ETB	51	3	79	O	07	k		
24	CAN	52	4	0	P	108	l		
25	EM	3	5	81	Q	109	m		
26	SUB	54	6	82	R	110	n		
27	ESC	55	7	83	S	111	o		

INDEX

1K, 346
1st Word Plus, 144, 226, 262, 292
    alternating headers and footers, 240
    block menu, 237
    character pitch, 230
    clipboard, 238
    defaults, 243
    DICMERGE.APP, 247
    dictionary, 228, 245, 247
    direction change in search/replace, 234
    edit menu, 230
    file menu, 231
    footnote window, 242, 243
    formats, 249
    graphics files, 247, 254
    graphics menu, 247
    help menu, 249
    image file resolution, 248
    keyboard commands, 250–252
    layout menu, 239
    mouseable keyboard, 227
    no open file area, 227
    page border, 228
    publication design, 255
    ruler, 229, 241, 242
    special characters, 228
    spill file, 228
    statistics, 235
    style menu, 244
    supplementary dictionary, 247
    "@" in search string, 233
3270 PC, 5
80286 microprocessor, 3
80386 microprocessor, 4
8088 microprocessor, 3

A

Alarm clock, 40
Alt key, 33
Amstrad, 204
Amstrad PC1512, 6
Arcs, 104, 134
Area graph, 150
Arranging the desktop, 37
ASCII files, 205, 216, 236, 262, 292, 334
AT&T DEB, 6
AT&T graphics adapters, 5, 6, 7
AT&T monochrome, 7
Avant Garde, 302

B

Background printing, 48
Bar and line graph, 151
Bar graph, 150, 151, 170, 172–173
Bitstream fonts, 302–304
Business graphics library, 127, 202

C

Calculator, 38
Call-outs, 130
Cameras, 48
Caption, 131
Centering, 306
Century Schoolbook, 303
CGA, 4, 261
Change configuration, 18
Character set, 60–61
Chart design, 190–202
Charter, 52, 181, 302
Clock, 39
Close box, 29
Clustered bar graph, 150
Color printers, 9
Compugraphic Intellifonts, 322
Concurrent DOS XM, 348
Concurrent DOS '386, 348
Configuring applications, 35
Control diagram symbols, 127
Convert application, 249
CORA, 322
Corel, 346–348
Courier, 303
CUT files, 341

D

Database publishing, 333
dBase III+, 144
DCA files, 262, 292
Desktop, 37
Desktop Publisher, 261
    attributes menu, 273
    clipboard, 270
    color printing, 275
    copying documents, 289
    copying print files, 291
    edit menu, 270
    embedded codes, 298–299

file menu, 268
fill attributes, 282
fonts, 274
graphics editing, 266
graphics files, 262
grid size, 289
header codes, 284
hyphenation, 277, 278, 293
image size, 288
keyboard commands, 294–297
keyboard mapping, 299–300
launching an application, 270
line attributes, 281
line spacing, 276
mini-selector, 267
mode icons, 264
page menu, 286
page numbers, 283–285
panner, 268
rectangles, 263, 265, 280
reversed type, 275
screen magnification, 268
setting preferences, 291
status, 294
style menu, 272
style sheets, 272
tabs, 278–279
tags, 266
text editing, 266
text grid, 277
toolkit, 264
tracking, 277
width tables, 275
word processor files, 262
Desktop keyboard commands, 41
DesqView, 262, 348–349
    Calculator, 349
    Datebook, 349
    Link, 349
    Notepad, 349
Diablo 630, 9
Diagonal point, 138
Dialog, 31
Diary, 41
Directories, 27
Disk drive installation, 35
Disk drives, 27
DOS, 32, 34, 35, 348
Dot matrix printers, 9, 16
Draw Plus, 85
    alignment menu, 96–97
    clip art, 126
    colors menu, 102
    file menu, 91–93
    flip horizontal, 95
    flip vertical, 96, 107
    grid, 90
    layering, 117
    lines menu, 99–100
    making page numbers for, 283–285
    modify menu, 94–96
    multiple files, 113
    page menu, 93–94
    panner, 89
    patterns menu, 100–102
    pointer, 89
    rulers, 89
    shadow pattern, 111
    toolkit, 85–88
    type menu, 97–99
    with Graph, 144
    zoomer, 88
Driver pack, 10, 11, 16
Dual vanishing point, 134, 141
Dutch, 52, 99, 181, 302
DXF files, 85

E

EEMS memory, 348
EGA, 5, 6, 261
EGA monochrome, 6
Electrical schematic symbols, 127
Encapsulated PostScript, 344, 345

F

Fat bits, 65
File handling, 30, 32, 34
File redirection, 47
Flow chart symbols, 127
Flyers, 78
Font codes, 56–59
FontMerge, 59
Fontware, 50
    font codes, 56–59
    installation, 50
    making fonts, 53
Formatting diskettes, 34
Full box, 29
Futura, 303

G

Galliard, 303
Garamond, 303
GEM international character set, 60–61
GEMAPPS/FONTS, 55
GEMPREP, 14, 18
GEMSCRAP, 14
Graph, 144, 336
    area graph, 150
    bar and line graph, 151
    bar graph, 150, 151
    clustered bar graph, 150

data entry, 145
edit menu, 155–157
file menu, 152–155
font menu, 164
keyboard commands, 144, 147, 148
line graph, 149
map chart, 151
map editor, 164
options menu, 160–164
pie chart, 148
stacked bar graph, 150
symbol graph, 151
toolkit, 158–160
Graphics Link, 263, 341–342
Grid based design, 307–319

H

HALO DPE, 2, 65, 262, 339–341
Headline, 346
Hercules graphics adapter, 5, 123, 261, 268
Hewlett-Packard LaserJet, 8, 55
HPGL, 10

I

Icons, 24
Illuminated letters, 82
Installation, 14
Installing disk drive, 35
Isometric projection, 134
I-beam cursor, 212

K

Kerning, 322
Keyed illustration, 131
Korinna, 303

L

Laser printers, 8, 17, 230
Laser printers paper tray, 47
Layout thumbnail sketches, 83
Leaders, 313
Leading, 276–277, 306
Legend, 131
Line graph, 149
Logo creation, 102
Lotus 1-2-3, 144

M

Macintosh, 21, 327
Making fonts, 53
Map chart, 151
Map editor application, 164
    edit menu, 166
    file menu, 165
    font menu, 167
MasterPlan, 334–337
Menus, 30
Micro Display Systems Genius, 7
Microsoft Windows, 326, 348
Microsoft Word, 262, 292
Mouse, 11, 12, 17, 207
Mouse techniques, 21–23
Multimate, 262, 292
Multi-column design, 307–319

N

NewFont, 323, 325, 346
Newsletters, 307–315

O

Office Publisher, 302, 321–325
Okidata Microline, 17
Organizational chart, 110, 127
Output application, 34, 42
    background printing, 48
    camera preferences, 48
    file menu, 44
    file redirection, 47
    global menu, 45
    page scaling, 46
    paper trays, 47
    preferences menu, 45

P

Page, 46
Paint II, 65
    drawing tools, 69–72
    file menu, 72–73
    fonts, 68
    patterns menu, 75–76
    resolution, 65
    tools menu, 74–75
Palatino, 304
PC Quick-Art, 263, 342–344
PC Technologies, 348
PCX files, 343
Pels, 65
PICT files, 85
Pie chart, 148, 170, 172
Pixels, 65
Plotters, 10, 270
Points, 98
PostScript, 8, 40, 55, 226, 266, 274, 275, 344, 345
Preferences, 36
Print spooler, 40
Protractor, 136
Psprint, 347
PS/2 computer, 4

Pull-down menus, 30

Q

Quadram Prosync, 5

R

RamRacer, 348
Readability, 255–256, 276–277, 305–306

S

Saving the desktop, 37
Scan, 27, 341
Scroll bar, 29
Shadowing, 77
Single column design, 304–306
Single vanishing point, 134, 136, 138, 140
Slide show, 46
Slider, 28
Snapshot, 40
Souvenir, 304
Specific Solutions fonts, 85, 144
Spill file, 218, 228
Stacked bar graph, 150
Standard.kys, 300
Starting GEM, 23
Stationery, 254
Style sheets, 272
Styler, 347
SuperBase, 332–334
Supercalc, 144
Swiss, 52, 99, 180, 302
Symbol graph, 151

T

Tabin, 347
Thirty degree triangle, 134
TIFF files, 341
Timeout, 347
Tombstoning, 314
Tracking, 277, 322
T/Maker, 334, 344–345

U

Univers, 303
University Roman, 304

V

Vanishing point, 138
Vcopy, 347
Ventura Publisher, 261, 302, 325–332
Ventura Users of North America, 325

Verticom 480, 7
VGA, 5
Video Seven Vega Deluxe, 5
Viking 1, 7
Visicalc, 144
Volkswriter, 204
Vpop, 347

W

White space, 305, 306
WordChart, 127, 177
    borders, 184, 187
    decimal tabs, 195
    edit menu, 183
    file menu, 182
    font limitations, 178
    keyboard commands, 179, 189–190
    options menu, 186
    outlines, 195
    template menu, 185
    text fields, 178
    using GEM Draw Plus to create borders, 197, 201
    zones, 178
WordPerfect, 262, 292
WordStar, 2, 204, 219, 220, 262, 292
Write, 204, 262, 292
    control characters in files, 213, 219
    dot-dot commands, 222–224
    draft printing, 210
    edit menu, 211
    file extensions, 205
    file menu, 208
    font menu, 214
    format menu, 215
    graphics files, 209, 215
    keyboard commands, 220–222
    mouse techniques, 207
    options menu, 217
    page menu, 214
    ruler, 218
    search and replace menu, 212–214
Wyse WY-700, 7

X

X height, 276, 303
Xerox 4020, 9
Xerox full page display, 7
Xmodem, 349

Z

Zaph Calligraphic, 304
Zaph Humanist, 304